Kitchen Princess

9

Natsumi Ando

Story by Miyuki Kobayashi

Translated by Satsuki Yamashita

Adapted by Nunzio DeFilippis and Christina Weir

Lettered by North Market Street Graphics

Ballantine Books • New York

A Del Rey Manga/Kodansha Trade Paperback Original

Kitchen Princess volume 9 copyright © 2008 by Natsumi Ando and Miyuki Kobayashi
English translation copyright © 2009 by Natsumi Ando and Miyuki Kobayashi

Published in the United States by Del Rey Books, an imprint of The Random House Publishing Group, a division of Random House, Inc., New York.

DEL REY is a registered trademark and the Del Rey colophon is a trademark of Random House, Inc.

Publication rights arranged through Kodansha Ltd.

First published in Japan in 2008 by Kodansha Ltd., Tokyo.

ISBN 978-0-345-51026-6

Printed in the United States of America

www.delreymanga.com

9 8 7 6 5 4 3 2 1

Translator: Satsuki Yamashita
Adaptors: Nunzio DeFilippis and Christina Weir
Lettering: North Market Street Graphics
Original cover design by Akiko Omo

Contents

While I was working on this volume,
there was a shortage in raw produce—which
caused a problem because I couldn't buy
butter! I couldn't make snacks! (> <)
—Natsumi Ando

Honorifics Explained

Throughout the Del Rey Manga books, you will find Japanese honorifics left intact in the translations. For those not familiar with how the Japanese use honorifics and, more important, how they differ from American honorifics, we present this brief overview.

Politeness has always been a critical facet of Japanese culture. Ever since the feudal era, when Japan was a highly stratified society, use of honorifics—which can be defined as polite speech that indicates relationship or status—has played an essential role in the Japanese language. When addressing someone in Japanese, an honorific usually takes the form of a suffix attached to one's name (example: "Asuna-san"), is used as a title at the end of one's name, or appears in place of the name itself (example: "Negi-sensei," or simply "Sensei!").

Honorifics can be expressions of respect or endearment. In the context of manga and anime, honorifics give insight into the nature of the relationship between characters. Many English translations leave out these important honorifics and therefore distort the feel of the original Japanese. Because Japanese honorifics contain nuances that English honorifics lack, it is our policy at Del Rey not to translate them. Here, instead, is a guide to some of the honorifics you may encounter in Del Rey Manga.

-*san*: This is the most common honorific and is equivalent to Mr., Miss, Ms., or Mrs. It is the all-purpose honorific and can be used in any situation where politeness is required.

-*sama*: This is one level higher than "-san" and is used to confer great respect.

-*dono*: This comes from the word "tono," which means "lord." It is an even higher level than "-sama" and confers utmost respect.

-*kun*: This suffix is used at the end of boys' names to express familiarity or endearment. It is also sometimes used by men among friends, or when addressing someone younger or of a lower station.

-chan: This is used to express endearment, mostly toward girls. It is also used for little boys, pets, and even among lovers. It gives a sense of childish cuteness.

Bozu: This is an informal way to refer to a boy, similar to the English terms "kid" and "squirt."

**Sempai/
Senpai:** This title suggests that the addressee is one's senior in a group or organization. It is most often used in a school setting, where underclassmen refer to their upperclassmen as "sempai." It can also be used in the workplace, such as when a newer employee addresses an employee who has seniority in the company.

Kohai: This is the opposite of "sempai" and is used toward underclassmen in school or newcomers in the workplace. It connotes that the addressee is of a lower station.

Sensei: Literally meaning "one who has come before," this title is used for teachers, doctors, or masters of any profession or art.

-[blank]: This is usually forgotten in these lists, but it is perhaps the most significant difference between Japanese and English. The lack of honorific means that the speaker has permission to address the person in a very intimate way. Usually, only family, spouses, or very close friends have this kind of permission. Known as *yobisute,* it can be gratifying when someone who has earned the intimacy starts to call one by one's name without an honorific. But when that intimacy hasn't been earned, it can be very insulting.

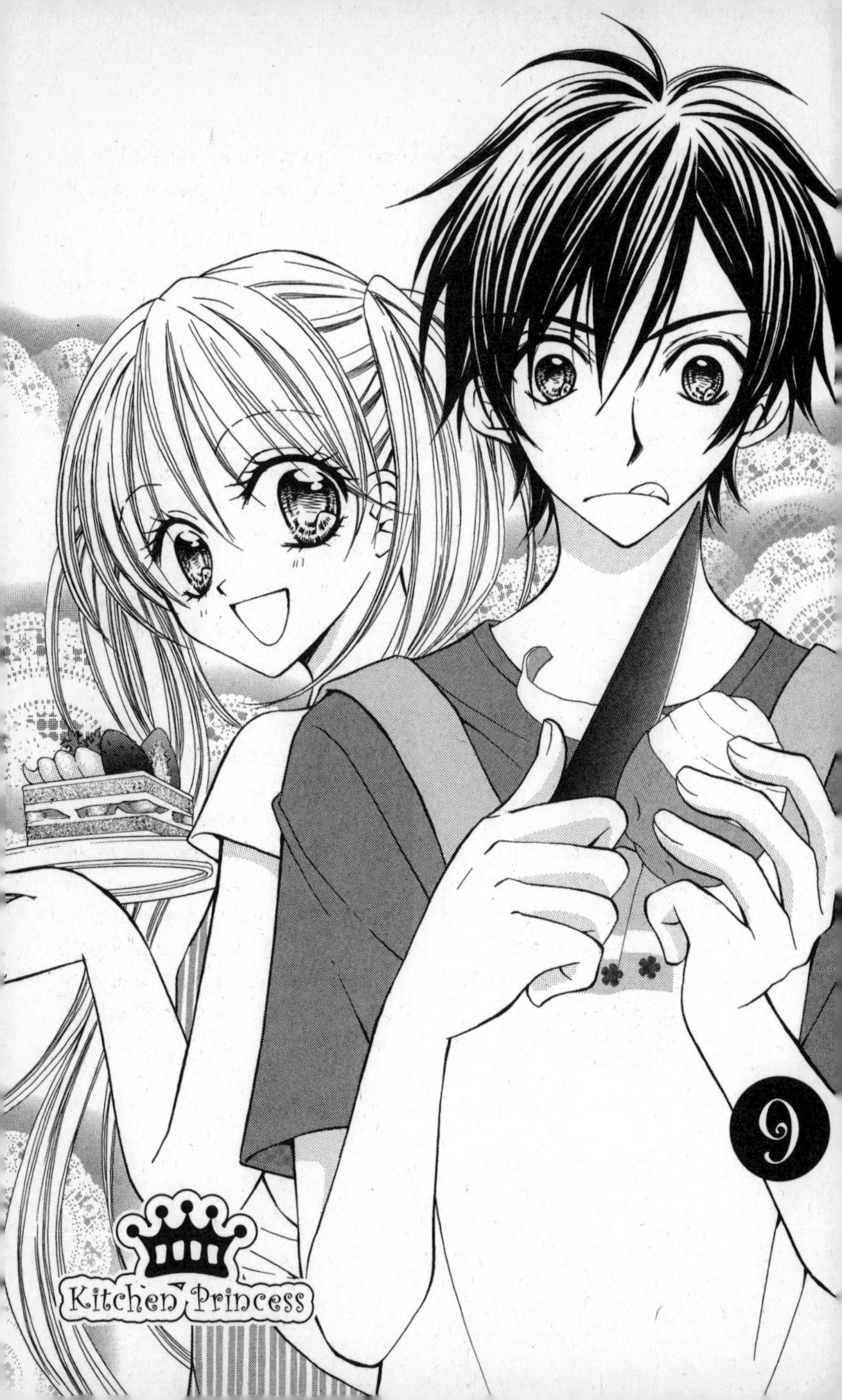
Kitchen Princess
9

Kitchen Princess

Table of Contents

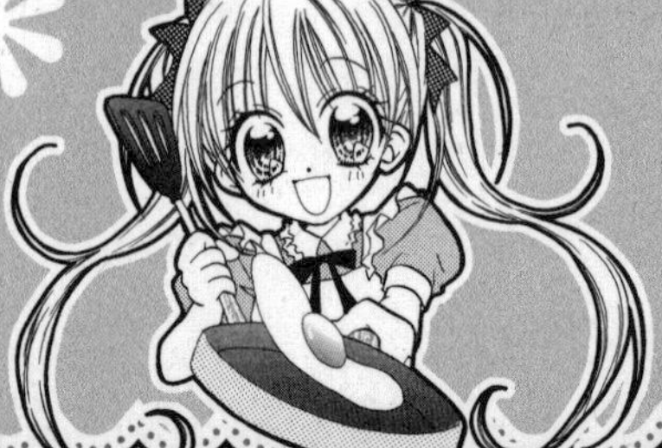

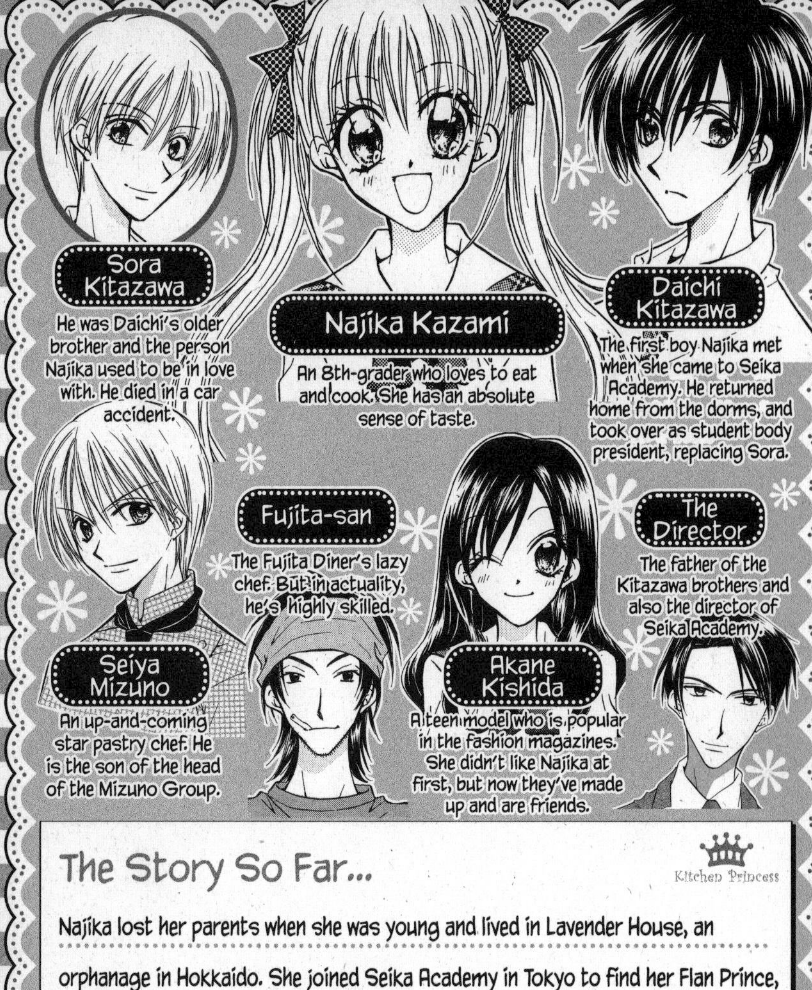
Sora Kitazawa
He was Daichi's older brother and the person Najika used to be in love with. He died in a car accident.
Najika Kazami
An 8th-grader who loves to eat and cook. She has an absolute sense of taste.
Daichi Kitazawa
The first boy Najika met when she came to Seika Academy. He returned home from the dorms, and took over as student body president, replacing Sora.
Fujita-san
The Fujita Diner's lazy chef. But in actuality, he's highly skilled.
The Director
The father of the Kitazawa brothers and also the director of Seika Academy.
Seiya Mizuno
An up-and-coming star pastry chef. He is the son of the head of the Mizuno Group.
Akane Kishida
A teen model who is popular in the fashion magazines. She didn't like Najika at first, but now they've made up and are friends.

The Story So Far...

Kitchen Princess

Najika lost her parents when she was young and lived in Lavender House, an orphanage in Hokkaido. She joined Seika Academy in Tokyo to find her Flan Prince, the boy who saved her from drowning when she was little. There she met Sora, Daichi, and Akane. Najika entered the National Confectionary Competition but lost in the finals, owing to Sora's death. She was able to recover, and worked hard even though the director tried to kick her out and Seiya has challenged her to countless cooking showdowns. She has started to develop feelings for Daichi, but then Seiya asked her out!

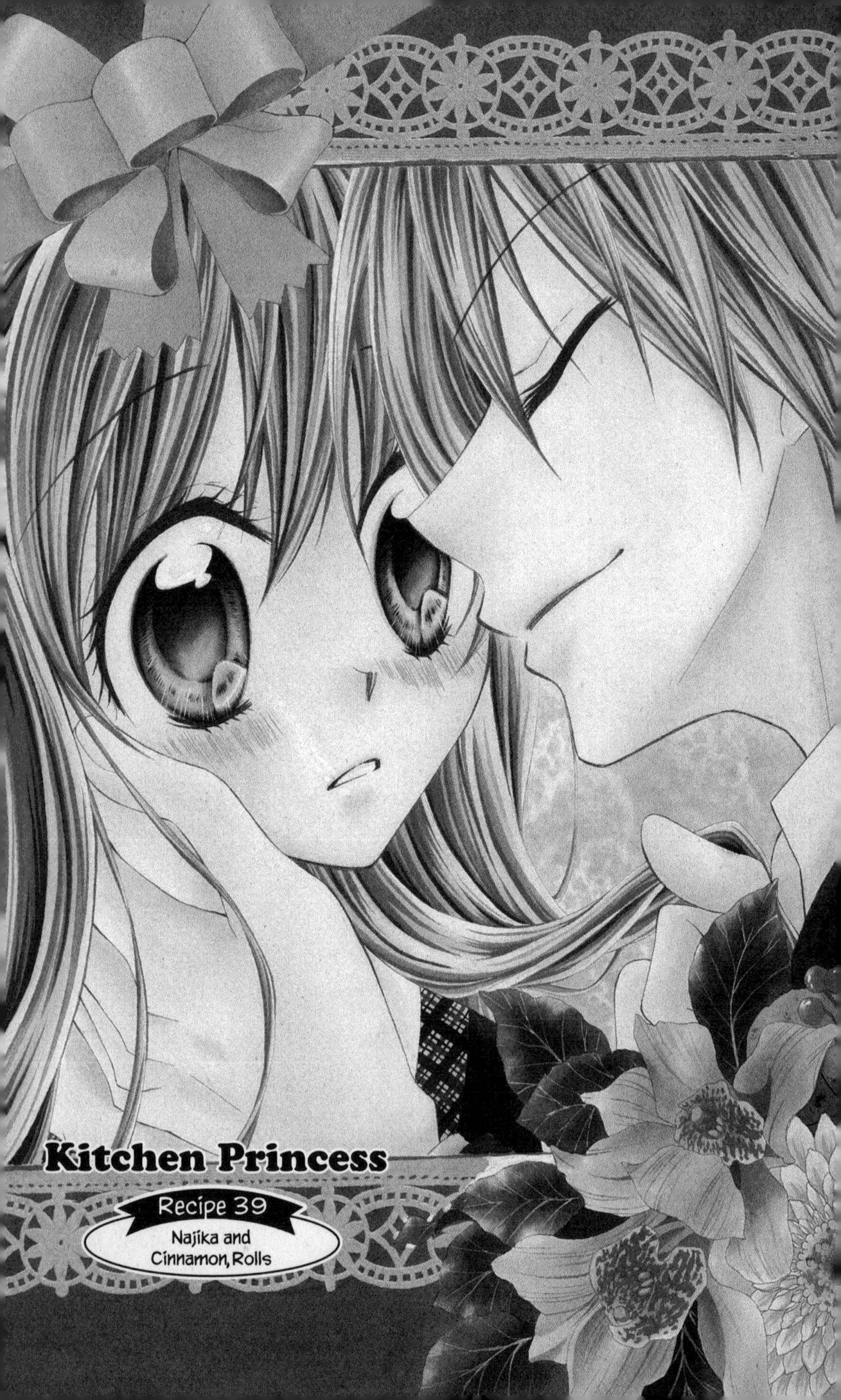
Kitchen Princess
Recipe 39
Najika and Cinnamon Rolls

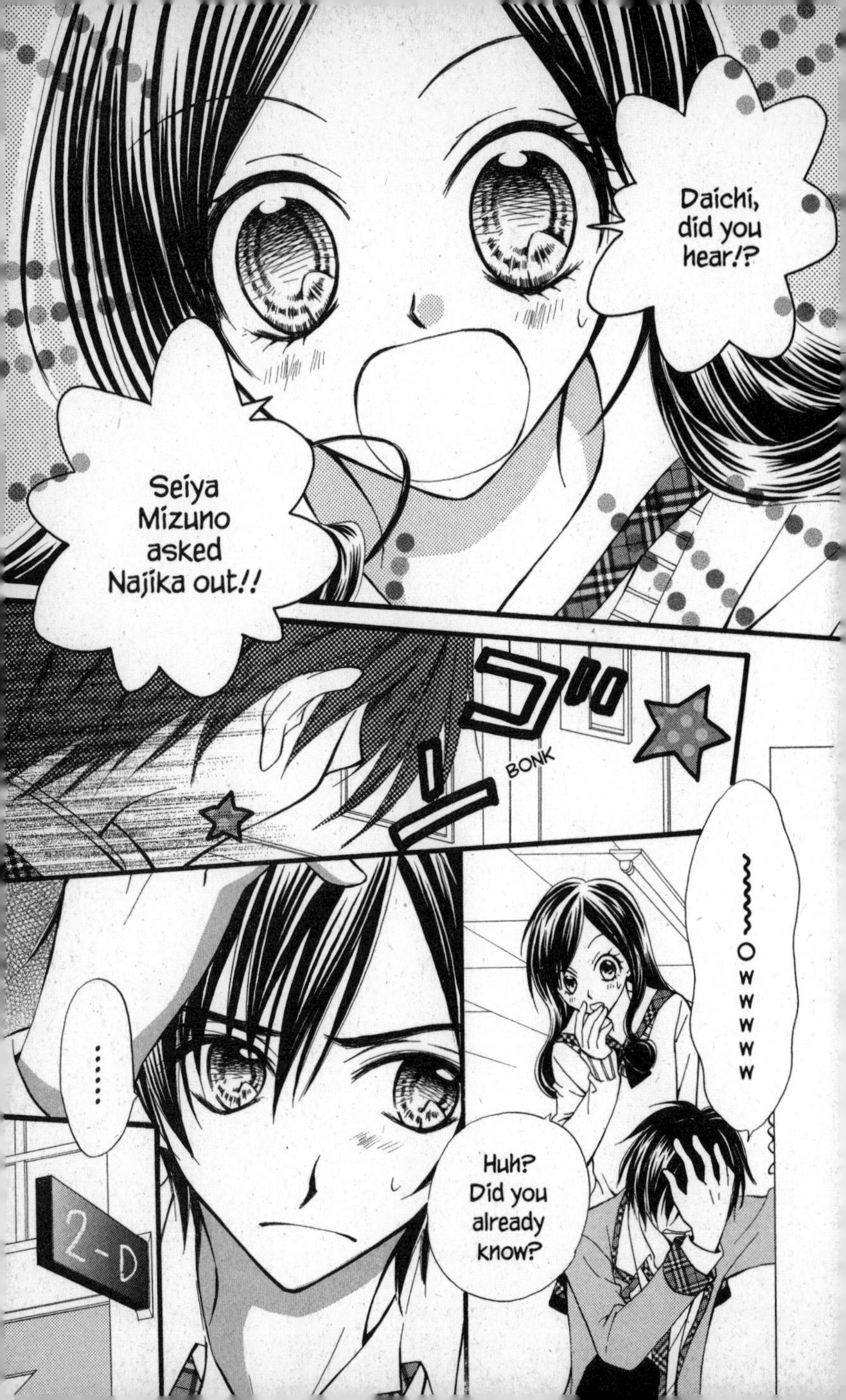
Daichi, did you hear!?
Seiya Mizuno asked Najika out!!
BONK
Owwwwww
Huh? Did you already know?
......
2-D

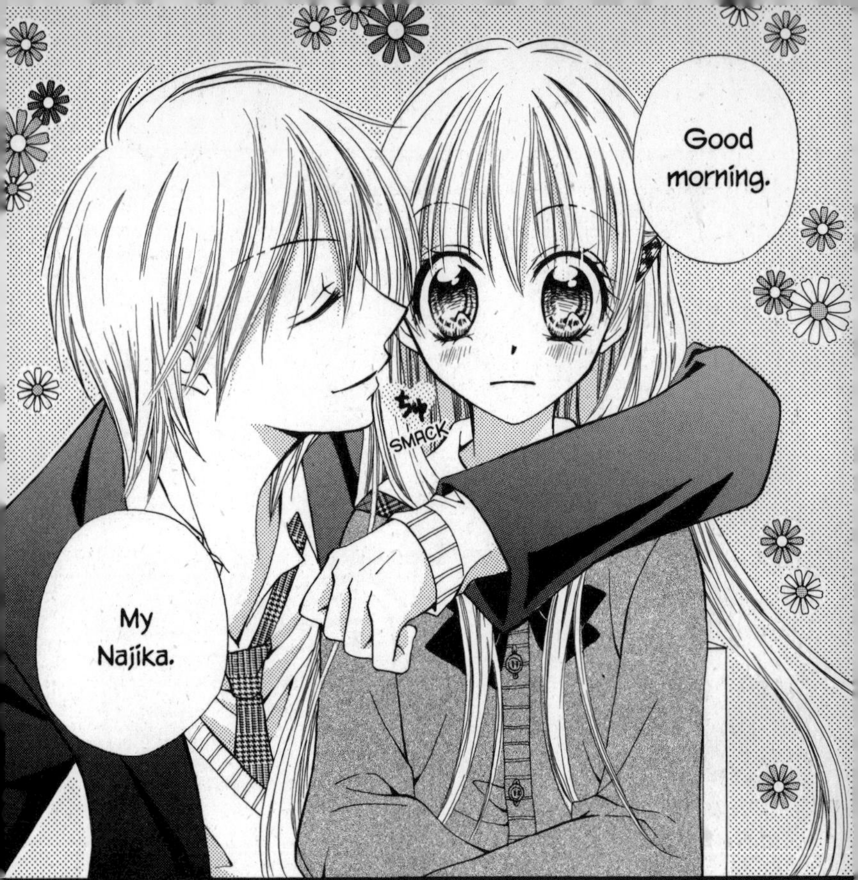
Good morning.
SMACK
My Najika.

About the Splash Pages

Recipe 39

This chapter was featured after a month's break in the magazine serialization, so I thought that it would be a good idea to have the splash page remind the readers what the previous chapter was about. So it shows Seiya being aggressive. I thought it would be boring with only the two of them, so I added some flowers. I worked really hard on them!!

Recipe 40

Since the chapter was about Valentine's Day, I wanted to draw chocolate and have Najika holding some. I wanted to draw a bigger chocolate, but it didn't quite fit in with the composition so I had to make it smaller.
We've done Valentine's Day recipes before, but this is the first time it's been featured in the main story, isn't it?

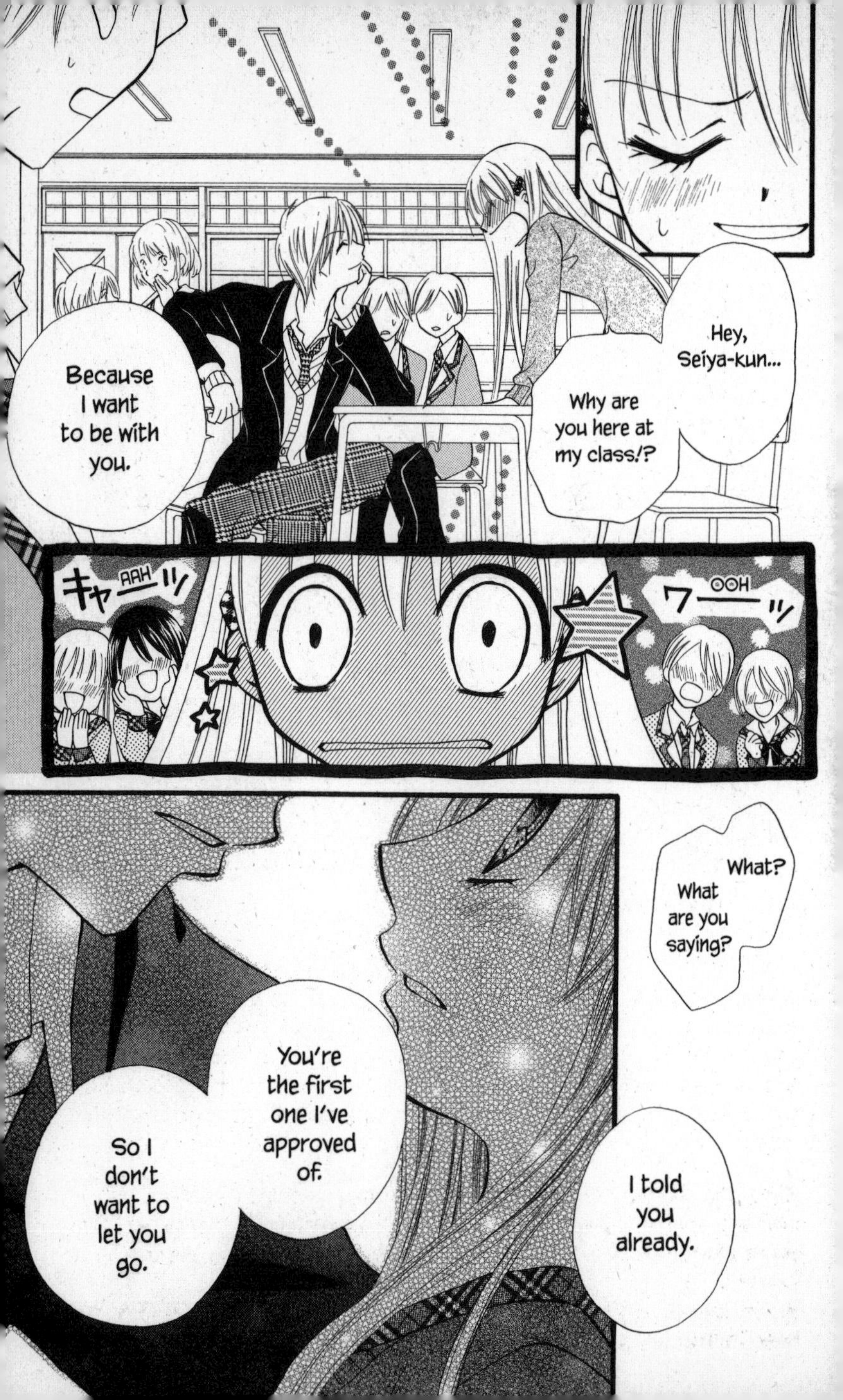
Hey, Seiya-kun...
Why are you here at my class!?
Because I want to be with you.
ワーーッ
OOH
キャーーッ
AAH
What? What are you saying?
I told you already.
You're the first one I've approved of.
So I don't want to let you go.

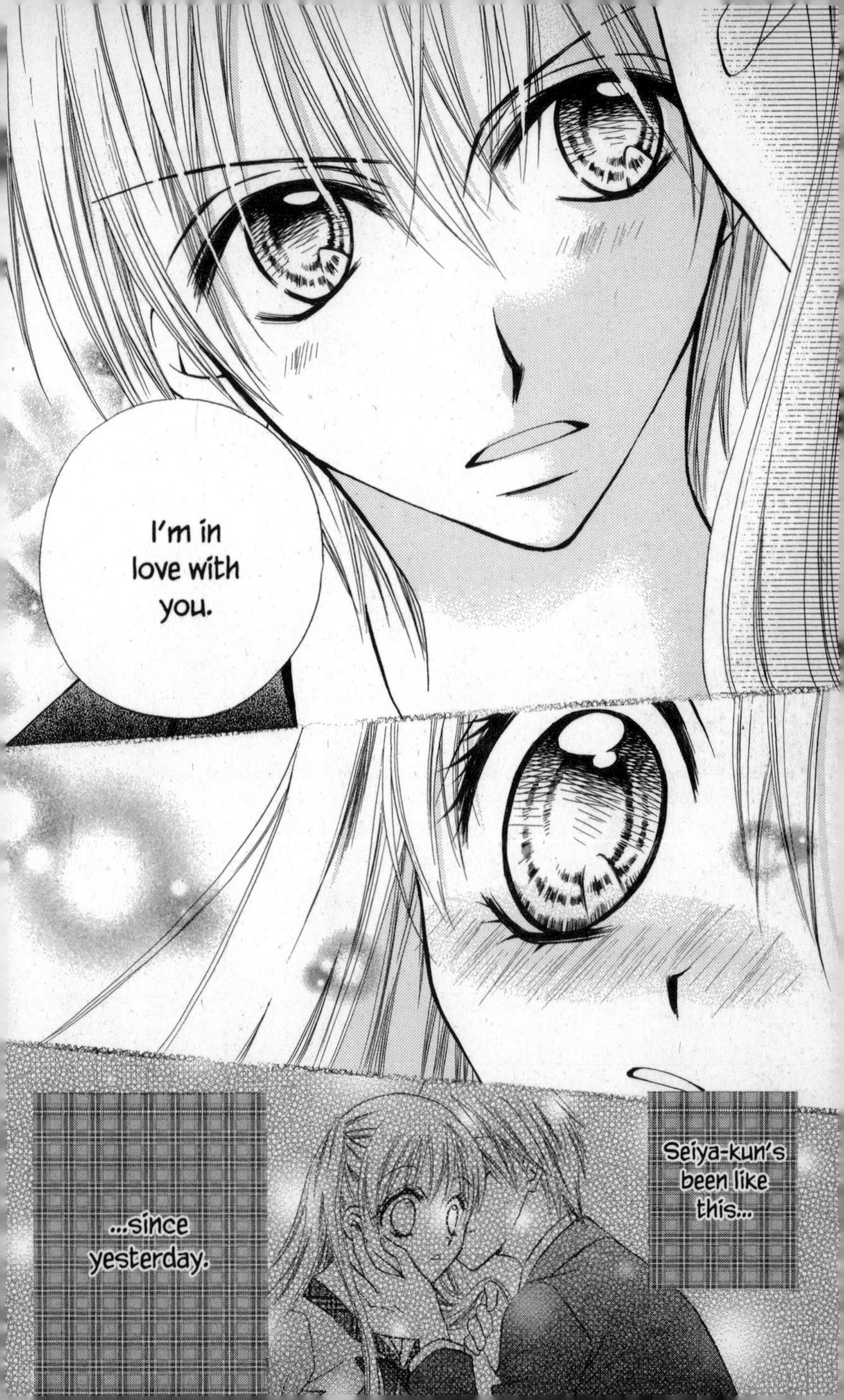
I'm in love with you.
Seiya-kun's been like this...
...since yesterday.

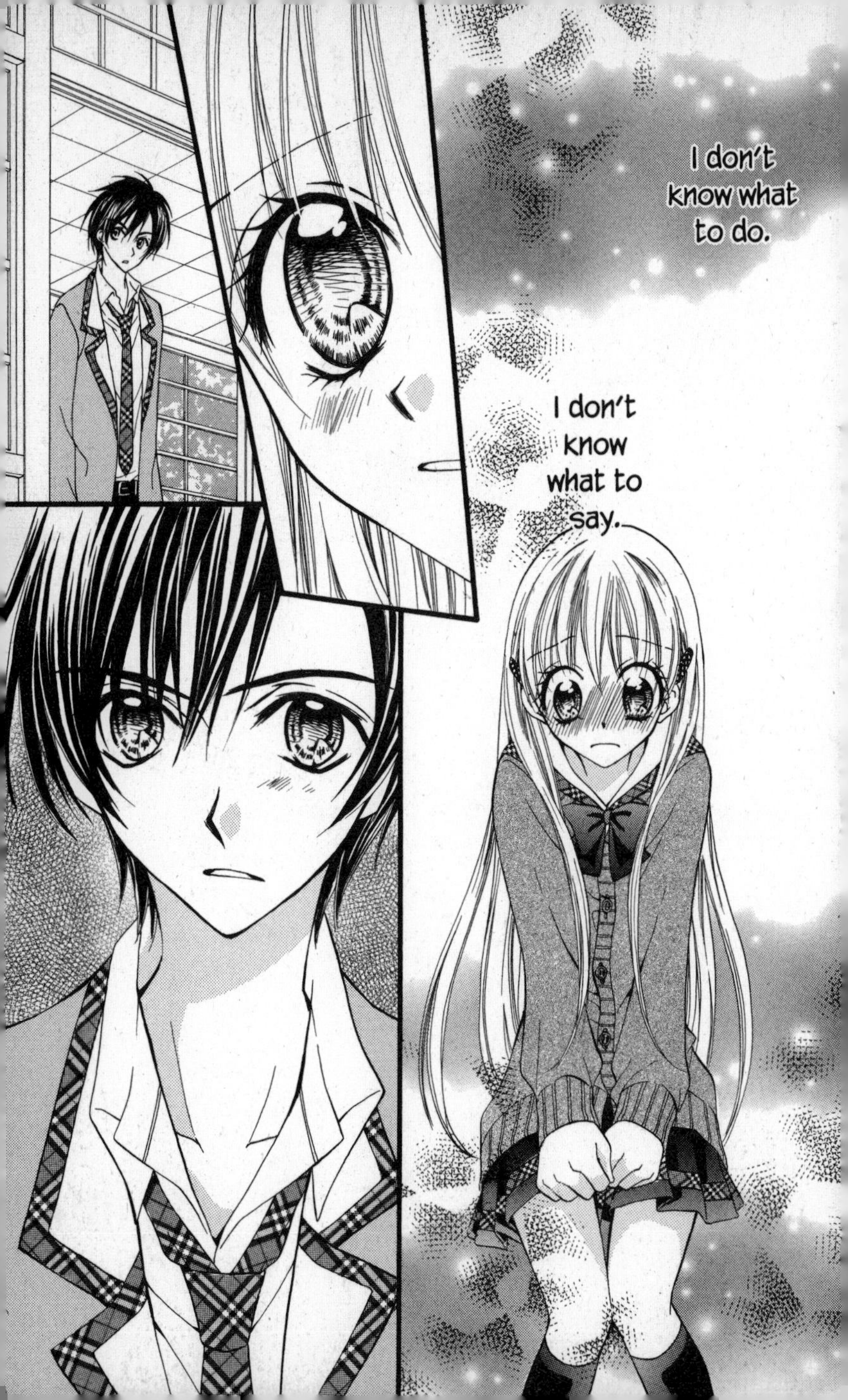
I don't know what to do.
I don't know what to say.

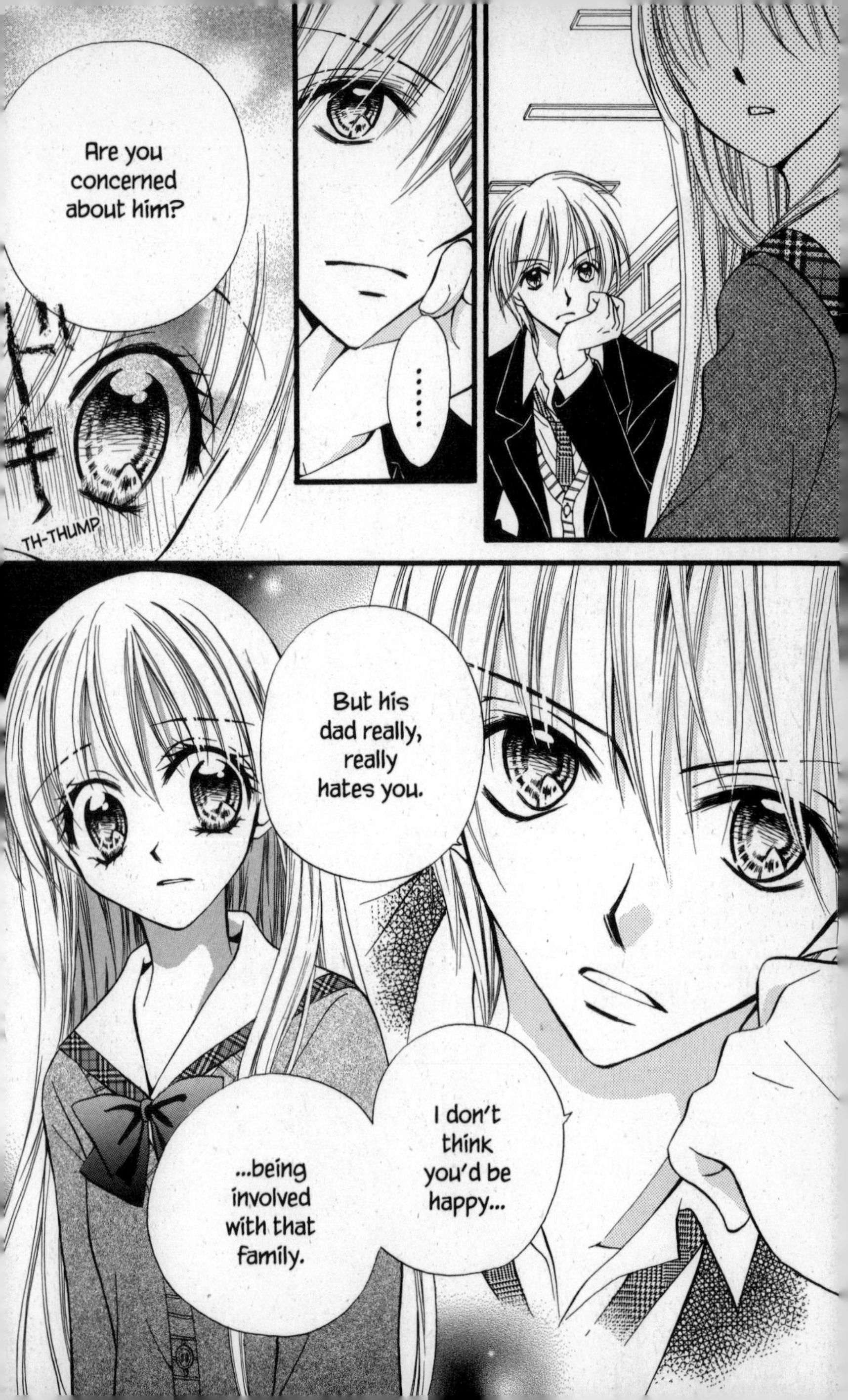
......
Are you concerned about him?
TH-THUMP
But his dad really, really hates you.
I don't think you'd be happy...
...being involved with that family.

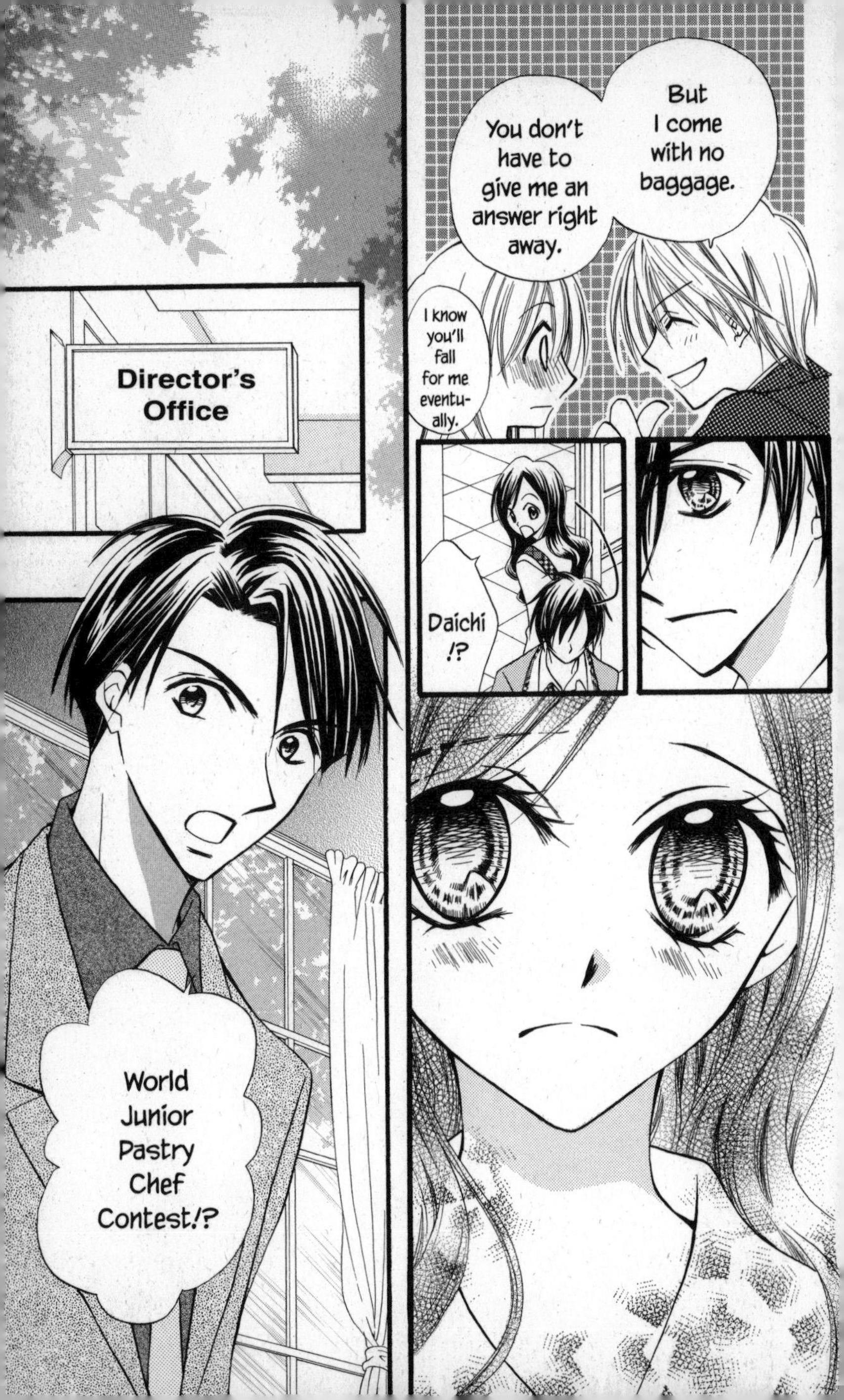
But I come with no baggage.
You don't have to give me an answer right away.
I know you'll fall for me eventu-ally.
Daichi!?
Director's Office
World Junior Pastry Chef Contest!?

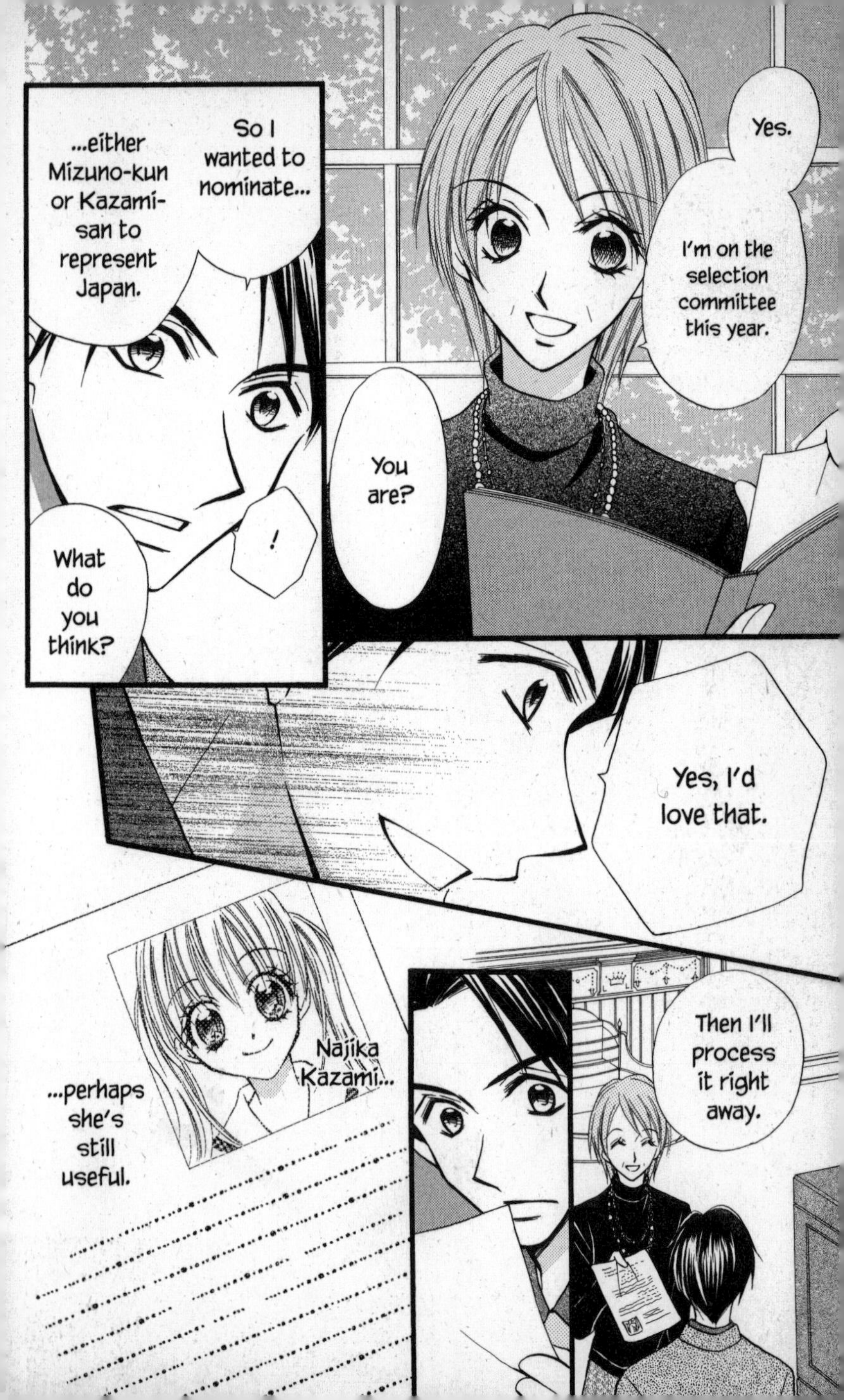
Yes.
I'm on the selection committee this year.
You are?
So I wanted to nominate...
...either Mizuno-kun or Kazami-san to represent Japan.
!
What do you think?
Yes, I'd love that.
Then I'll process it right away.
Najika Kazami...
...perhaps she's still useful.

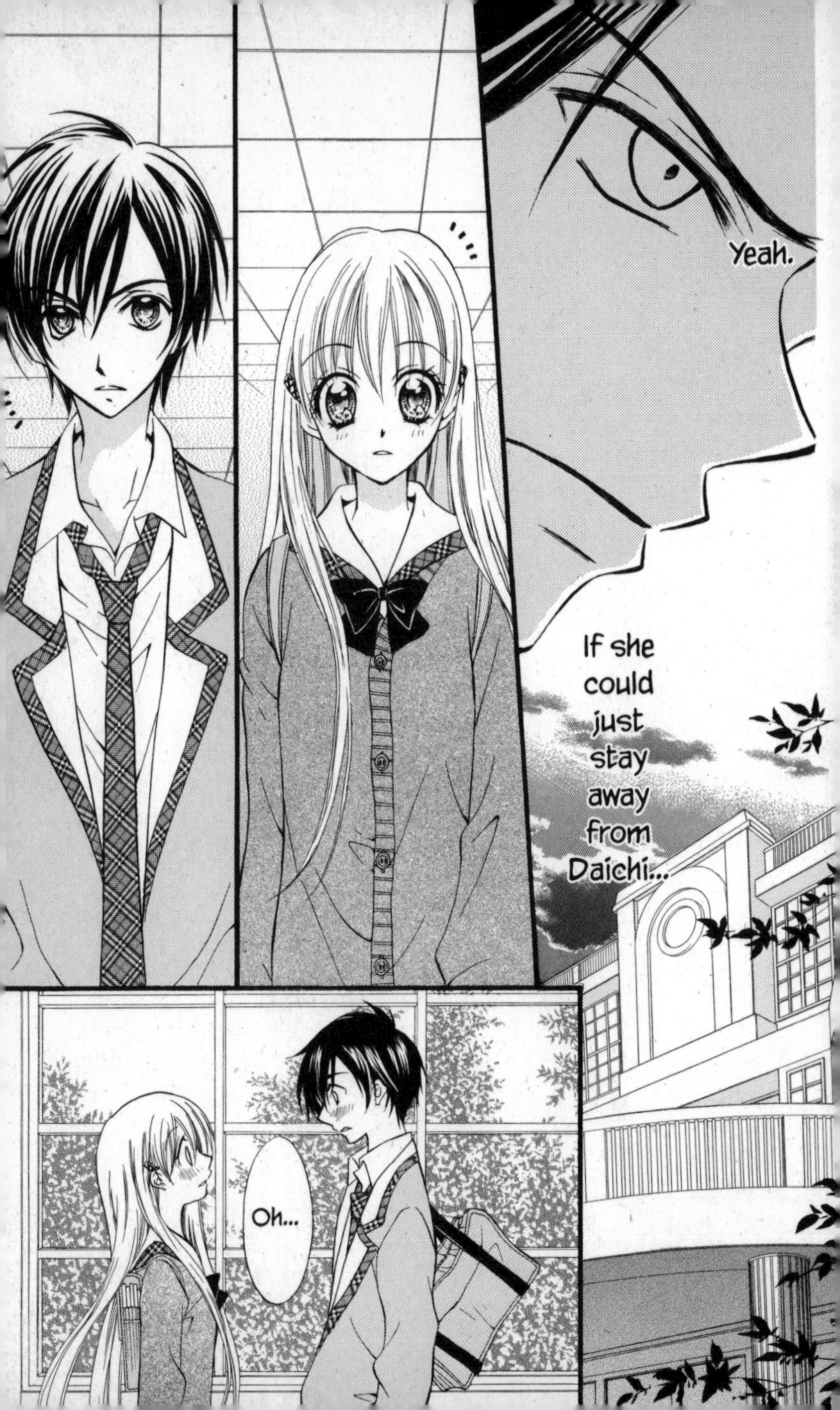
Yeah.
If she could just stay away from Daichi...
Oh...

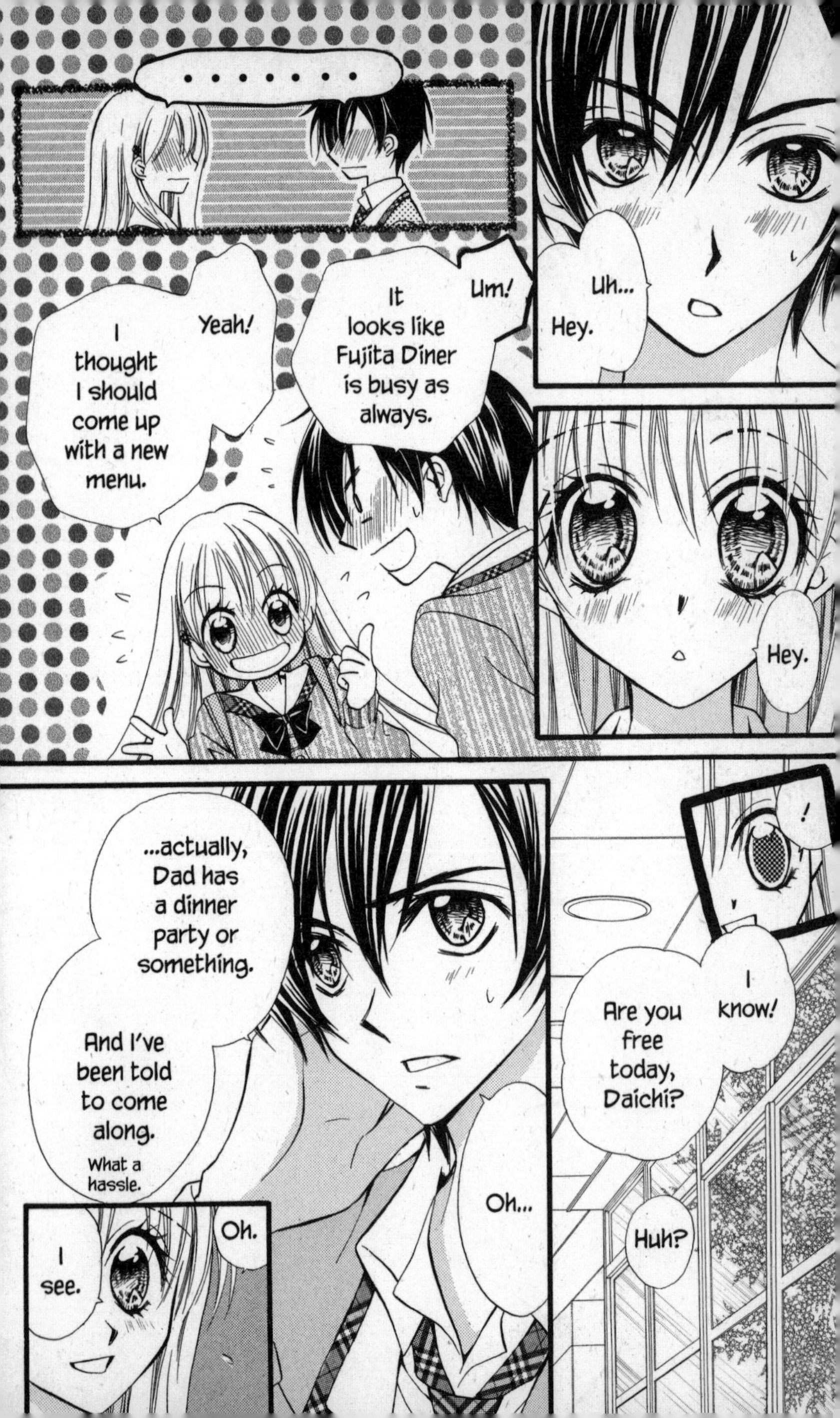
Uh... Hey.
Hey.
....
Um! It looks like Fujita Diner is busy as always.
Yeah! I thought I should come up with a new menu.
!
I know! Are you free today, Daichi?
Huh?
Oh...
...actually, Dad has a dinner party or something.
And I've been told to come along. What a hassle.
Oh. I see.

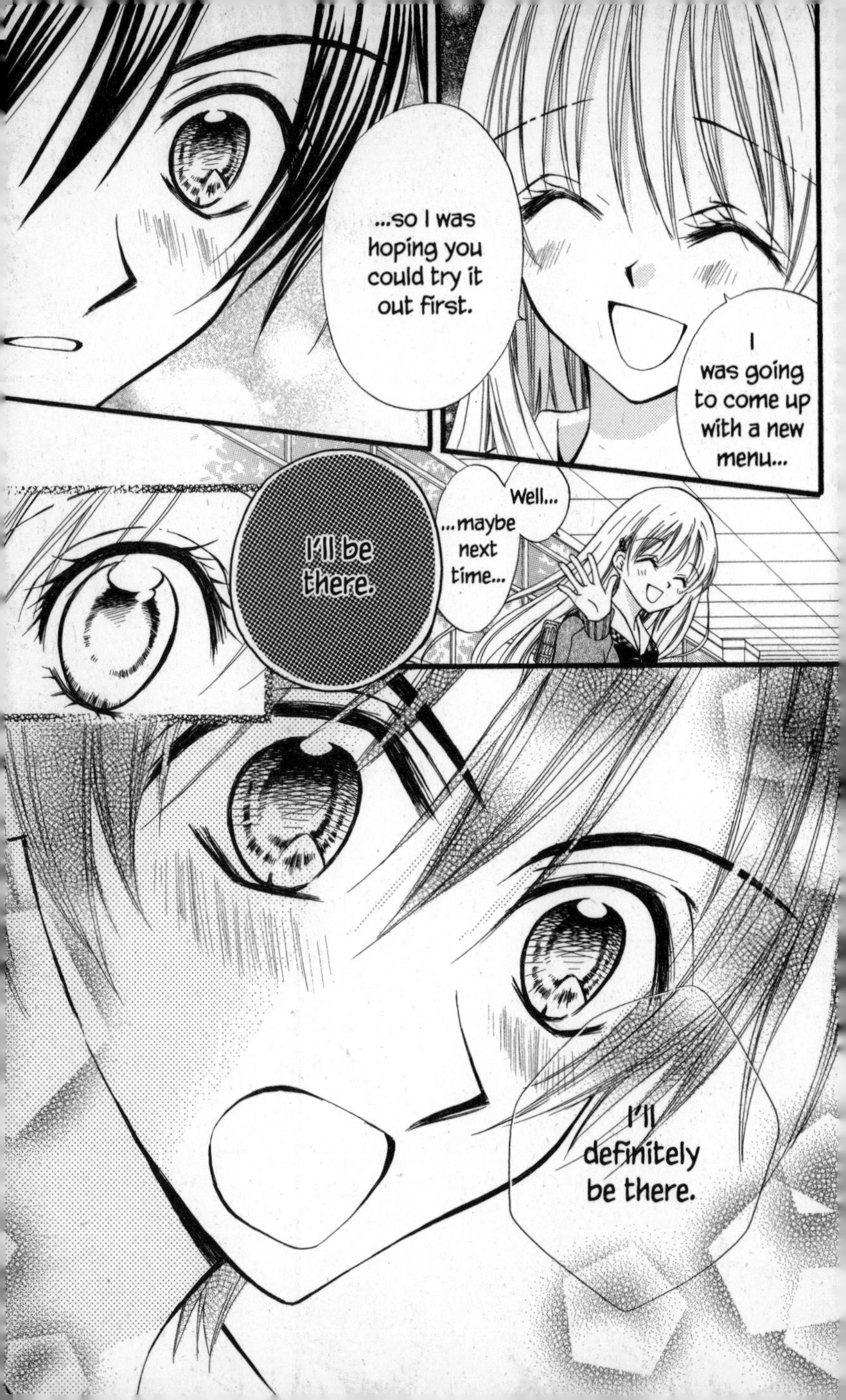
I was going to come up with a new menu...
...so I was hoping you could try it out first.
Well...
...maybe next time...
I'll be there.
I'll definitely be there.

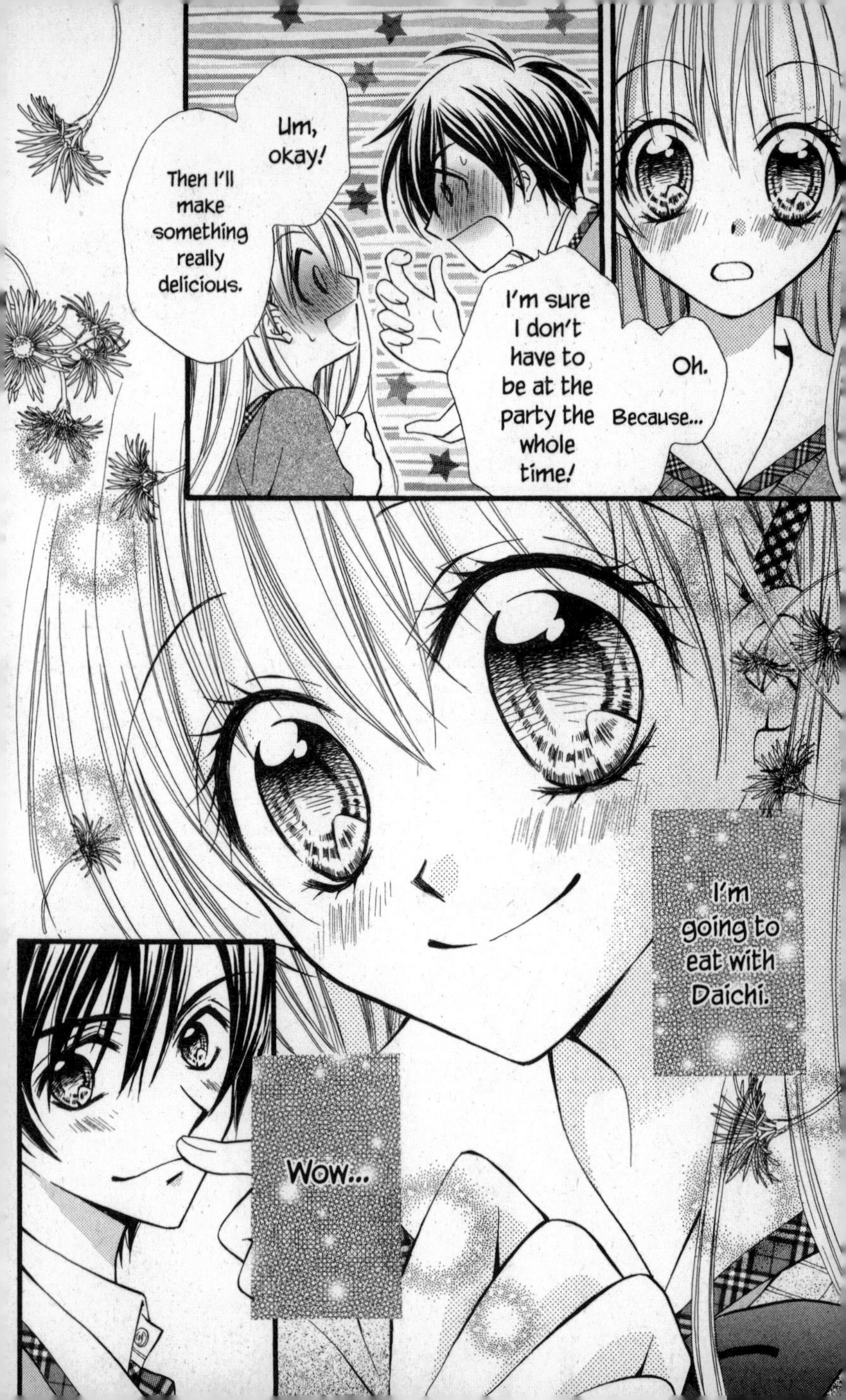
Oh.
Because...
I'm sure I don't have to be at the party the whole time!
Um, okay!
Then I'll make something really delicious.
I'm going to eat with Daichi.
Wow...

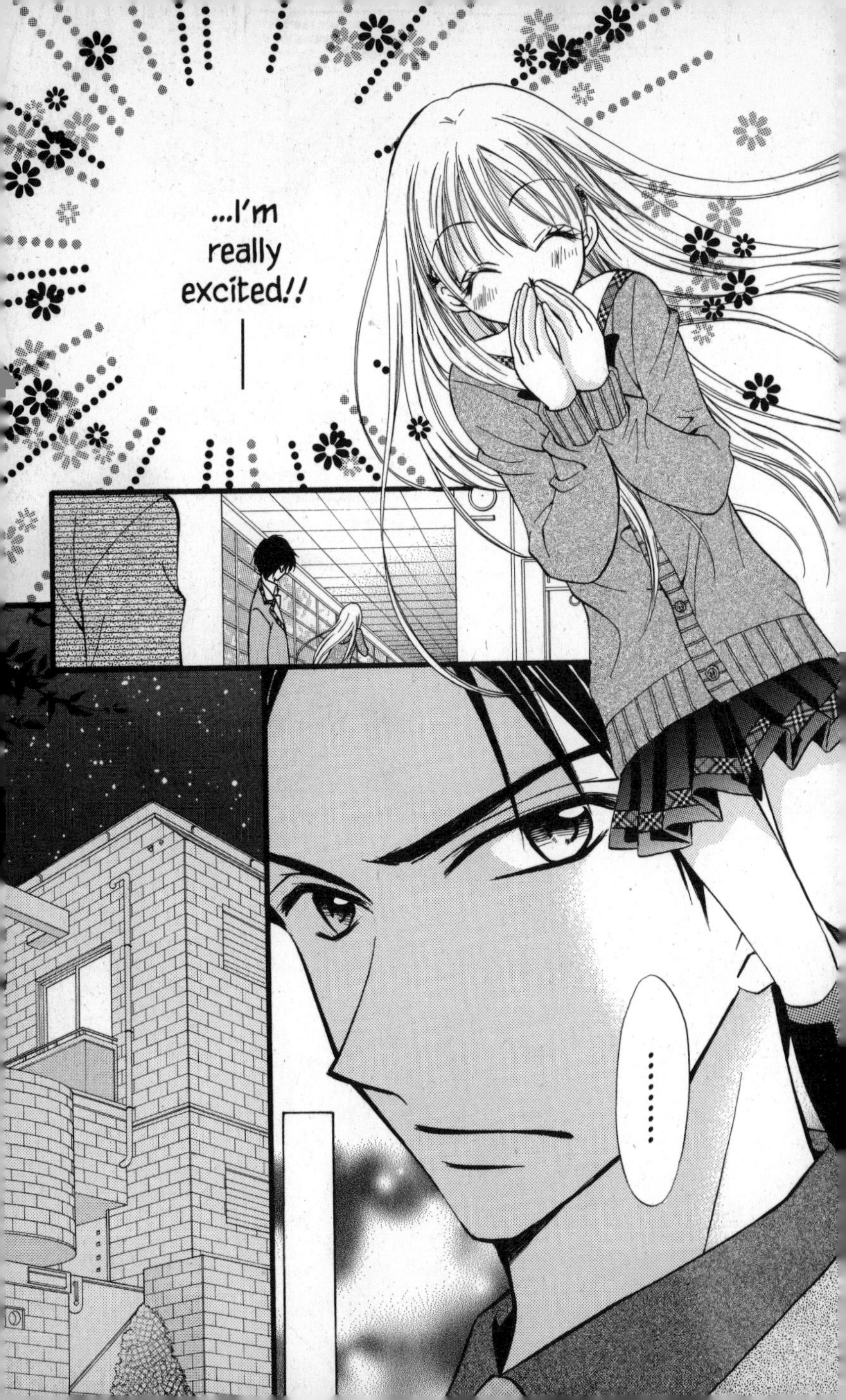
...I'm really excited!!
......

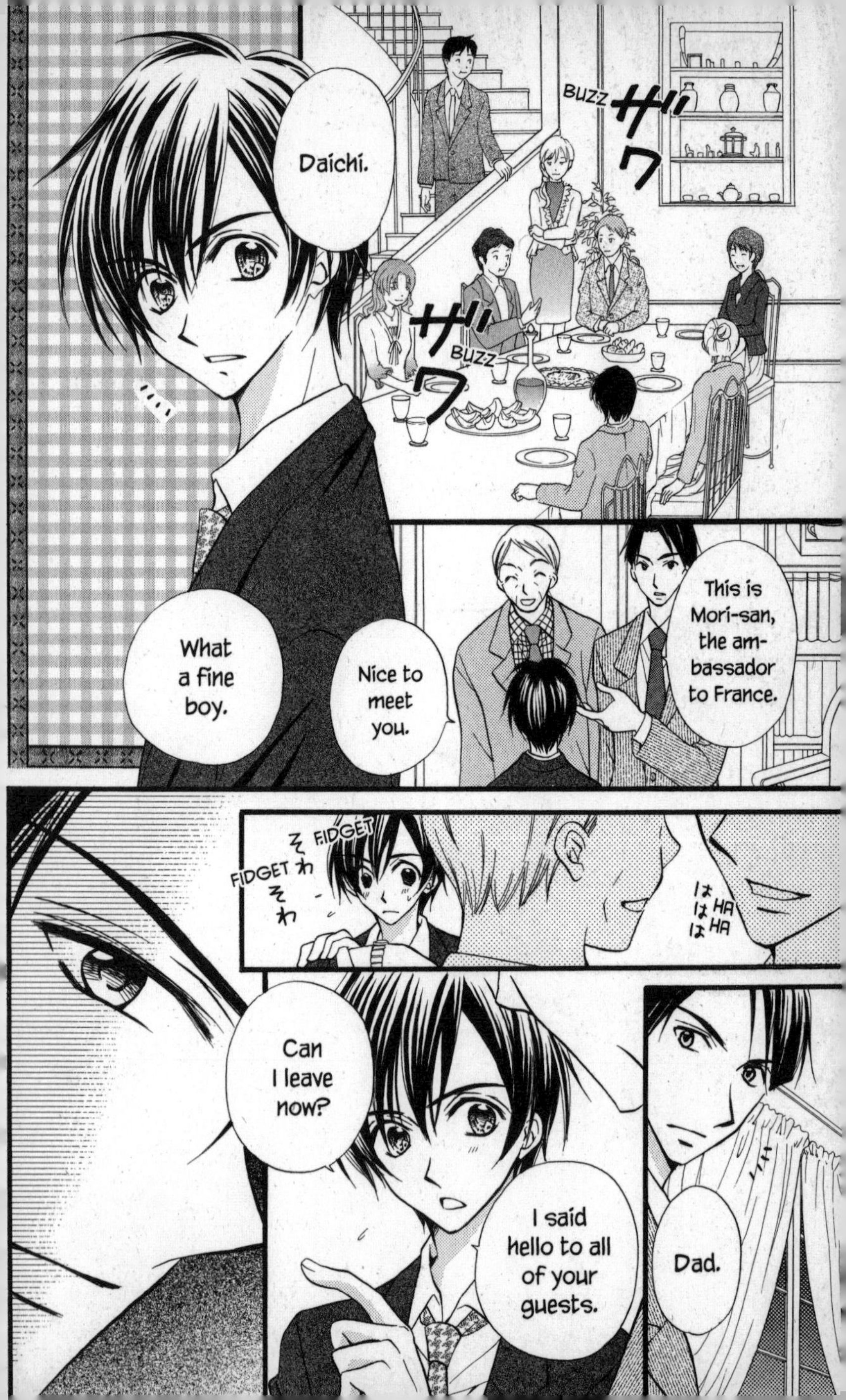

ザワ BUZZ
ザワ BUZZ
Daichi.
……
This is Mori-san, the am-bassador to France.
Nice to meet you.
What a fine boy.
ははは HA HA
そわそわ FIDGET FIDGET
Dad.
I said hello to all of your guests.
Can I leave now?

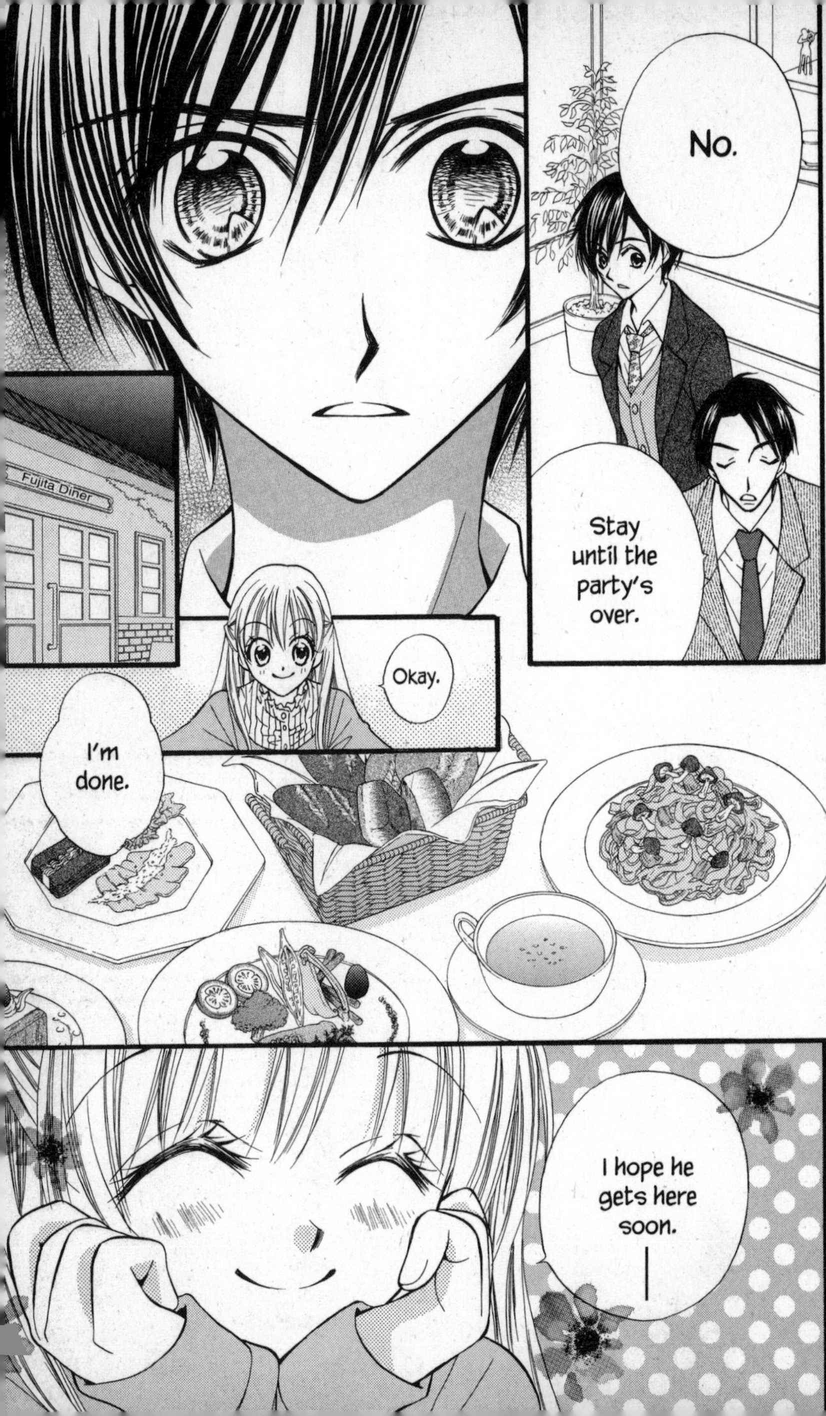
No.
Stay until the party's over.
Fujita Diner
Okay.
I'm done.
I hope he gets here soon.

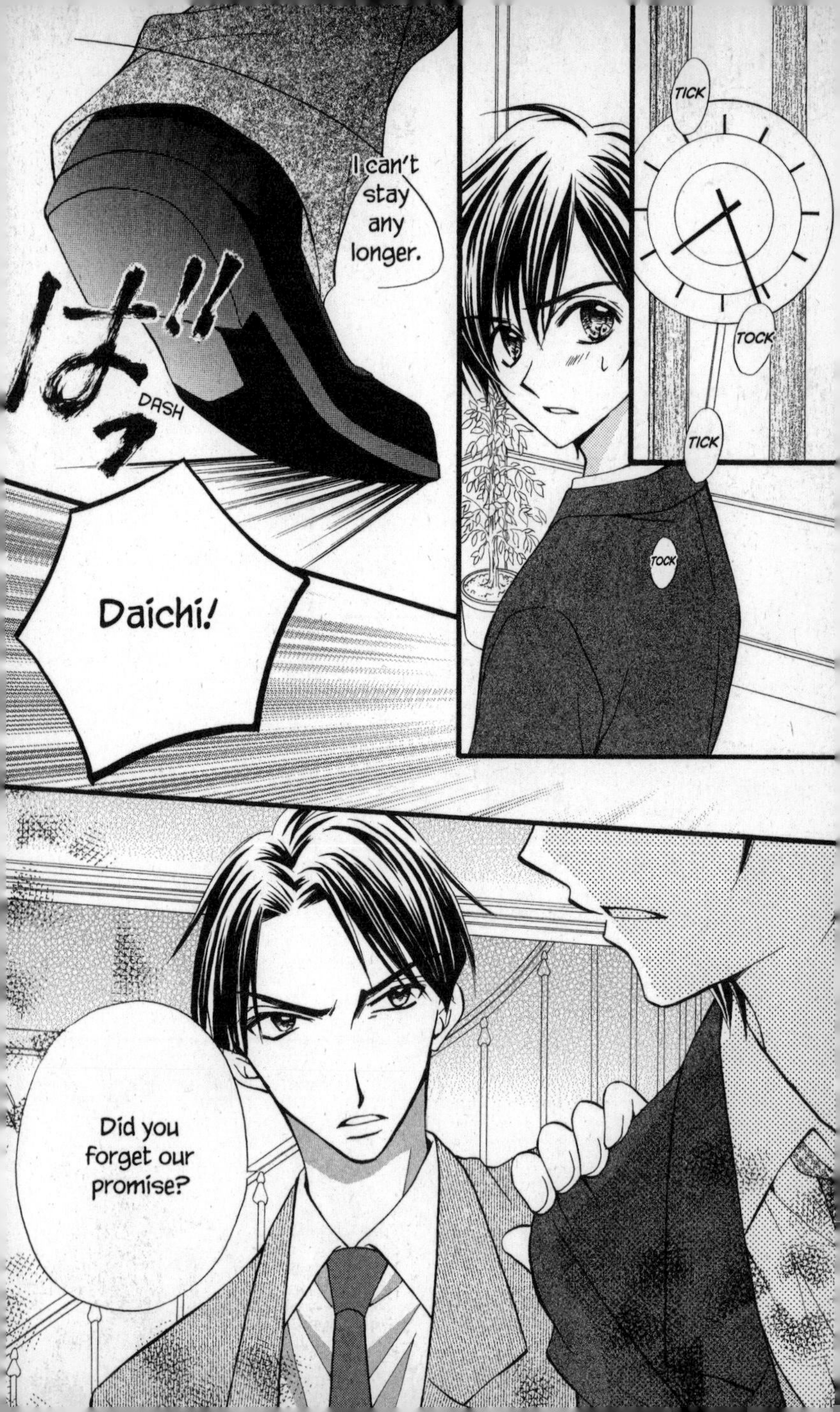
TICK
TOCK
TICK
TOCK
I can't stay any longer.
はっ!!
DASH
Daichi!
Did you forget our promise?

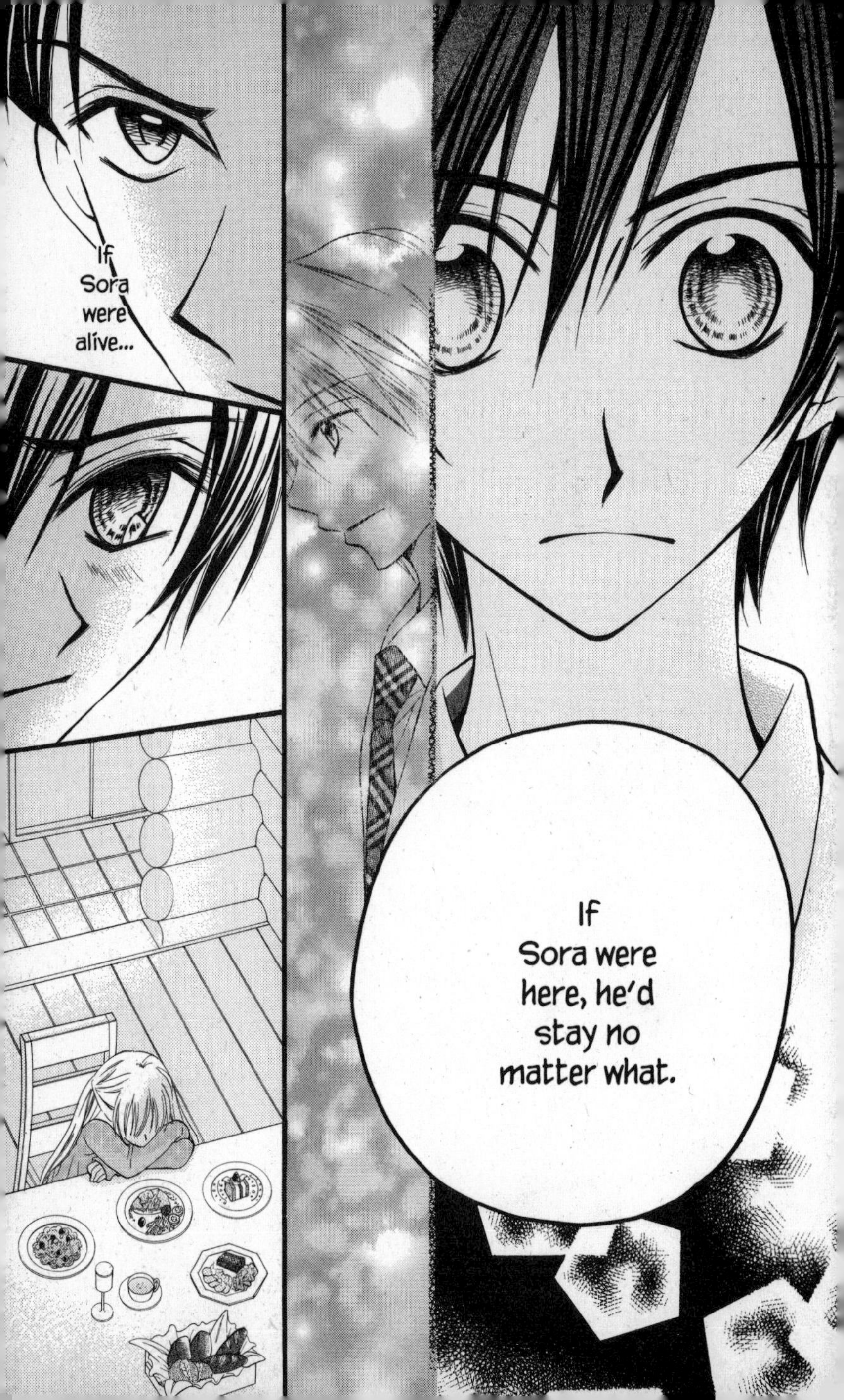
If Sora were here, he'd stay no matter what.
If Sora were alive...

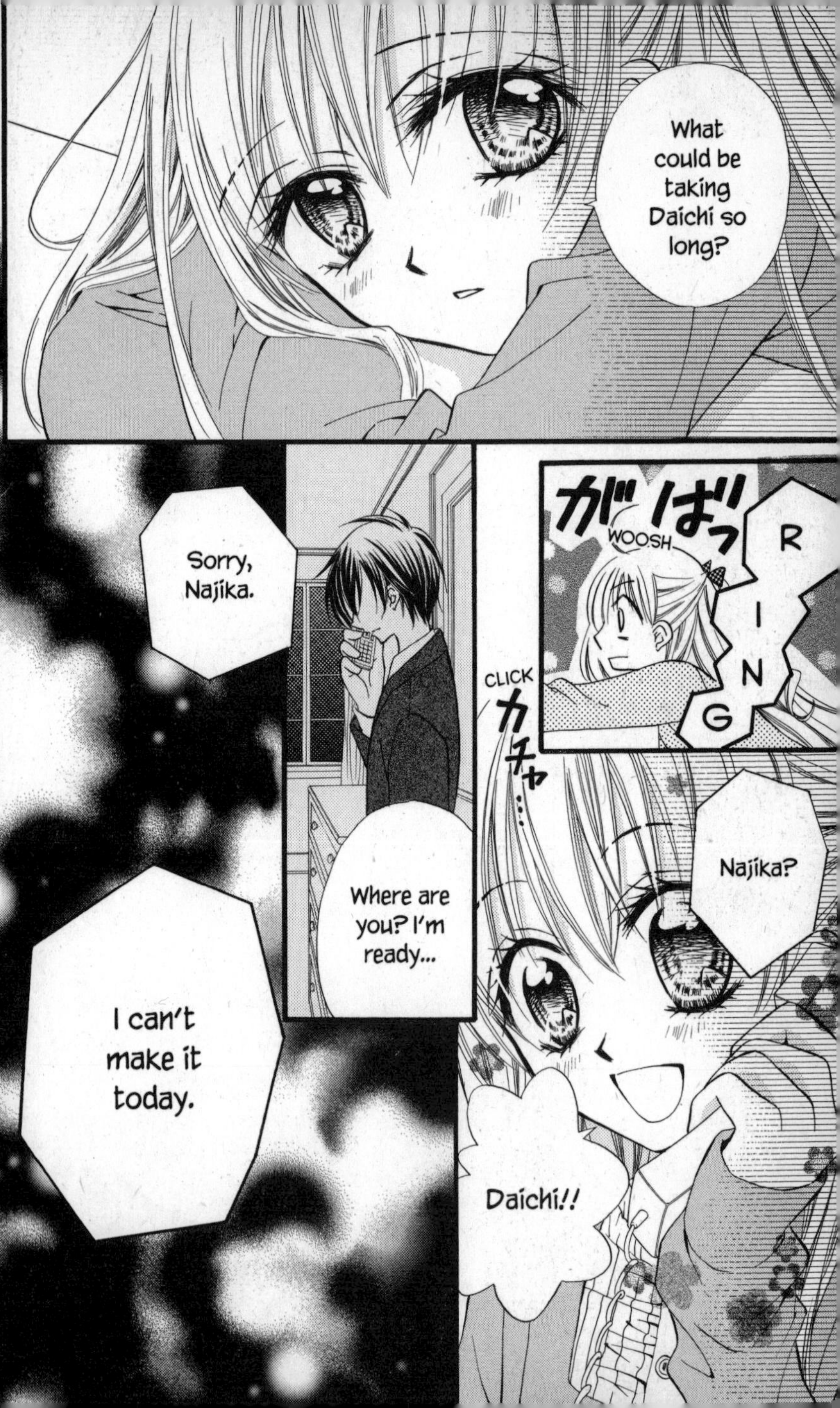
What could be taking Daichi so long?
RING
ガバッ
WOOSH
CLICK
カチャ
Najika?
Daichi!!
Where are you? I'm ready...
Sorry, Najika.
I can't make it today.

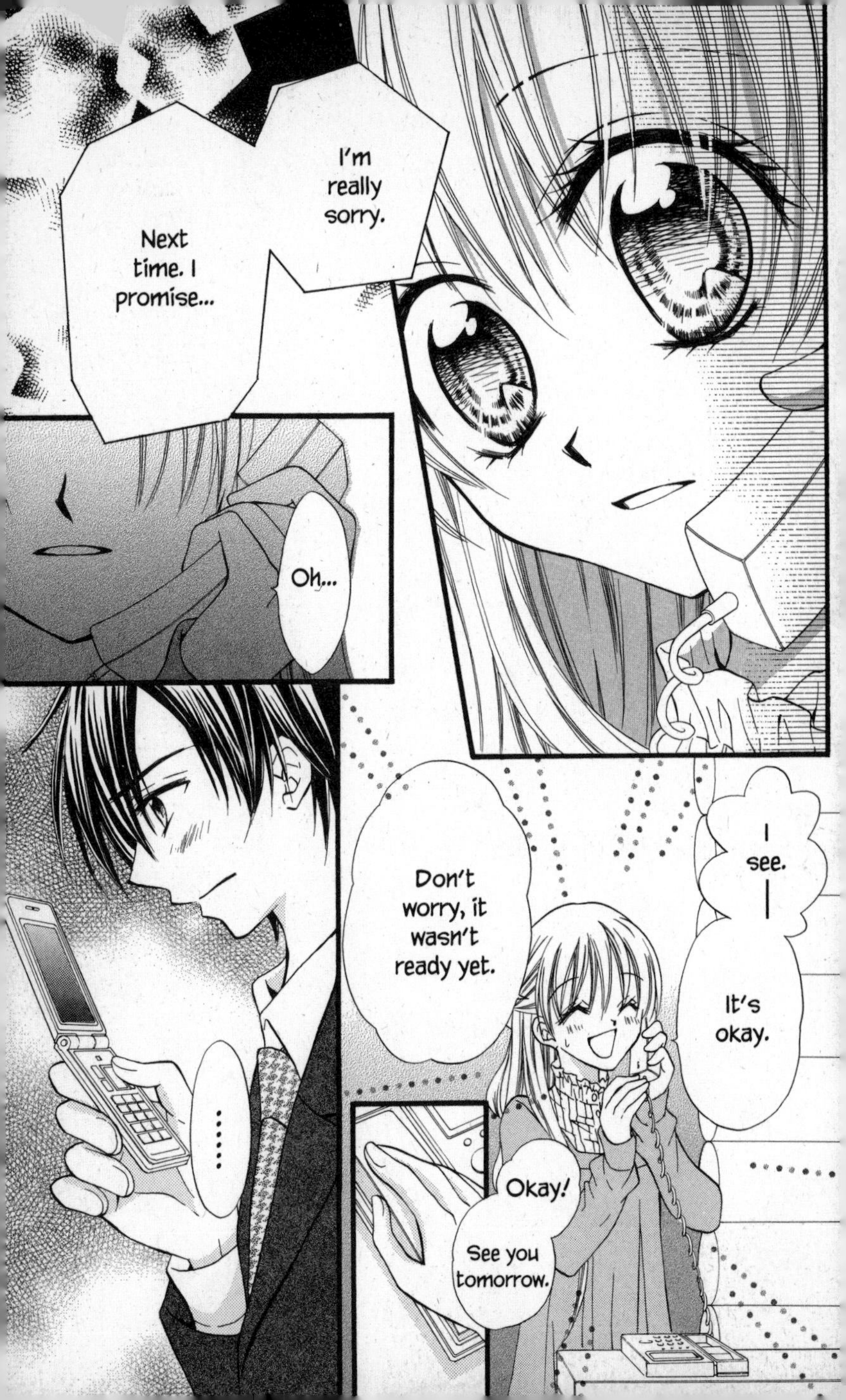
I'm really sorry.
Next time. I promise...
Oh...
I see.
It's okay.
Don't worry, it wasn't ready yet.
Okay!
See you tomorrow.
......

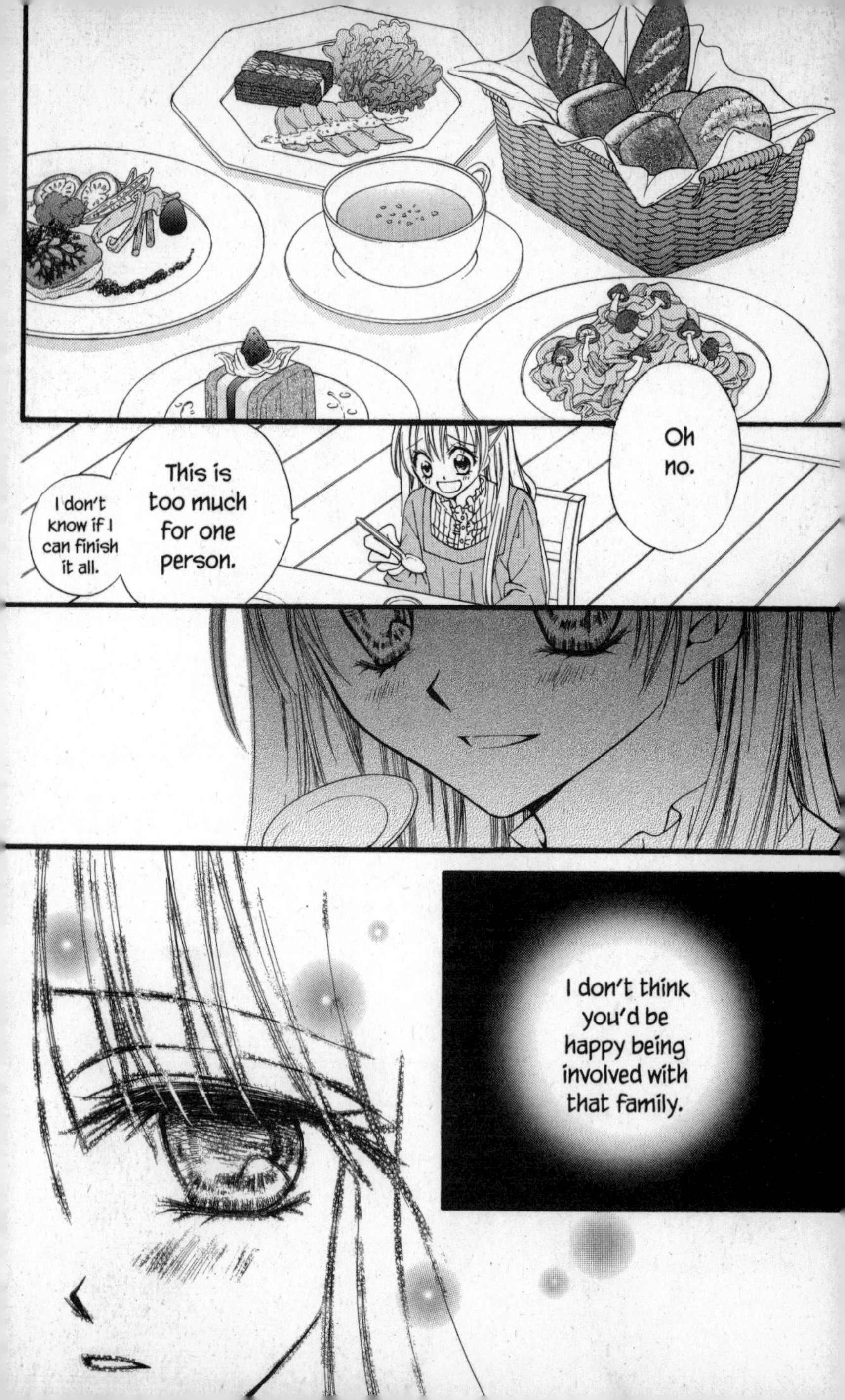
Oh no.
This is too much for one person.
I don't know if I can finish it all.
I don't think you'd be happy being involved with that family.

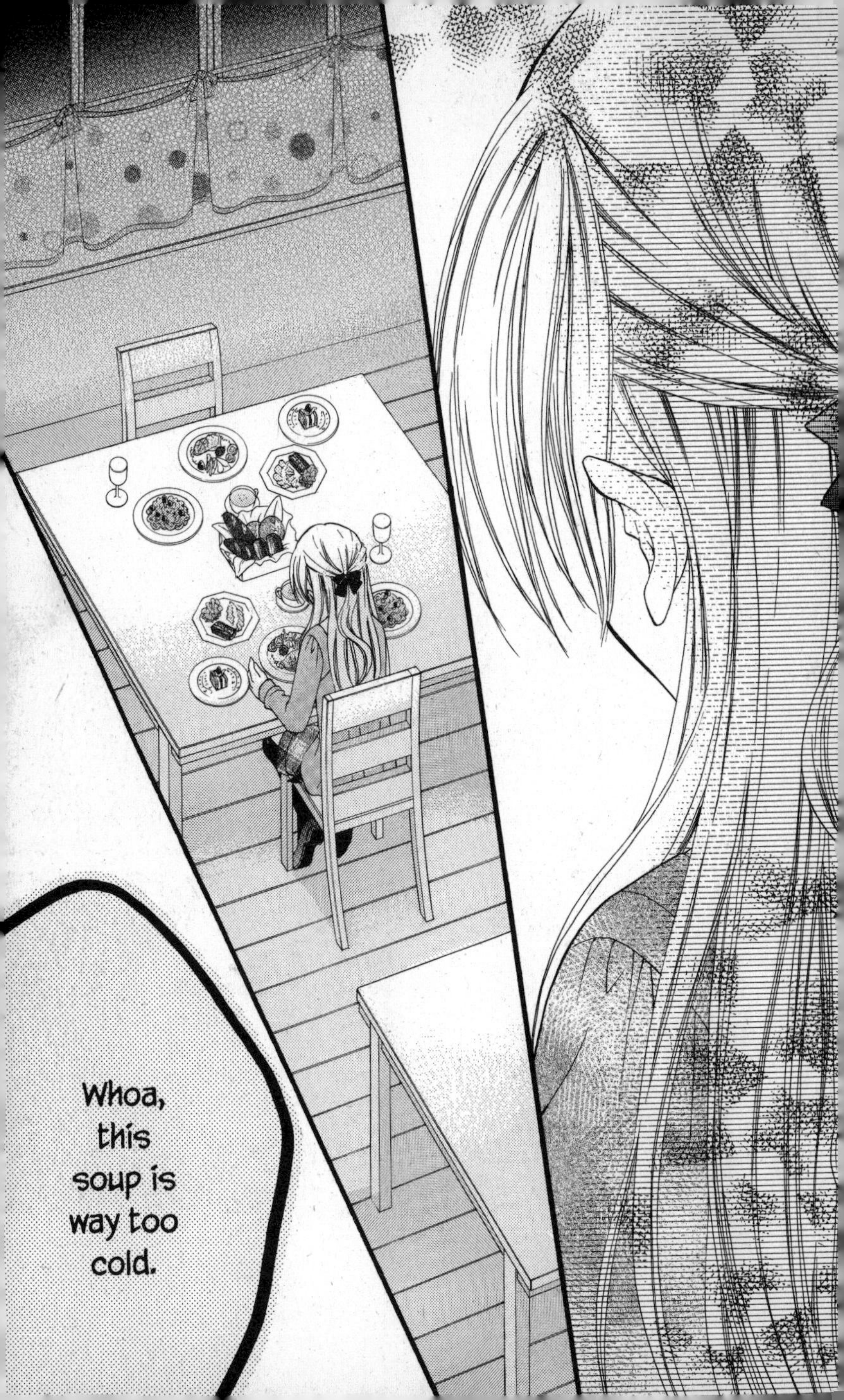
Whoa, this soup is way too cold.

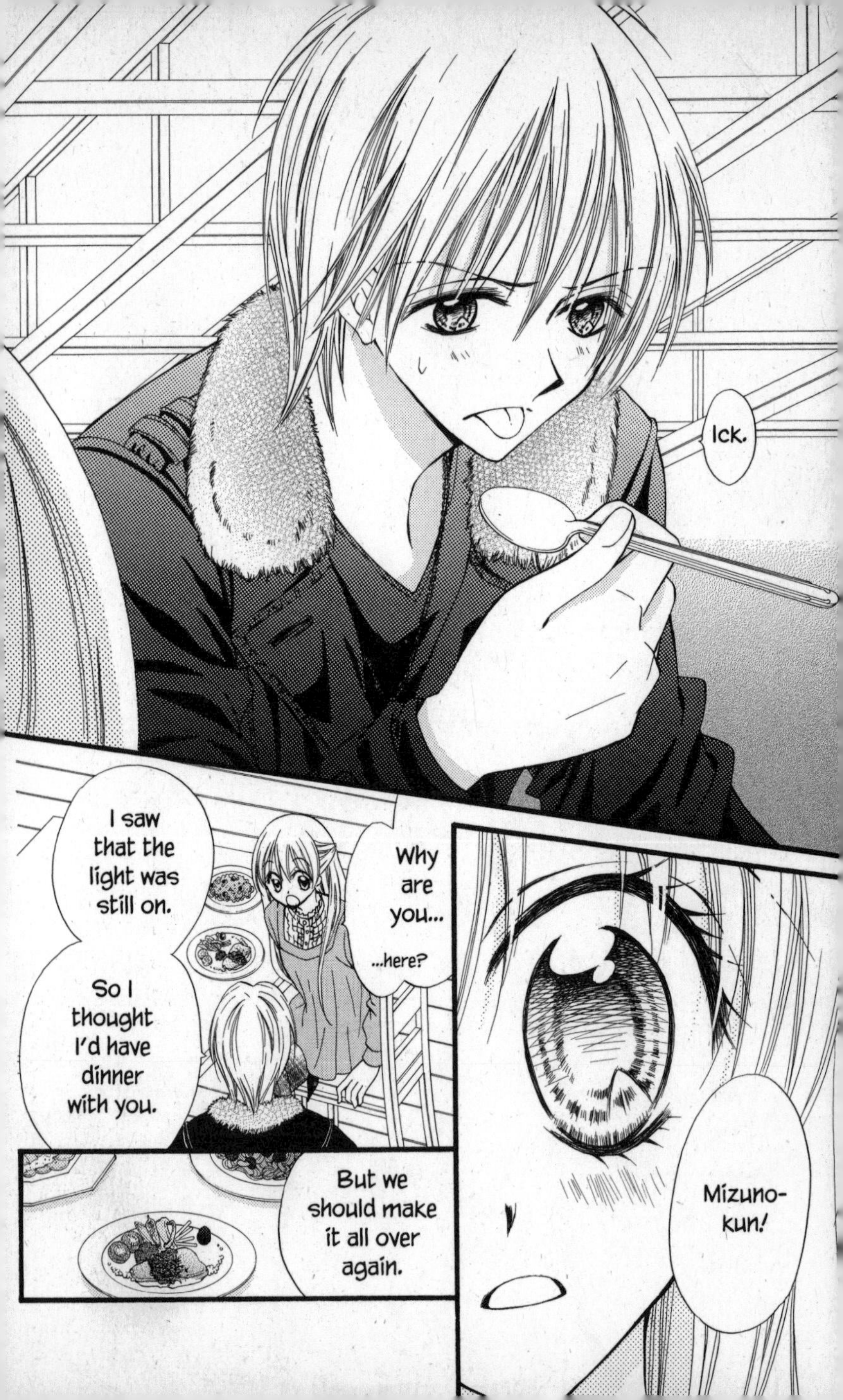
Ick.
Mizuno-kun!
Why are you...
...here?
I saw that the light was still on.
So I thought I'd have dinner with you.
But we should make it all over again.

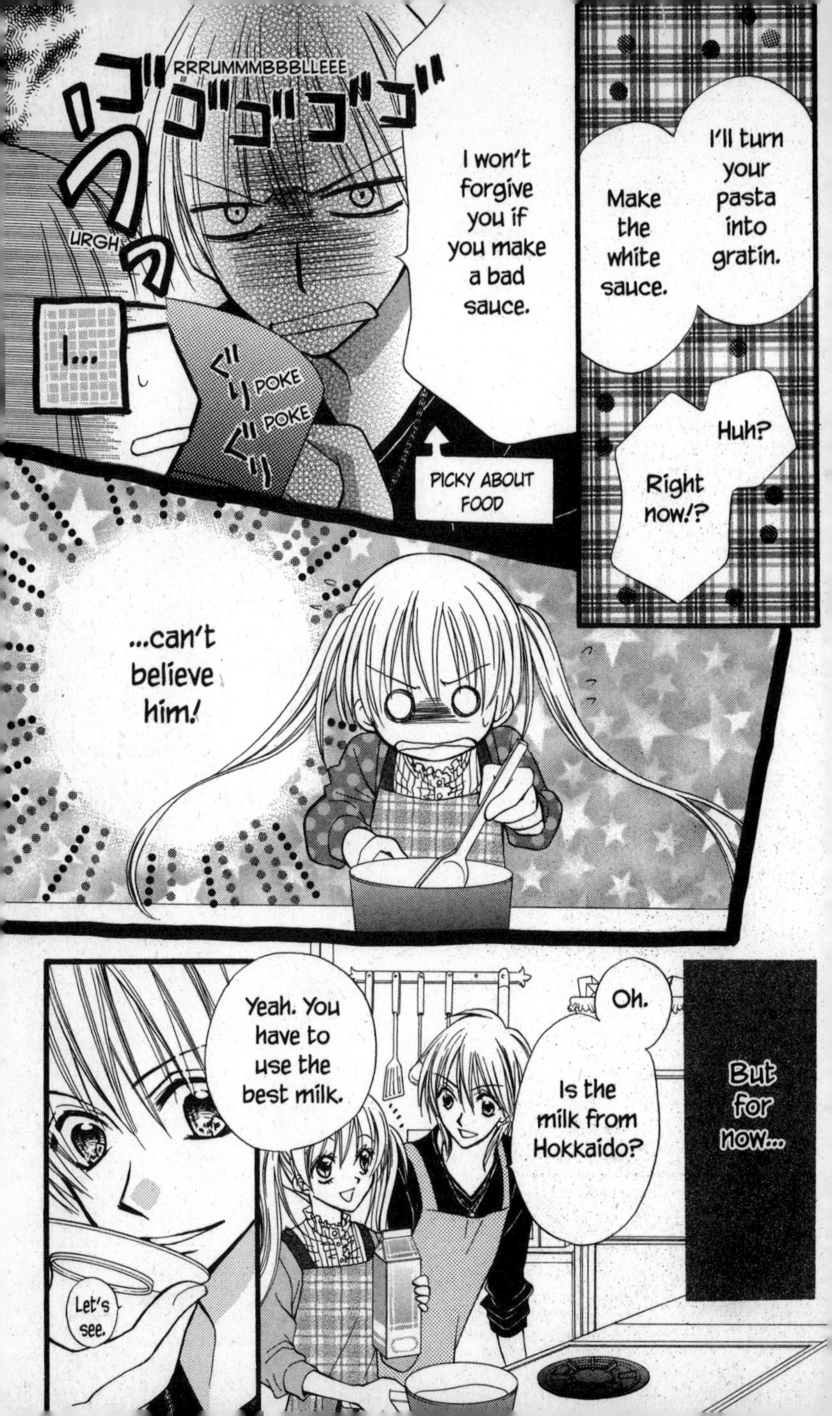
I'll turn your pasta into gratin.
Make the white sauce.
Huh?
Right now!?
RRRUMMMBBBLLEEE
I won't forgive you if you make a bad sauce.
URGH
I...
POKE POKE
PICKY ABOUT FOOD
...can't believe him!
But for now...
Oh.
Is the milk from Hokkaido?
Yeah. You have to use the best milk.
Let's see.

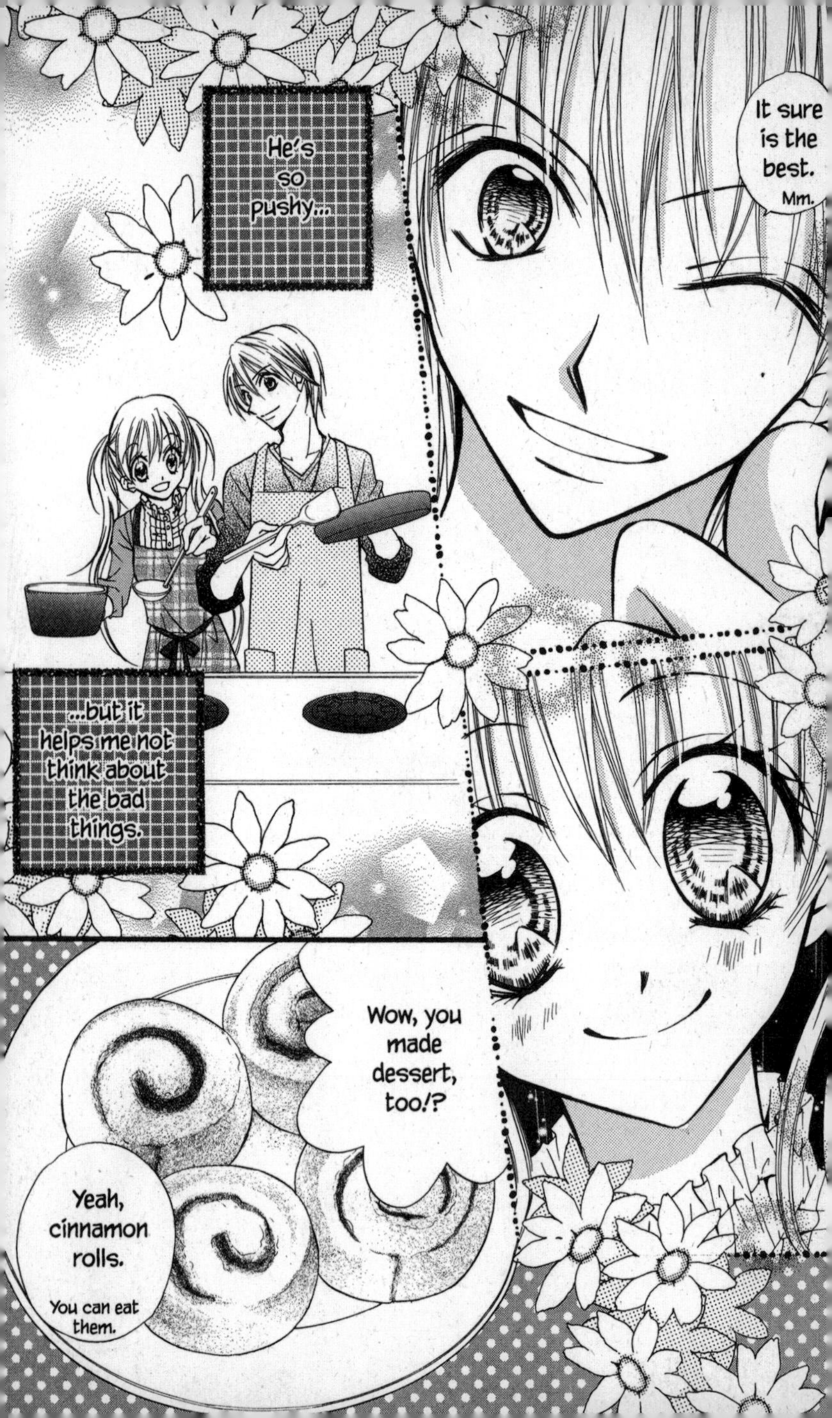
It sure is the best.
Mm.
He's so pushy...
...but it helps me not think about the bad things.
Wow, you made dessert, too!?
Yeah, cinnamon rolls.
You can eat them.

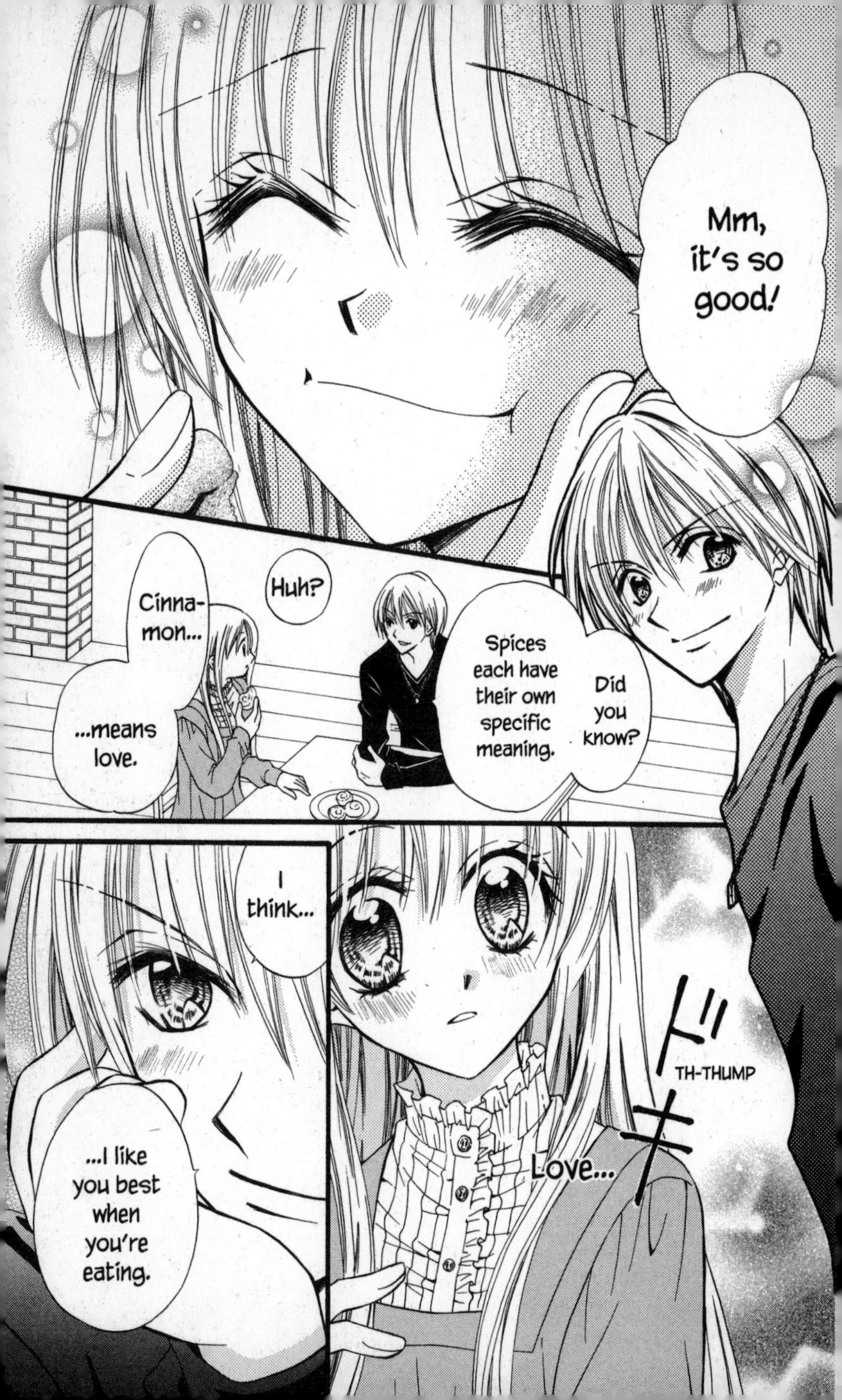

Mm, it's so good!
Did you know?
Spices each have their own specific meaning.
Huh?
Cinnamon...
...means love.
ドキ
TH-THUMP
Love...
I think...
...I like you best when you're eating.

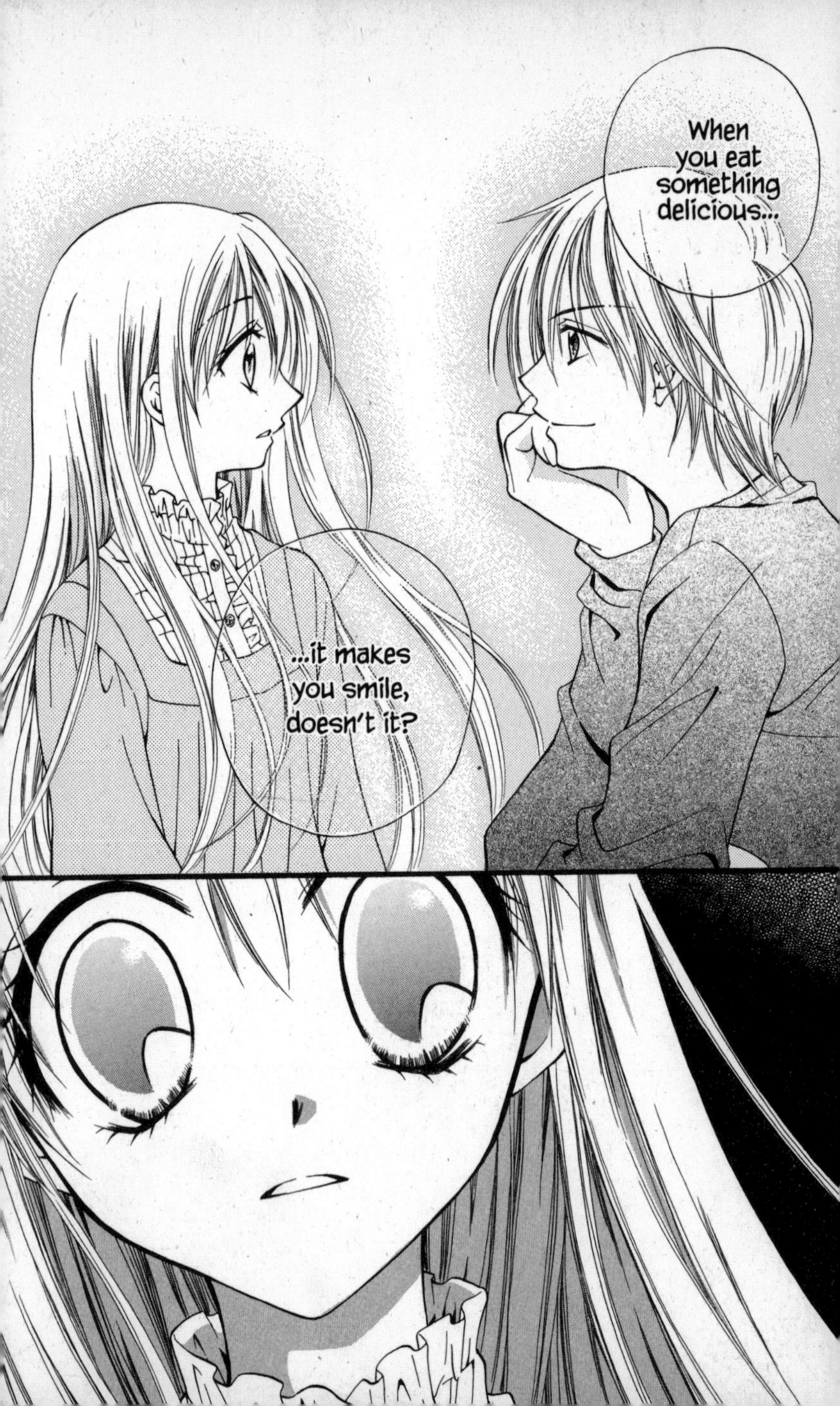
When you eat something delicious...
...it makes you smile, doesn't it?

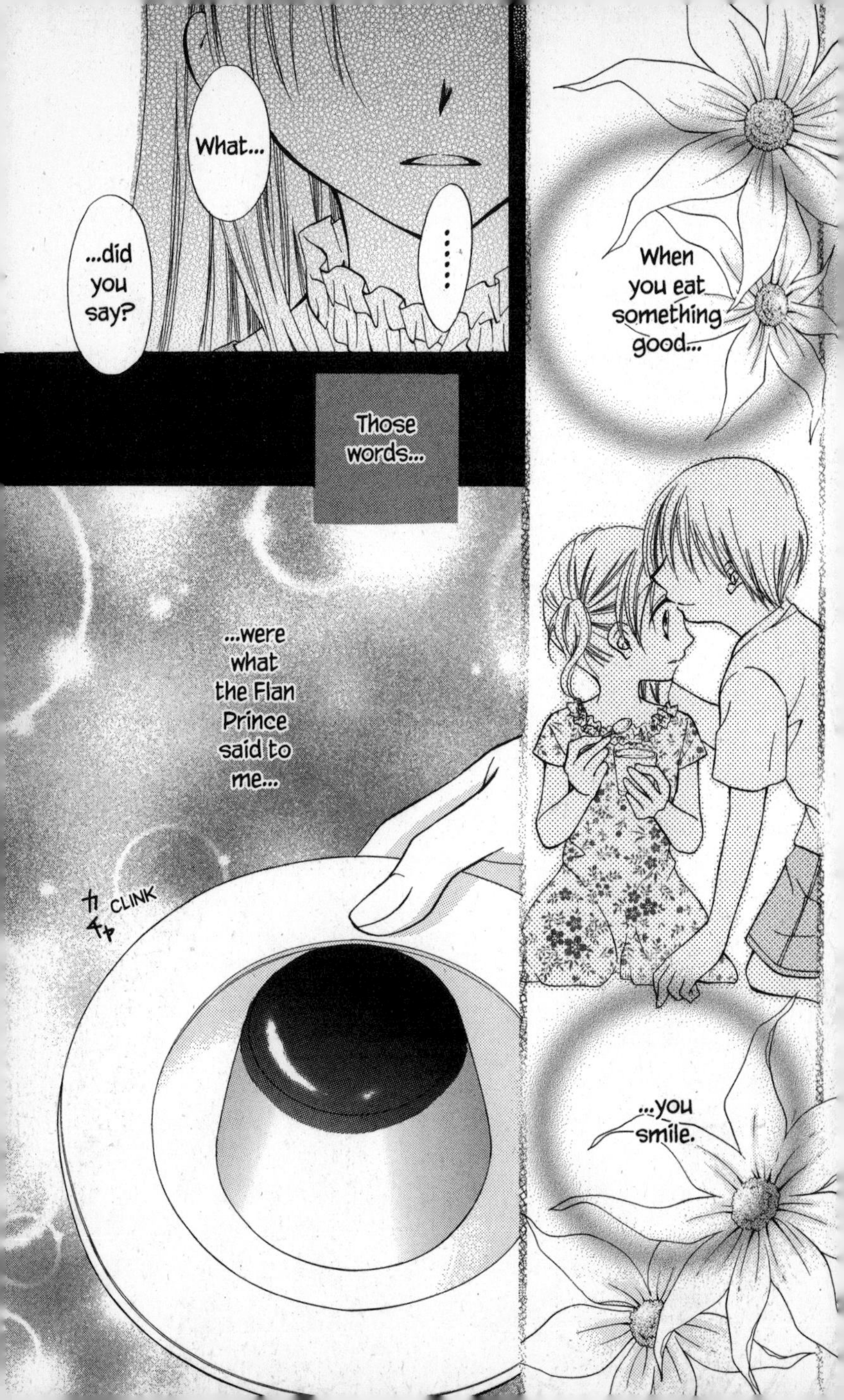

When you eat something good...
...you smile.
What...
...did you say?
......
Those words...
...were what the Flan Prince said to me...
CLINK

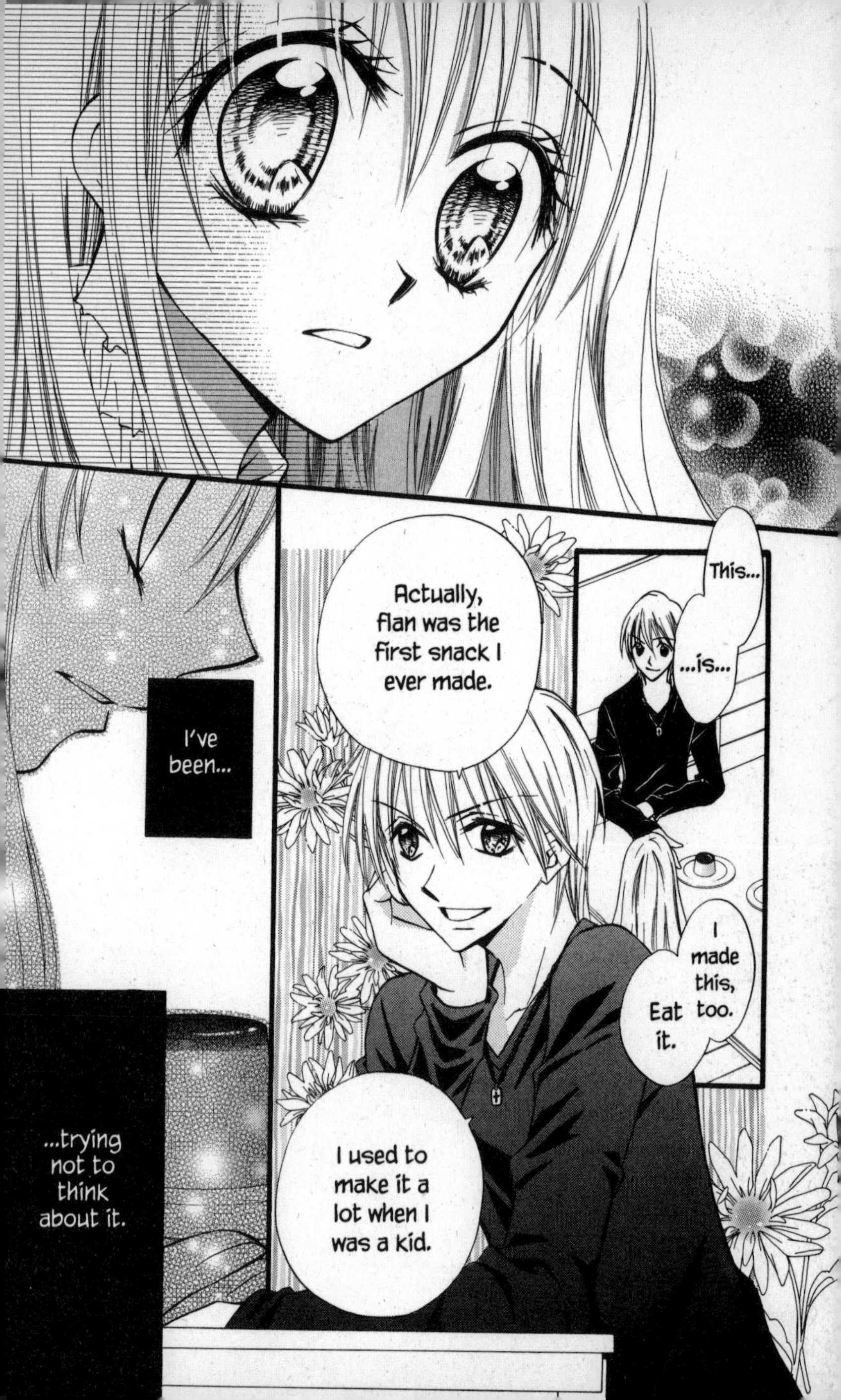
This...
...is...
I made this, too.
Eat it.
Actually, flan was the first snack I ever made.
I used to make it a lot when I was a kid.
I've been...
...trying not to think about it.

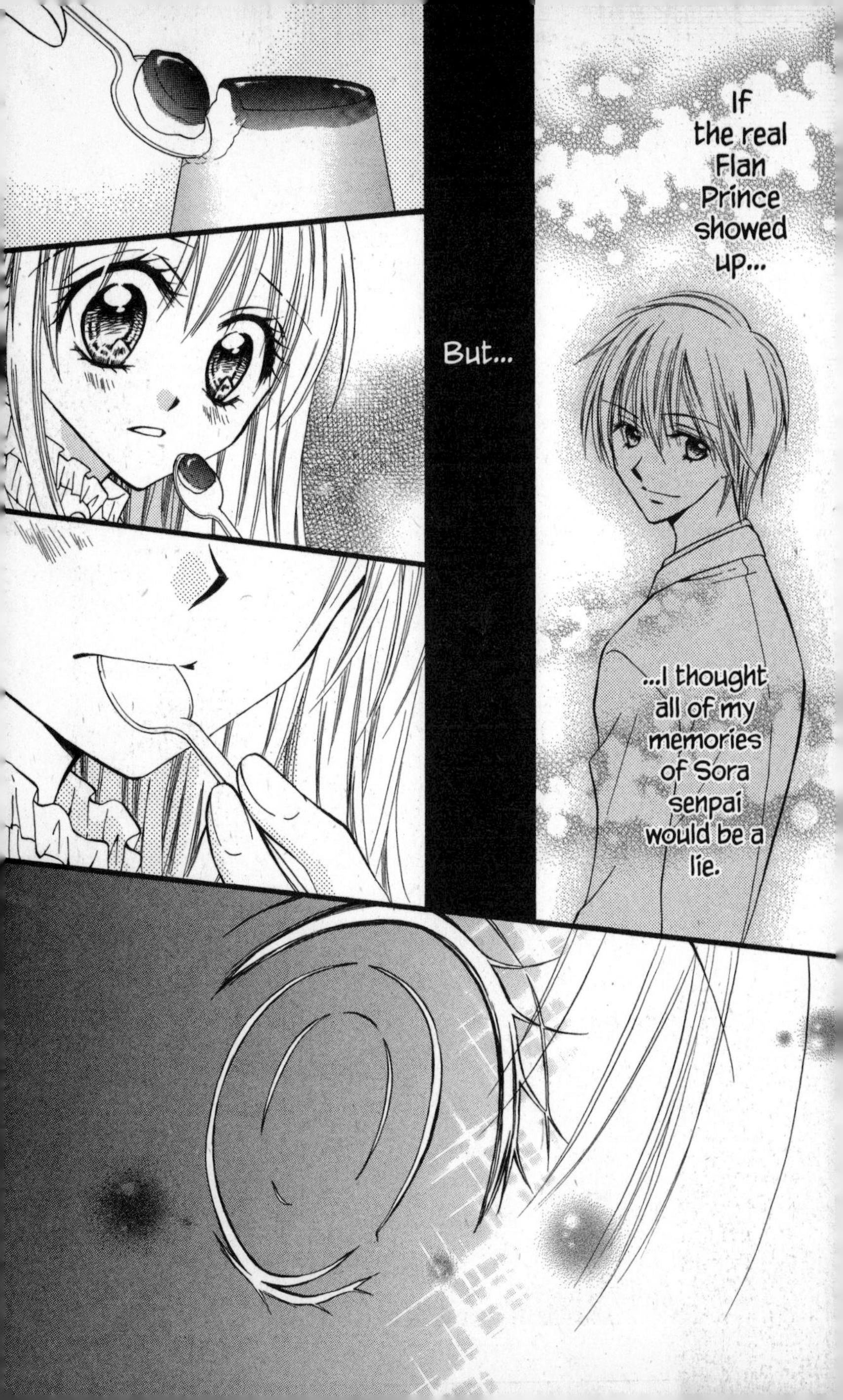
If the real Flan Prince showed up...
...I thought all of my memories of Sora senpai would be a lie.
But...

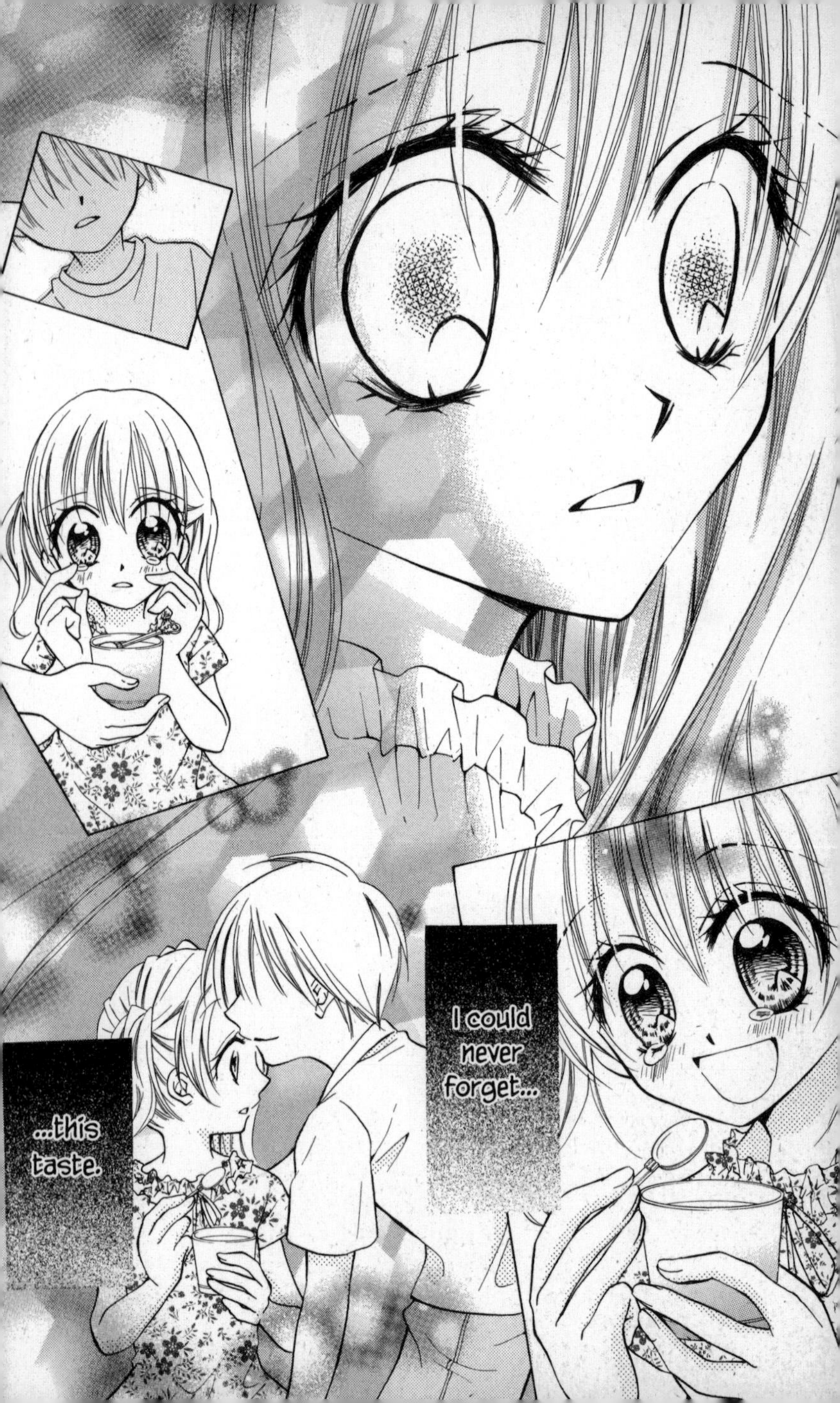
I could never forget...
...this taste.

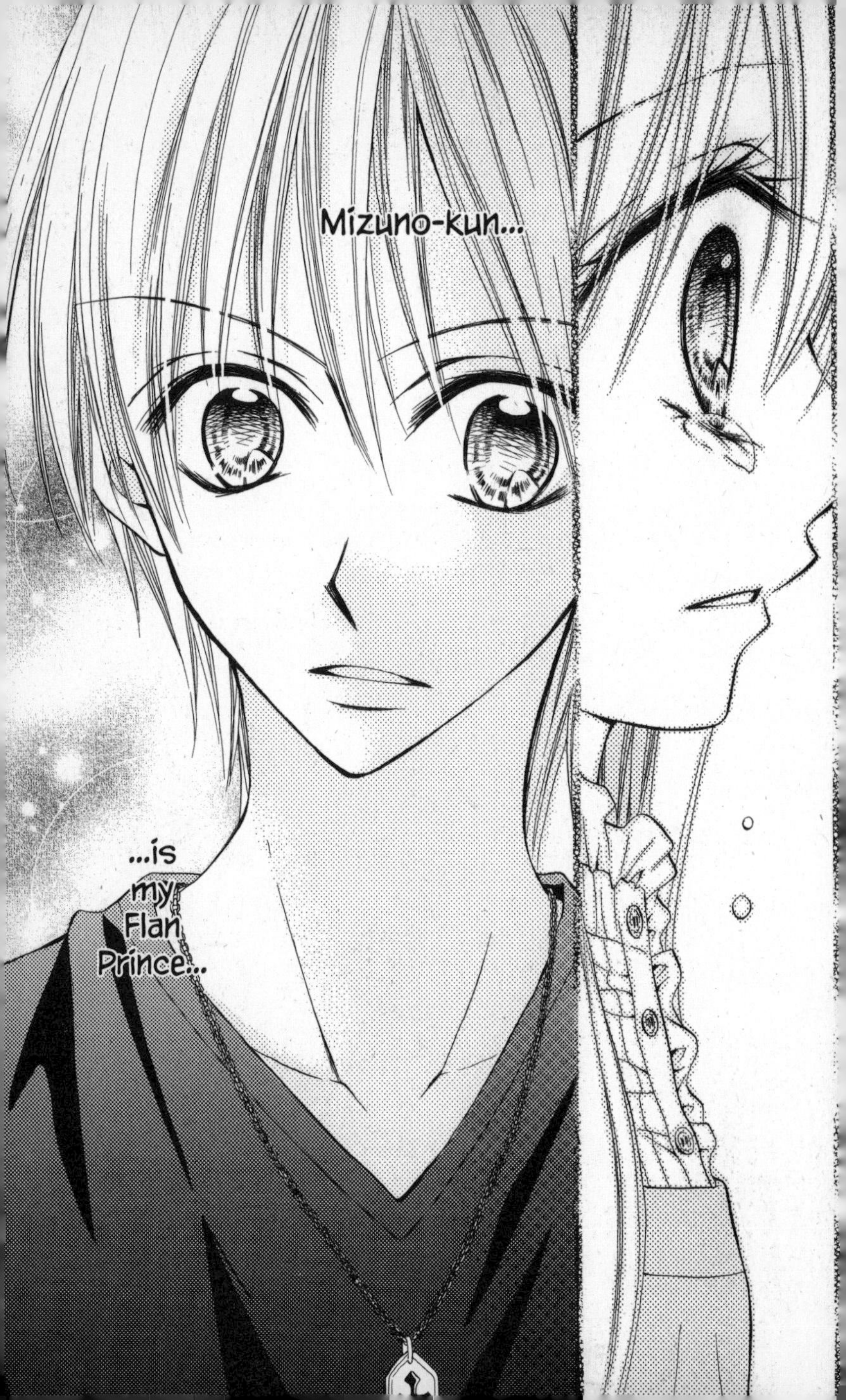
Mizuno-kun...
...is my Flan Prince...

Q & A

I would like to use this space to answer a few questions I received in the mail.

Q *Who is your favorite character?*

A It used to be Sora, but now it's Daichi. I'm completely in synch with Najika's feelings, aren't I...?

Q *What is your favorite dessert and your favorite food?*

A I like cheesecake and roll cakes for dessert.
For food...lately everything tastes good!
Pasta, curry, barbecue meat...I can't decide!!

Q *What are your hobbies lately?*

A I like to check out different restaurants. I look up the train maps to figure out how to get there, and that's the best part. I like the Tokyo train maps. They're so complicated.

OLD PHOTOGRAPHS:
NAJIKA AT THE SUMMER FESTIVAL

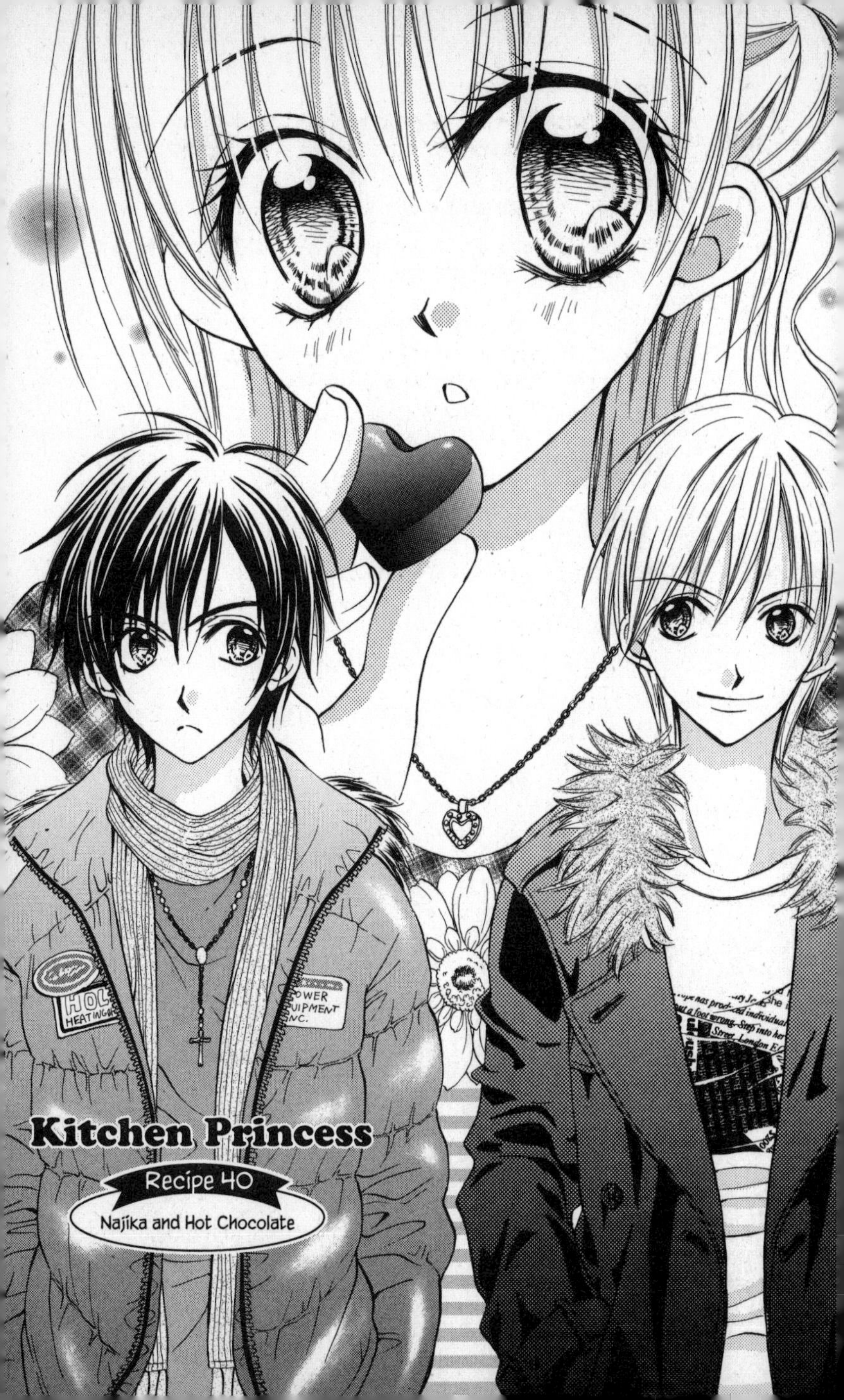
Kitchen Princess
Recipe 40
Najika and Hot Chocolate

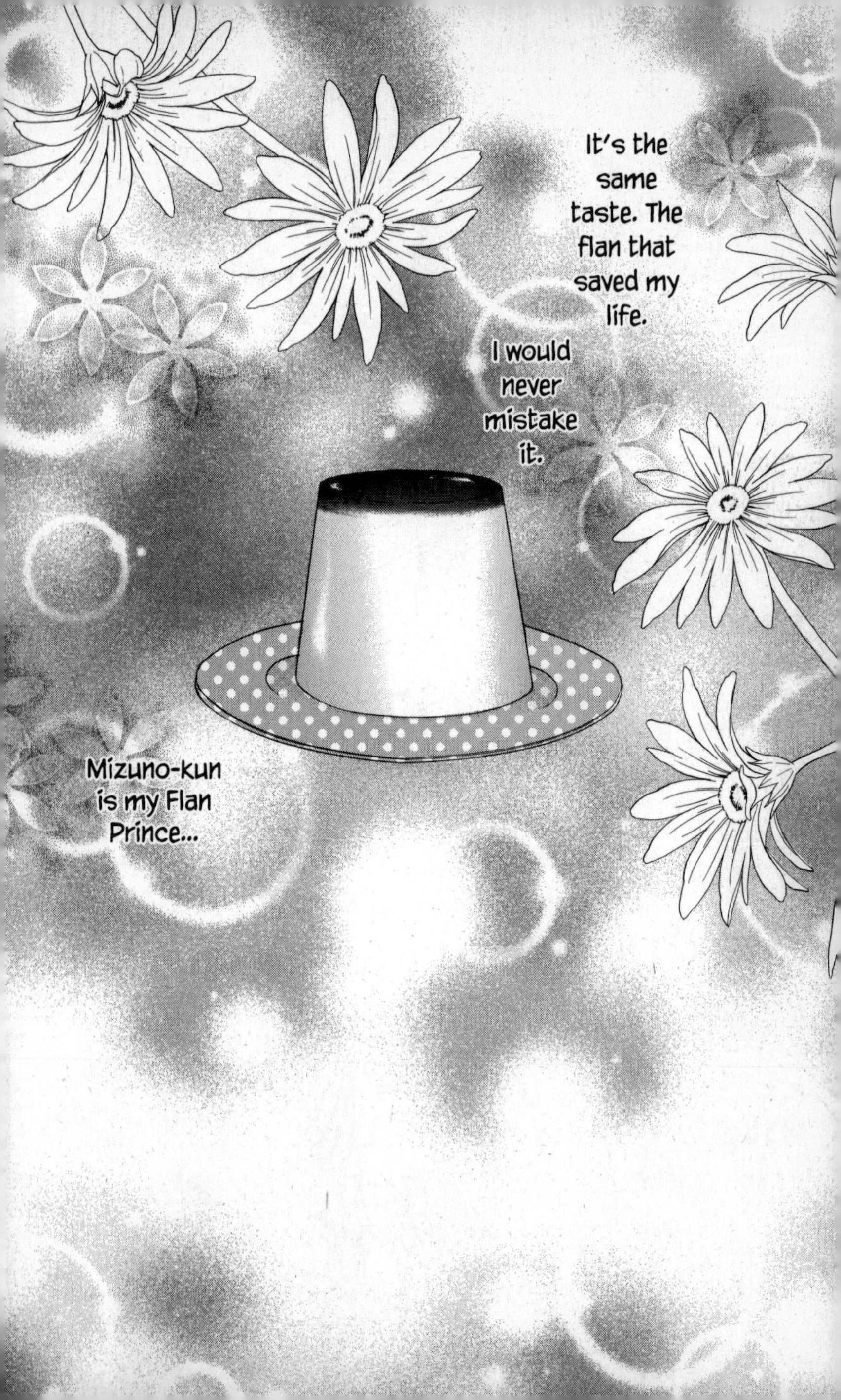
It's the same taste. The flan that saved my life.
I would never mistake it.
Mizuno-kun is my Flan Prince...

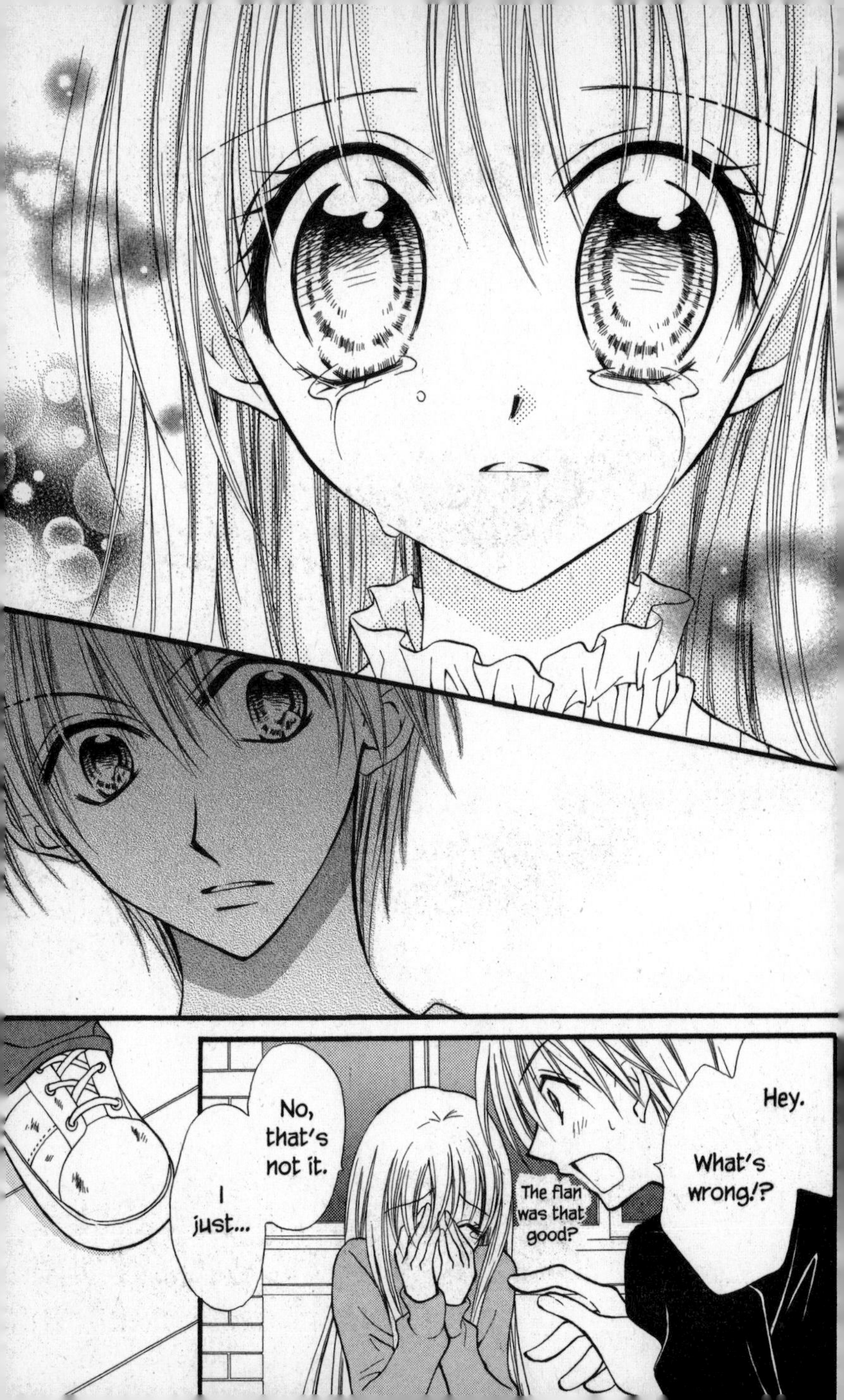
Hey.
What's wrong!?
The flan was that good?
No, that's not it.
I just...

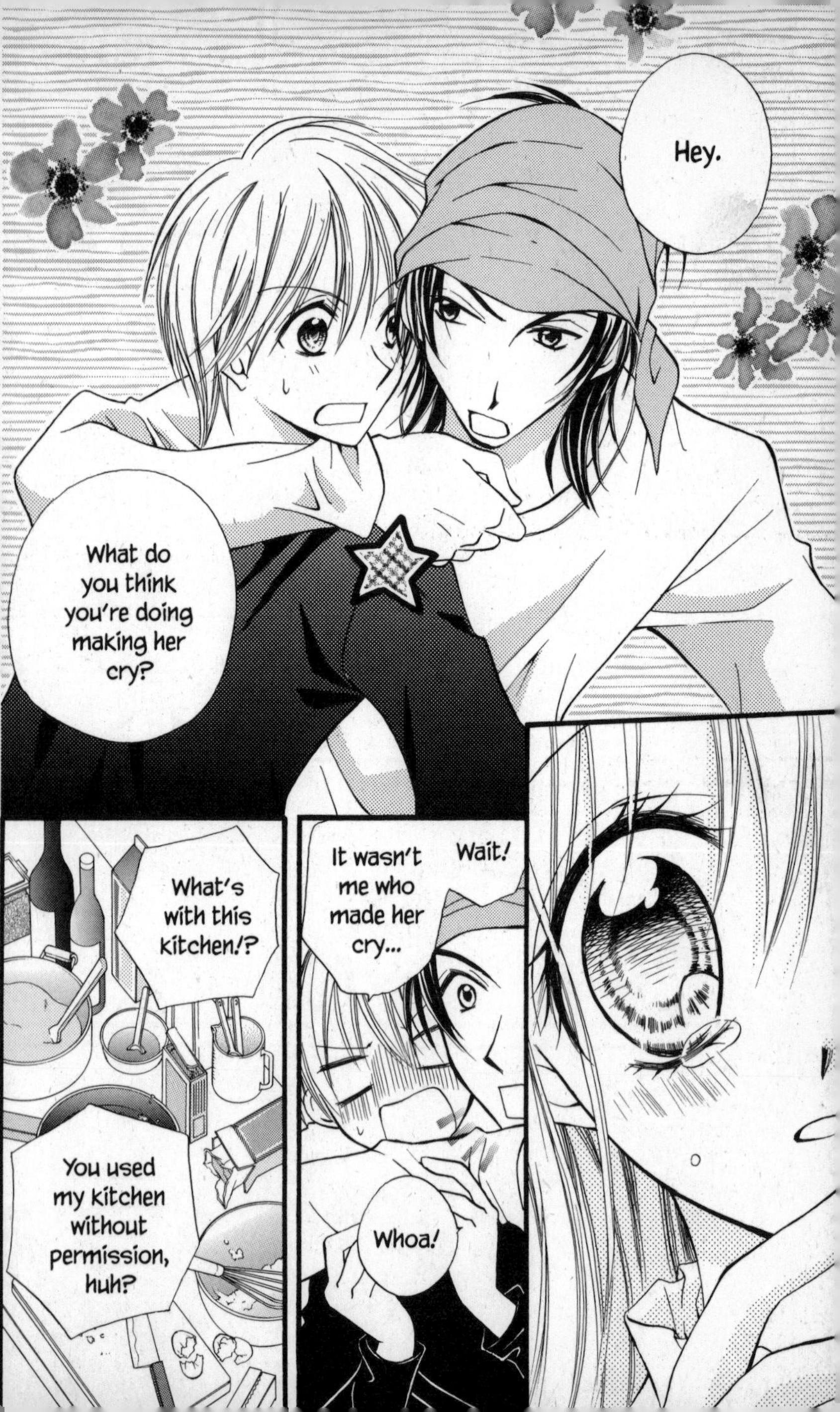
Hey.
What do you think you're doing making her cry?
Wait!
It wasn't me who made her cry...
Whoa!
What's with this kitchen!?
You used my kitchen without permission, huh?

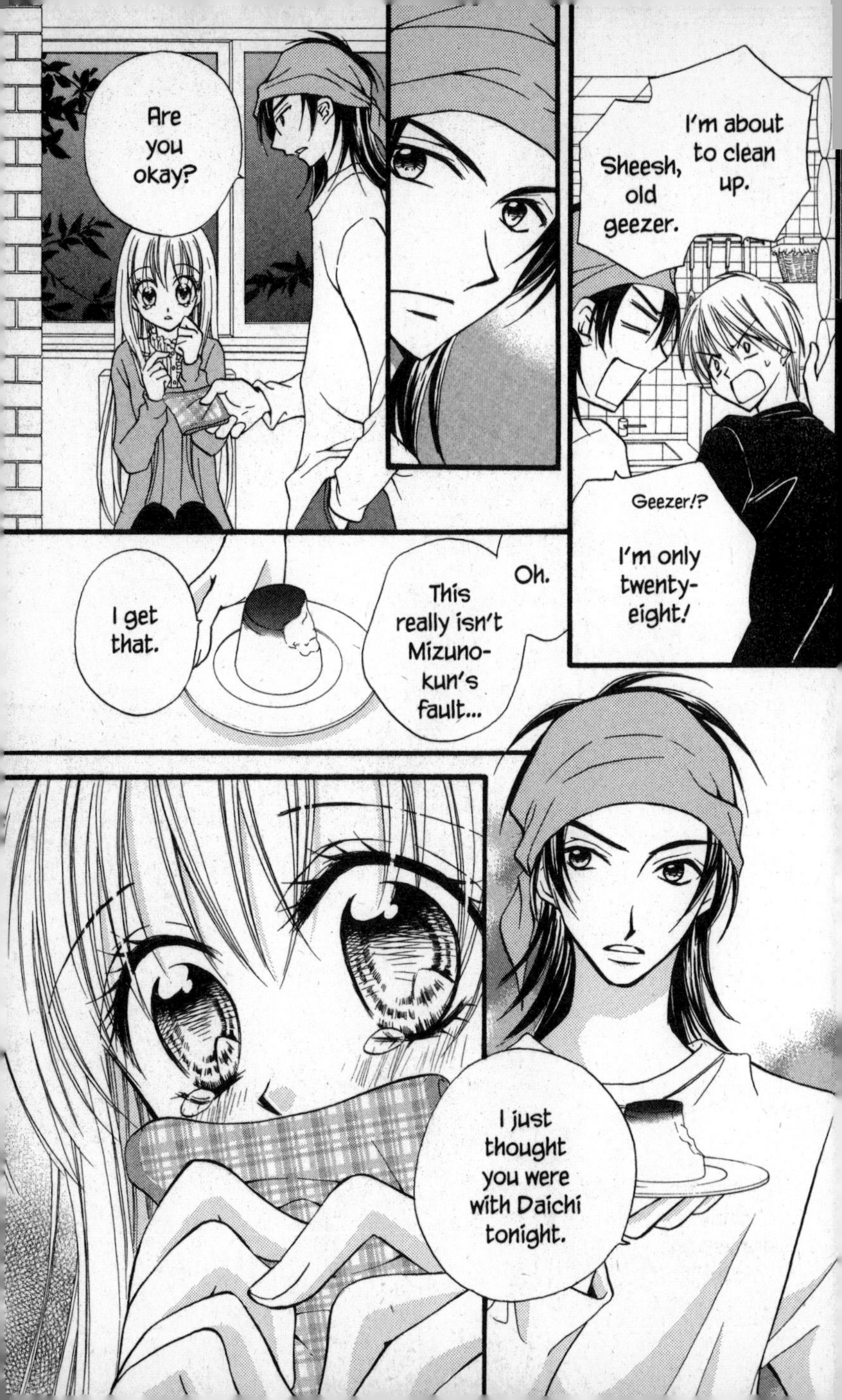

I'm about to clean up. Sheesh, old geezer.
Geezer!? I'm only twenty-eight!
Are you okay?
Oh. This really isn't Mizuno-kun's fault...
I get that.
I just thought you were with Daichi tonight.

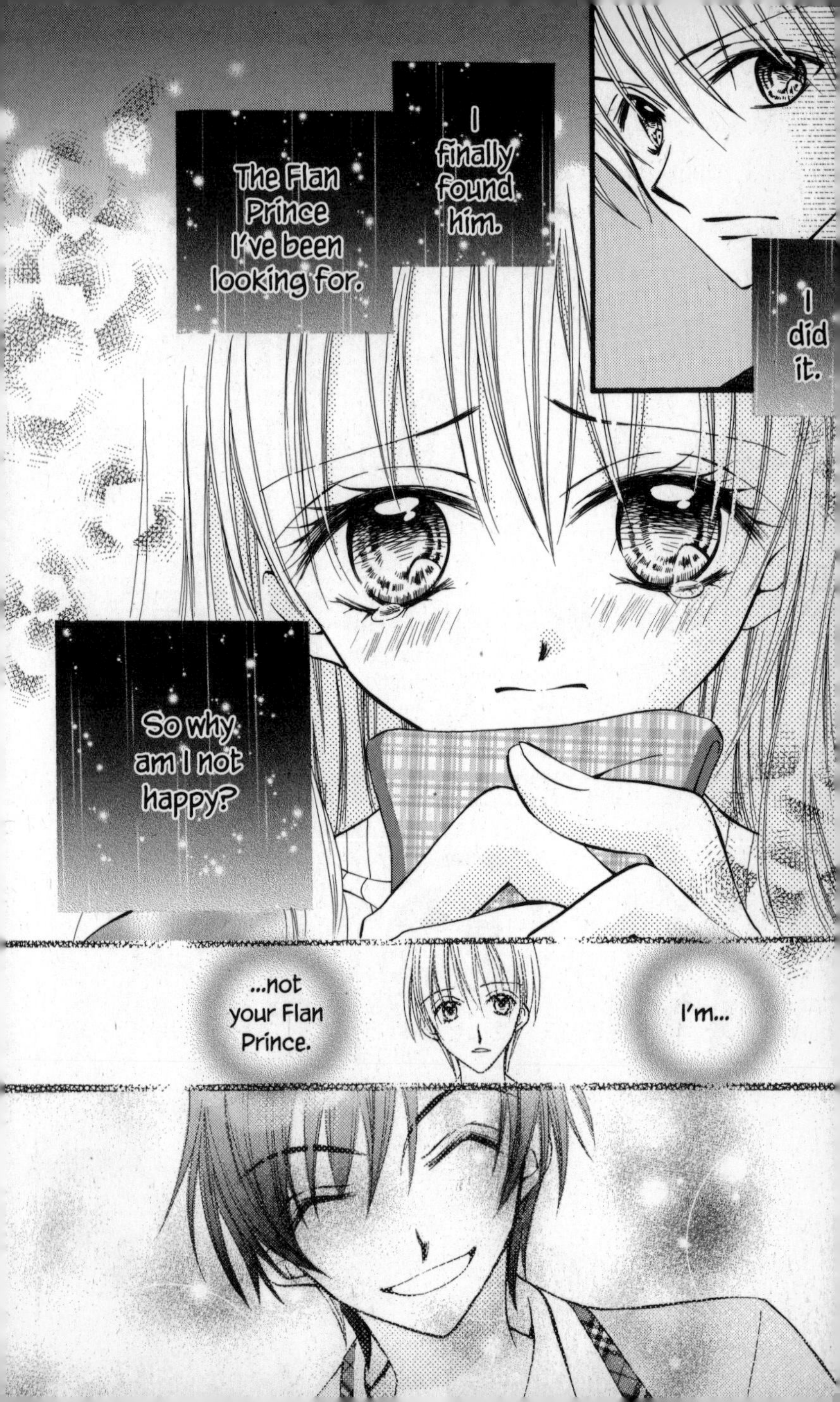
I did it.
I finally found him.
The Flan Prince I've been looking for.
So why am I not happy?
I'm...
...not your Flan Prince.

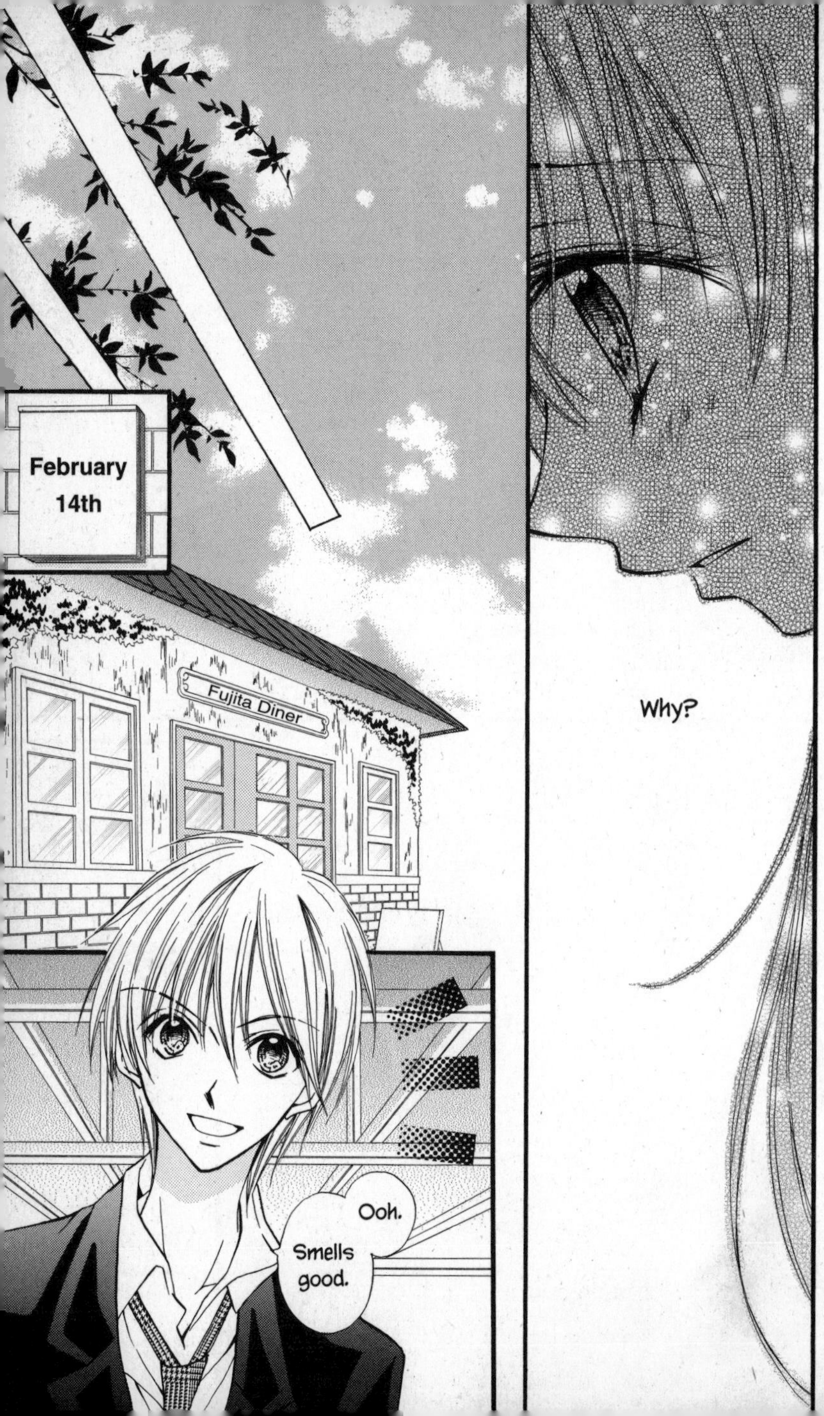
Why?
February 14th
Fujita Diner
Ooh.
Smells good.

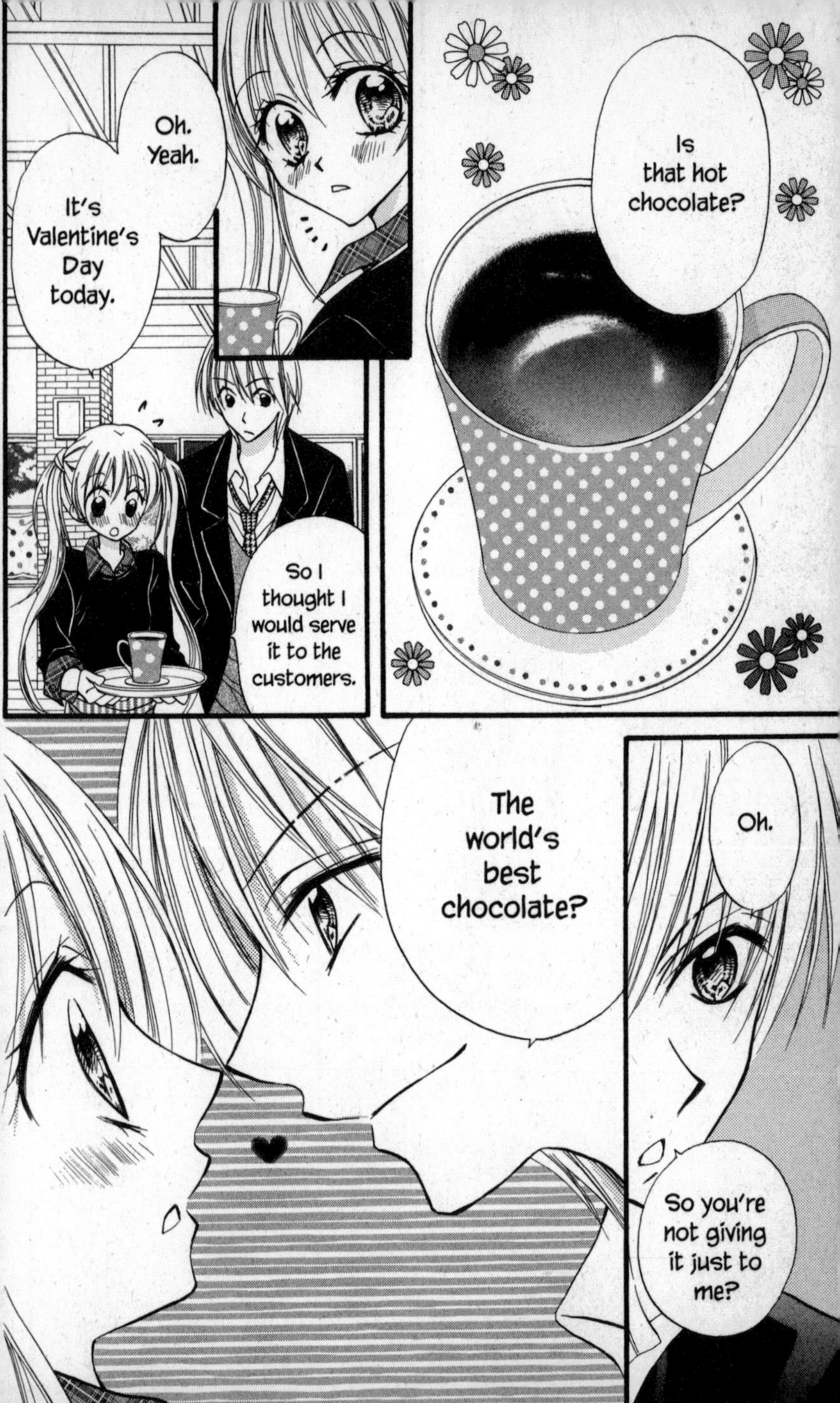

Is that hot chocolate?
Oh. Yeah.
It's Valentine's Day today.
So I thought I would serve it to the customers.
Oh.
So you're not giving it just to me?
The world's best chocolate?

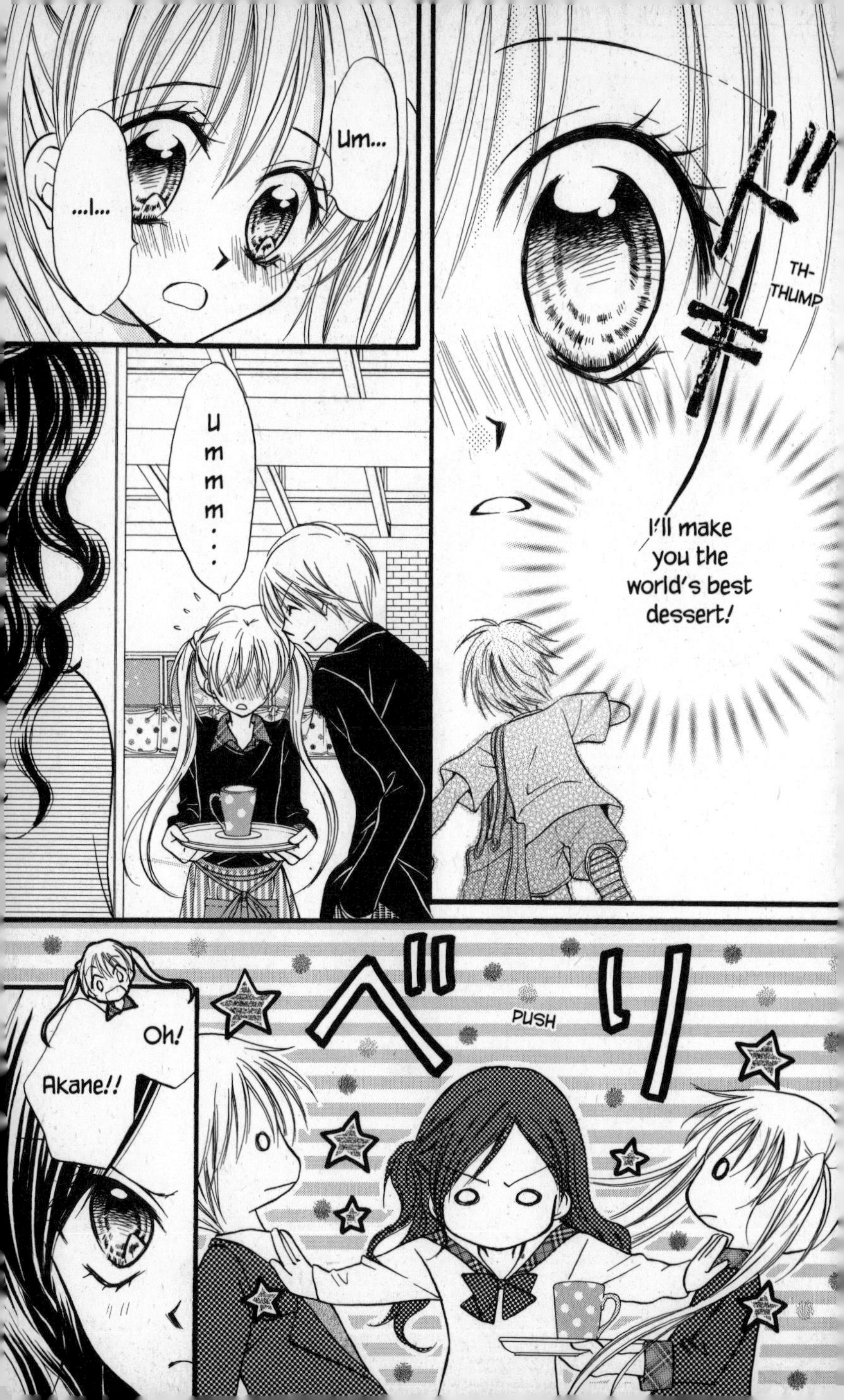
TH-THUMP
I'll make you the world's best dessert!
Um...
...I...
Ummm...
PUSH
Oh!
Akane!!

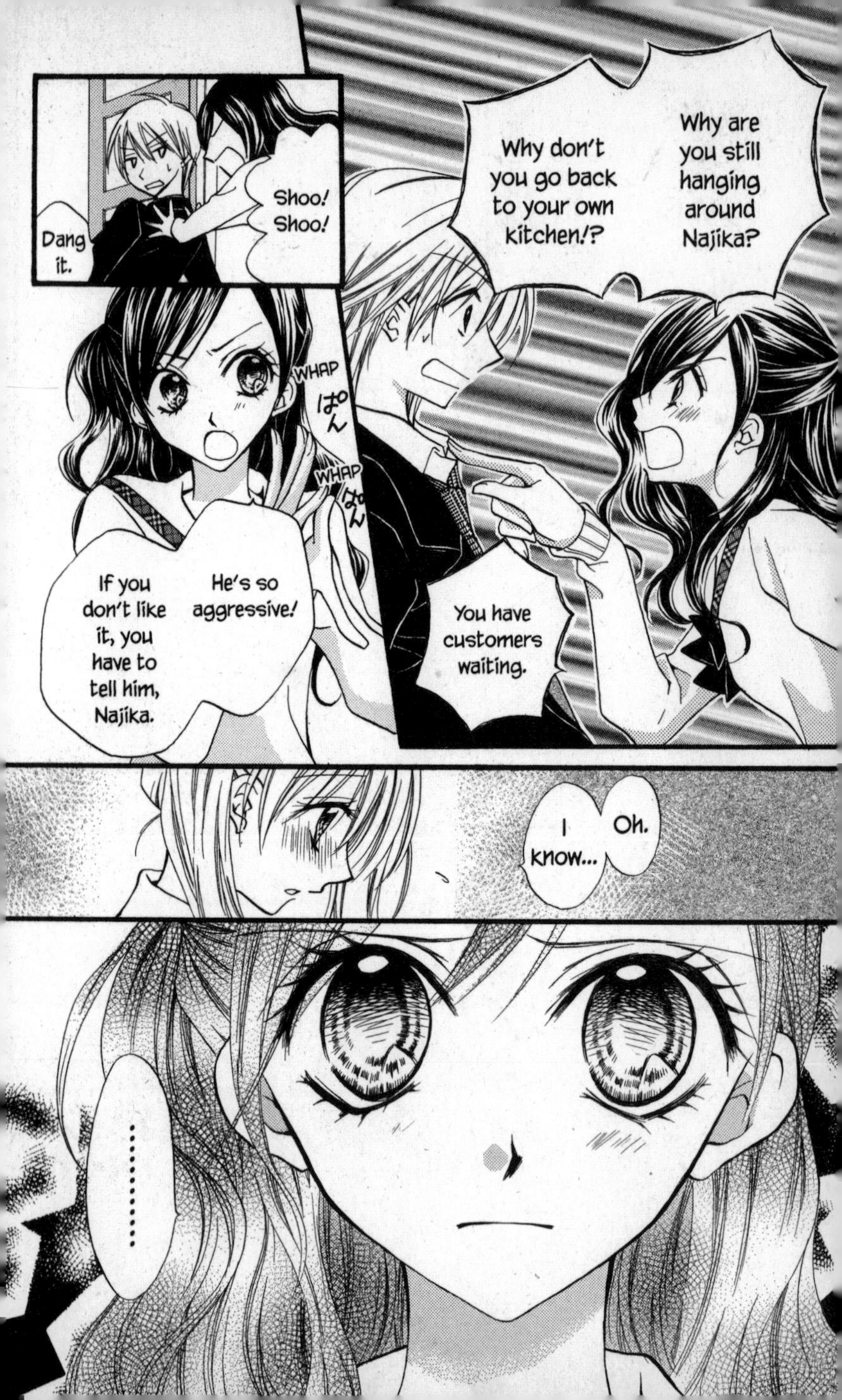
Why are you still hanging around Najika?
Why don't you go back to your own kitchen!?
You have customers waiting.
Shoo! Shoo!
Dang it.
WHAP
ぱん
WHAP
ぱん
He's so aggressive!
If you don't like it, you have to tell him, Najika.
Oh.
I know...
......

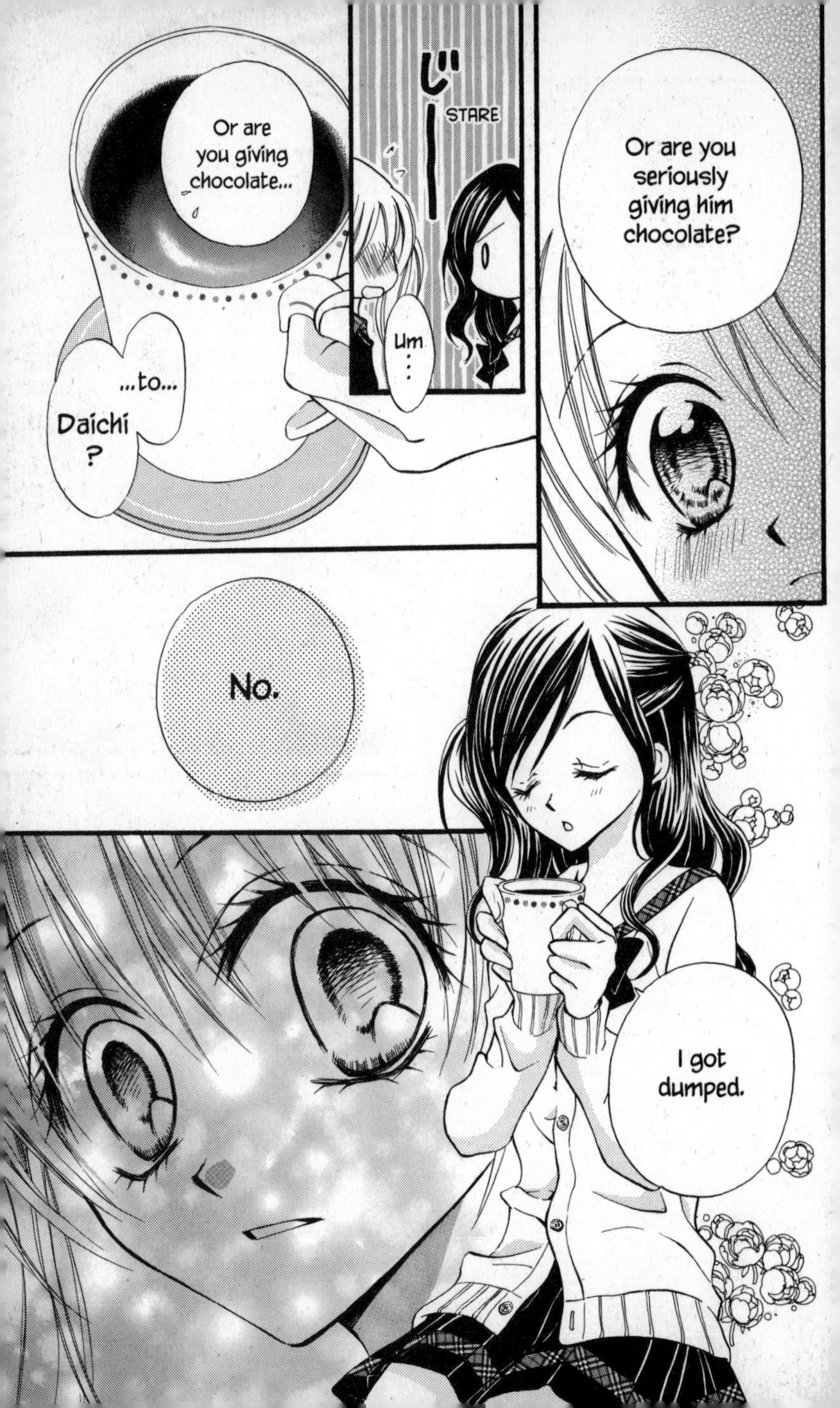
Or are you seriously giving him chocolate?
STARE
Um...
Or are you giving chocolate...
...to...
Daichi?
No.
I got dumped.

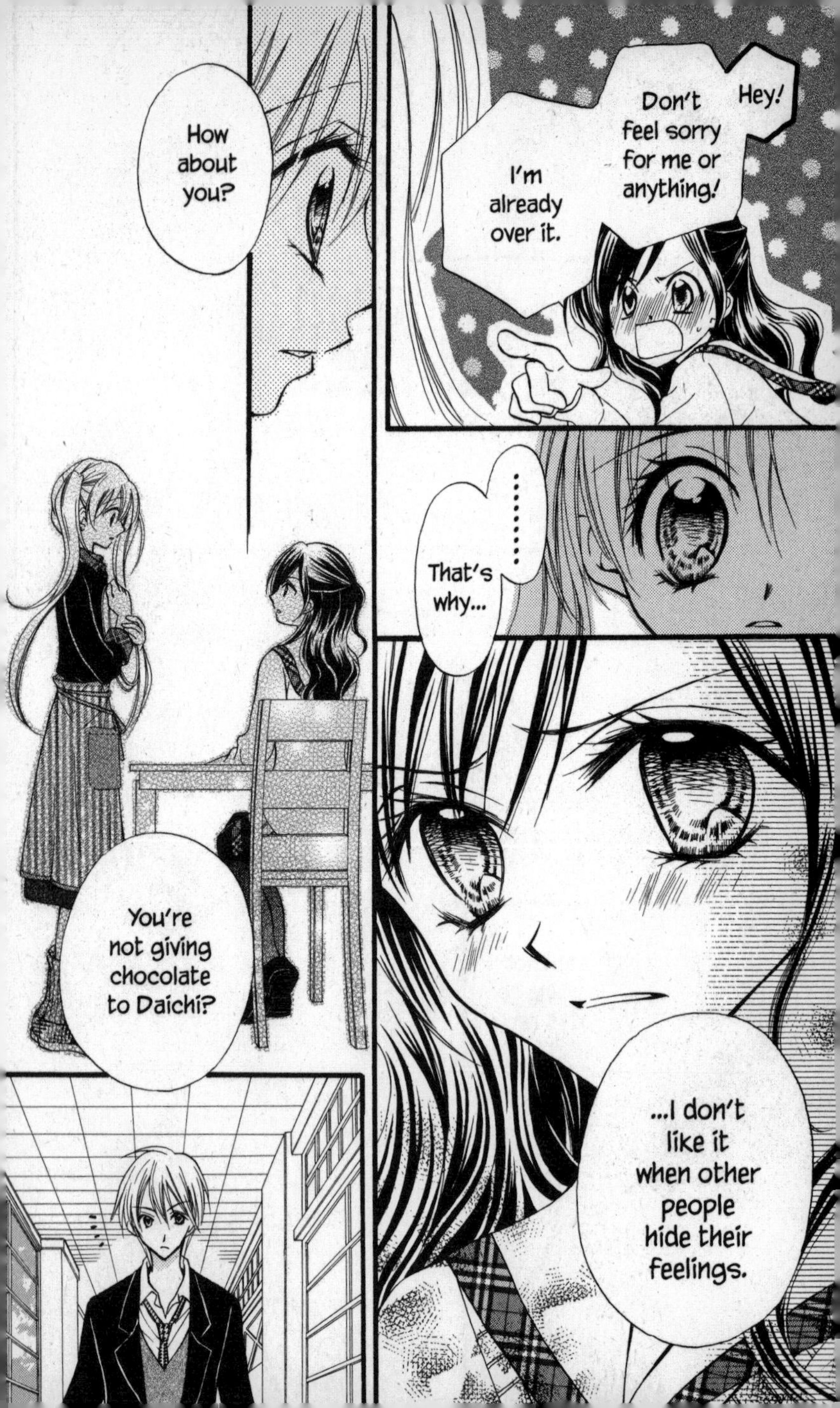
Hey!
Don't feel sorry for me or anything!
I'm already over it.
How about you?
......
That's why...
...I don't like it when other people hide their feelings.
You're not giving chocolate to Daichi?

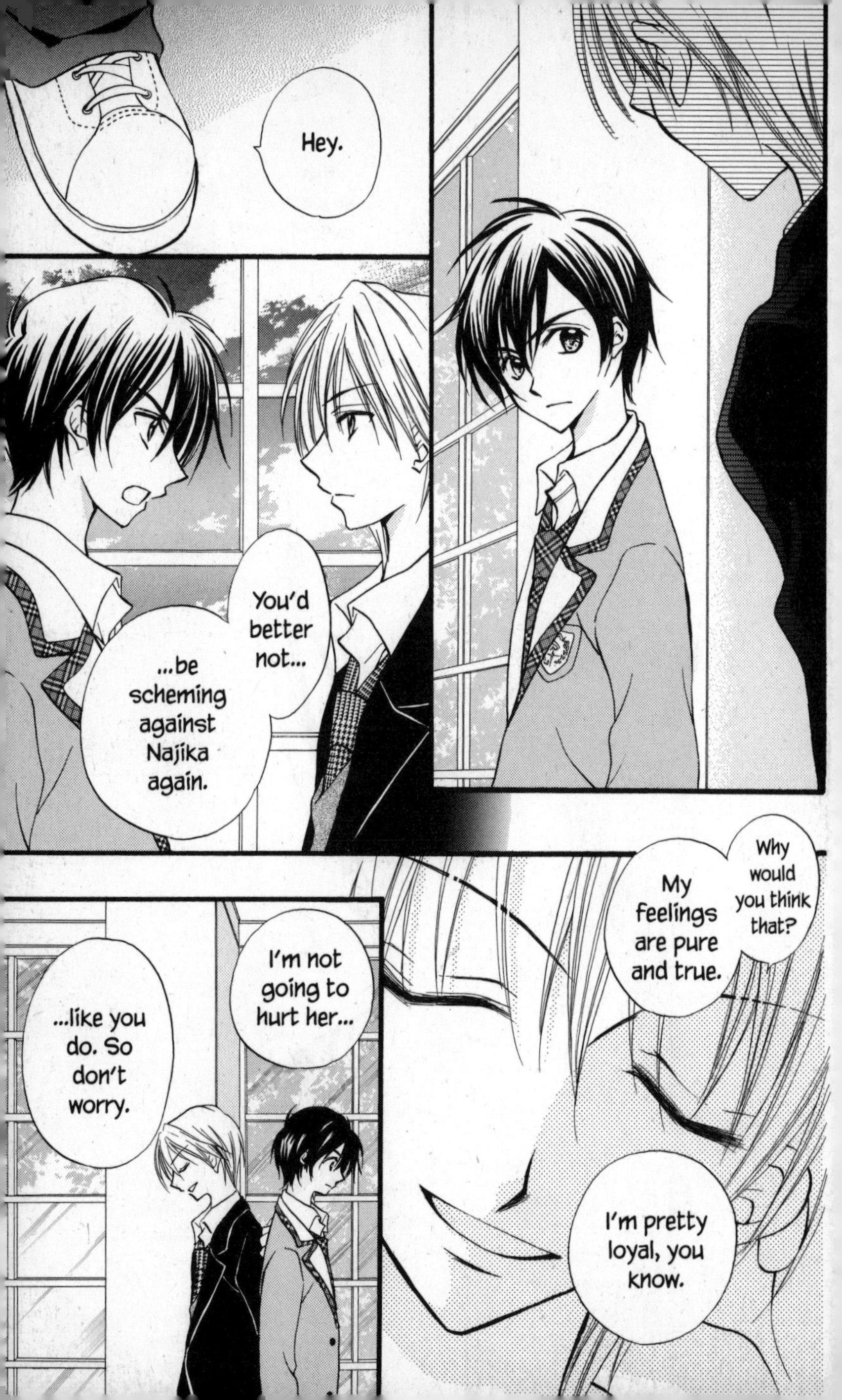
Hey.
You'd better not...
...be scheming against Najika again.
Why would you think that?
My feelings are pure and true.
I'm pretty loyal, you know.
I'm not going to hurt her...
...like you do. So don't worry.

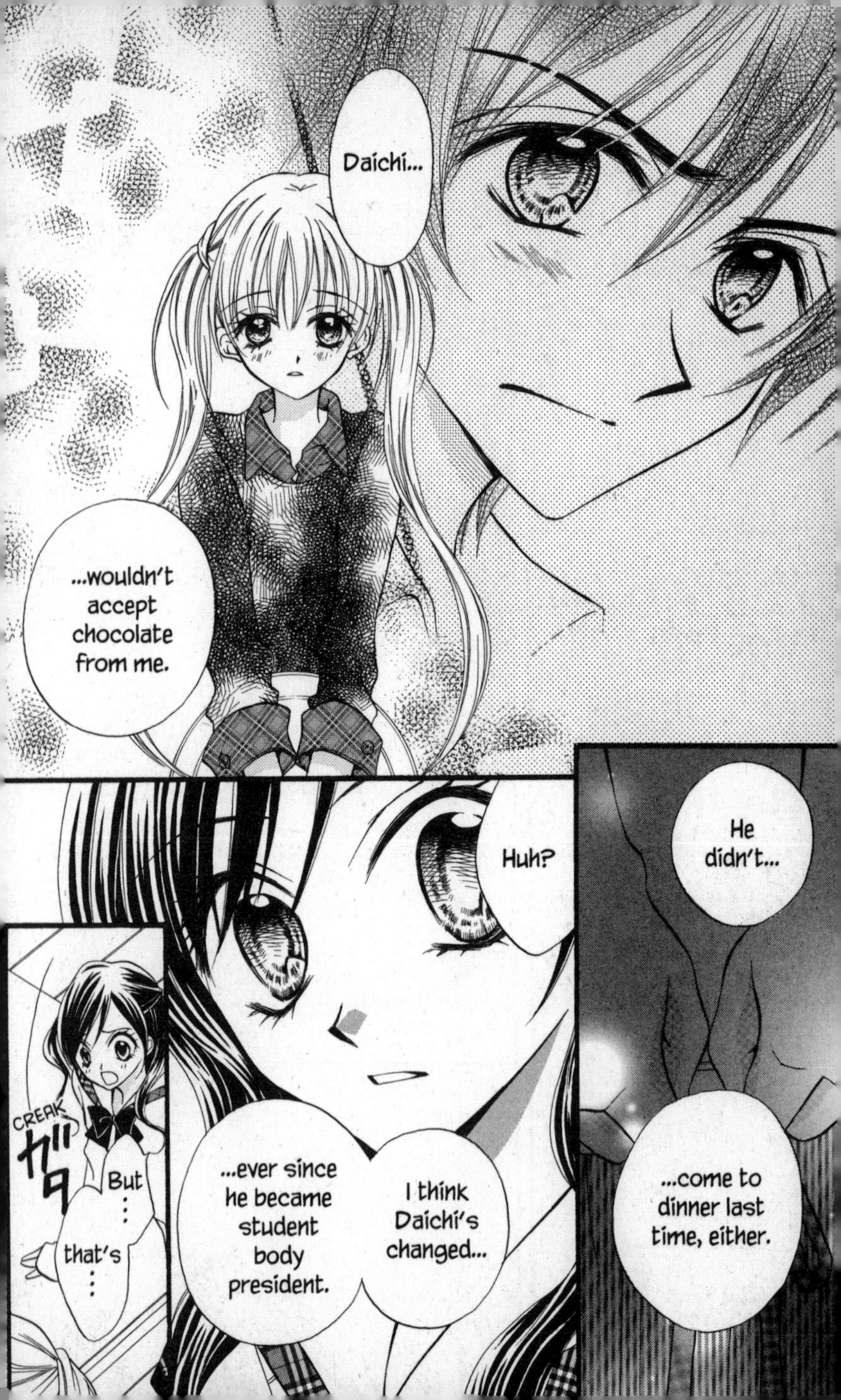

Daichi...
...wouldn't accept chocolate from me.
He didn't...
...come to dinner last time, either.
Huh?
I think Daichi's changed...
...ever since he became student body president.
CREAK
ガタ
But...
that's...

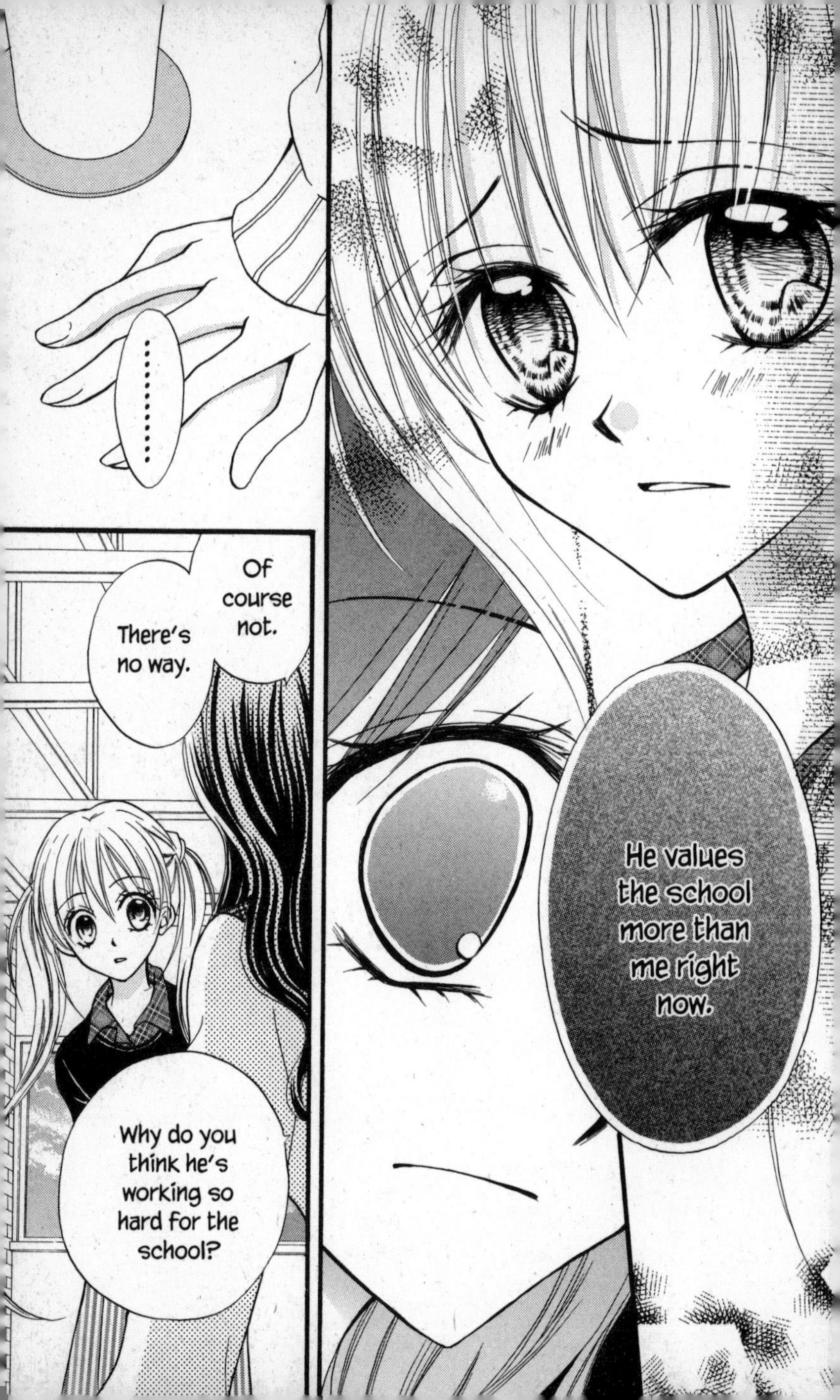
He values the school more than me right now.
……
Of course not.
There's no way.
Why do you think he's working so hard for the school?

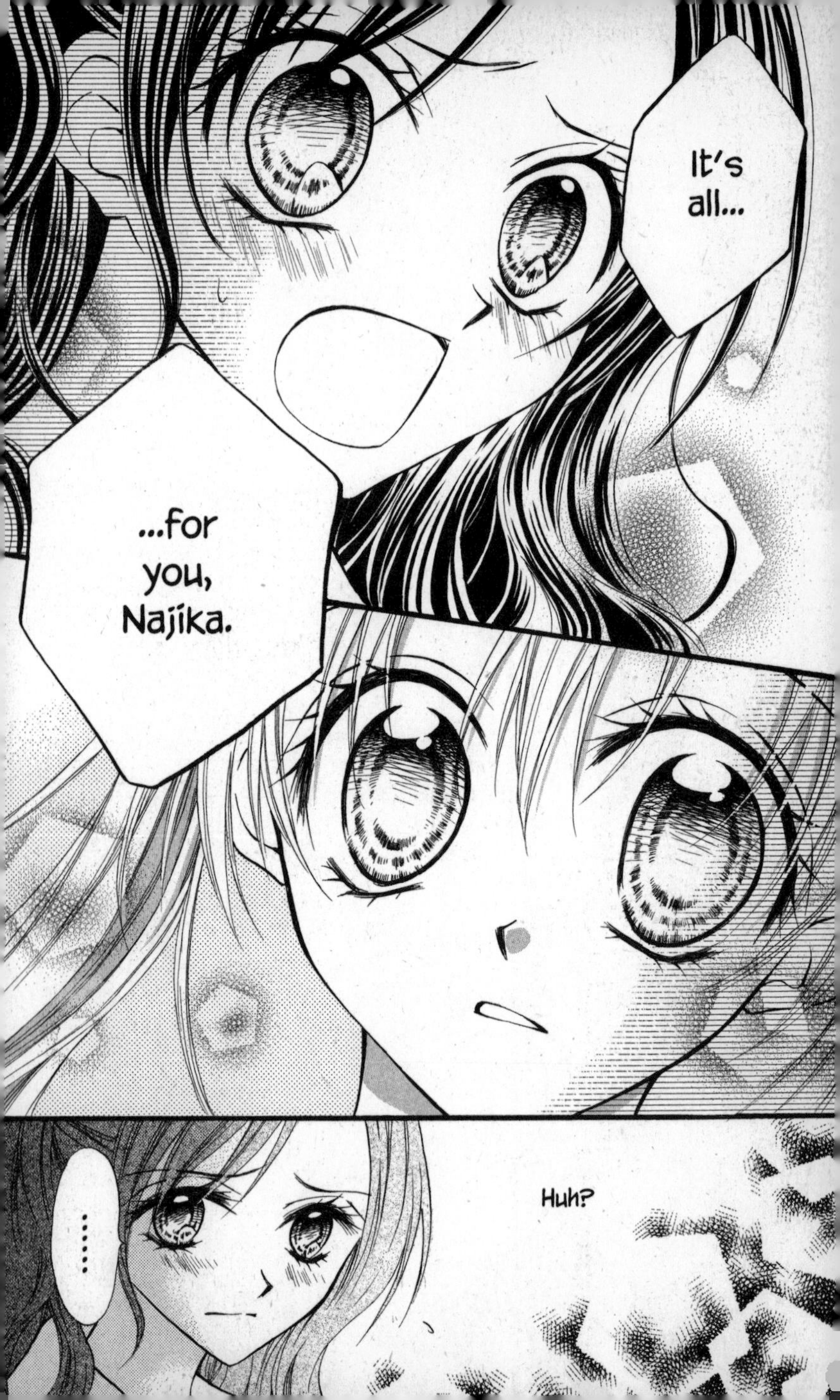
It's all...
...for you, Najika.
Huh?
......

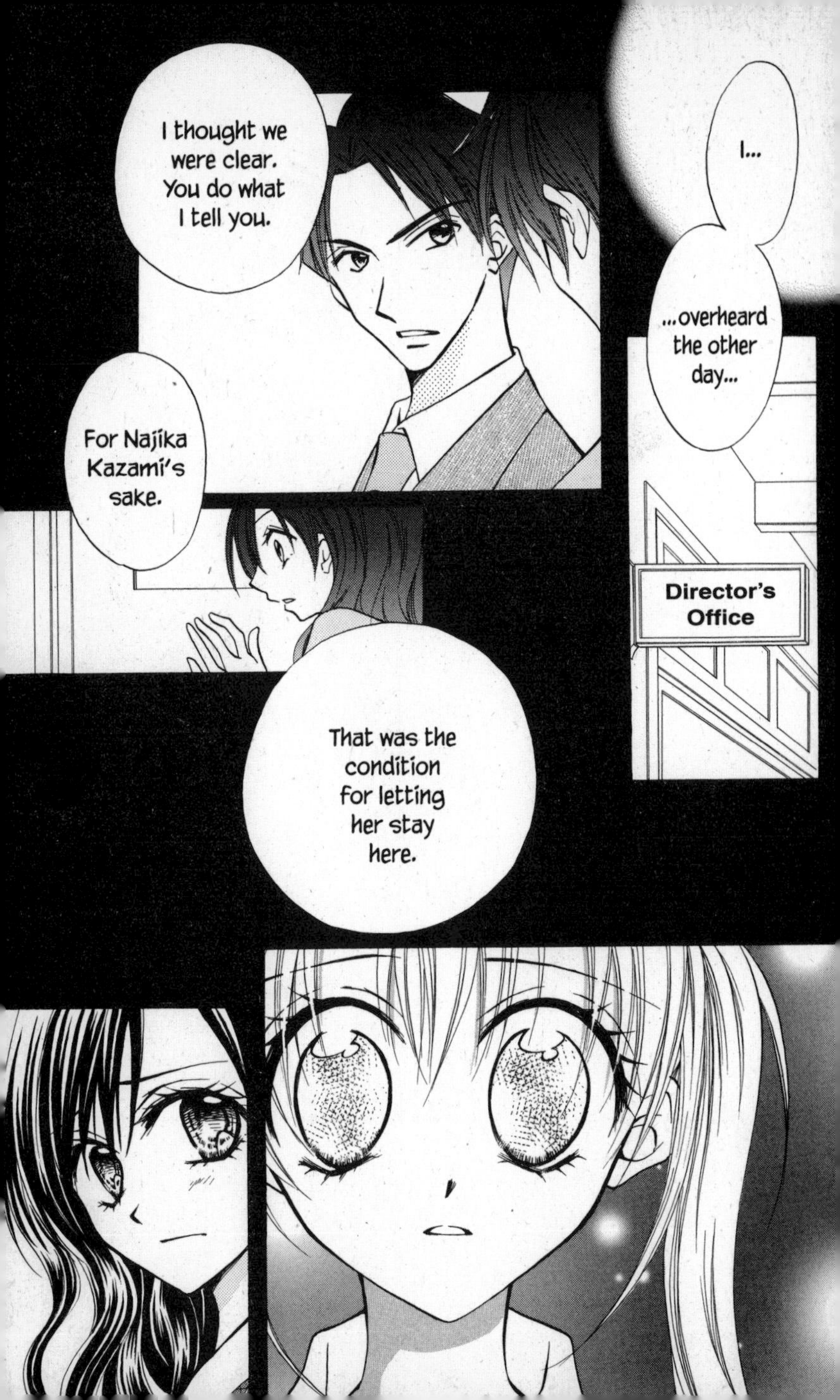
I...
...overheard the other day...
Director's Office
I thought we were clear. You do what I tell you.
For Najika Kazami's sake.
That was the condition for letting her stay here.

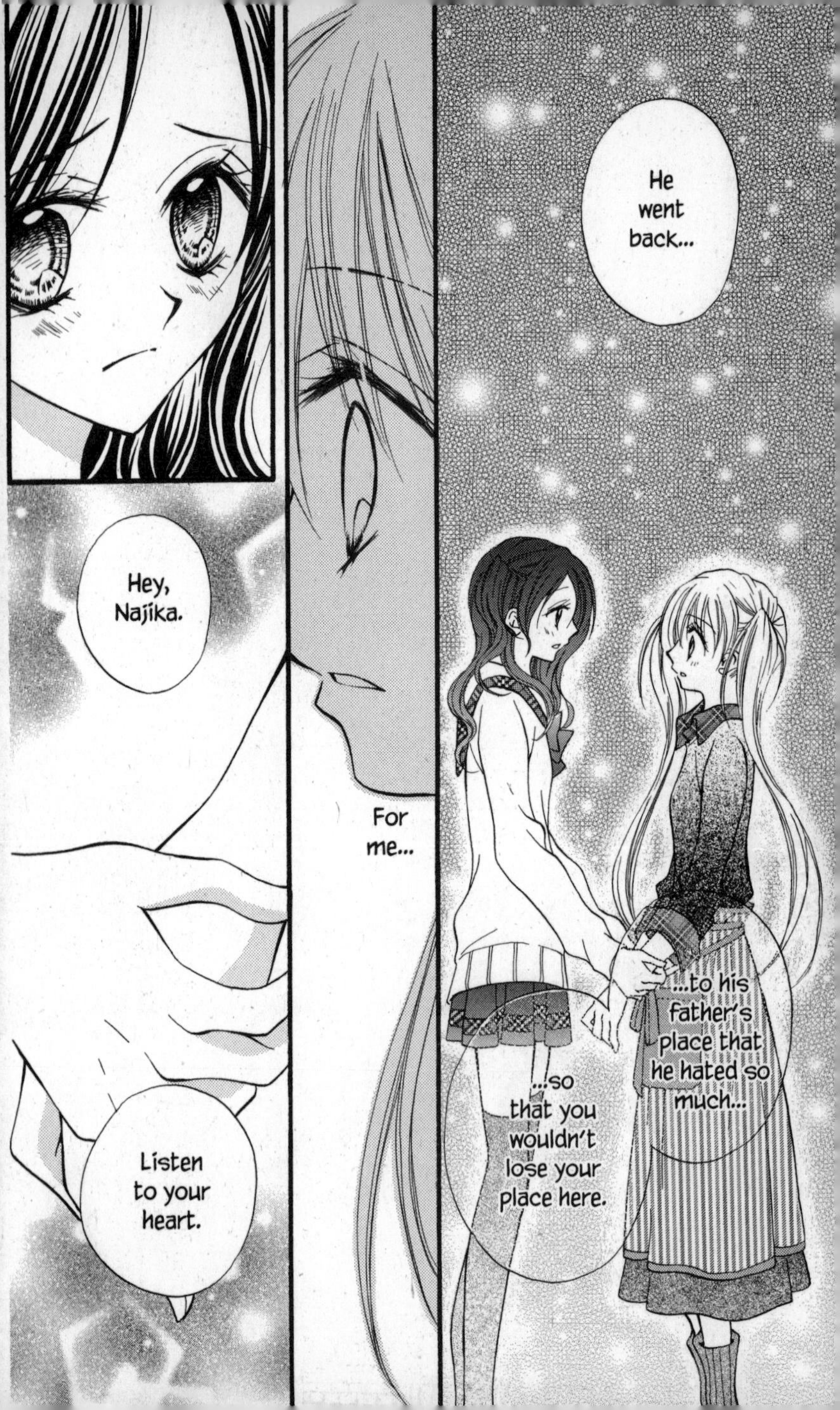

He went back...
...to his father's place that he hated so much...
...so that you wouldn't lose your place here.
For me...
Hey, Najika.
Listen to your heart.

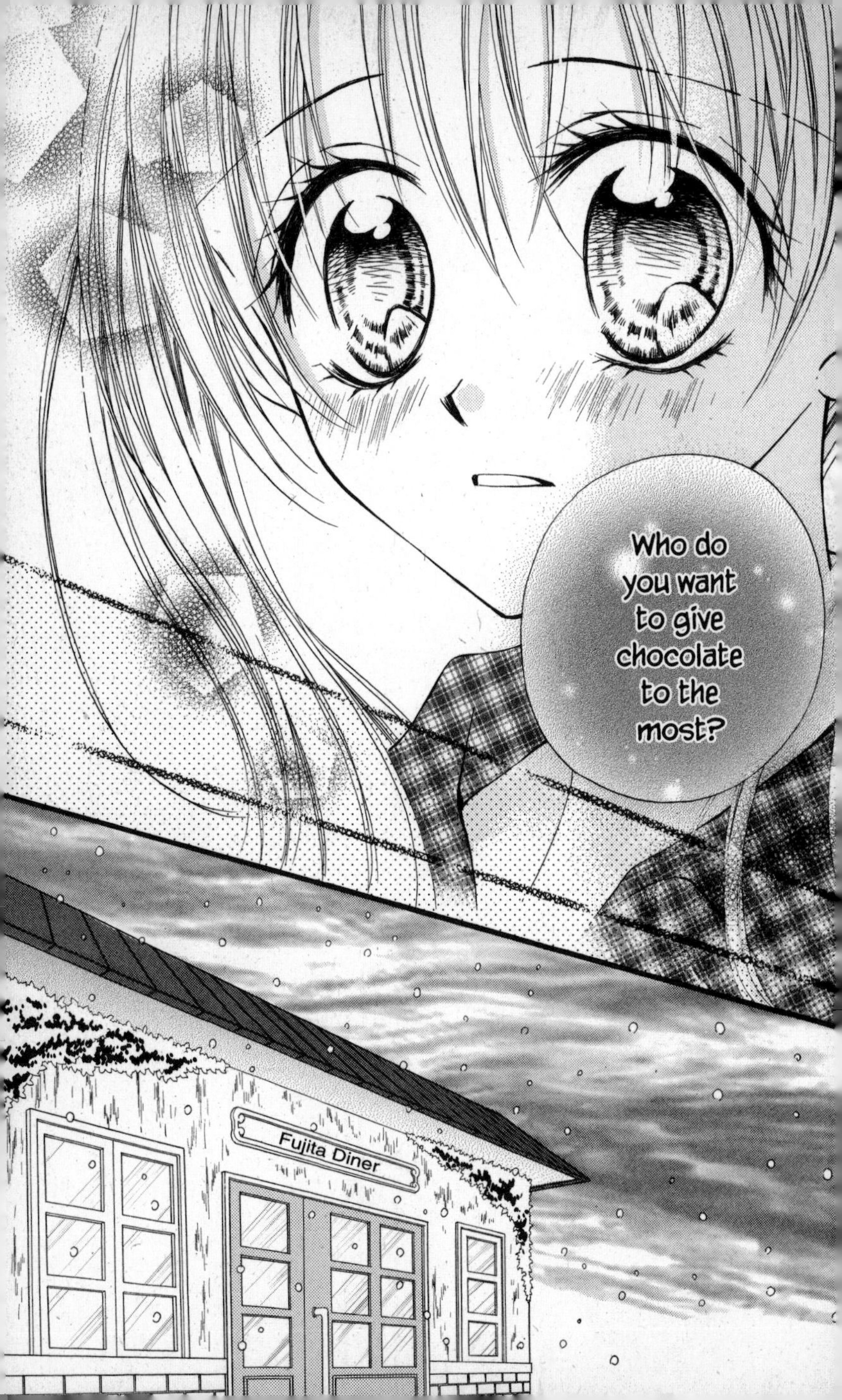
Who do you want to give chocolate to the most?
Fujita Diner

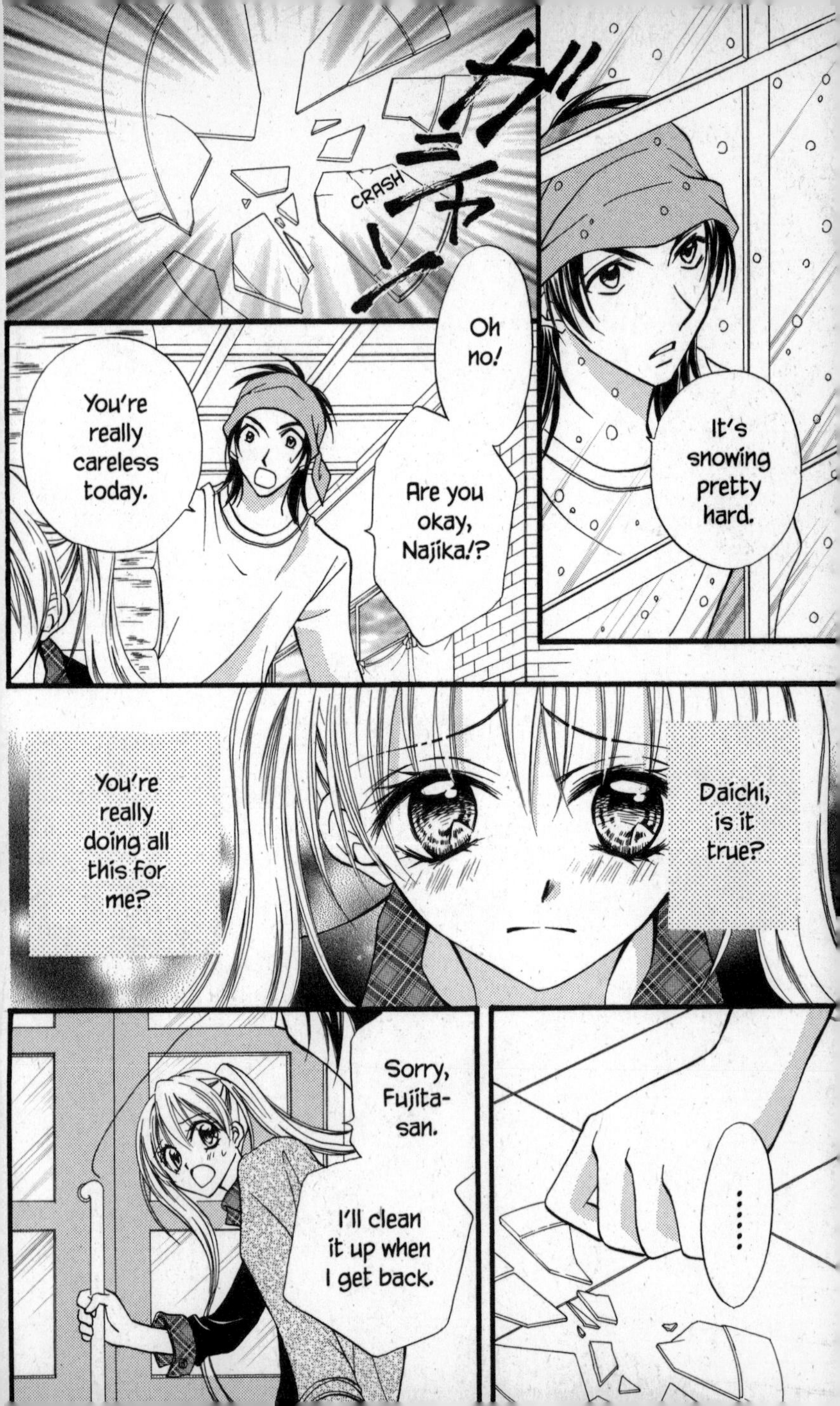
It's snowing pretty hard.
CRASH
Oh no!
Are you okay, Najika!?
You're really careless today.
Daichi, is it true?
You're really doing all this for me?
......
Sorry, Fujita-san.
I'll clean it up when I get back.

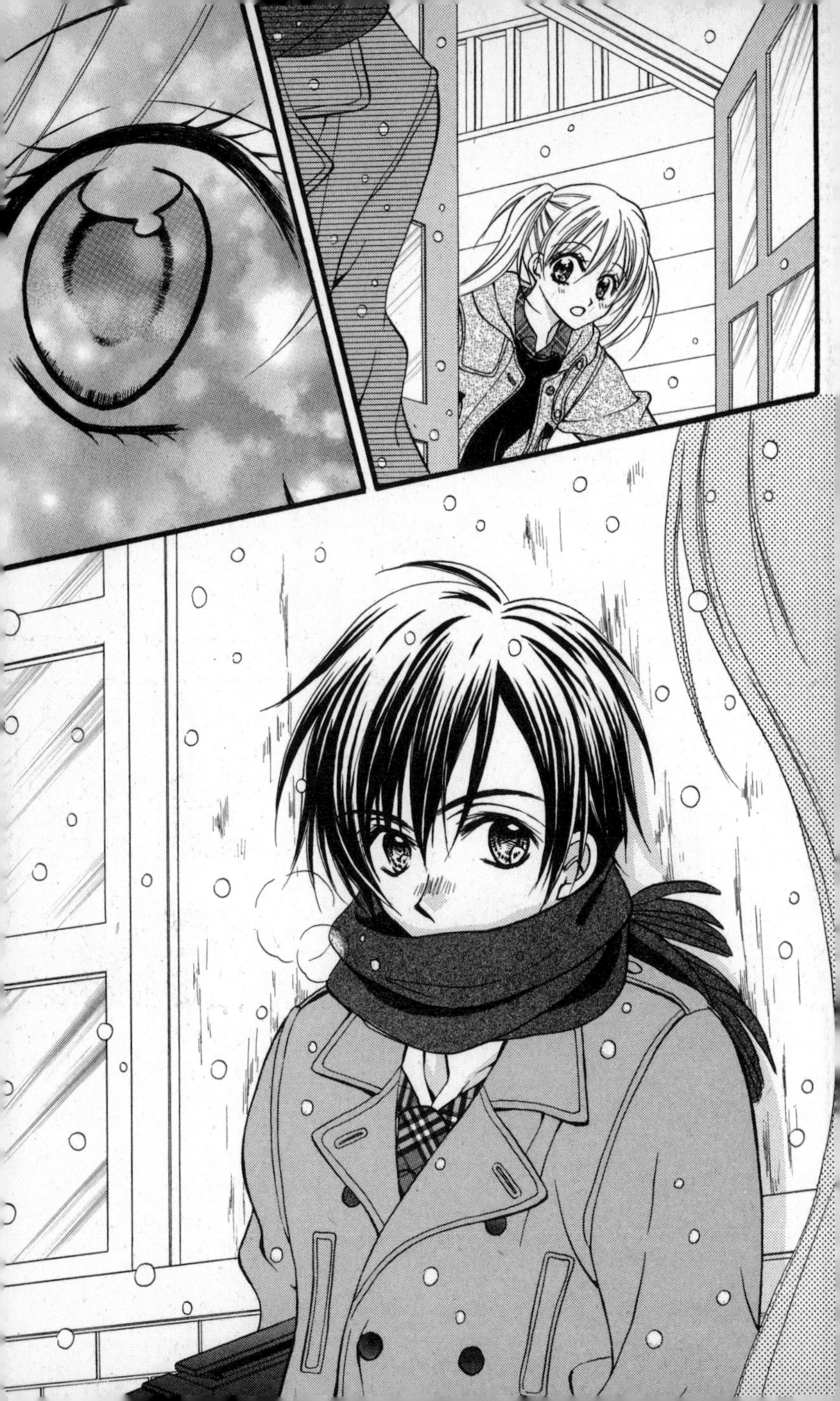

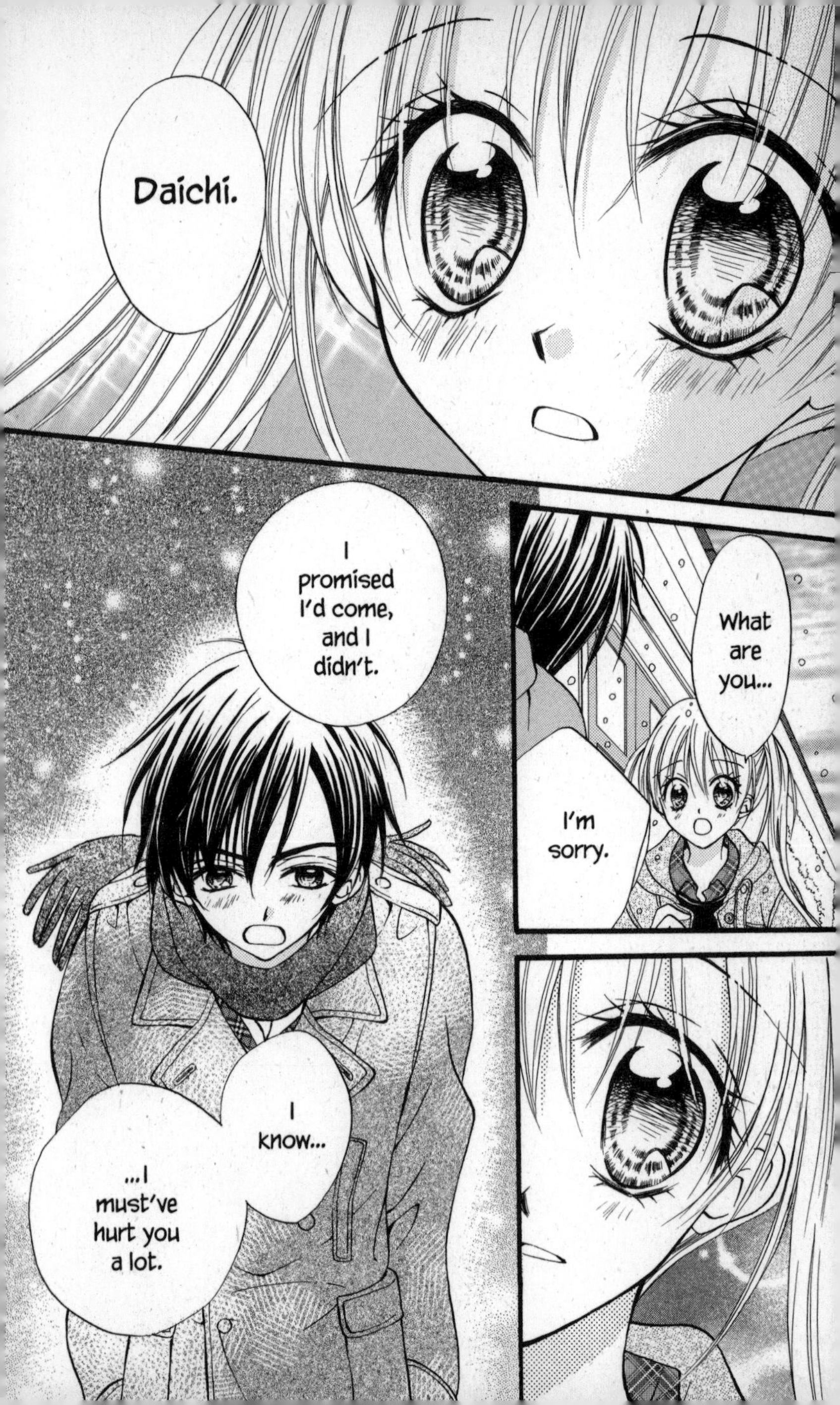
Daichi.
What are you...
I'm sorry.
I promised I'd come, and I didn't.
I know...
...I must've hurt you a lot.

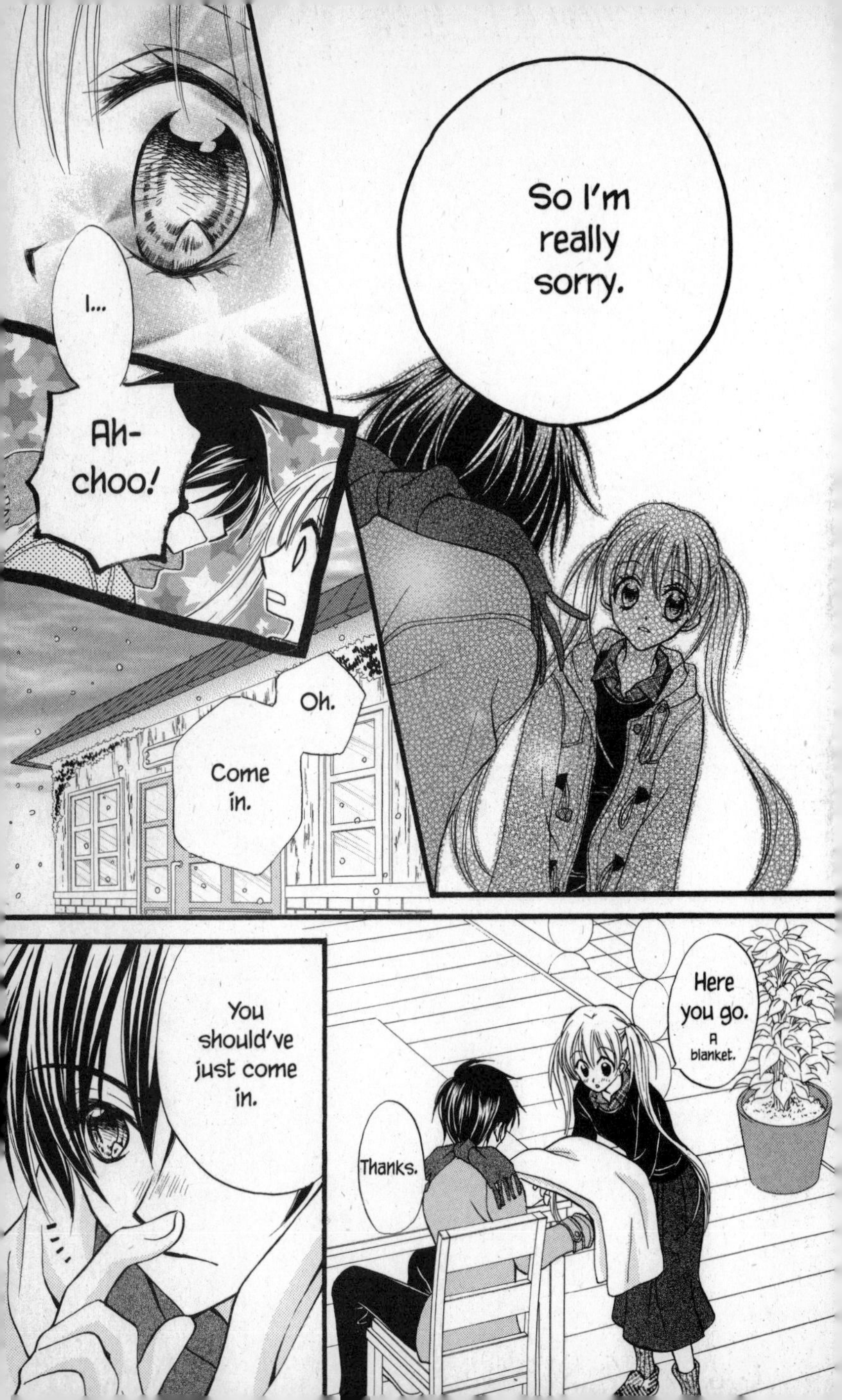

So I'm really sorry.
I...
Ah-choo!
Oh.
Come in.
Here you go.
A blanket.
Thanks.
You should've just come in.

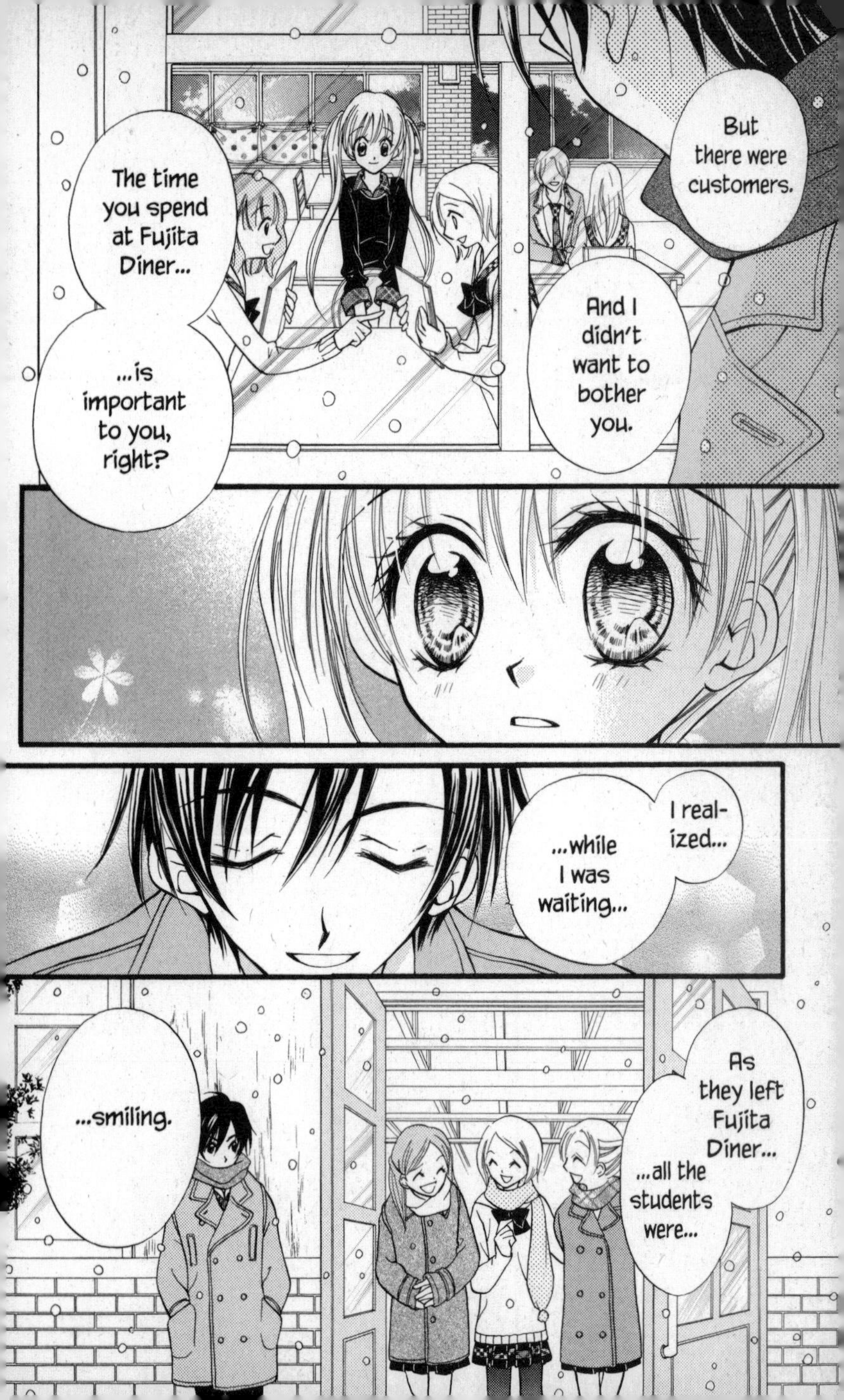
But there were customers.
And I didn't want to bother you.
The time you spend at Fujita Diner...
...is important to you, right?
I realized...
...while I was waiting...
As they left Fujita Diner...
...all the students were...
...smiling.

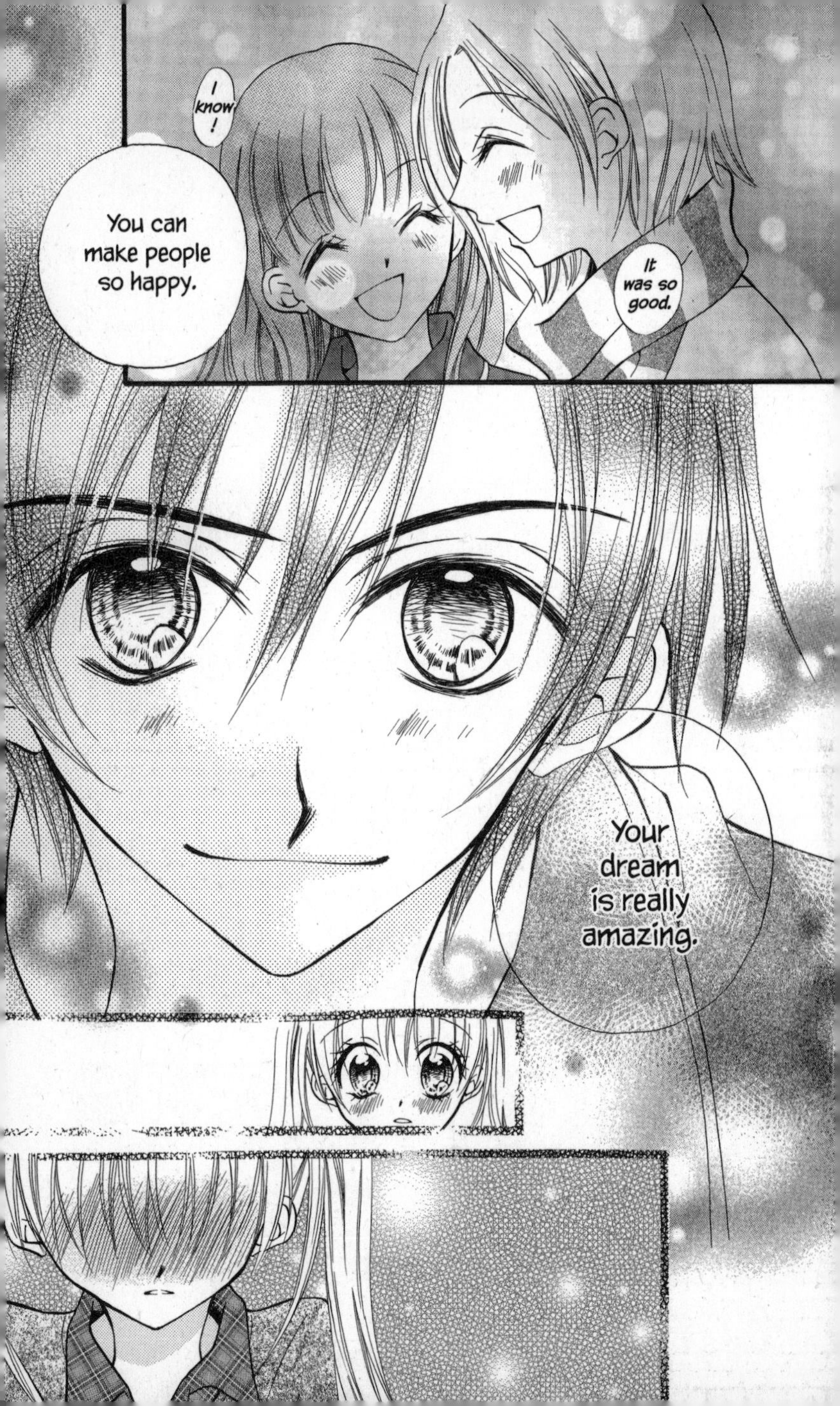
It was so good.
I know!
You can make people so happy.
Your dream is really amazing.

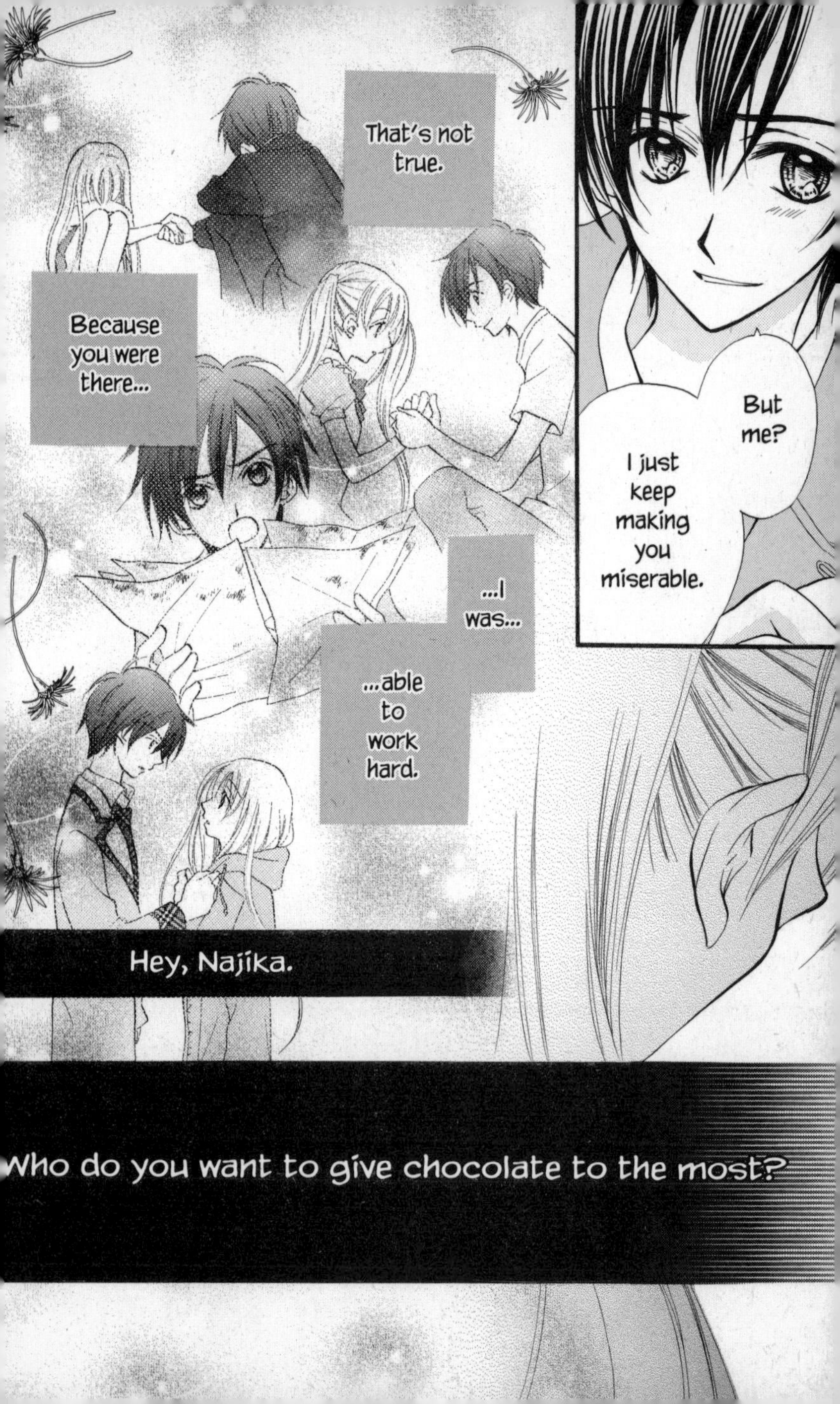
But me?
I just keep making you miserable.
That's not true.
Because you were there...
...I was...
...able to work hard.
Hey, Najika.
Who do you want to give chocolate to the most?

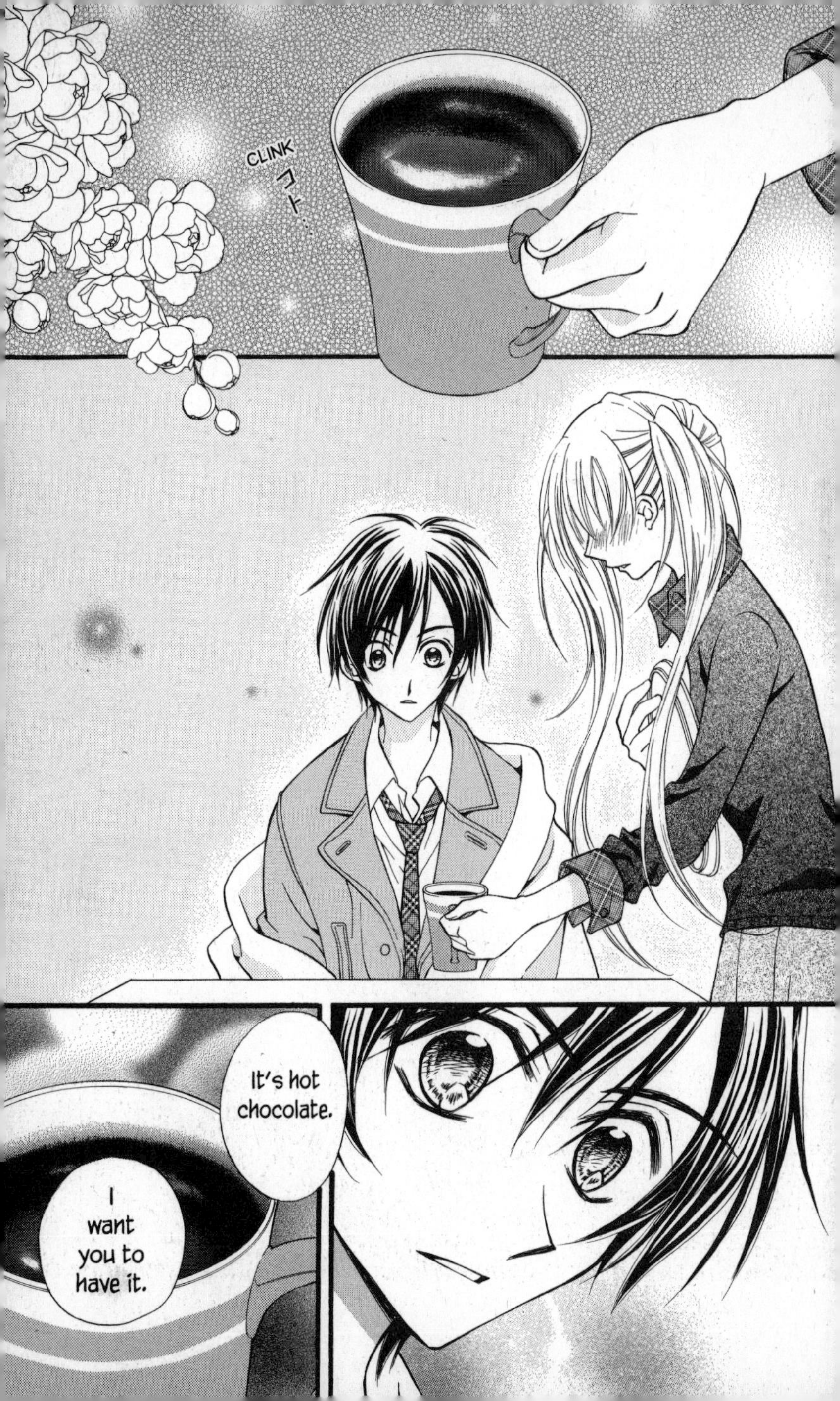
CLINK
コト…
It's hot chocolate.
I want you to have it.

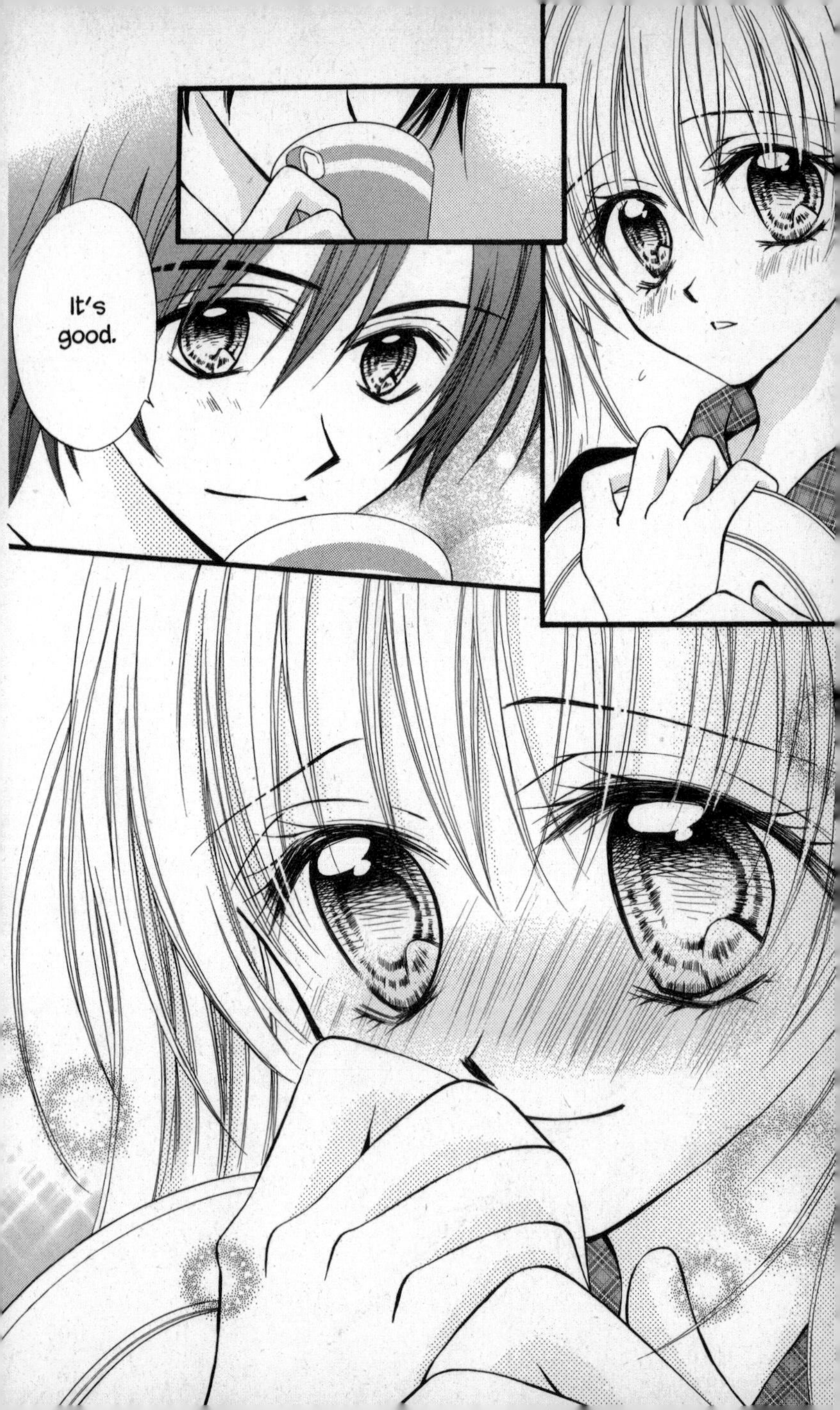
It's good.

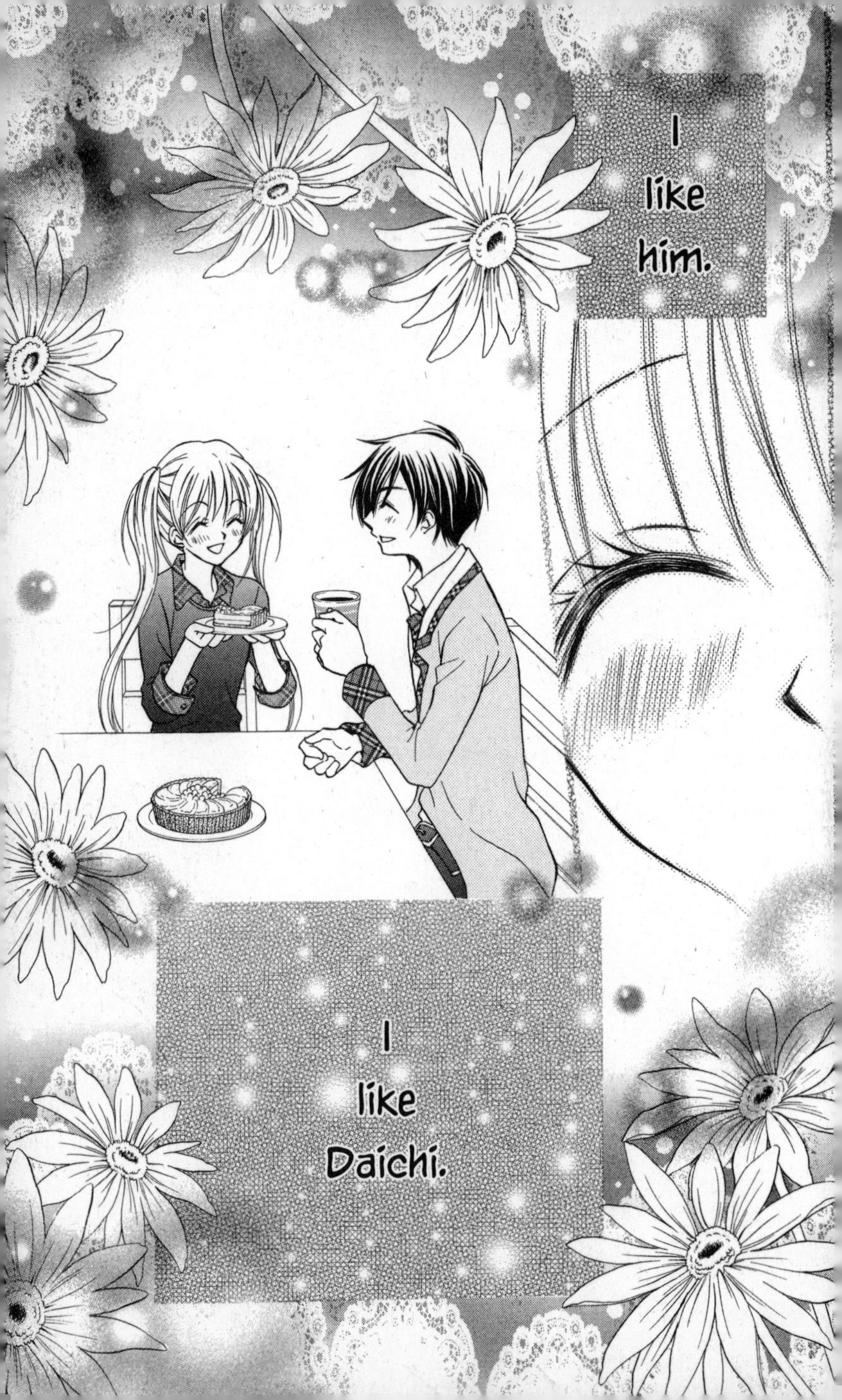
I like him.
I like Daichi.

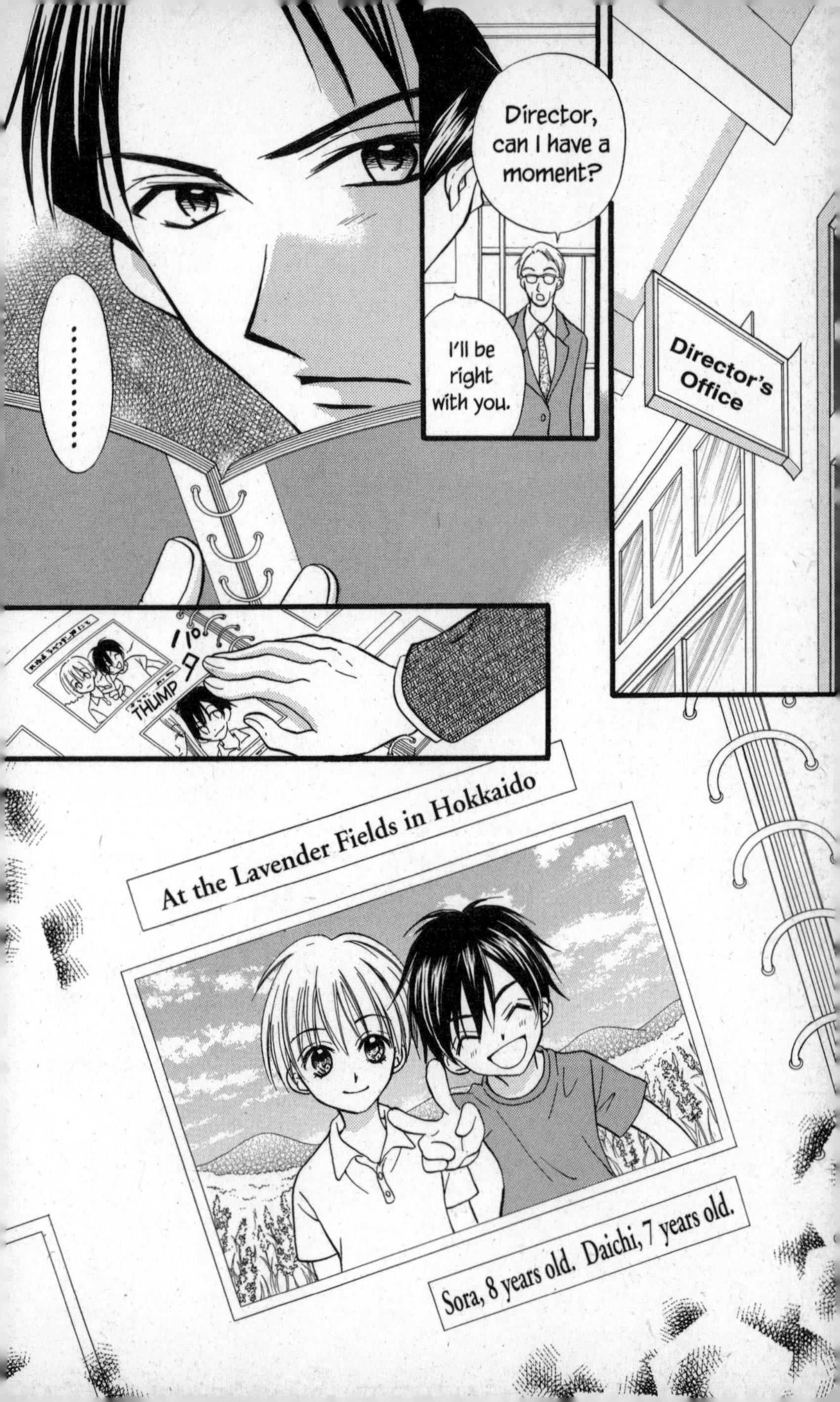
Director's Office
Director, can I have a moment?
I'll be right with you.
......
THUMP
At the Lavender Fields in Hokkaido
Sora, 8 years old. Daichi, 7 years old.

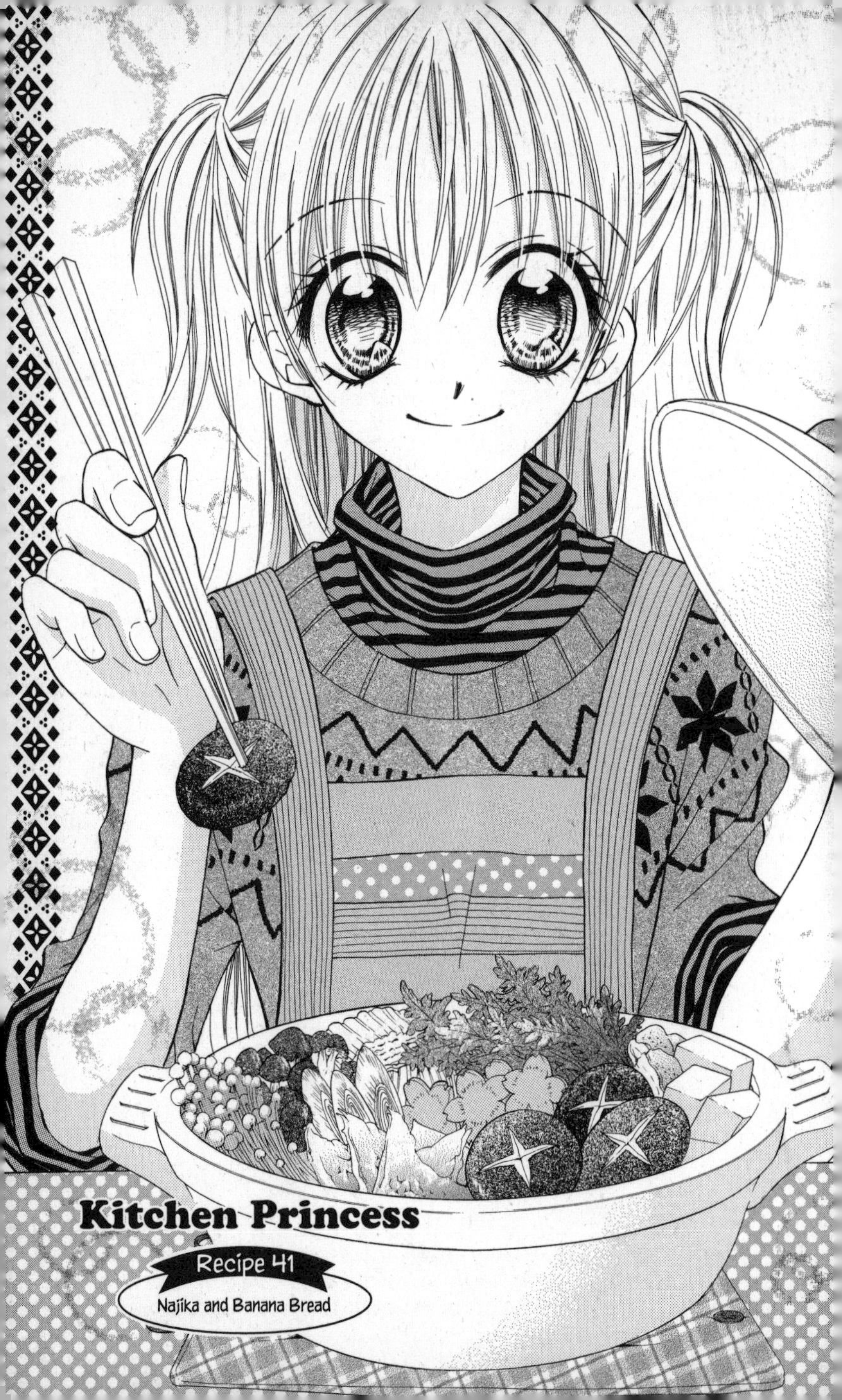
Kitchen Princess
Recipe 41
Najika and Banana Bread

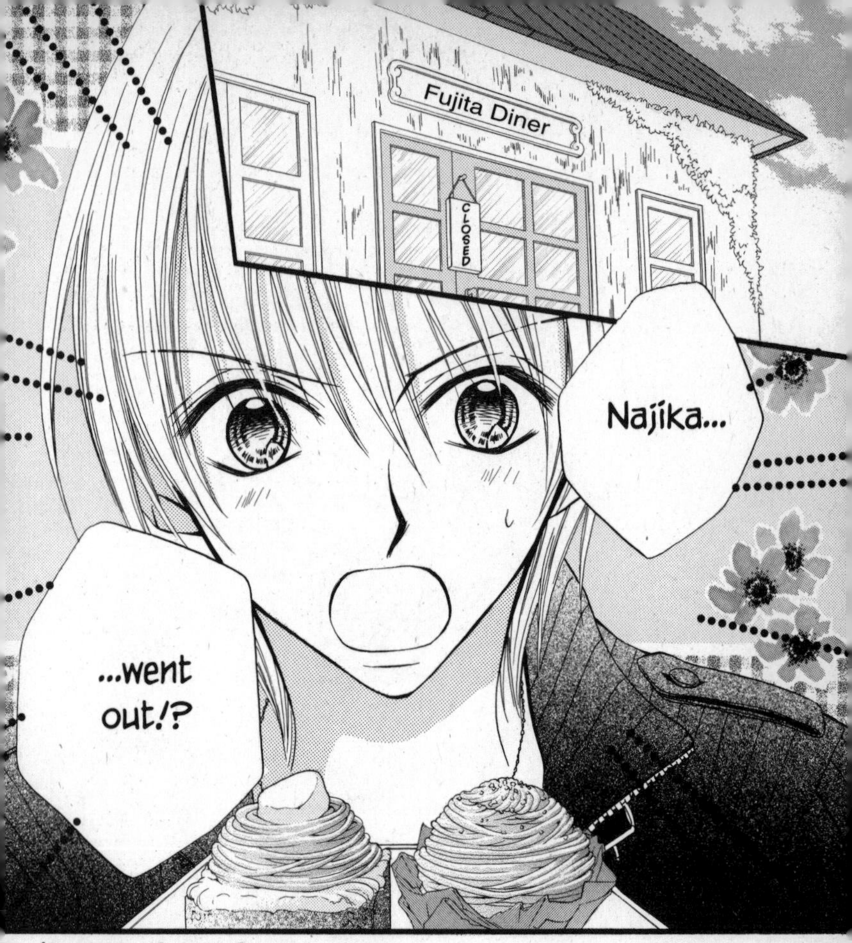
Fujita Diner
CLOSED
Najika...
...went out!?

About the Splash Pages

Recipe 41

When I drew this, I was really into nabe! I was constantly thinking about nabe (laugh). Nabe is easy to make, many people can eat it together, and you don't have to wash that many dishes, so when my assistants came over we ate it a lot (only during the winter, though).
Oh! And putting rice in at the end to make porridge is the best part. The taste is just so good!! I wonder what makes it *so good*...sigh...
I was really feeling the nabe love ♥

Recipe 42

This splash page might be my favorite among the black and white ones. I wasn't sure about including Fujita-san in the picture, but it balanced the composition so it turned out well. I remember I couldn't decide what to make him hold until the very end...In the end, I gave him a doughnut.

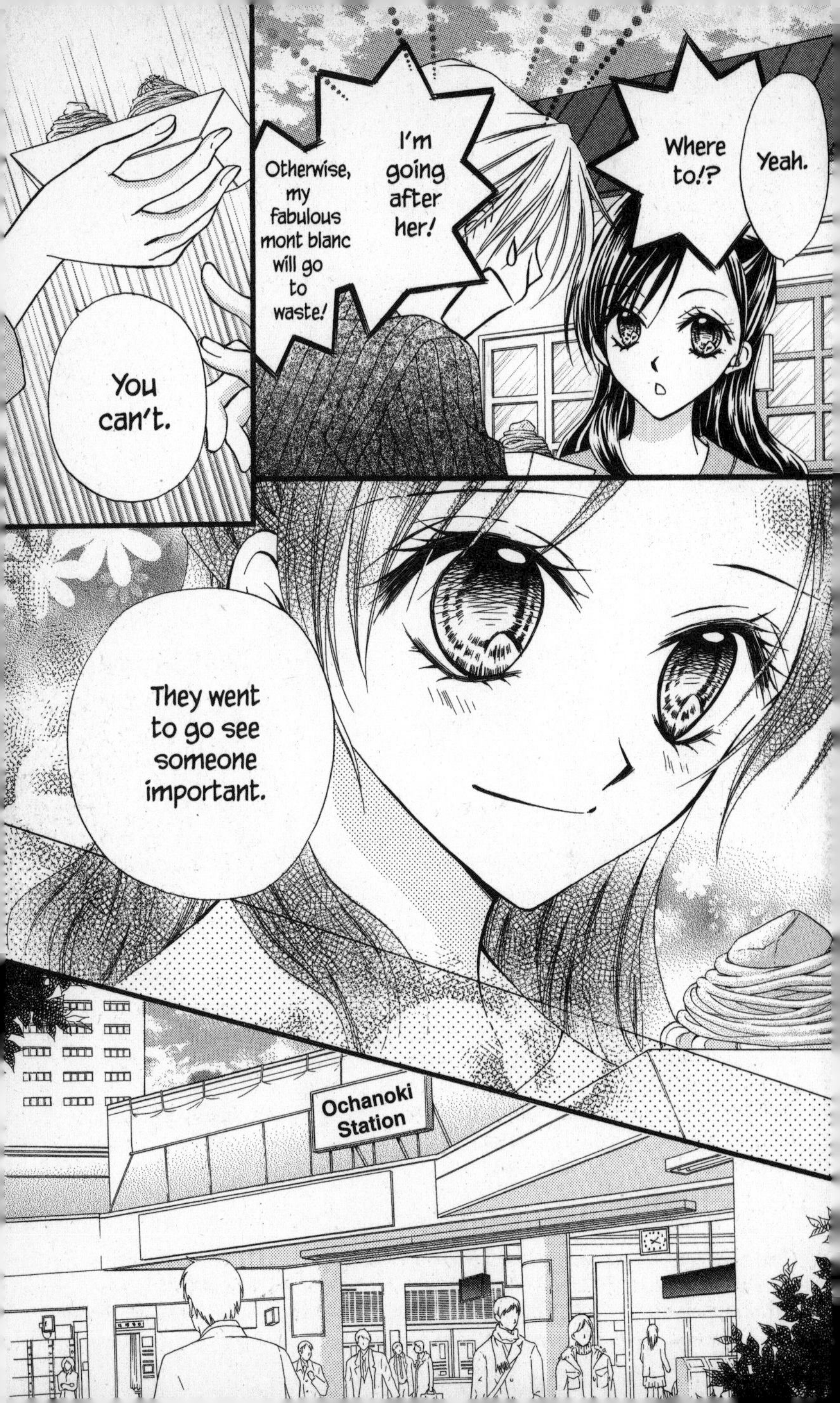
Yeah.
Where to!?
I'm going after her!
Otherwise, my fabulous mont blanc will go to waste!
You can't.
They went to go see someone important.
Ochanoki Station

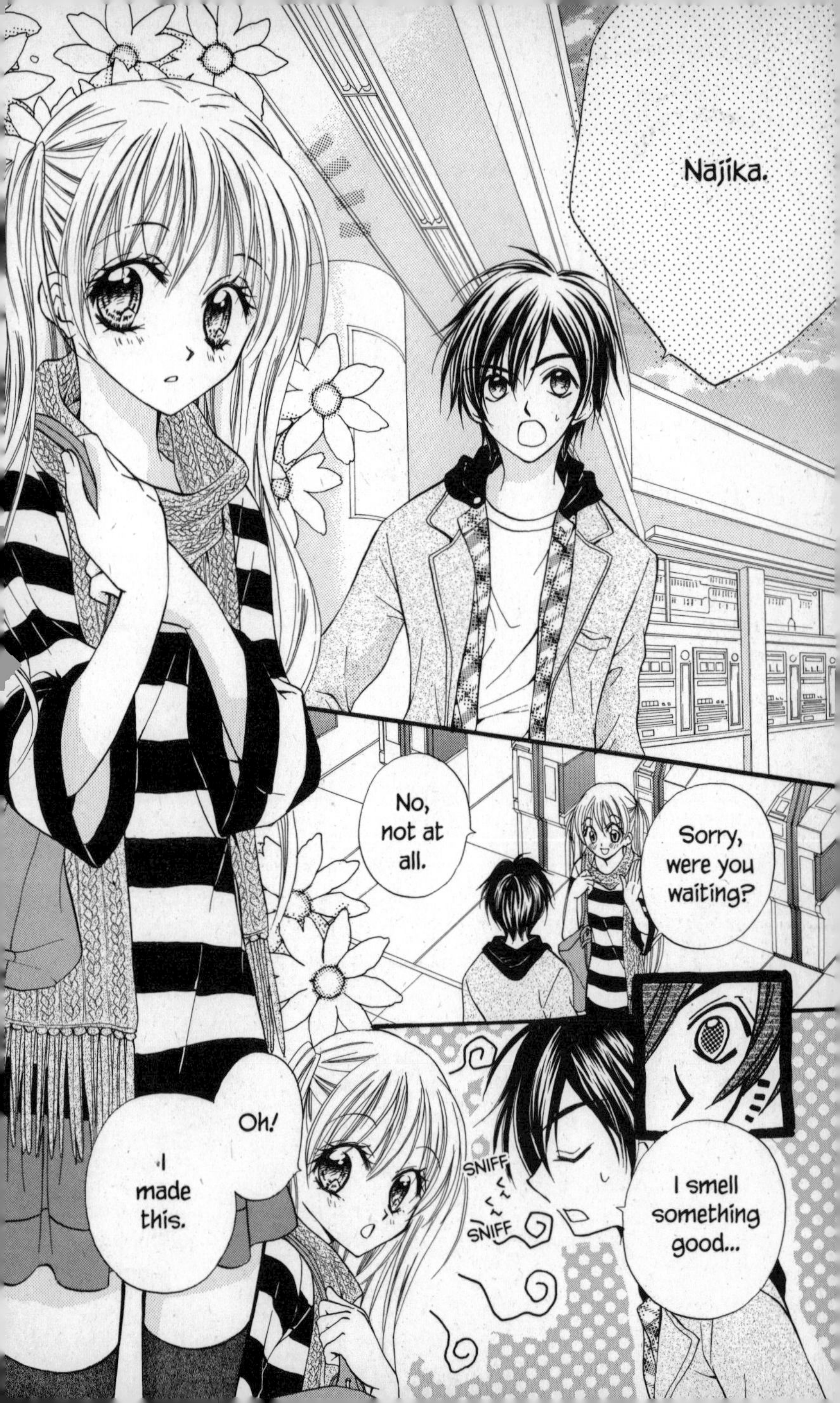

Najika.
Sorry, were you waiting?
No, not at all.
I smell something good...
SNIFF
SNIFF
Oh!
I made this.

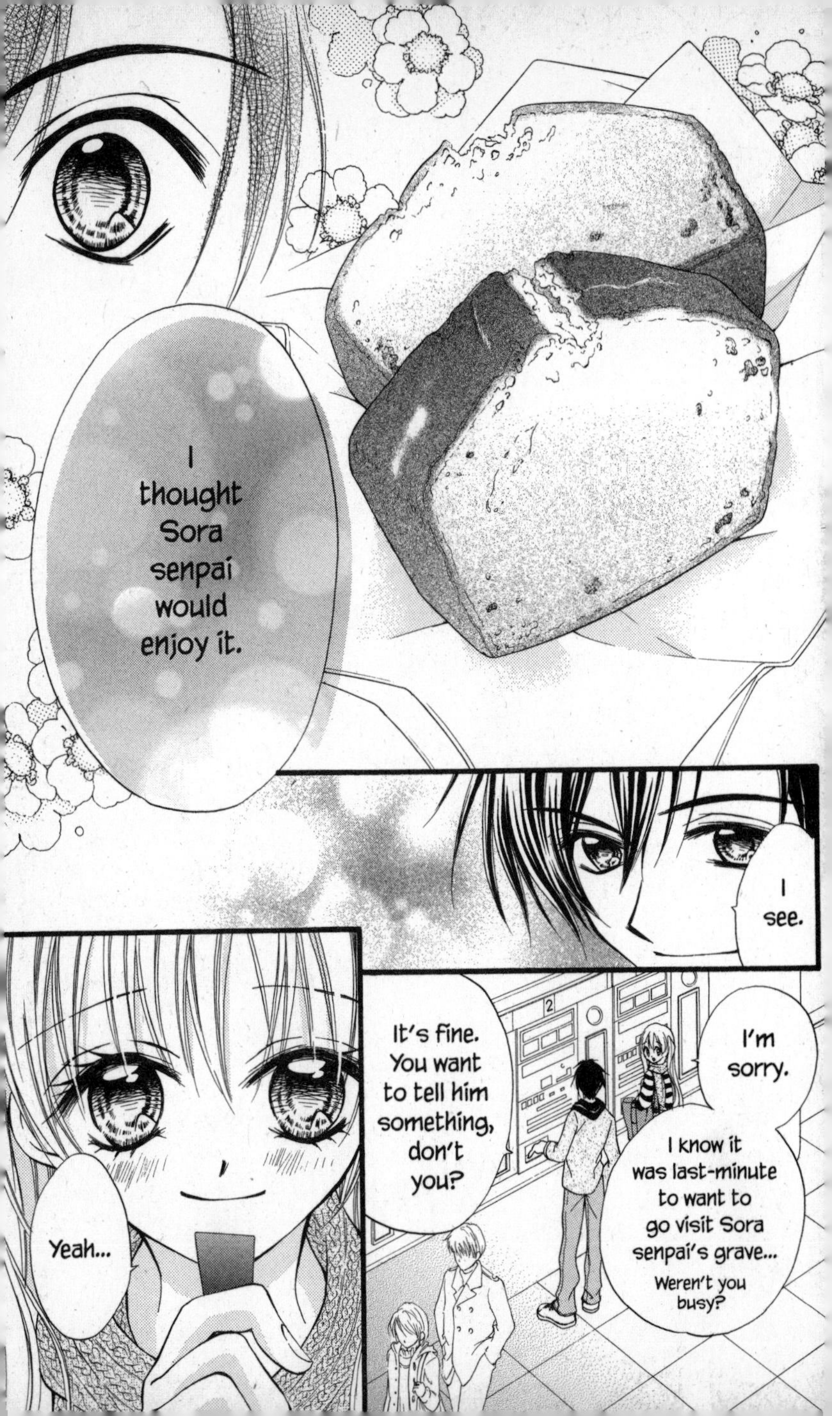
I thought Sora senpai would enjoy it.
I see.
I'm sorry.
I know it was last-minute to want to go visit Sora senpai's grave... Weren't you busy?
It's fine. You want to tell him something, don't you?
Yeah...

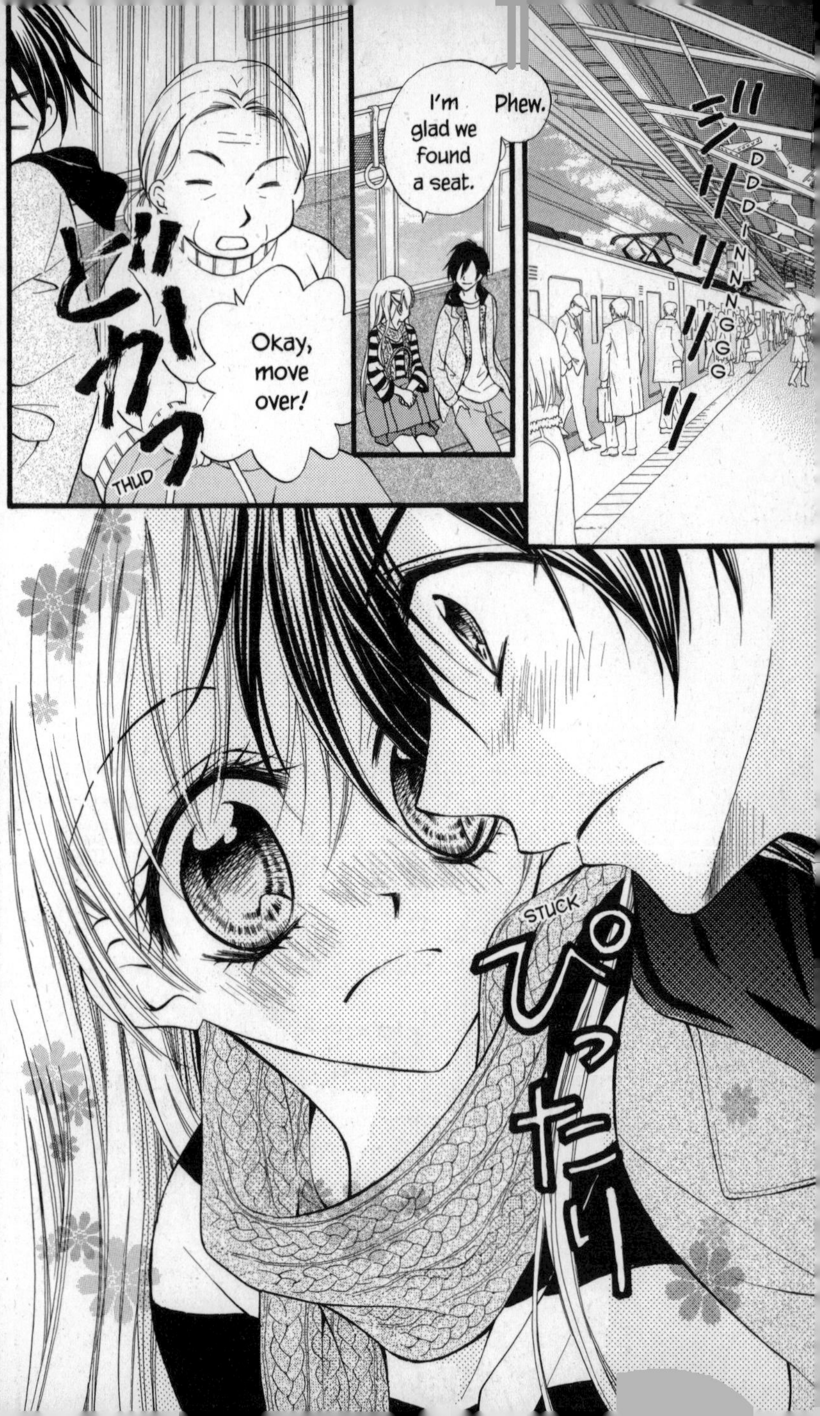
DDDINNNGGG
Phew.
I'm glad we found a seat.
Okay, move over!
THUD
STUCK

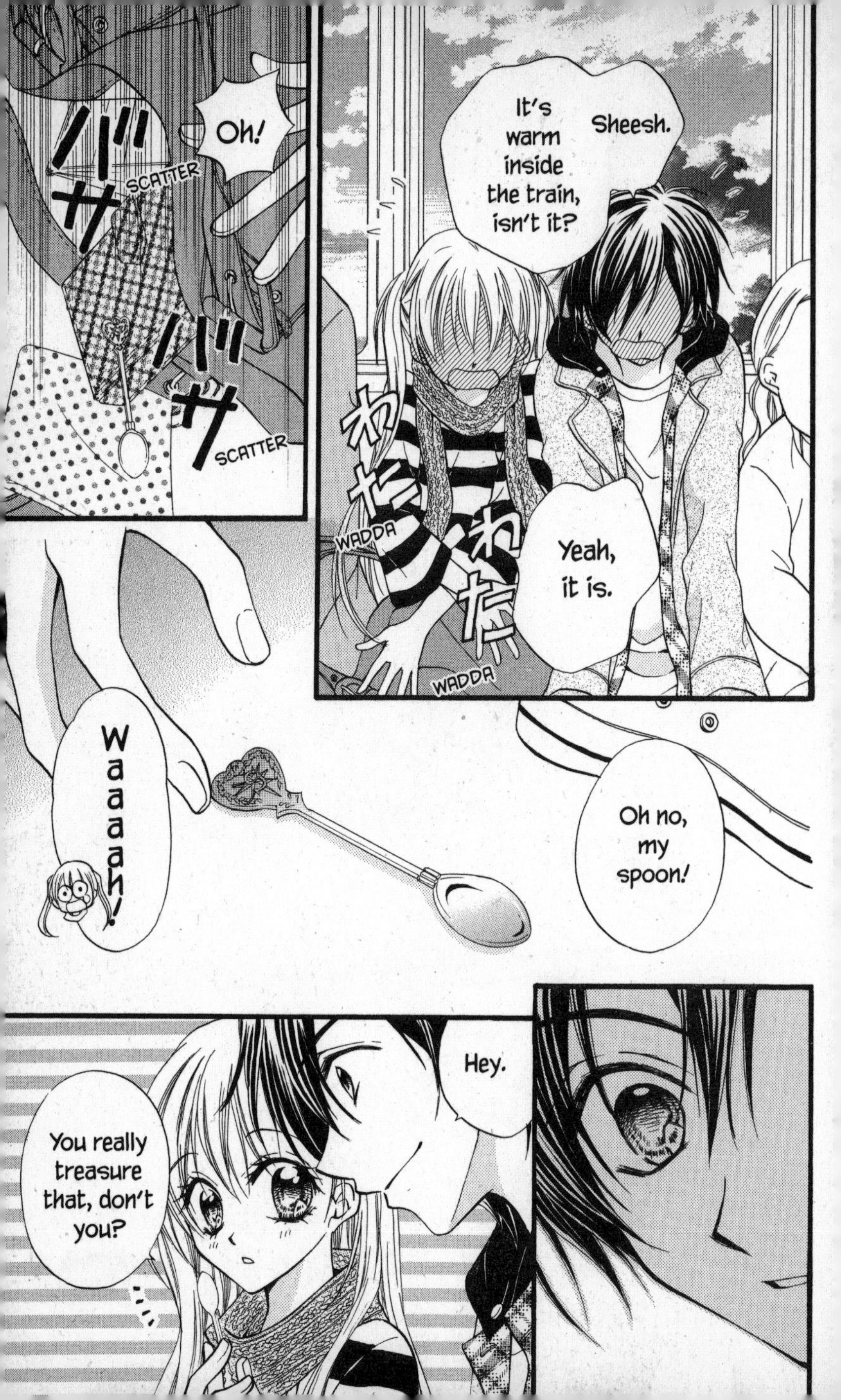
Sheesh.
It's warm inside the train, isn't it?
WADDA
WADDA
Yeah, it is.
Oh!
SCATTER
SCATTER
Oh no, my spoon!
Waaaaah!
Hey.
You really treasure that, don't you?
...

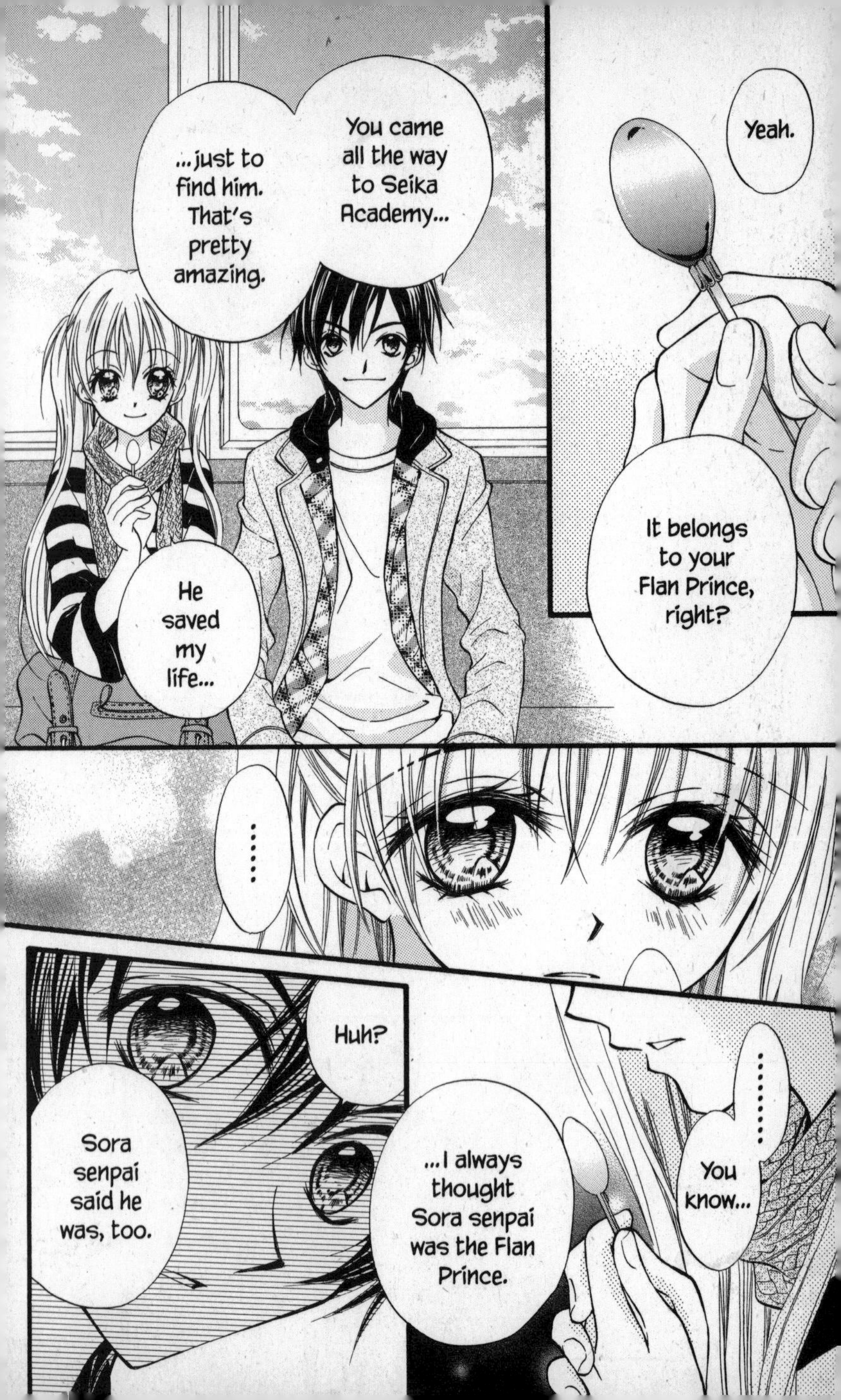
Yeah.
It belongs to your Flan Prince, right?
You came all the way to Seika Academy...
...just to find him. That's pretty amazing.
He saved my life...
......
......
You know...
...I always thought Sora senpai was the Flan Prince.
Huh?
Sora senpai said he was, too.

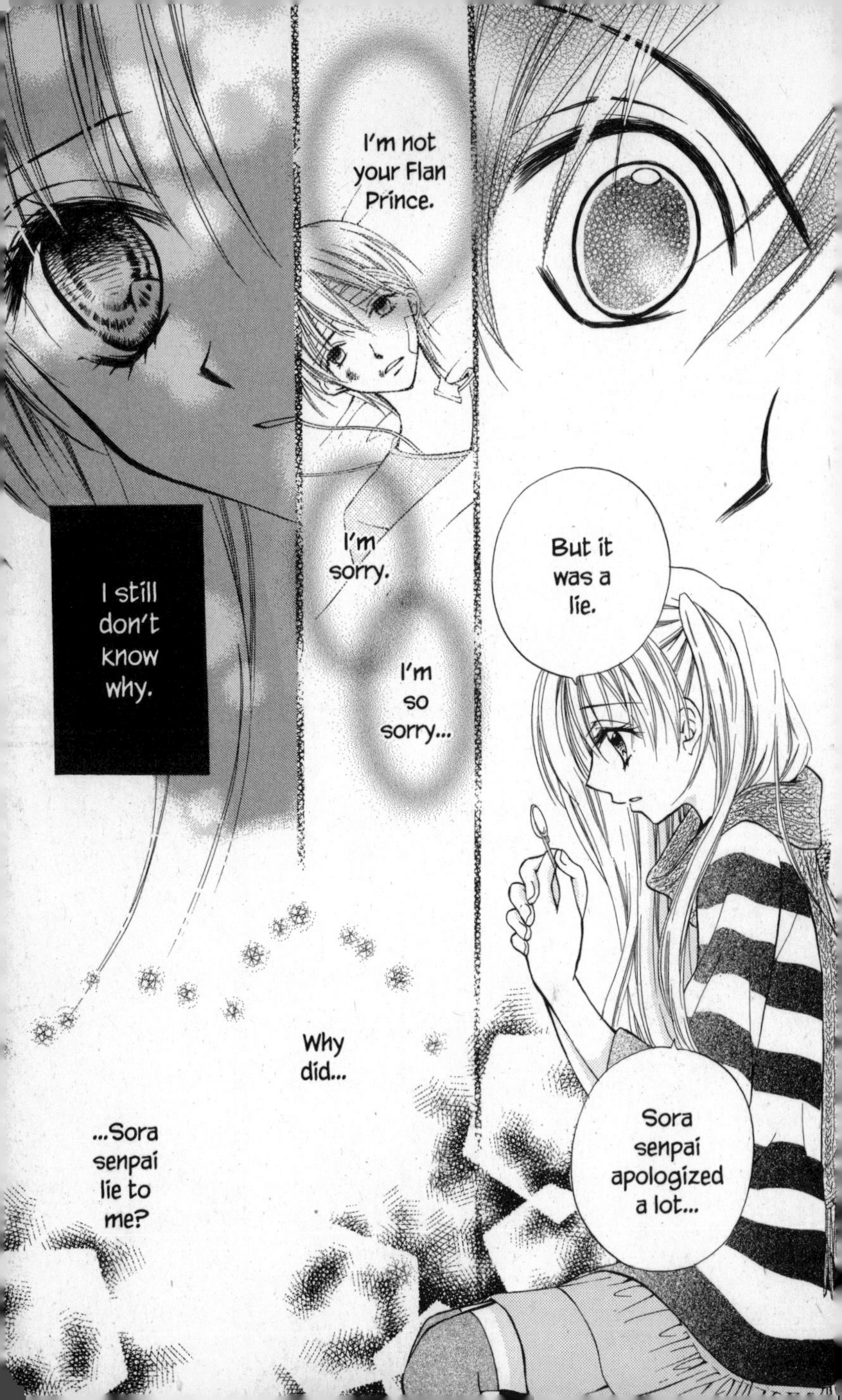
But it was a lie.
Sora senpai apologized a lot...
I'm not your Flan Prince.
I'm sorry.
I'm so sorry...
I still don't know why.
Why did...
...Sora senpai lie to me?

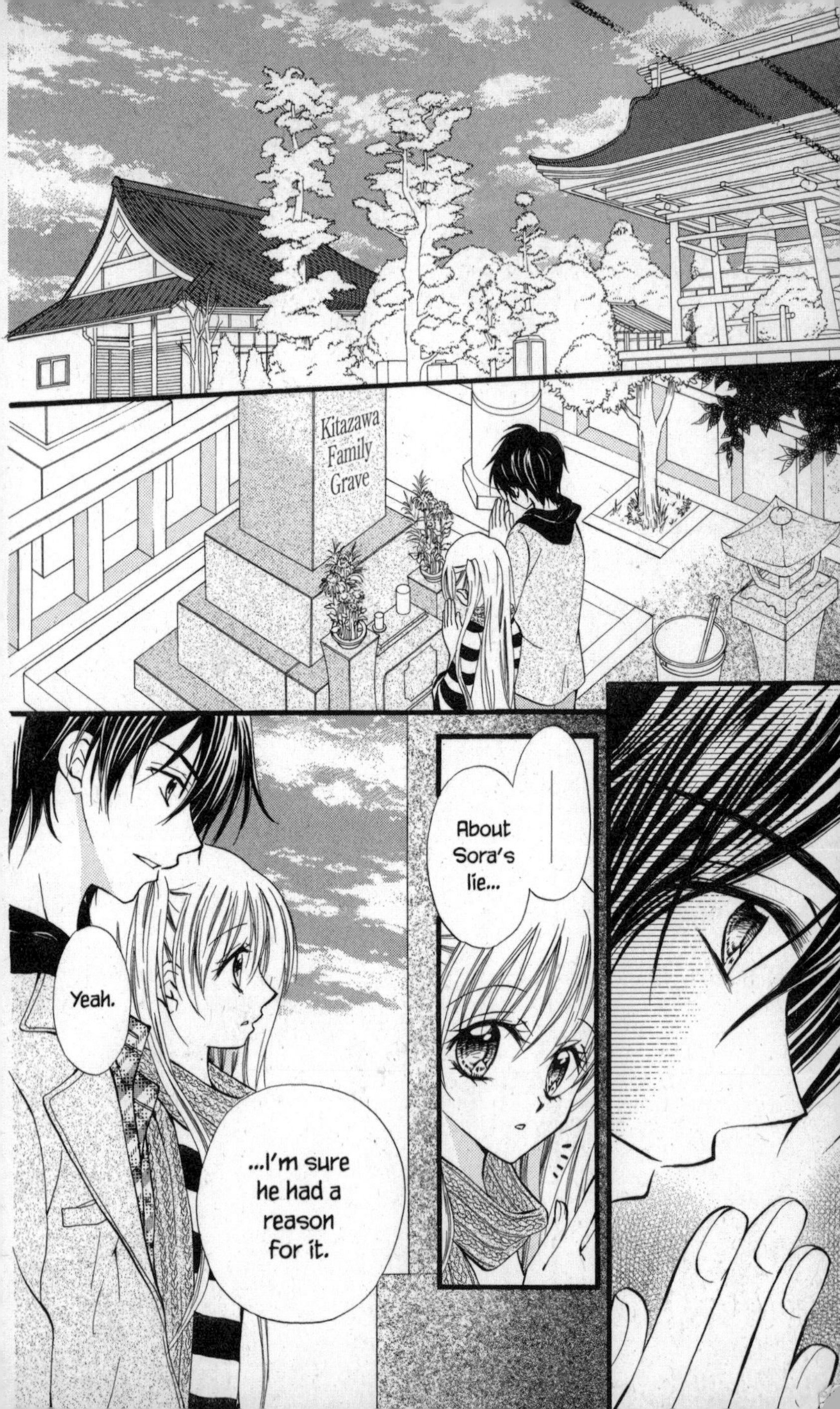
Kitazawa Family Grave
About Sora's lie...
Yeah.
...I'm sure he had a reason for it.

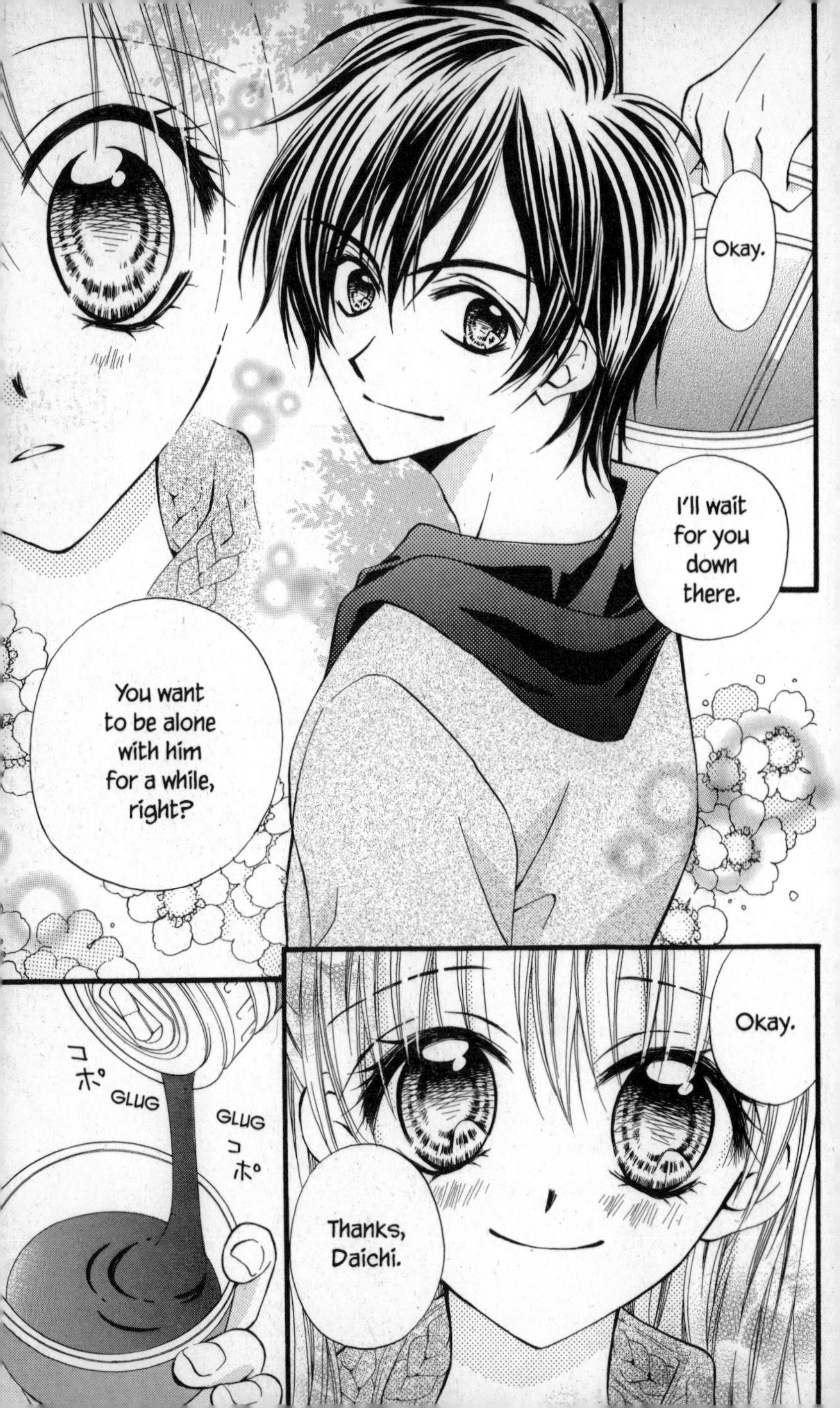
Okay.
I'll wait for you down there.
You want to be alone with him for a while, right?
Okay.
Thanks, Daichi.
コポ GLUG
GLUG コポ

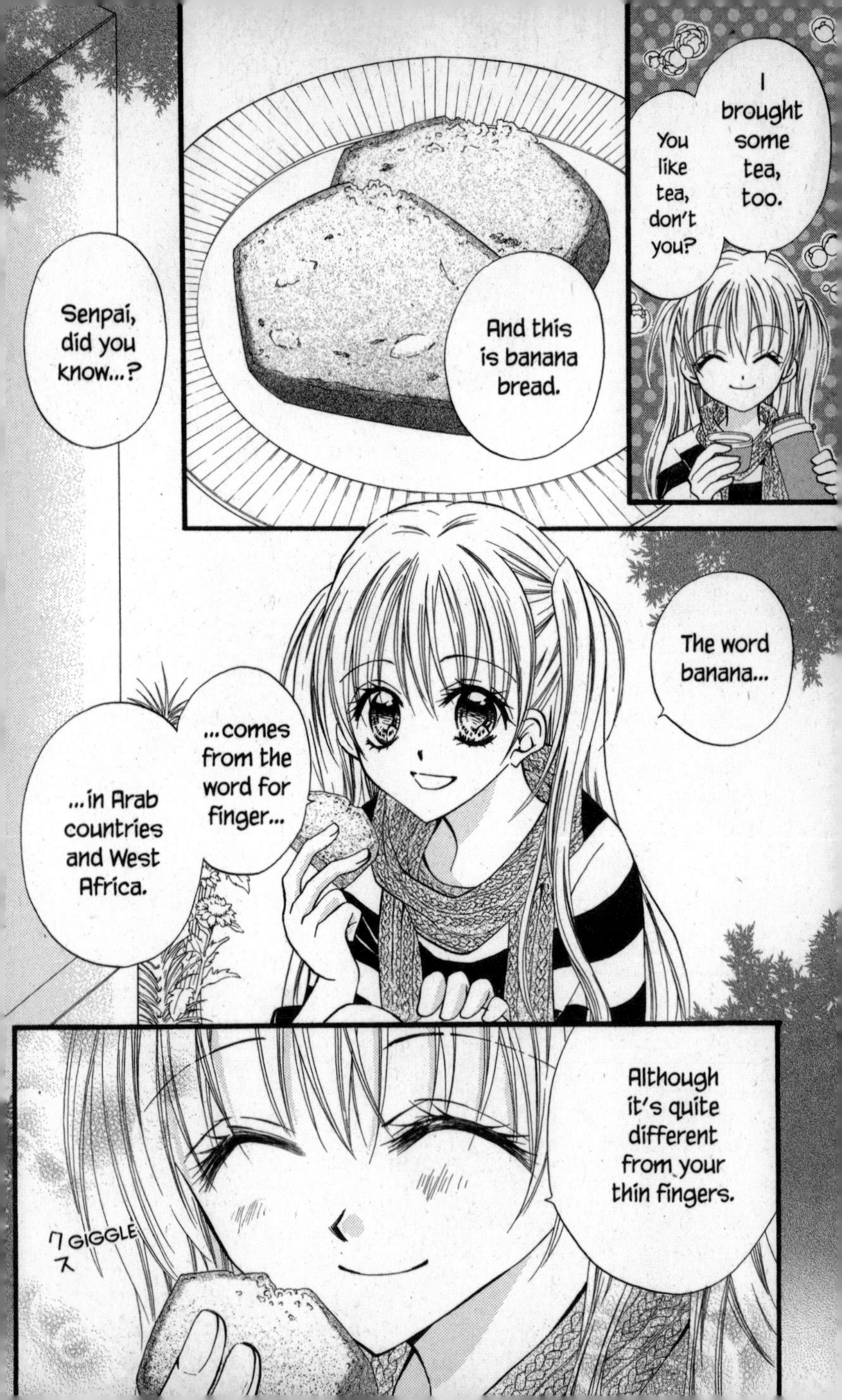
I brought some tea, too.
You like tea, don't you?
And this is banana bread.
Senpai, did you know...?
The word banana...
...comes from the word for finger...
...in Arab countries and West Africa.
Although it's quite different from your thin fingers.
GIGGLE

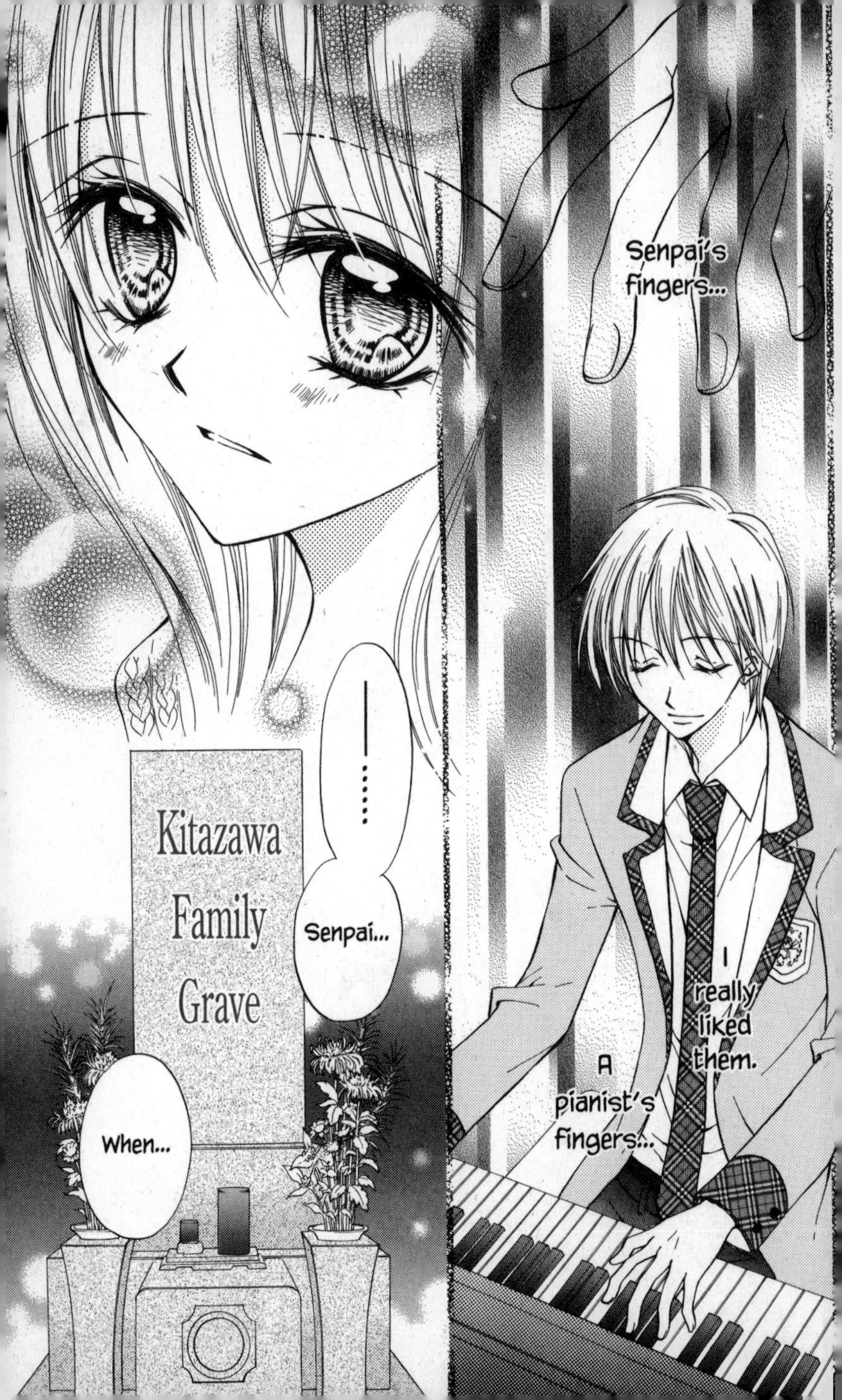
Senpai's fingers...
I really liked them.
A pianist's fingers...
—......
Senpai...
Kitazawa Family Grave
When...

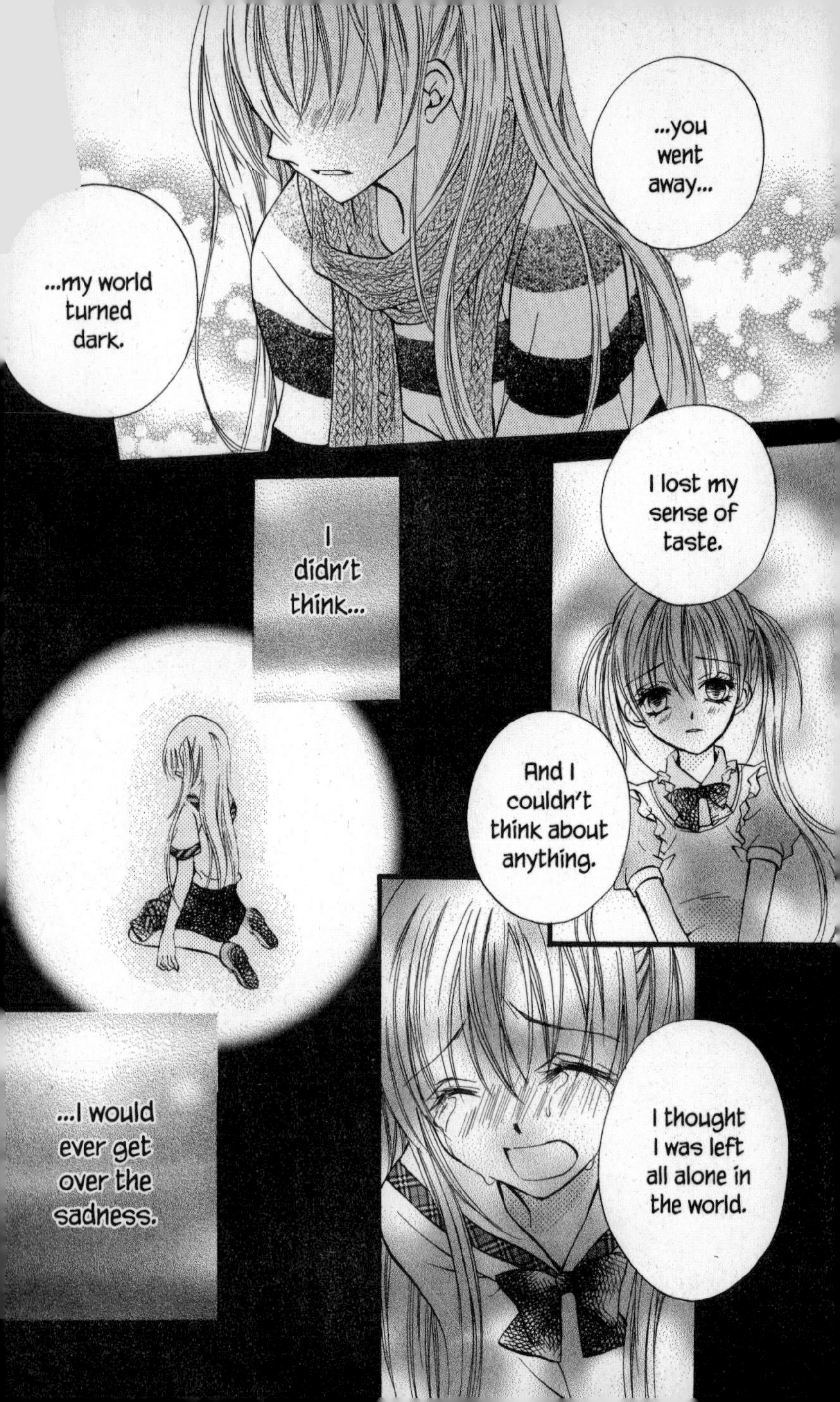
...you went away...
...my world turned dark.
I lost my sense of taste.
And I couldn't think about anything.
I didn't think...
I thought I was left all alone in the world.
...I would ever get over the sadness.

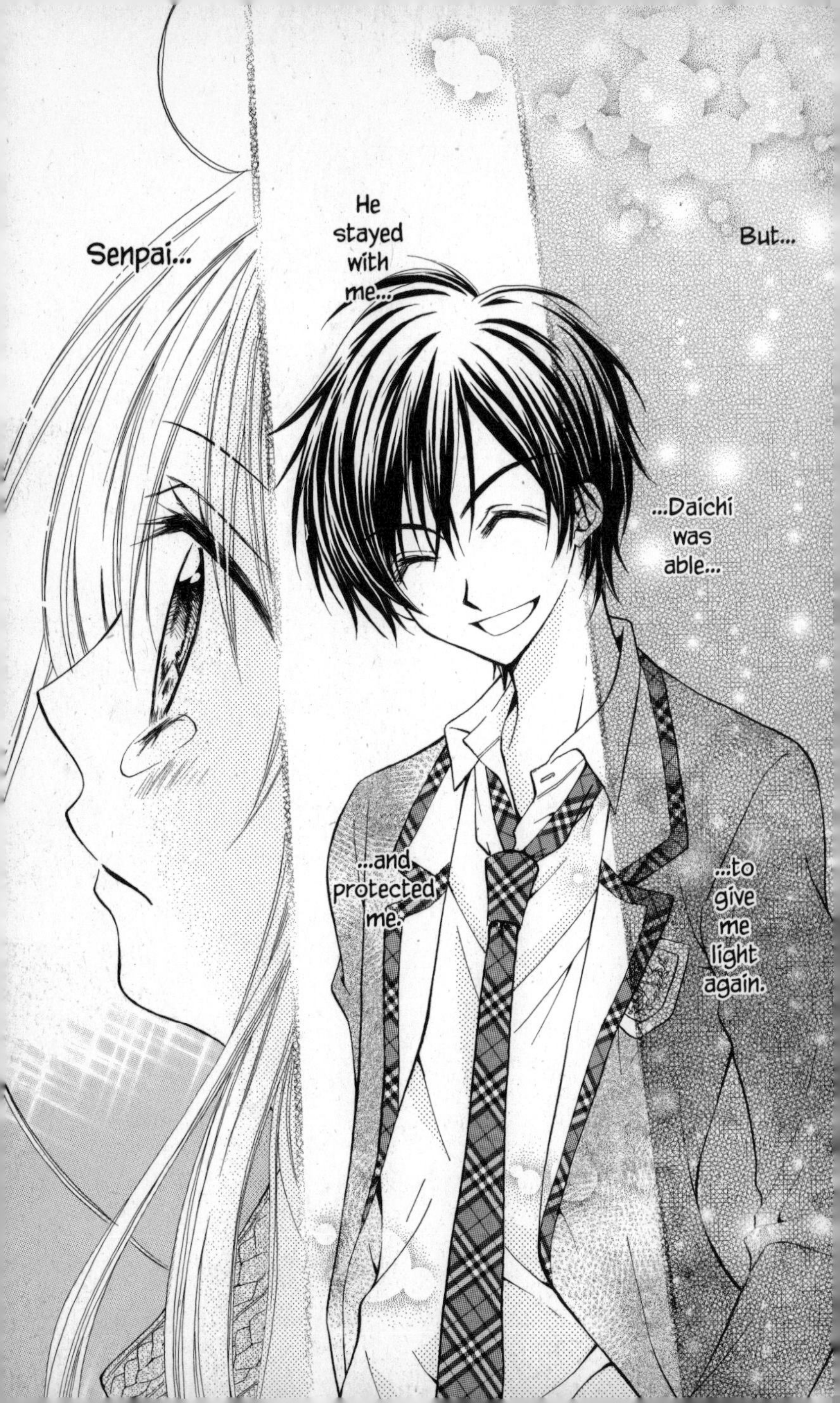
Senpai...
He stayed with me...
...and protected me.
But...
...Daichi was able...
...to give me light again.

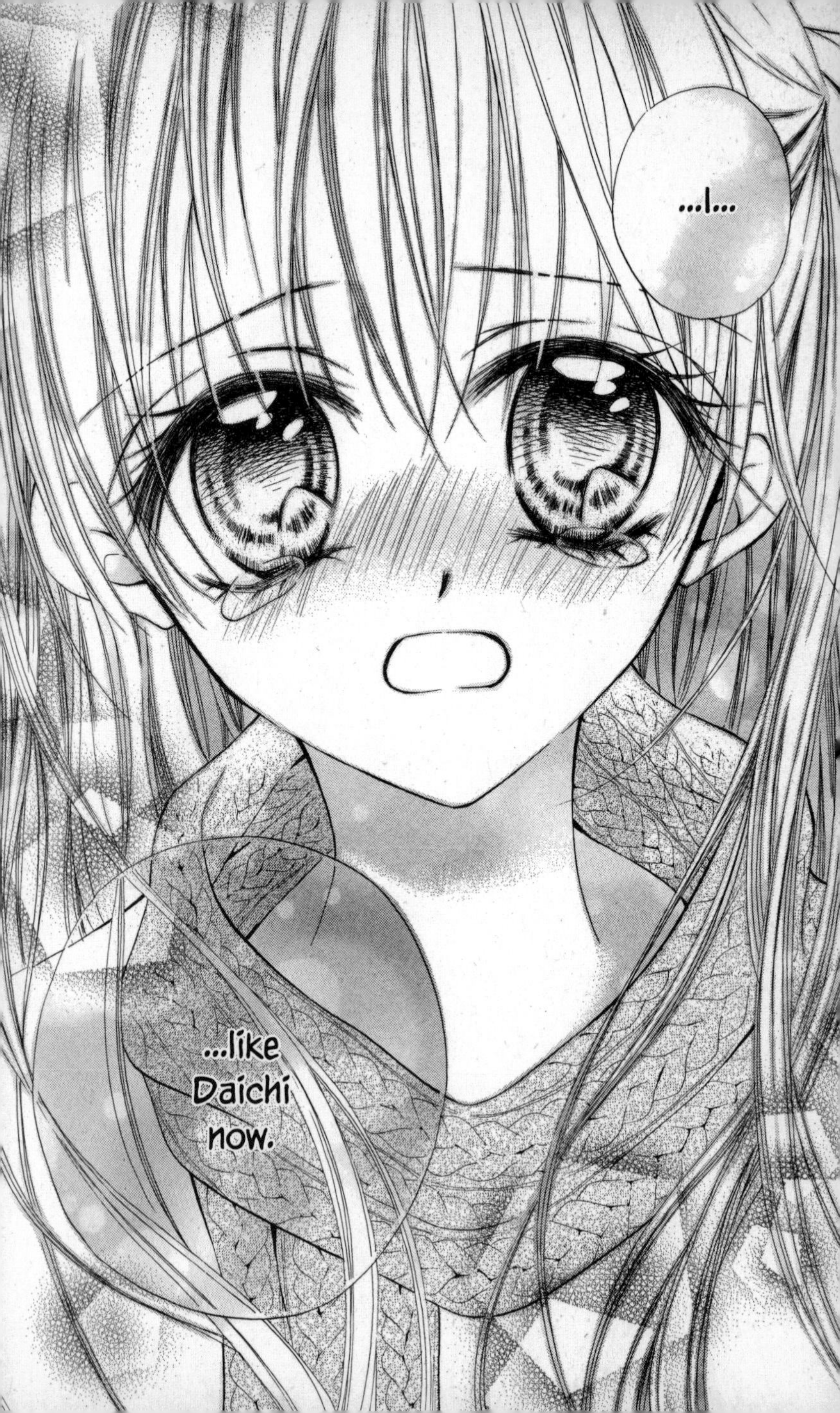
...I...
...like Daichi now.

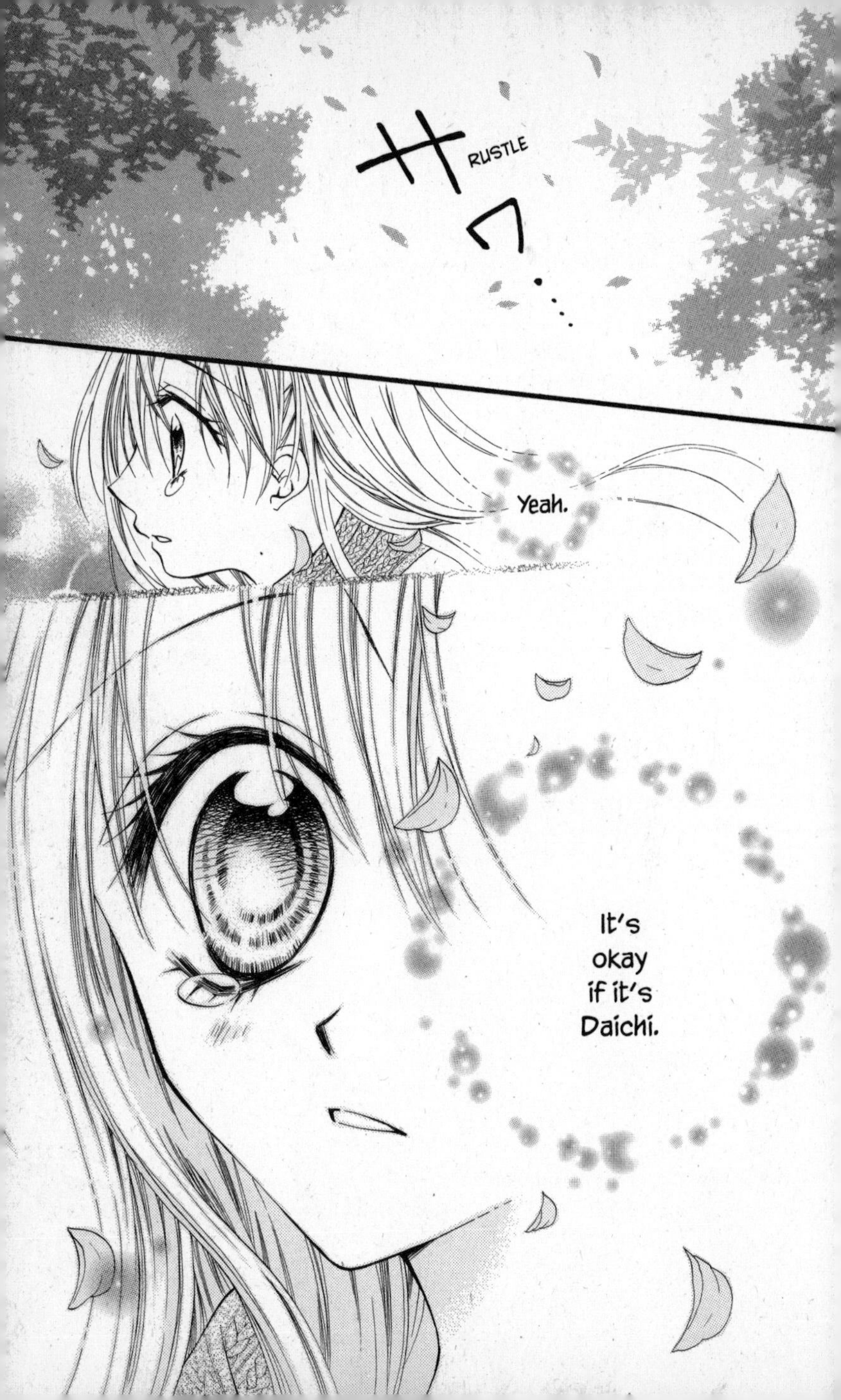
RUSTLE
Yeah.
It's okay if it's Daichi.

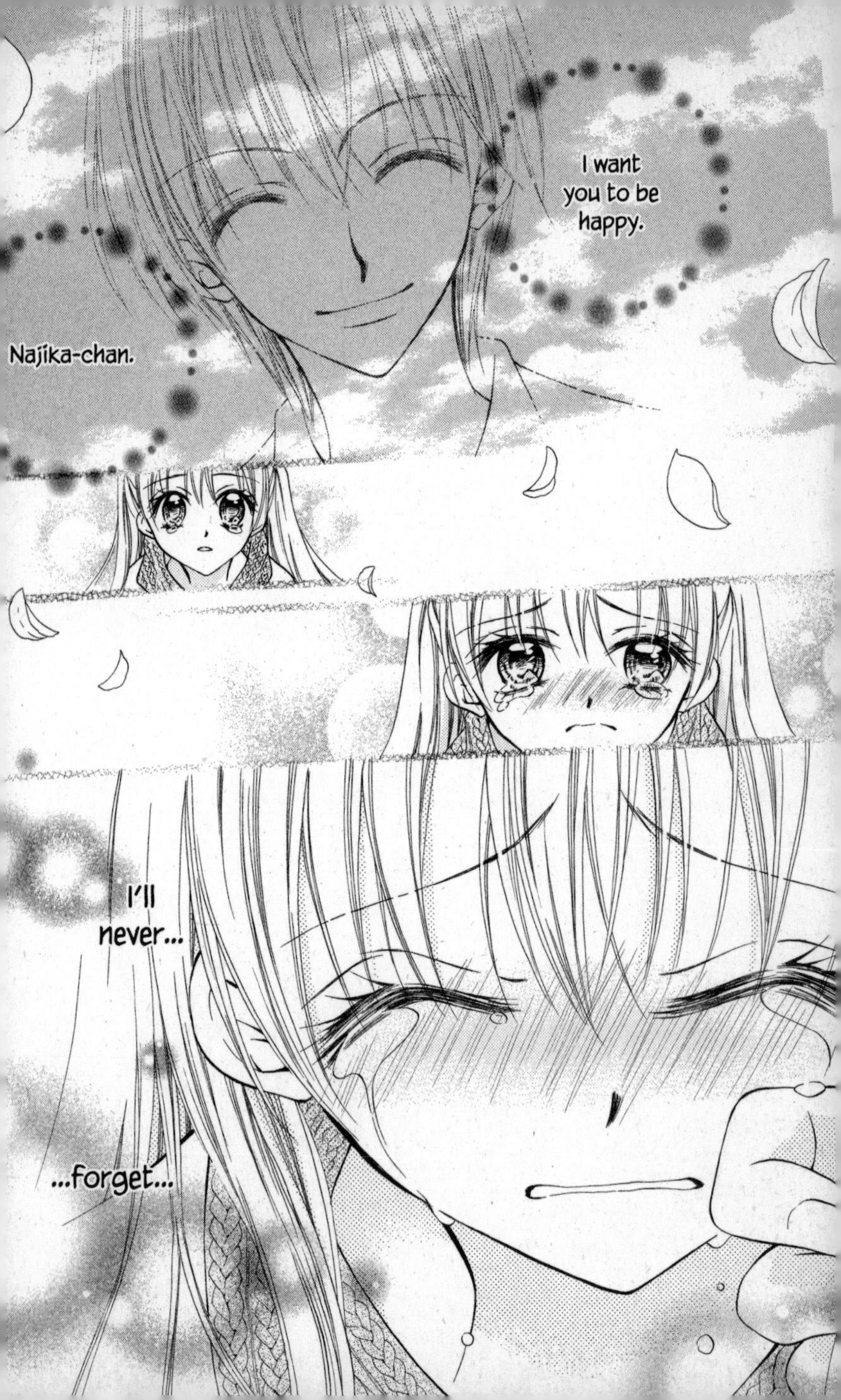
I want you to be happy.
Najika-chan.
I'll never...
...forget...

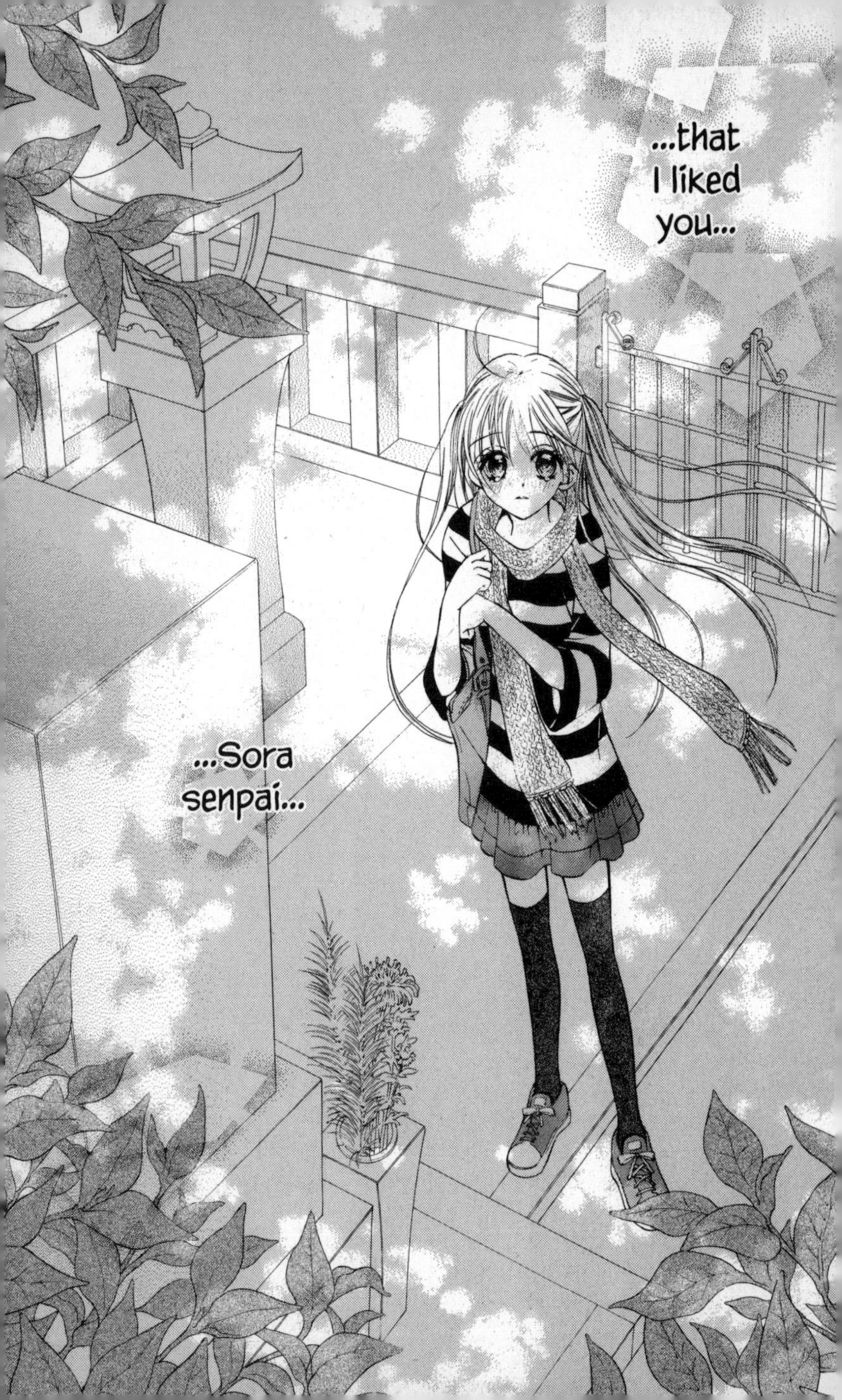
...that I liked you...
...Sora senpai...

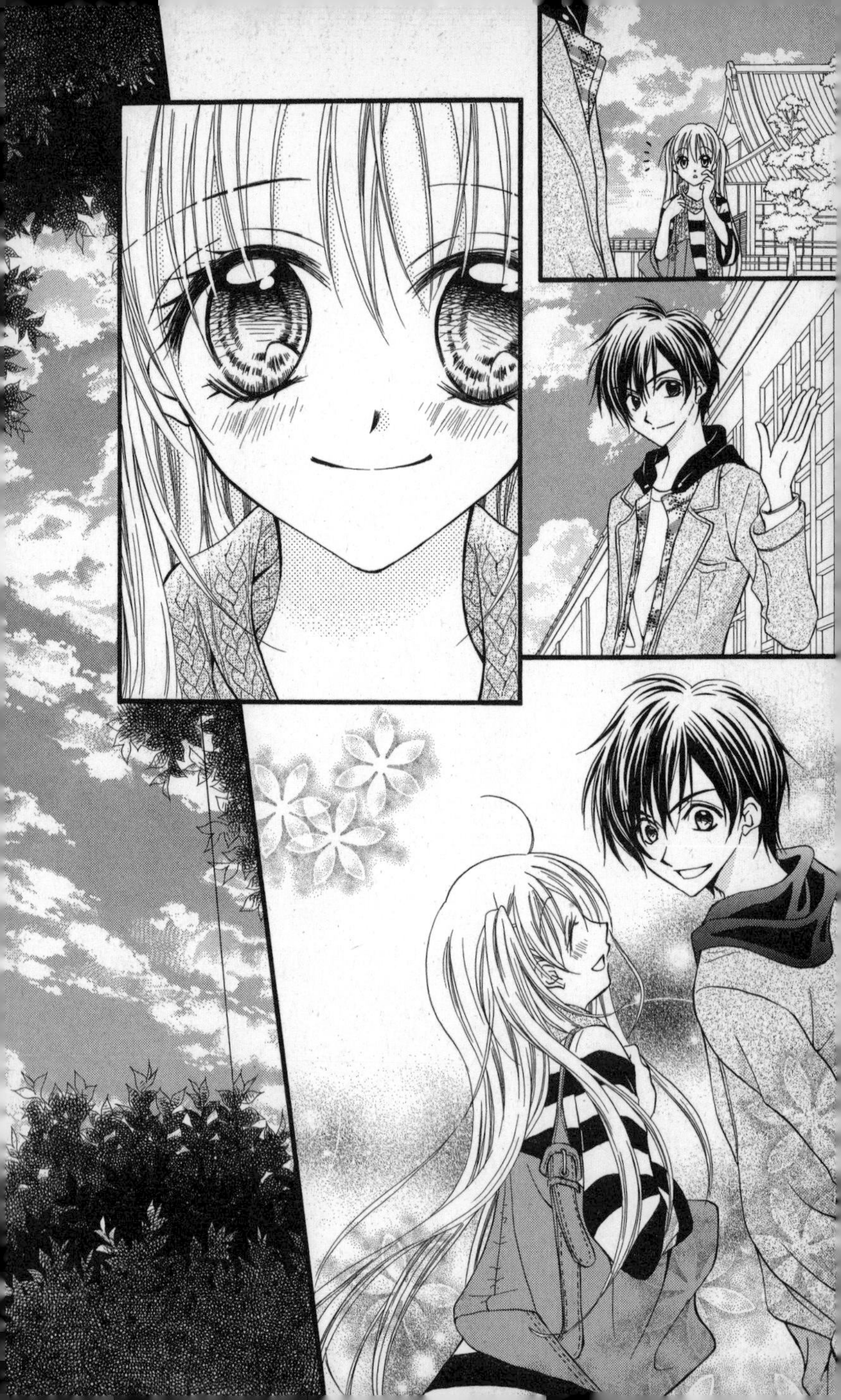

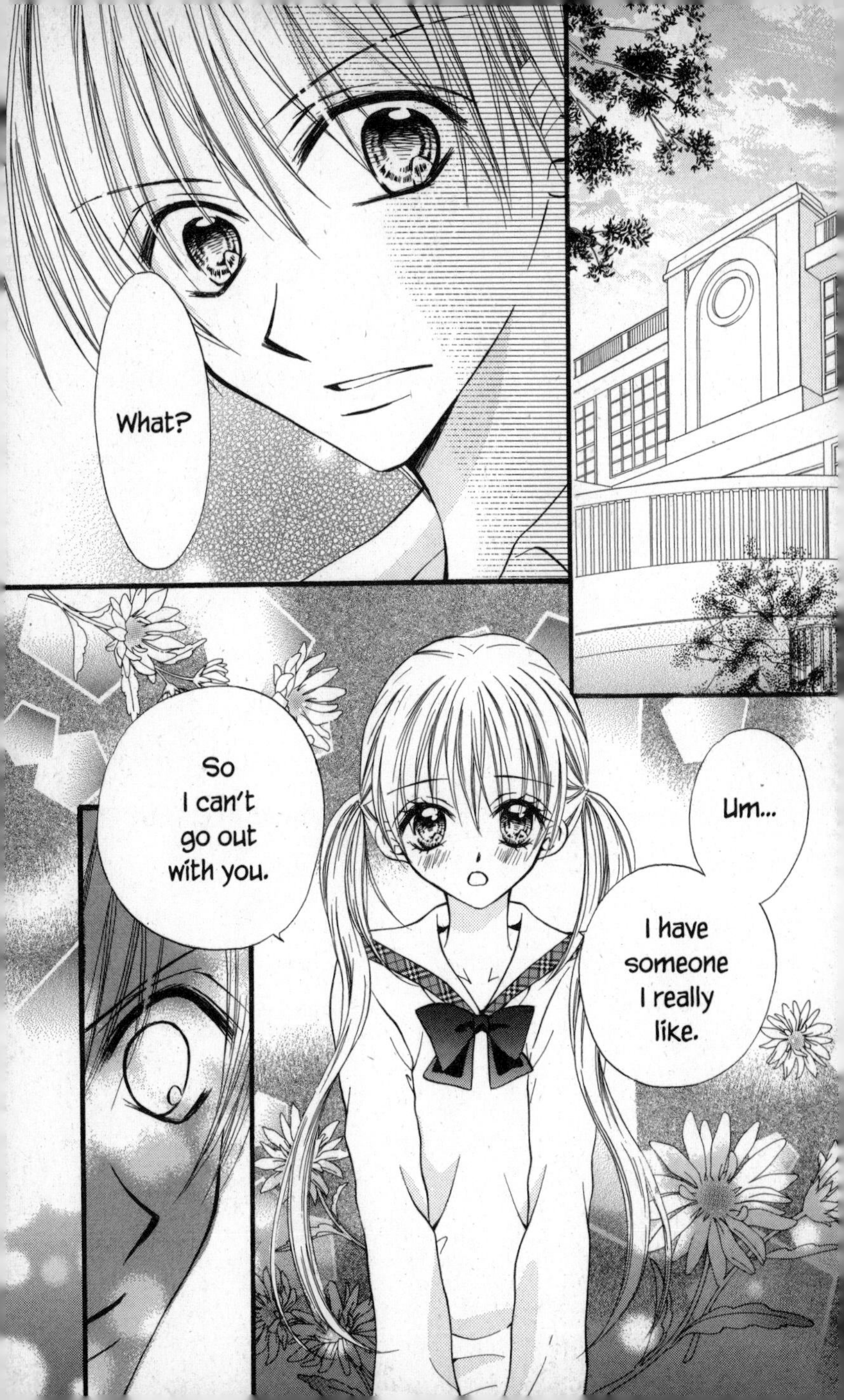
What?
Um...
I have someone I really like.
So I can't go out with you.

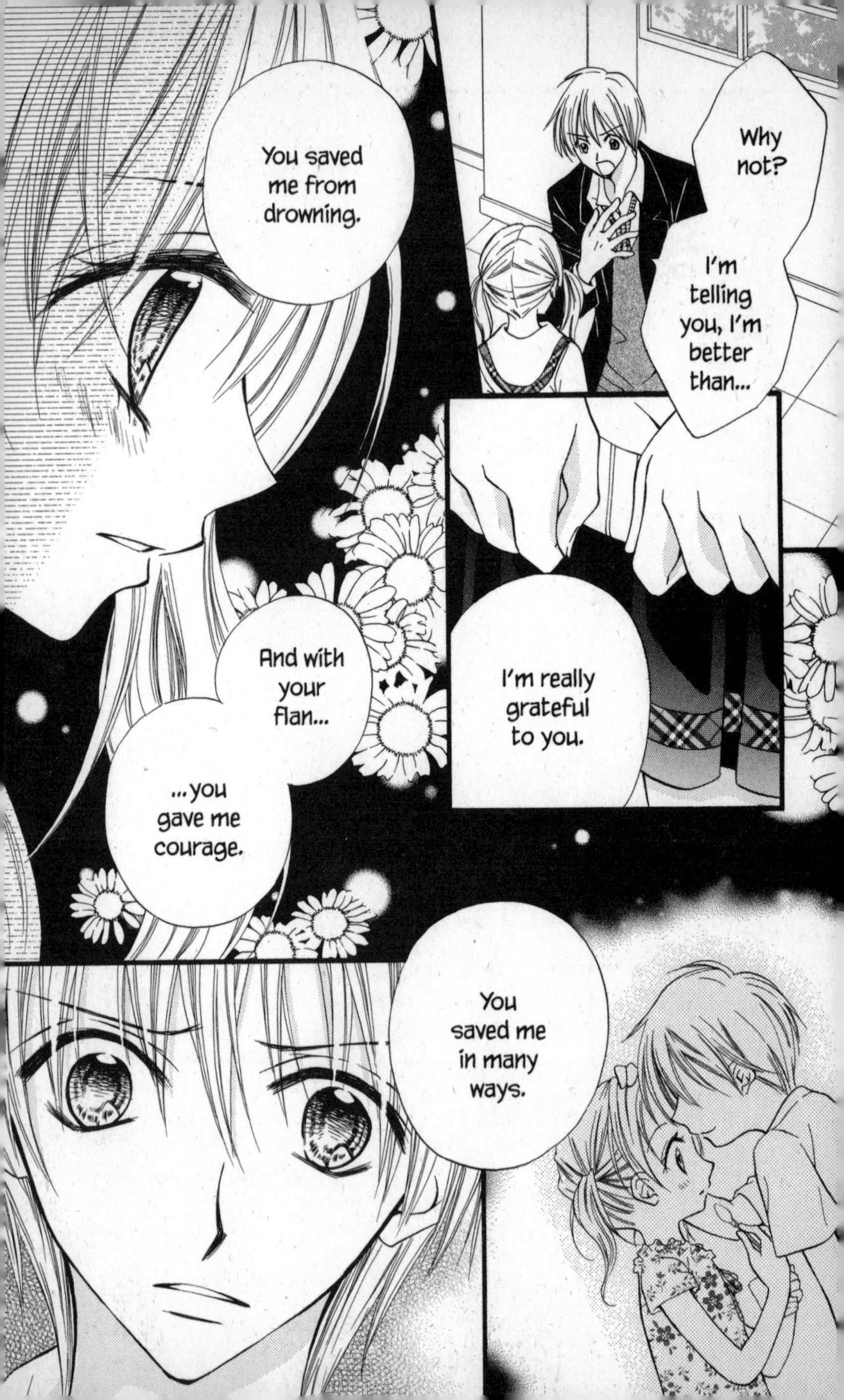
Why not?
I'm telling you, I'm better than...
I'm really grateful to you.
You saved me from drowning.
And with your flan...
...you gave me courage.
You saved me in many ways.

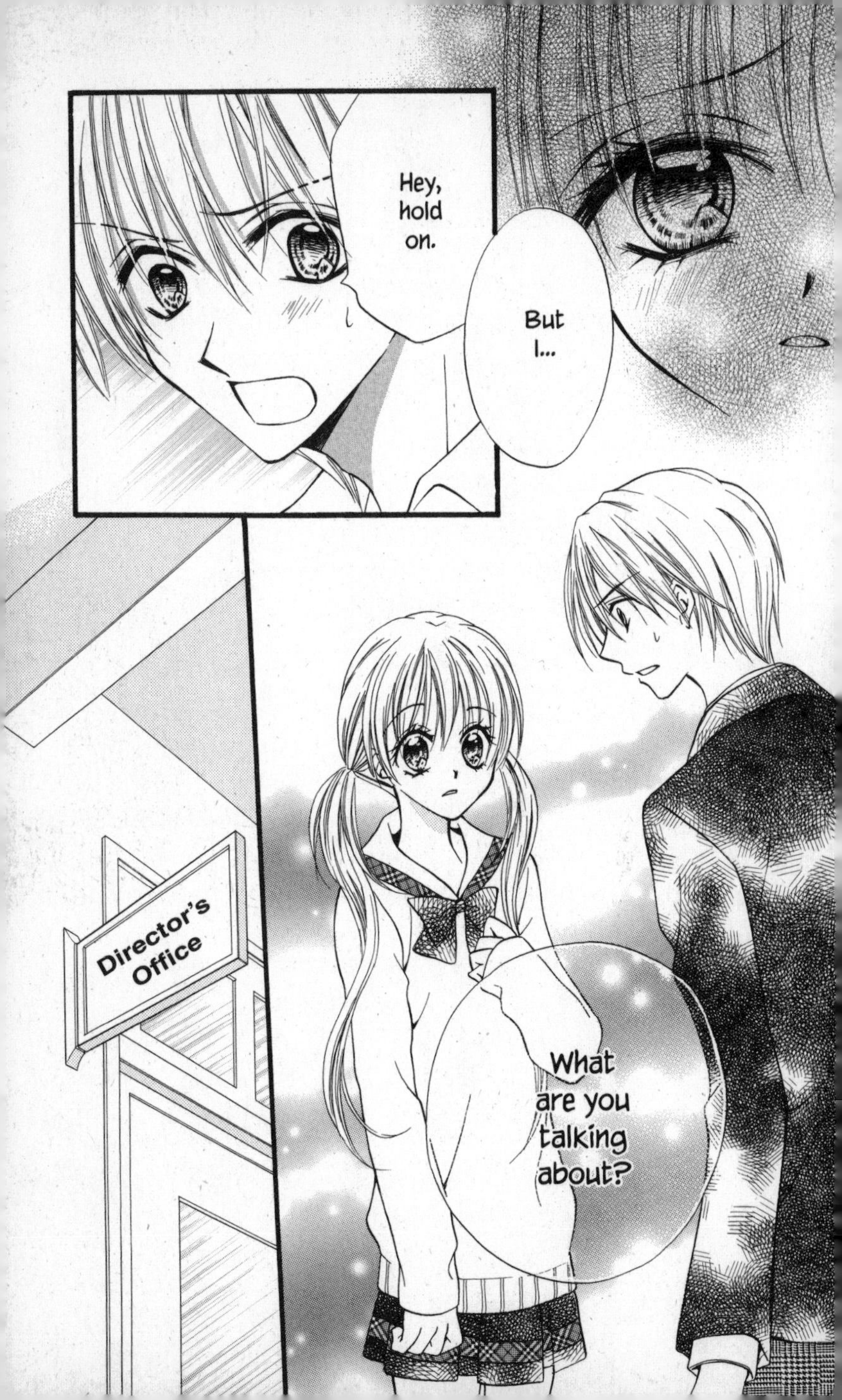
But I...
Hey, hold on.
What are you talking about?
Director's Office

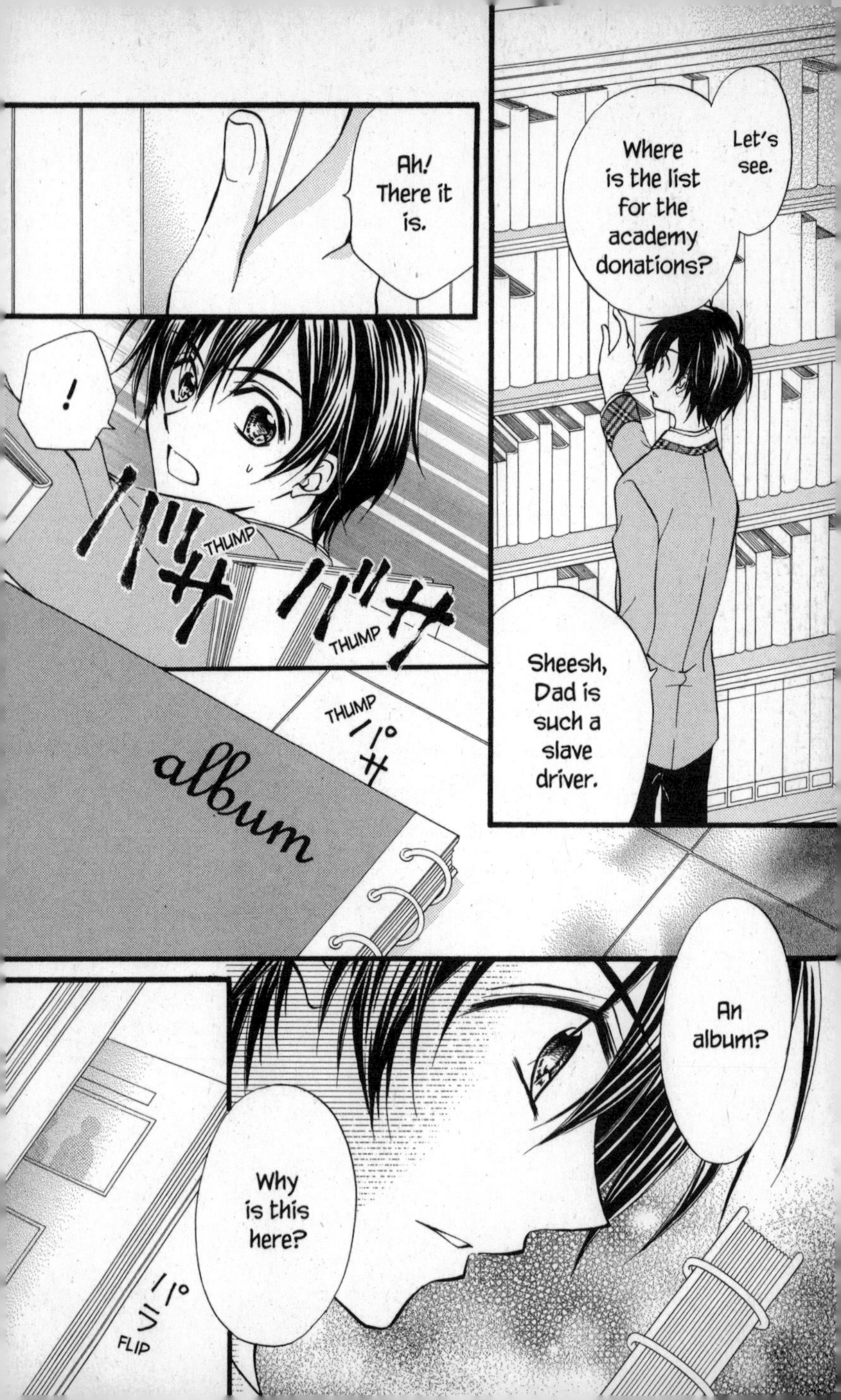
Let's see.
Where is the list for the academy donations?
Sheesh, Dad is such a slave driver.
Ah! There it is.
!
バサ
THUMP
バサ
THUMP
THUMP
パサ
album
An album?
Why is this here?
パラ
FLIP

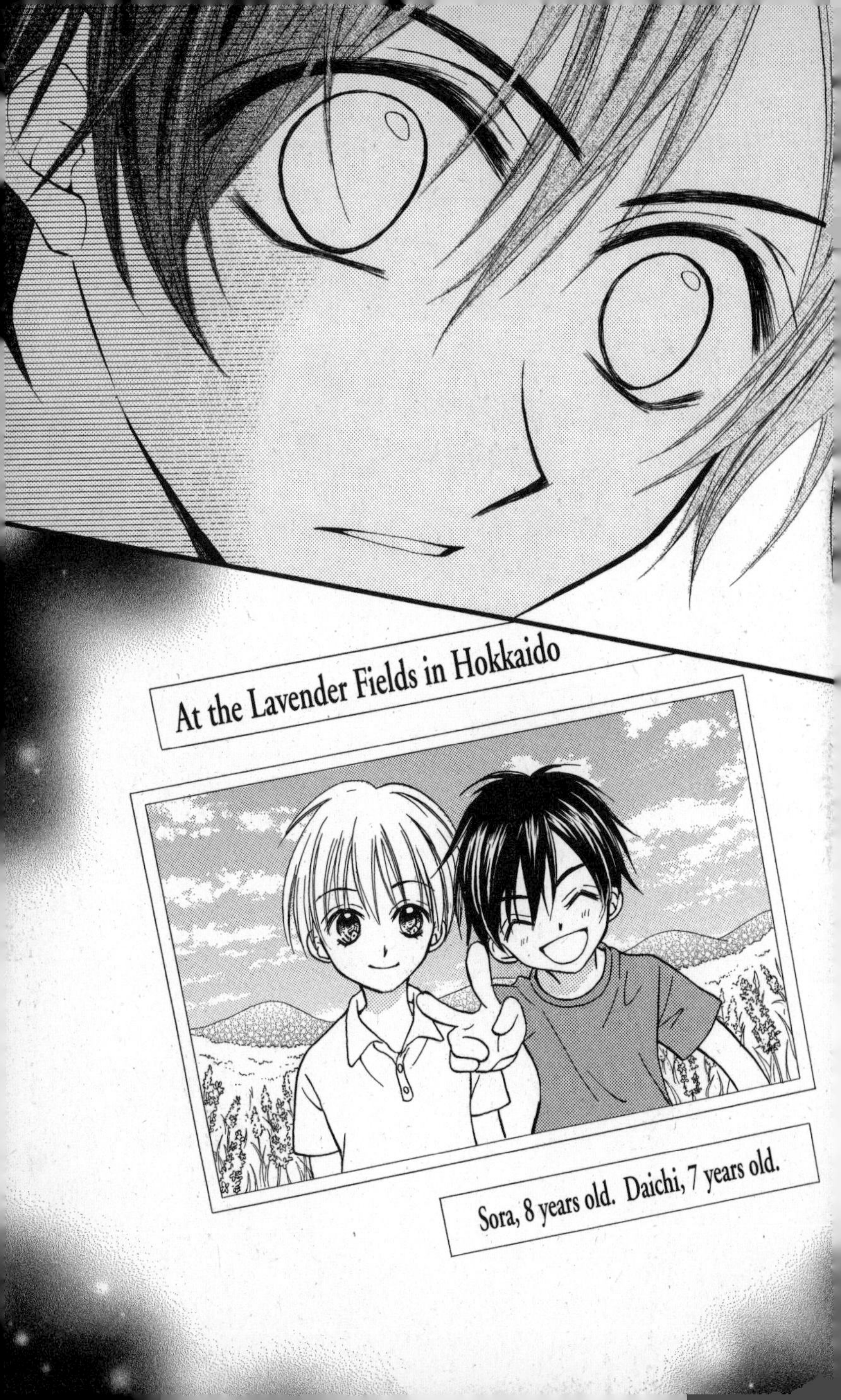
At the Lavender Fields in Hokkaido
Sora, 8 years old. Daichi, 7 years old.

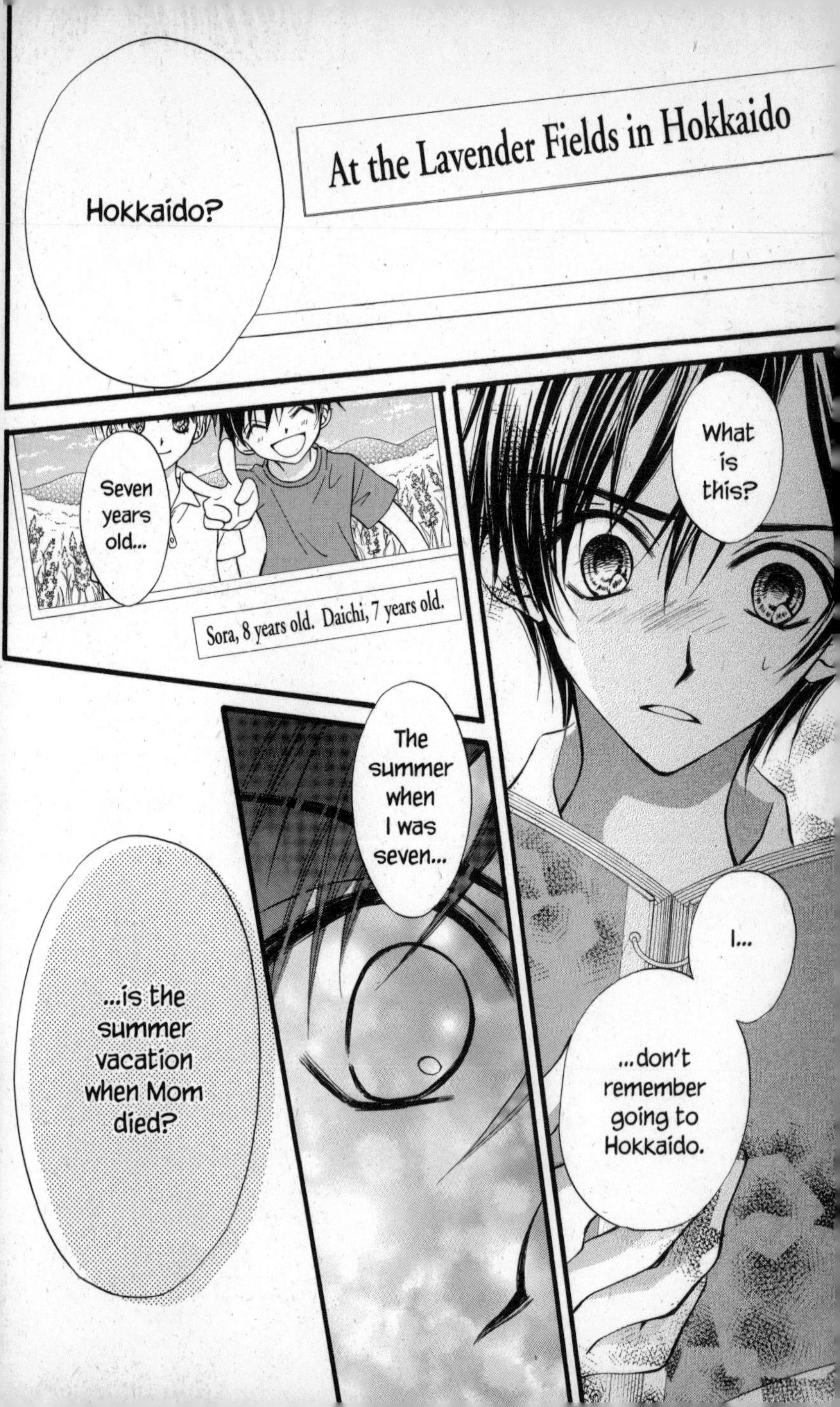
At the Lavender Fields in Hokkaido
Hokkaido?
What is this?
I...
...don't remember going to Hokkaido.
Seven years old...
Sora, 8 years old. Daichi, 7 years old.
The summer when I was seven...
...is the summer vacation when Mom died?

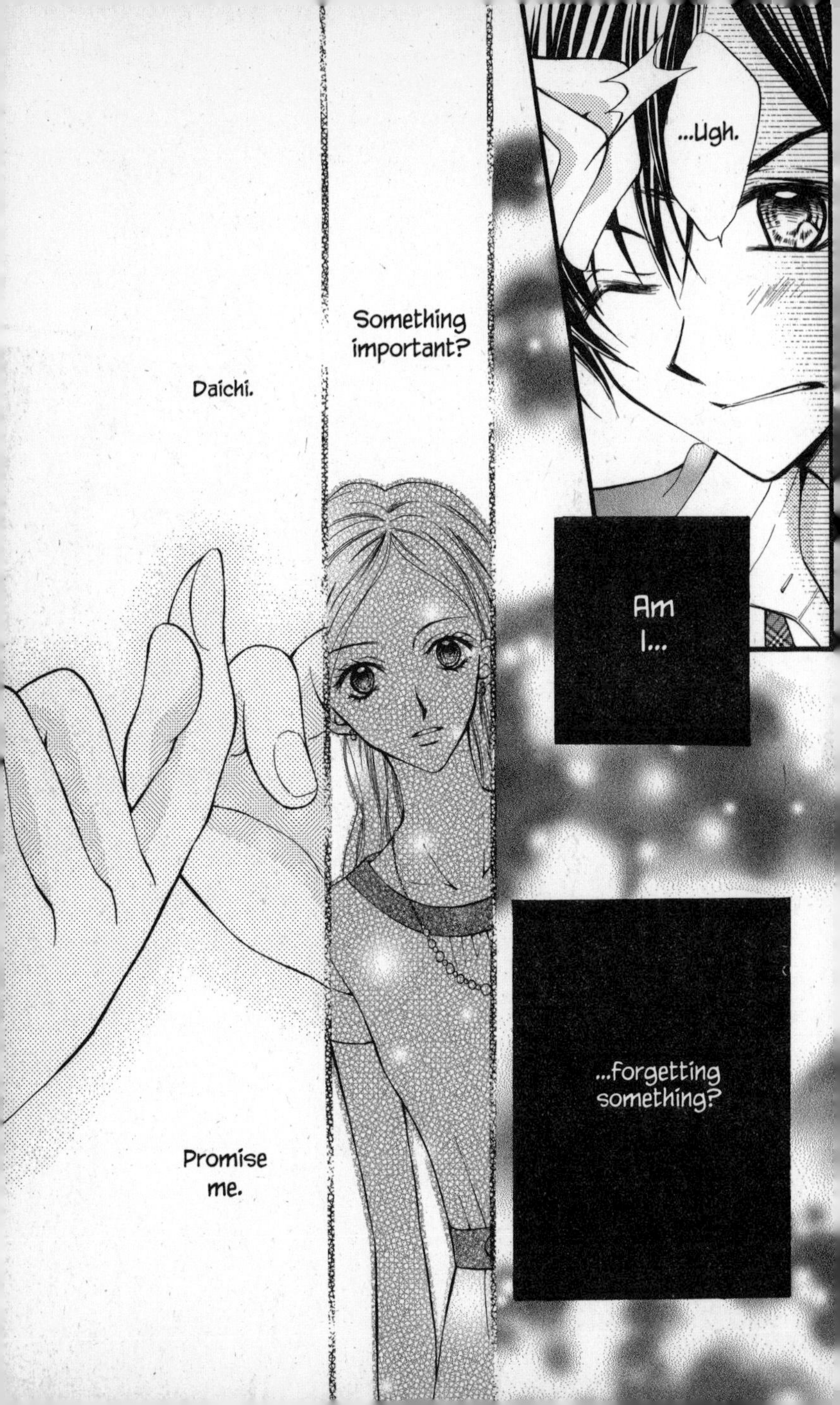
...Ugh.
Am I...
...forgetting something?
Something important?
Daichi.
Promise me.

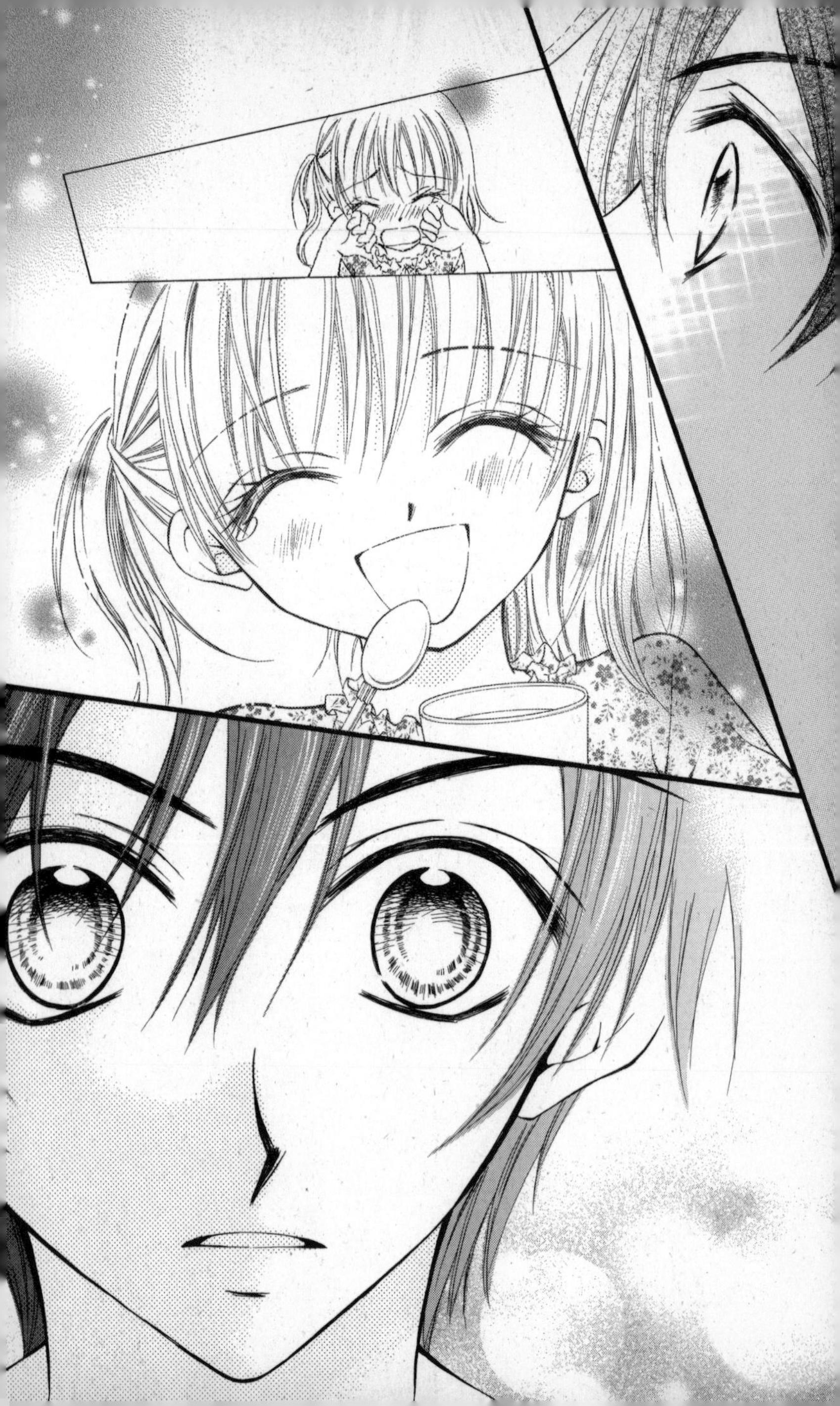

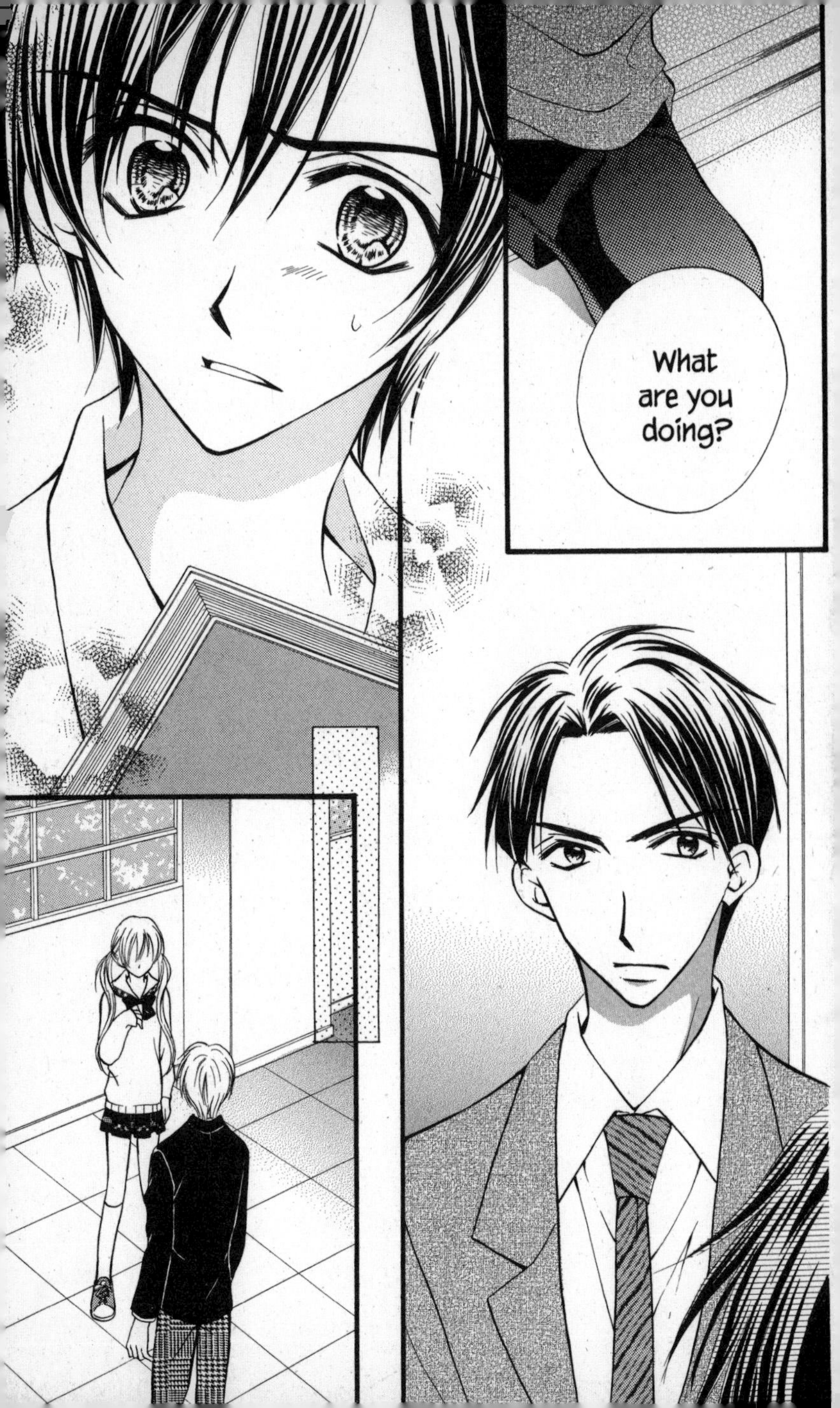
What are you doing?

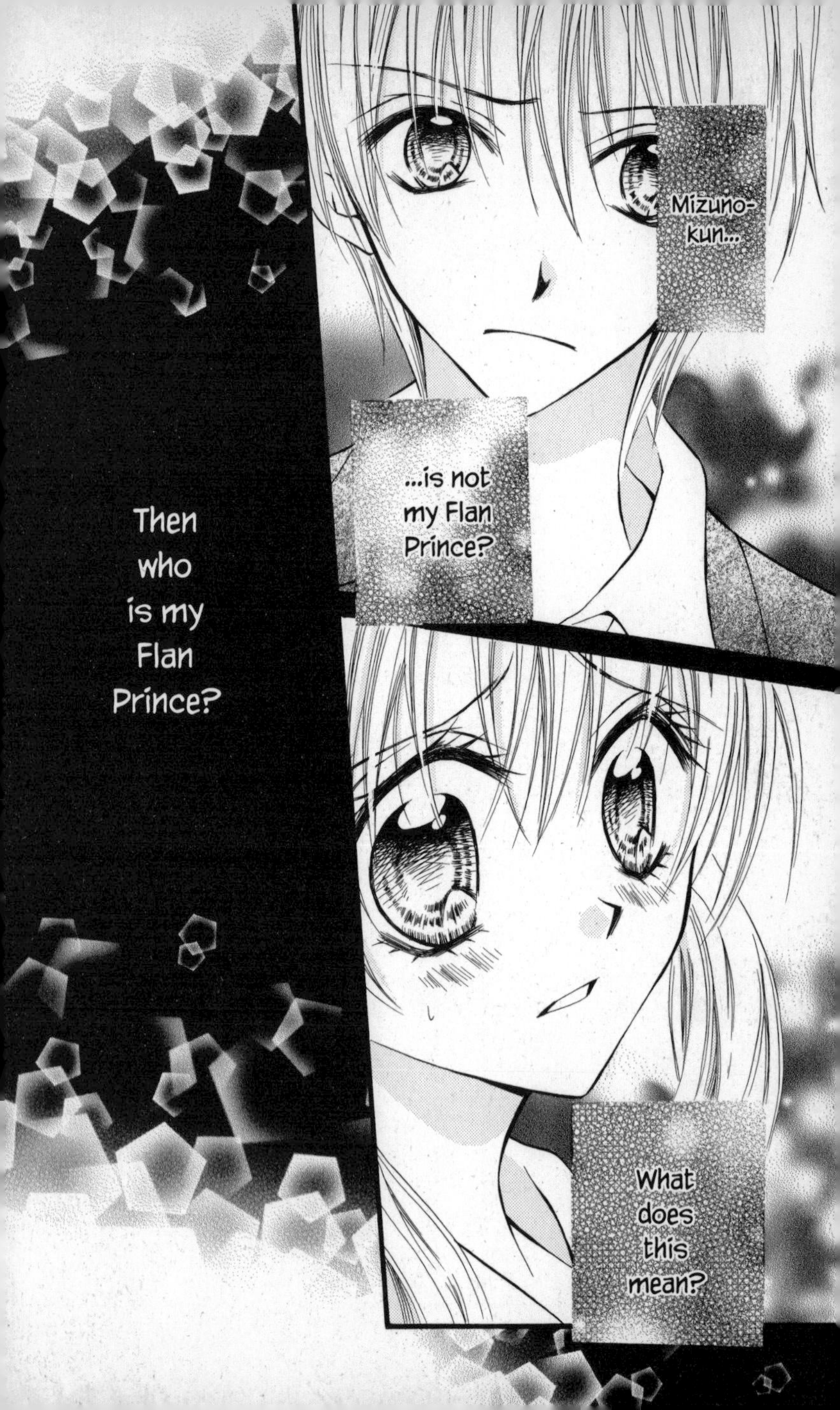
Mizuno-kun...
...is not my Flan Prince?
What does this mean?
Then who is my Flan Prince?

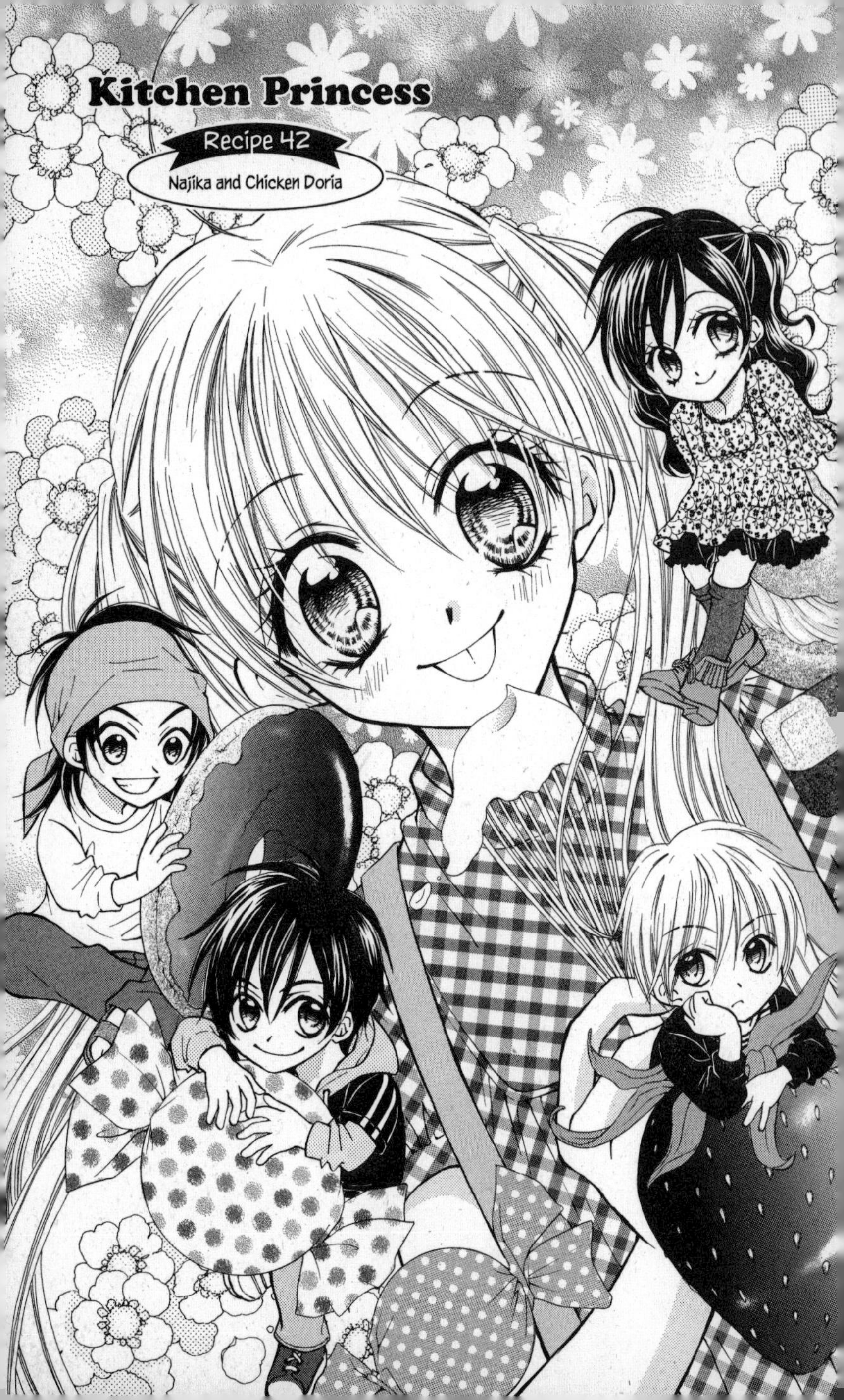
Kitchen Princess
Recipe 42
Najika and Chicken Doria

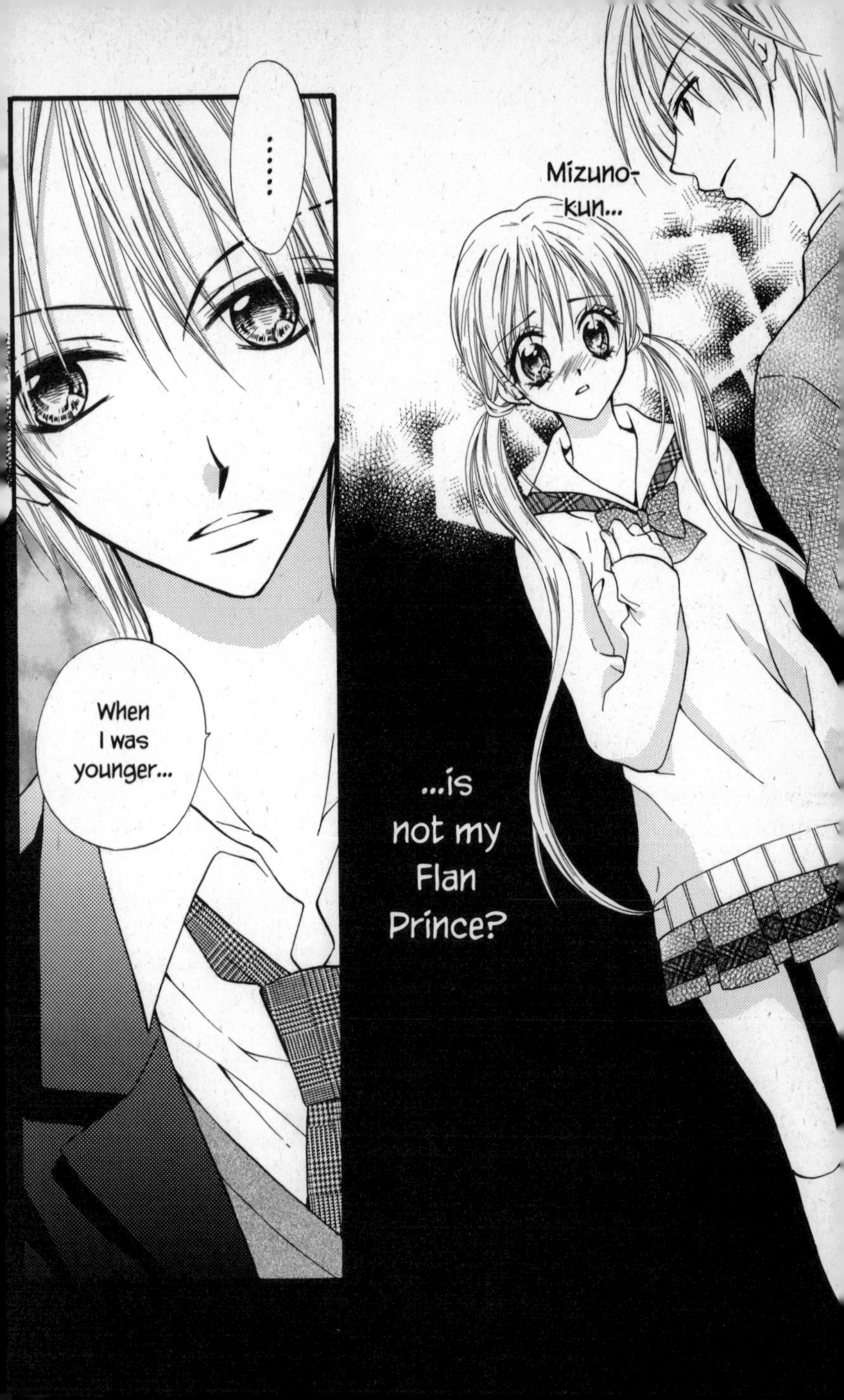
Mizuno-kun...
...is not my Flan Prince?
......
When I was younger...

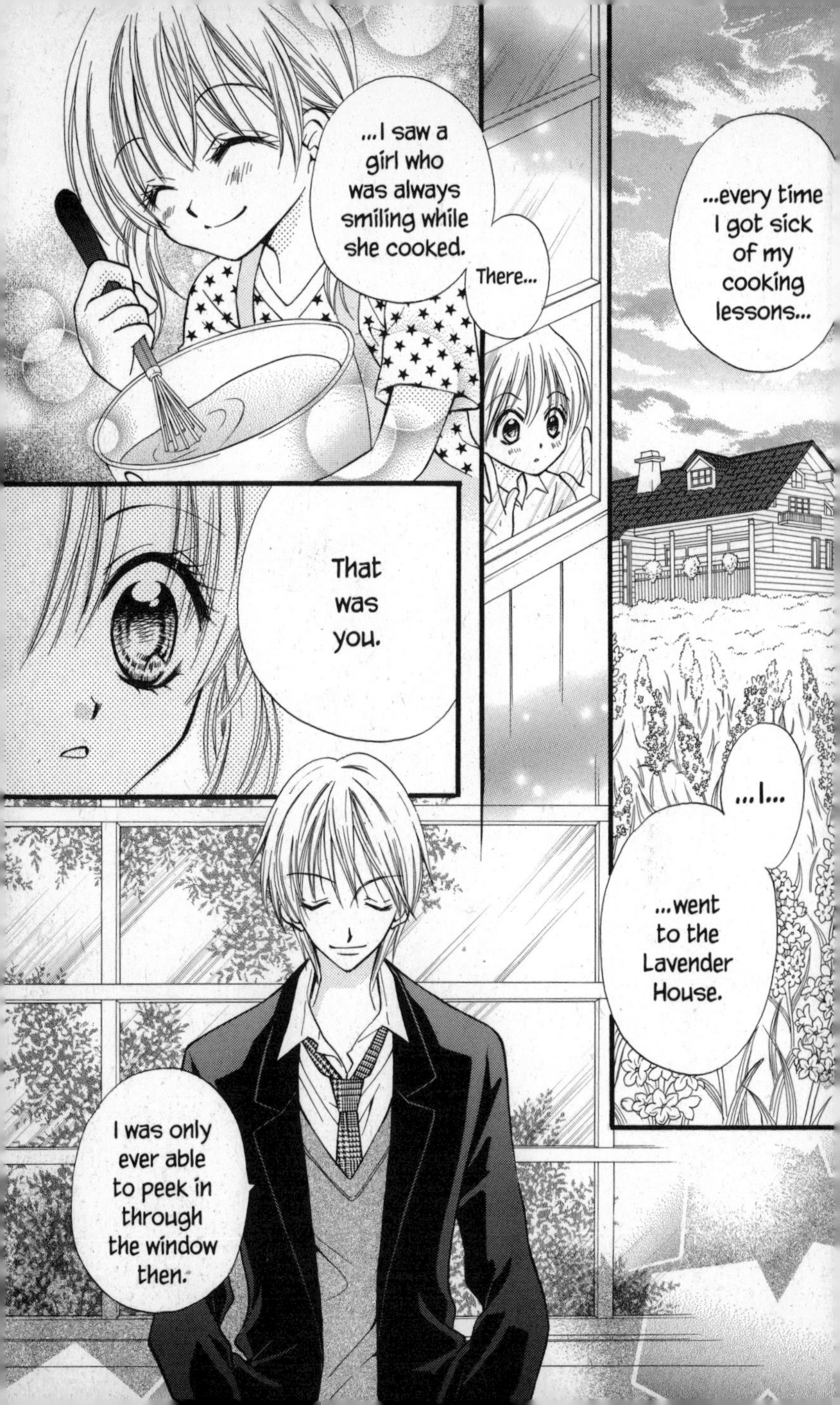
...every time I got sick of my cooking lessons...
...I...
...went to the Lavender House.
There...
...I saw a girl who was always smiling while she cooked.
That was you.
I was only ever able to peek in through the window then.

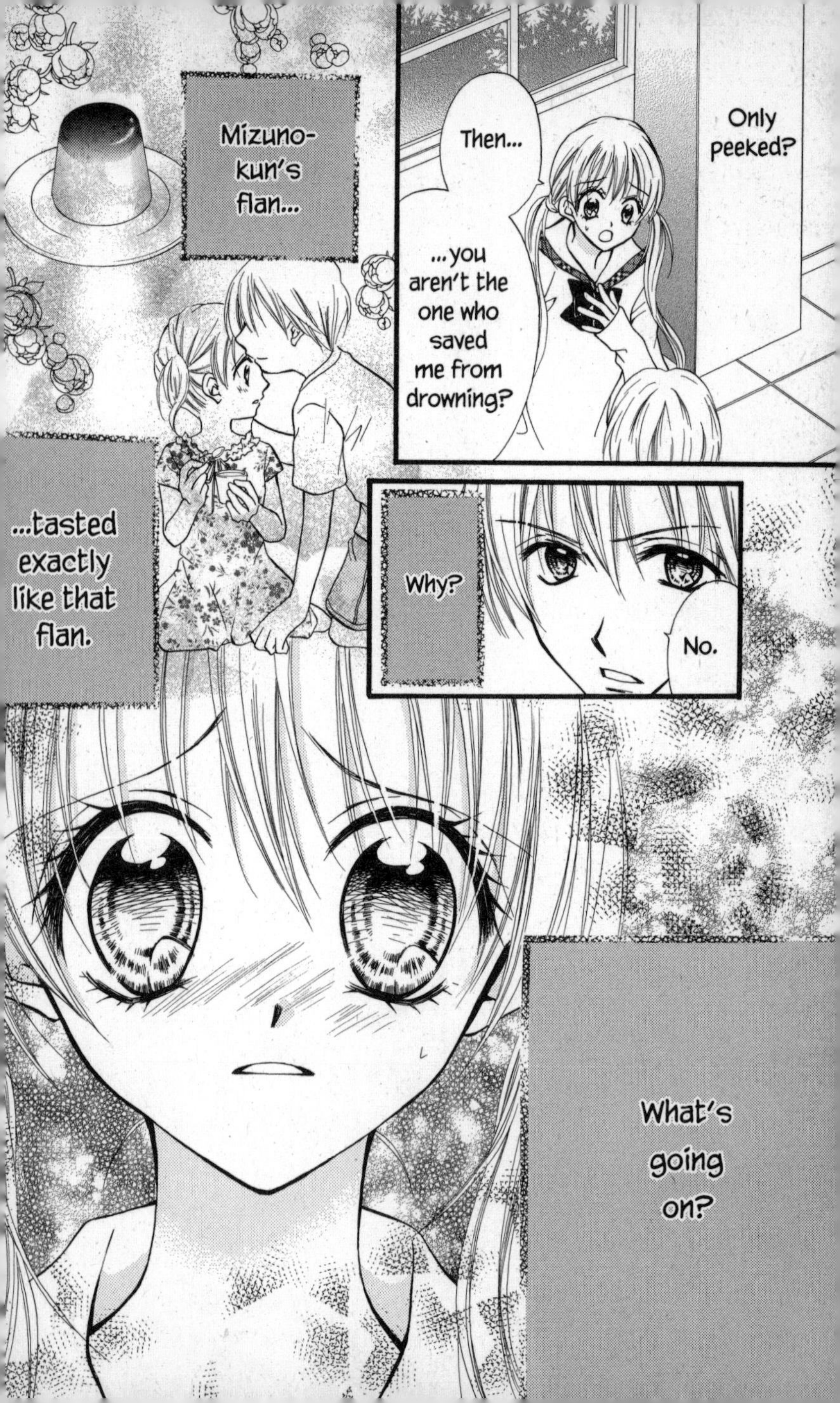

Only peeked?
Then...
...you aren't the one who saved me from drowning?
No.
Why?
Mizuno-kun's flan...
...tasted exactly like that flan.
What's going on?

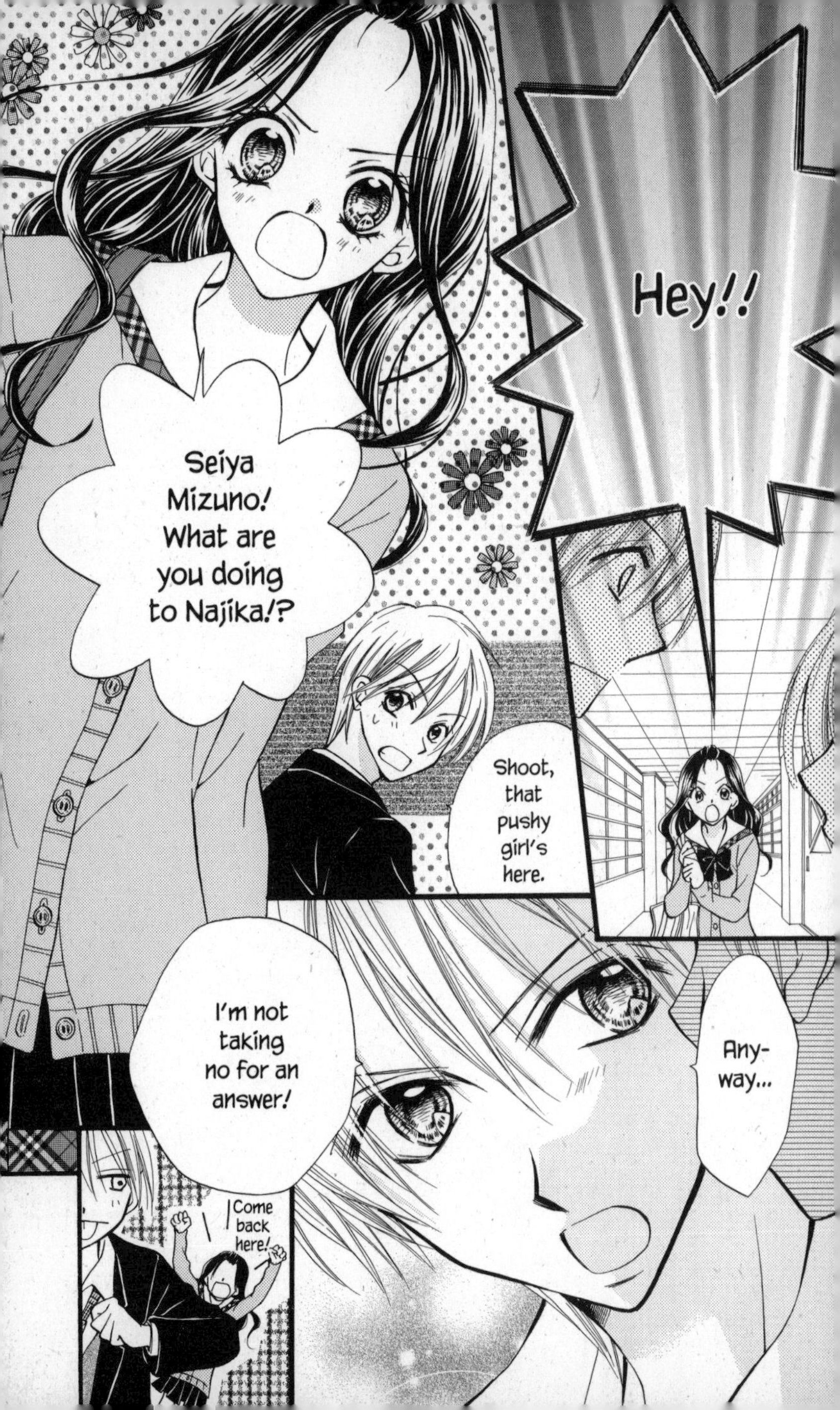
Hey!!
Seiya Mizuno! What are you doing to Najika!?
Shoot, that pushy girl's here.
Any-way...
I'm not taking no for an answer!
Come back here!

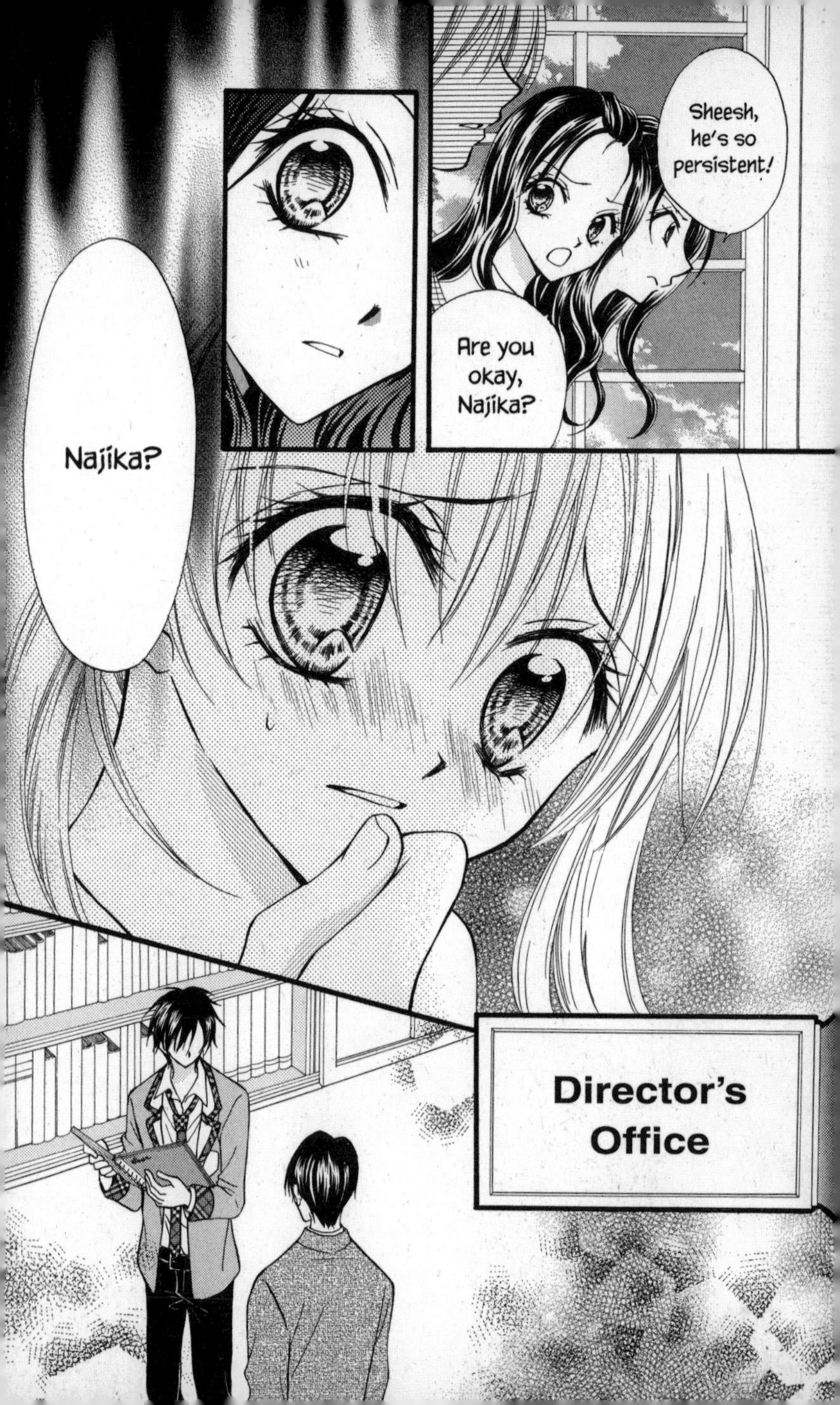
Sheesh, he's so persistent!
Are you okay, Najika?
Najika?
Director's Office

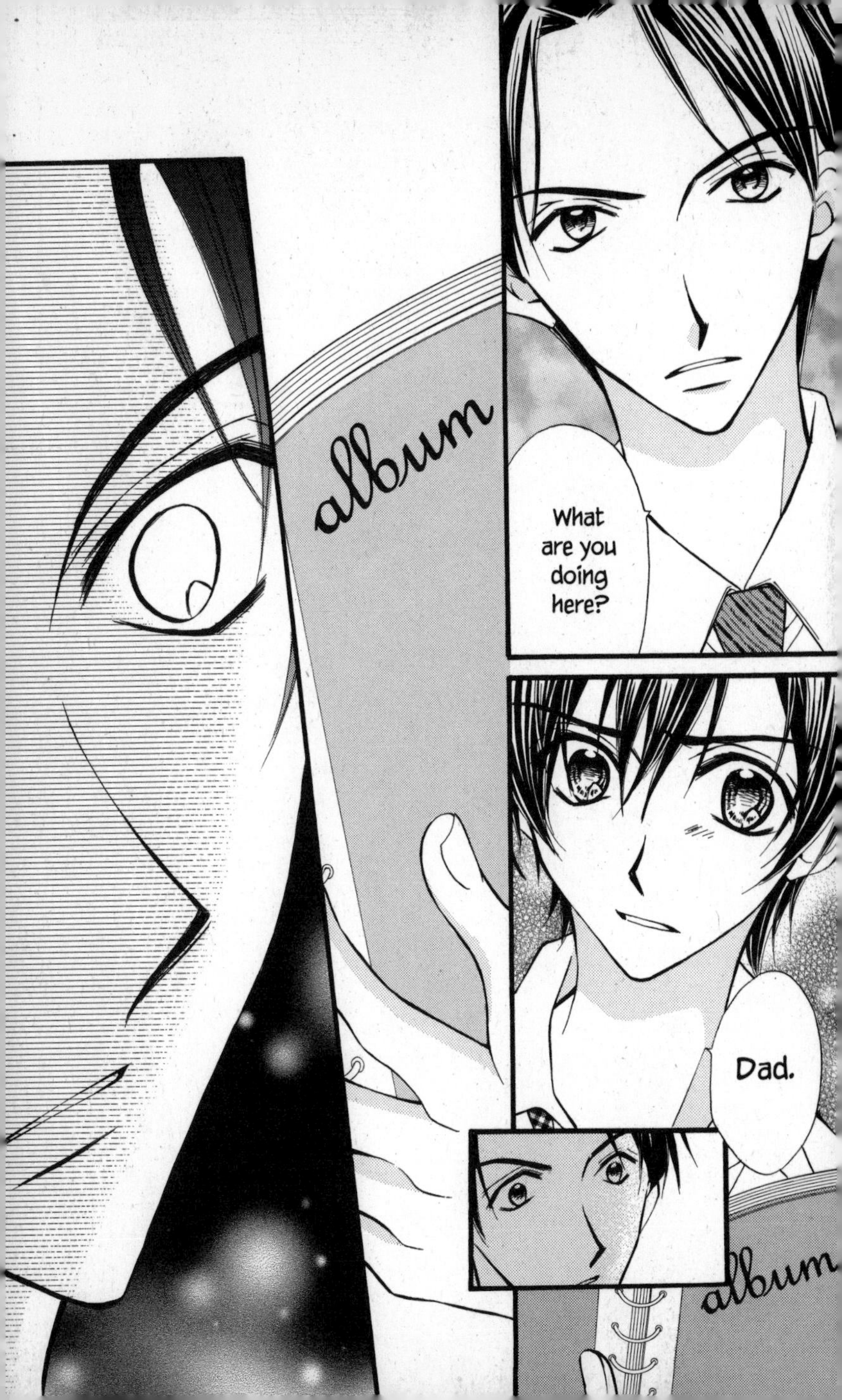
What are you doing here?
Dad.
album
album

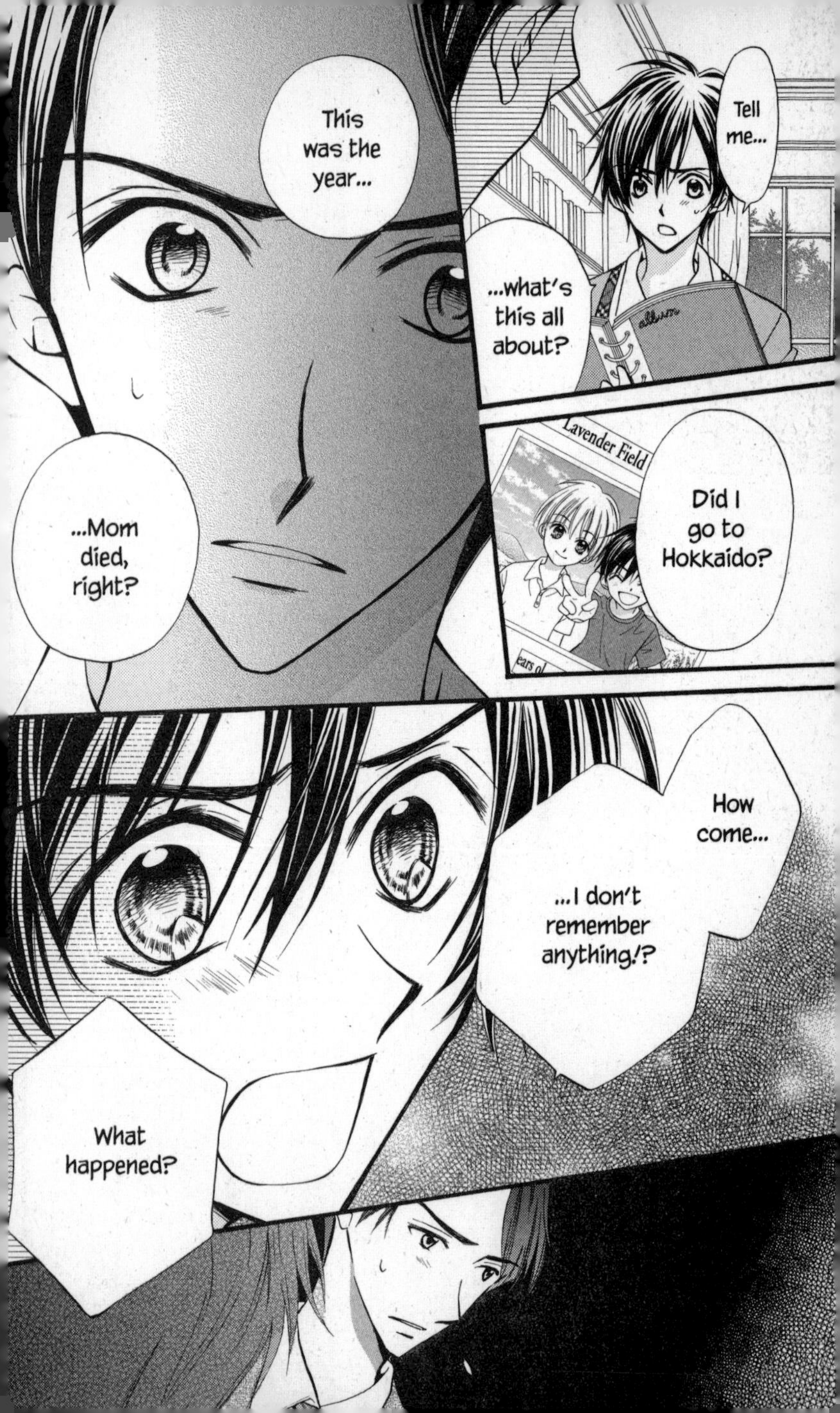
Tell me...
...what's this all about?
Lavender Field
Did I go to Hokkaido?
This was the year...
...Mom died, right?
How come...
...I don't remember anything!?
What happened?

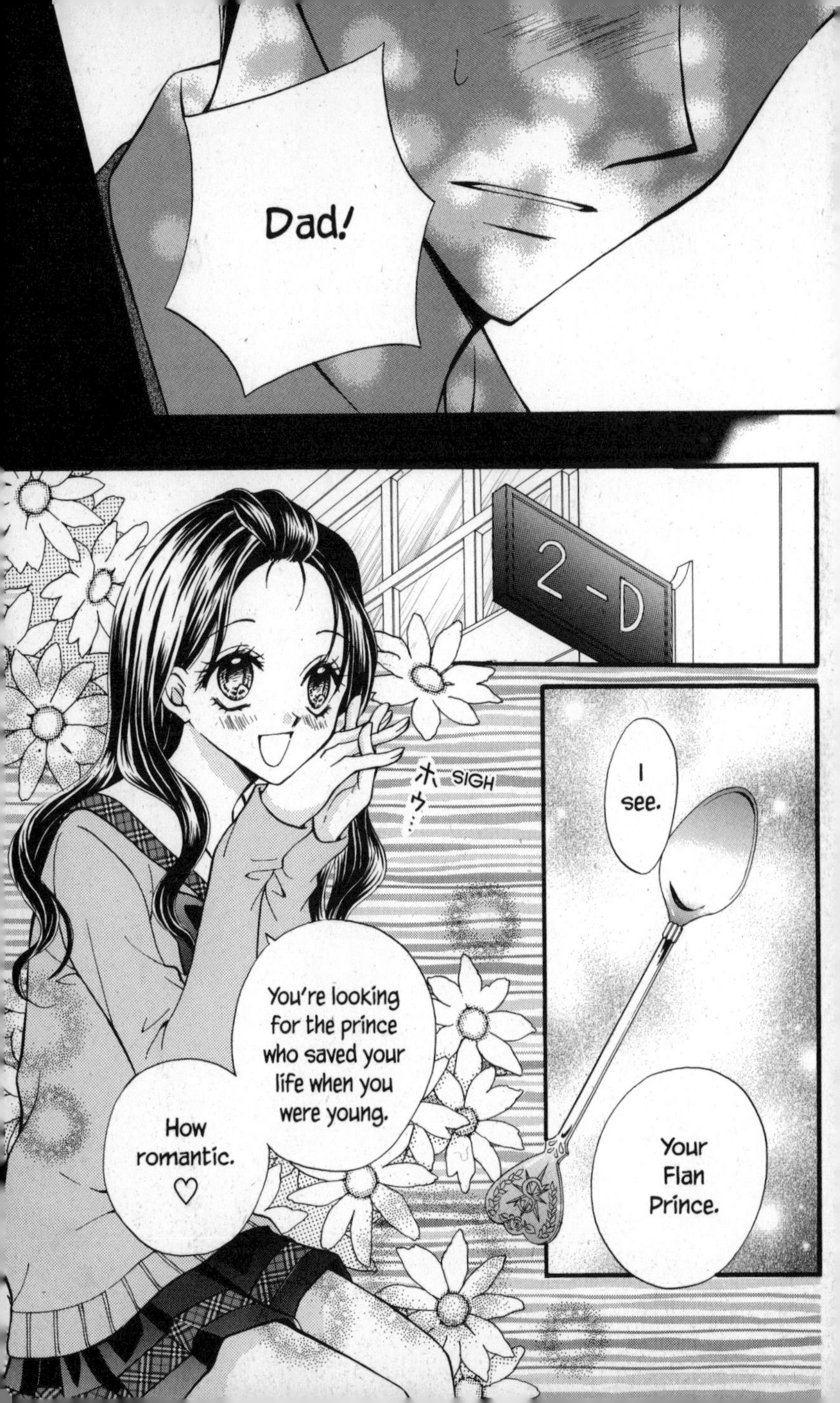
Dad!
2-D
I see.
Your Flan Prince.
ホウ…
SIGH
You're looking for the prince who saved your life when you were young.
How romantic. ♡

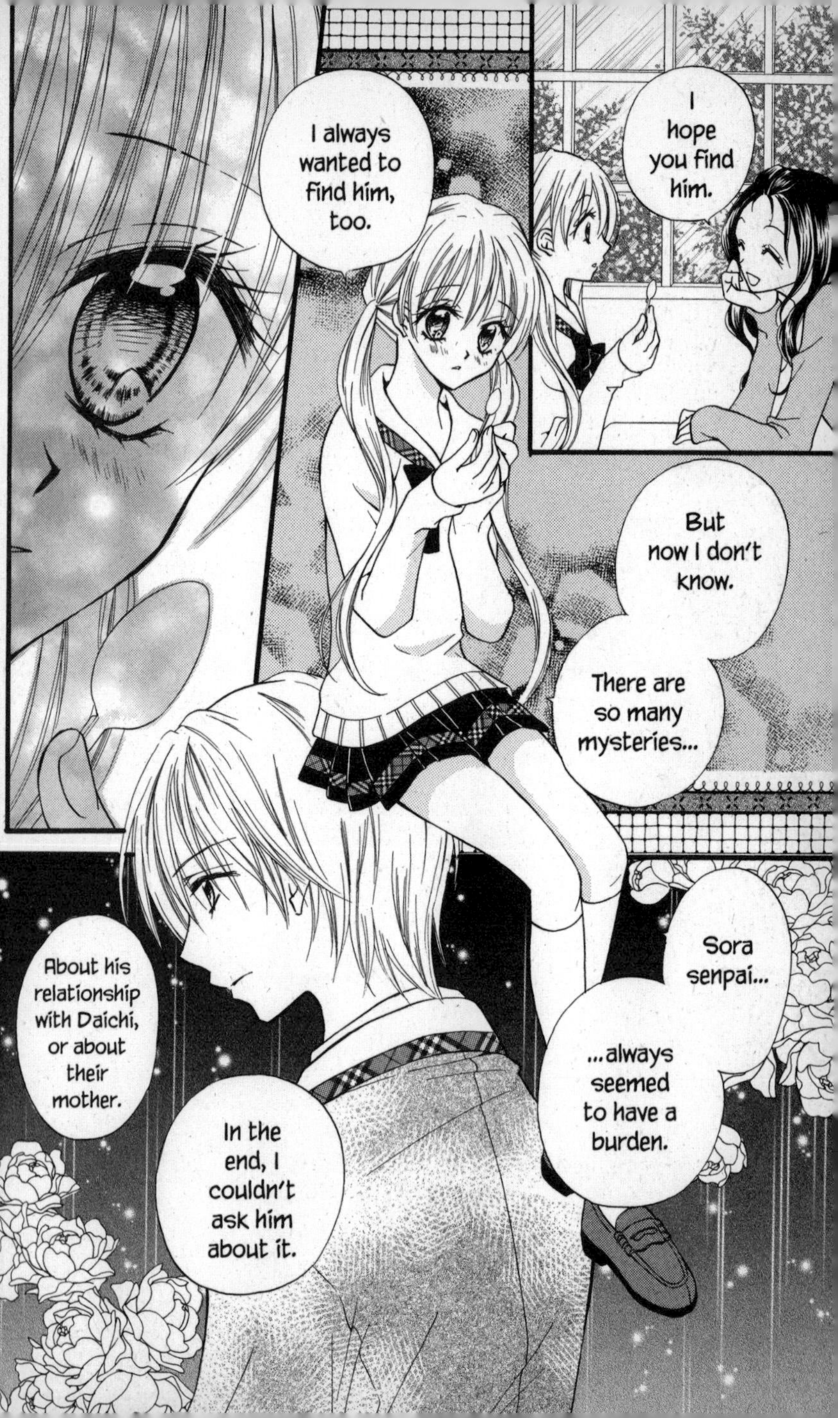
I hope you find him.
I always wanted to find him, too.
But now I don't know.
There are so many mysteries...
Sora senpai...
...always seemed to have a burden.
About his relationship with Daichi, or about their mother.
In the end, I couldn't ask him about it.

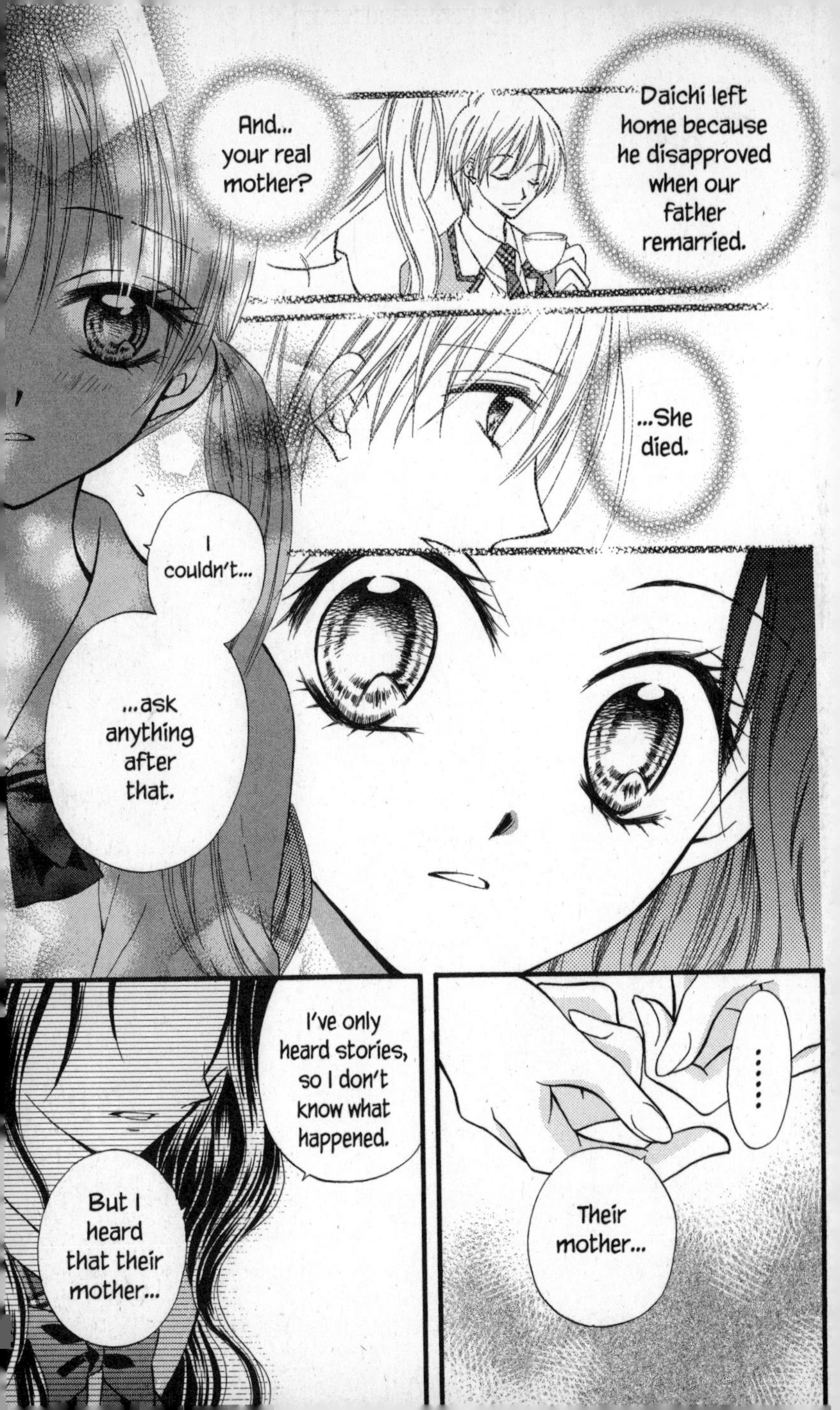
Daichi left home because he disapproved when our father remarried.
And... your real mother?
...She died.
I couldn't...
...ask anything after that.
......
Their mother...
I've only heard stories, so I don't know what happened.
But I heard that their mother...

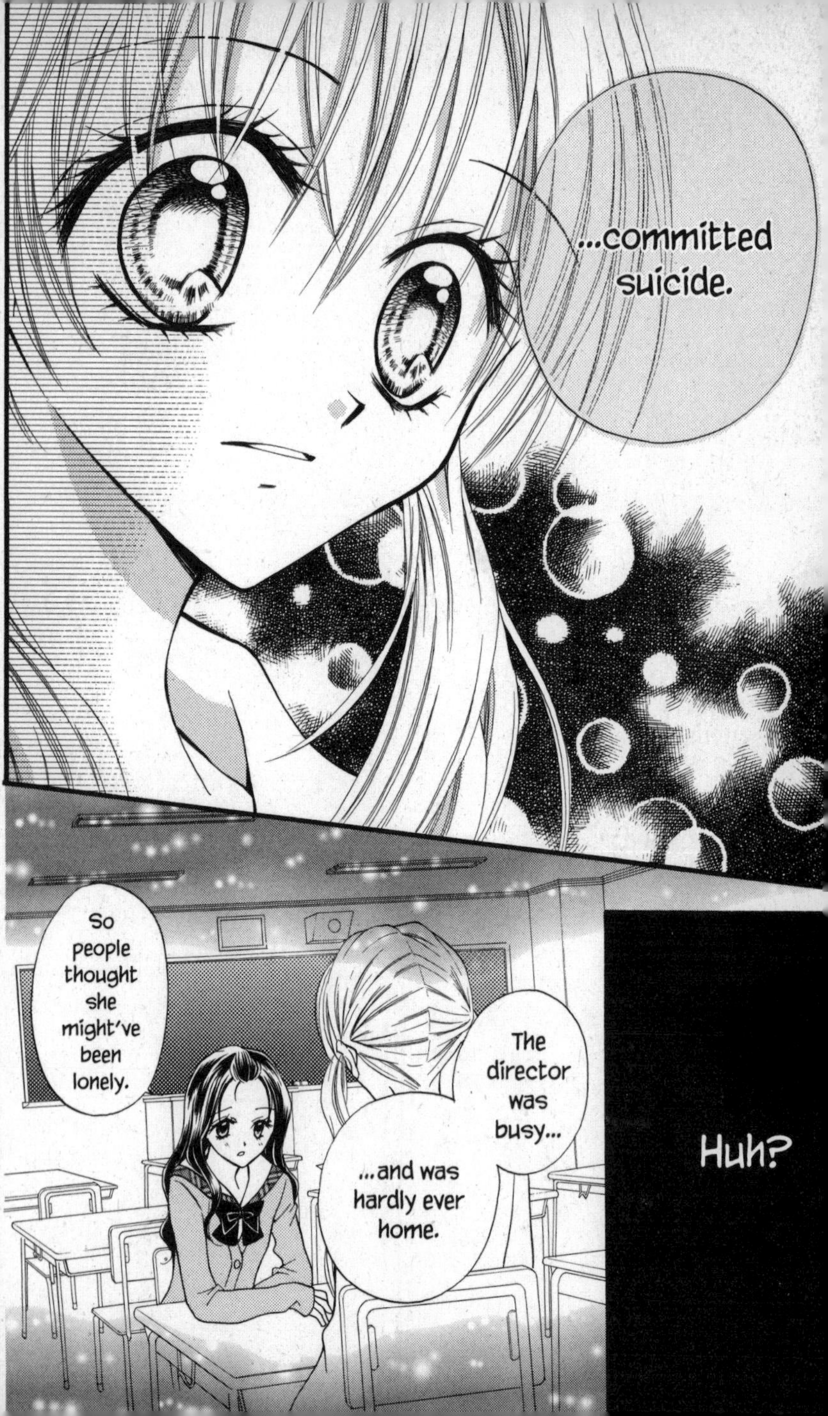
...committed suicide.
Huh?
The director was busy...
...and was hardly ever home.
So people thought she might've been lonely.

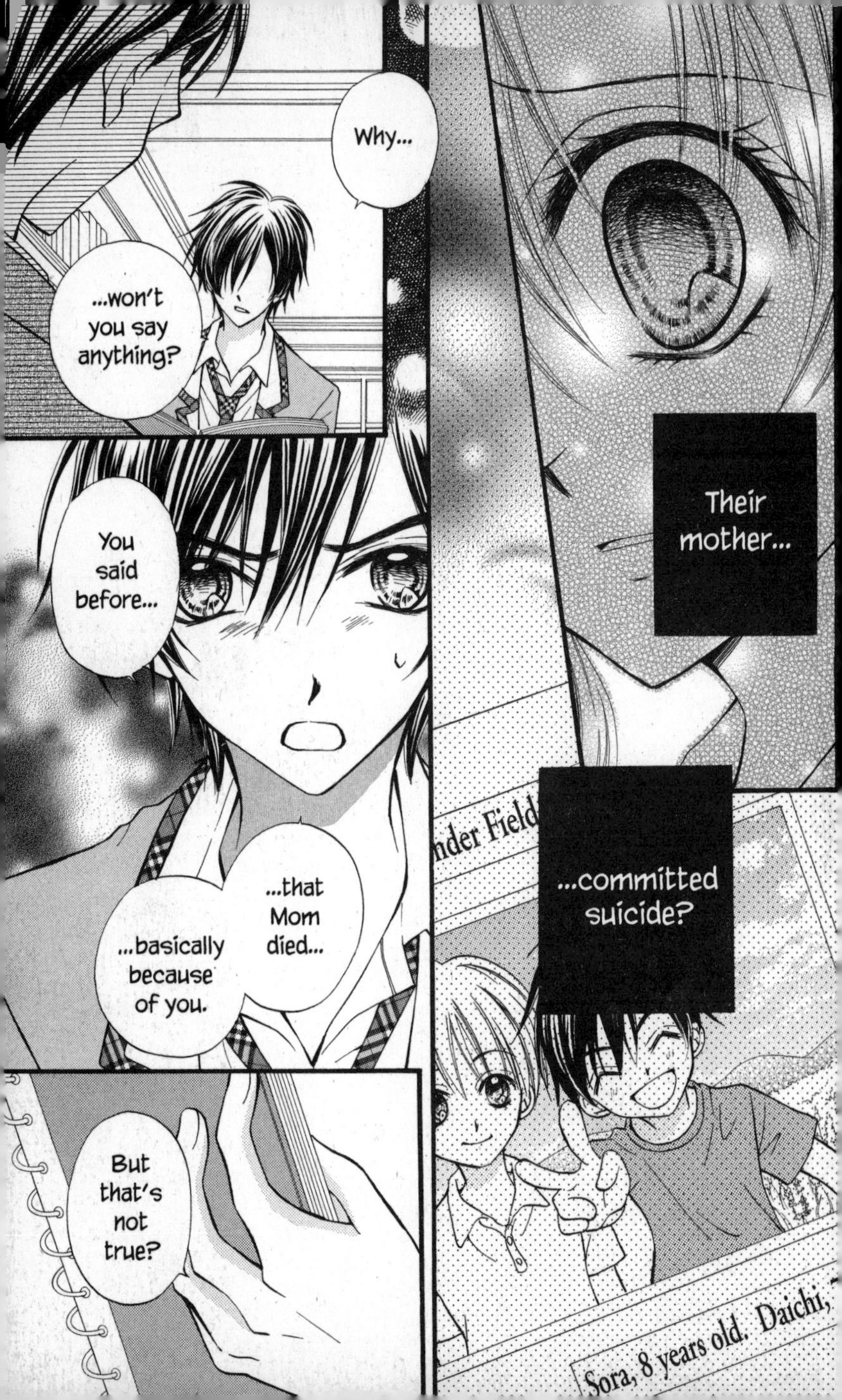
Why...
...won't you say anything?
You said before...
...that Mom died...
...basically because of you.
But that's not true?
Their mother...
...committed suicide?
Sora, 8 years old. Daichi,

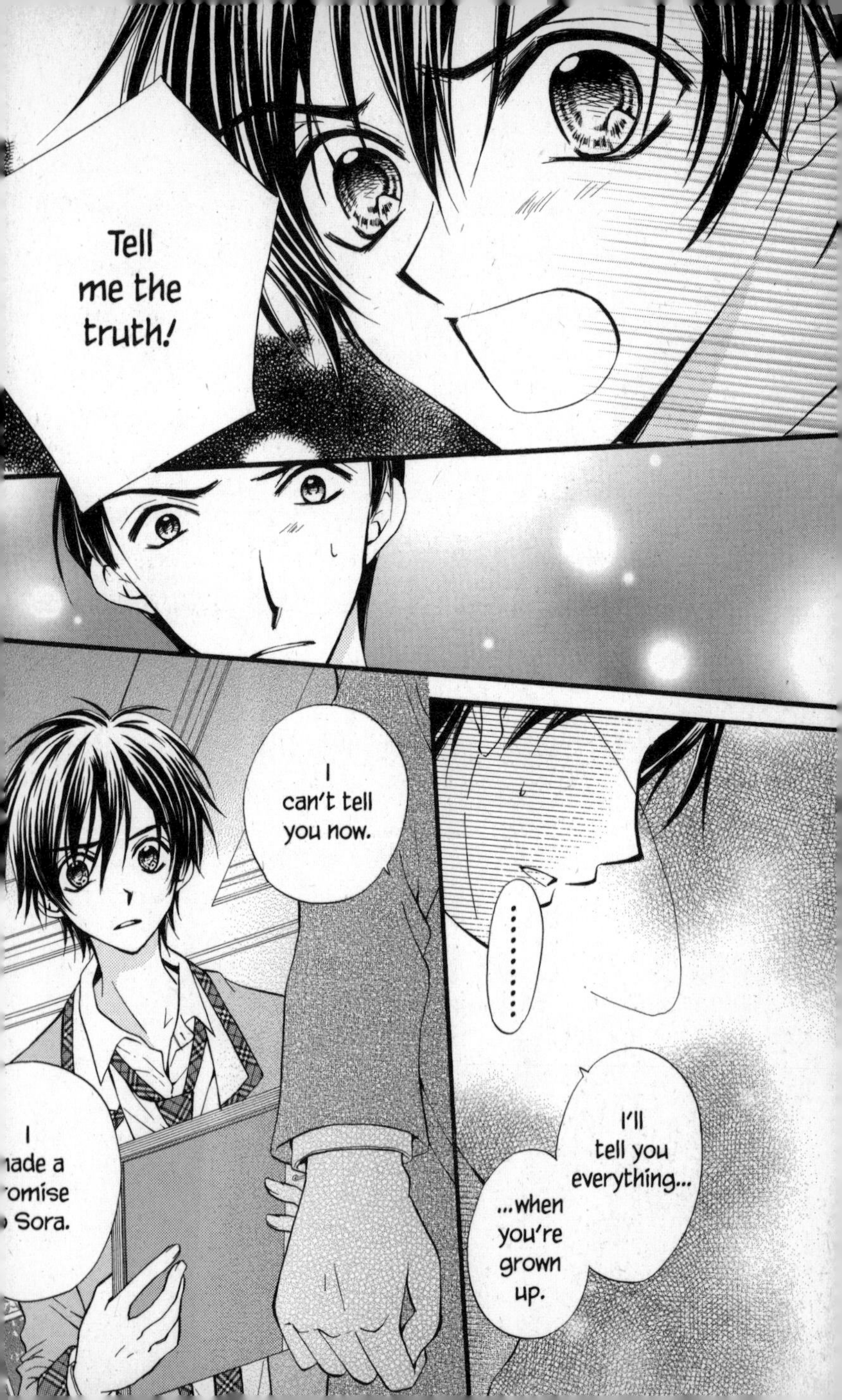
Tell me the truth!
......
I'll tell you everything...
...when you're grown up.
I can't tell you now.
I nade a romise Sora.

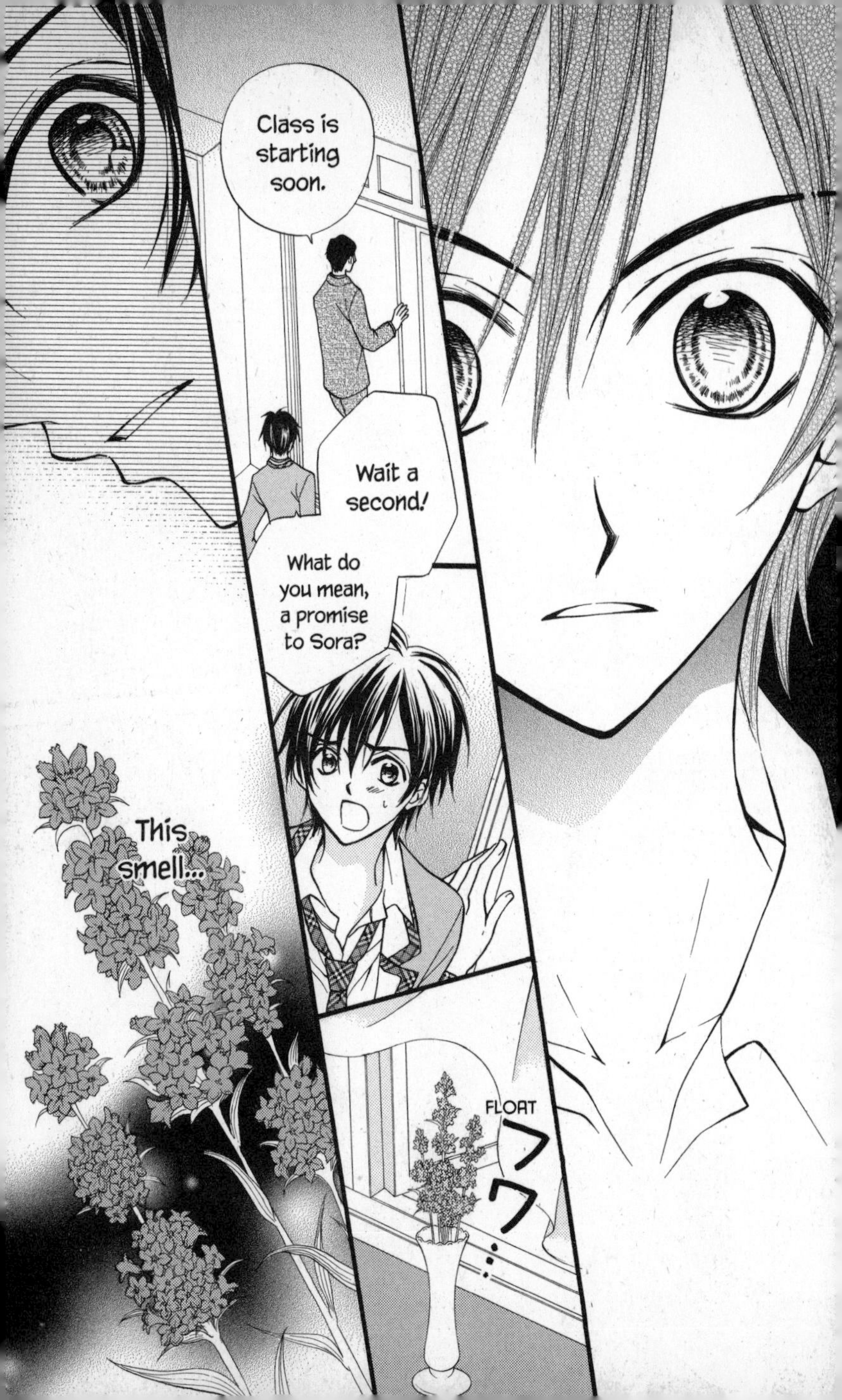

Class is starting soon.
Wait a second!
What do you mean, a promise to Sora?
FLOAT
フワ…
This smell...

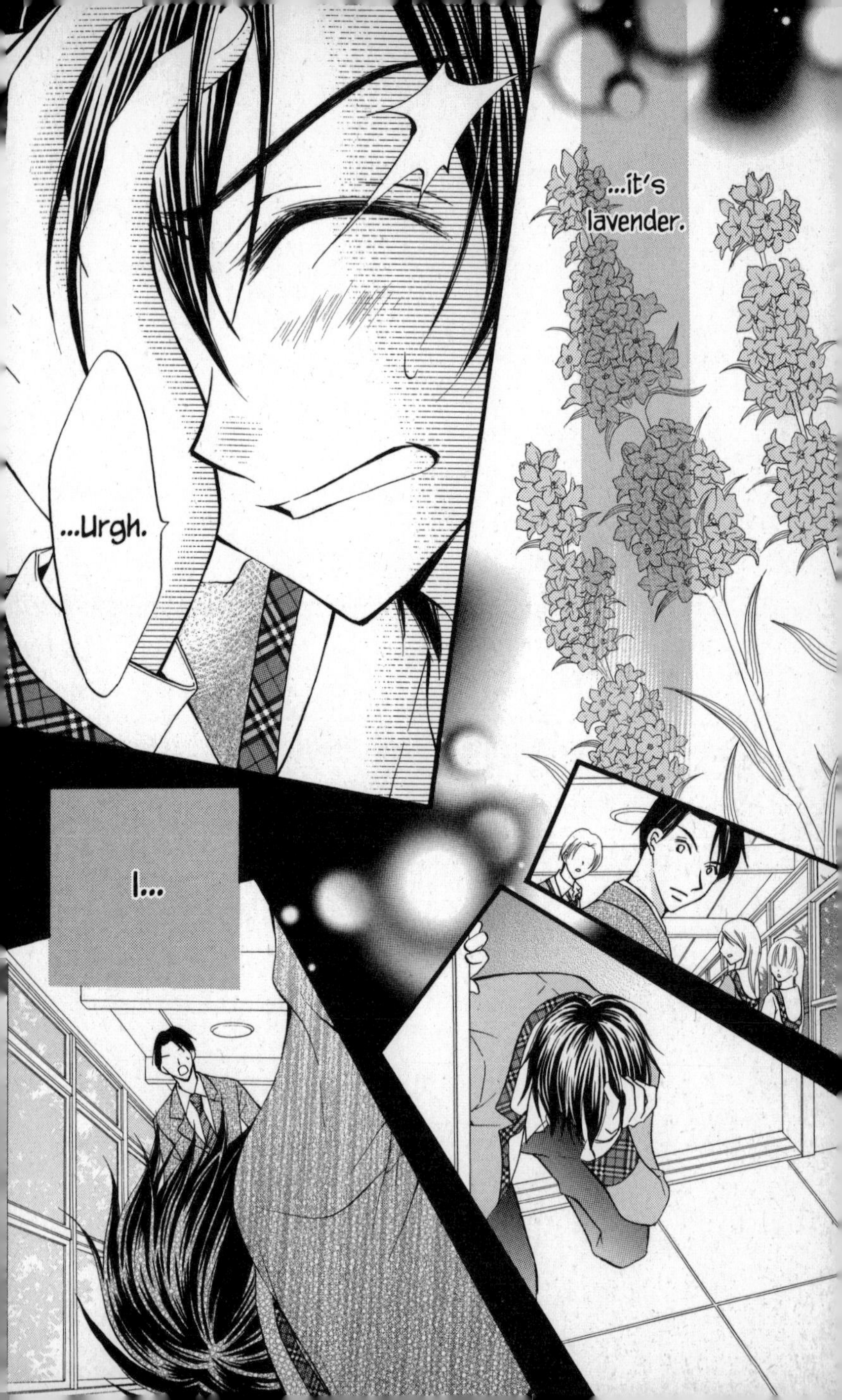

...it's lavender.
...Urgh.
I...

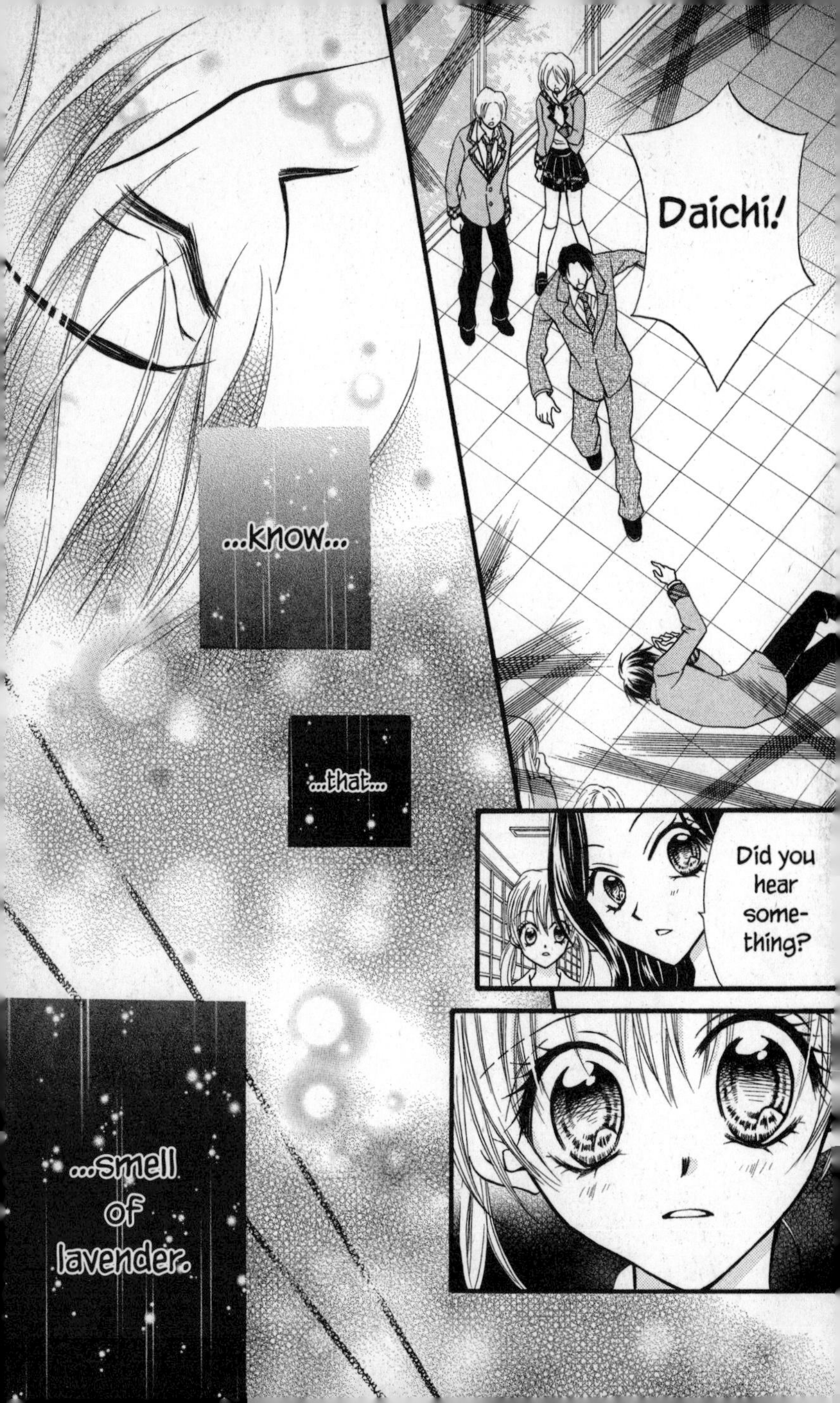

Daichi!
Did you hear something?
...know...
...that...
...smell of lavender.

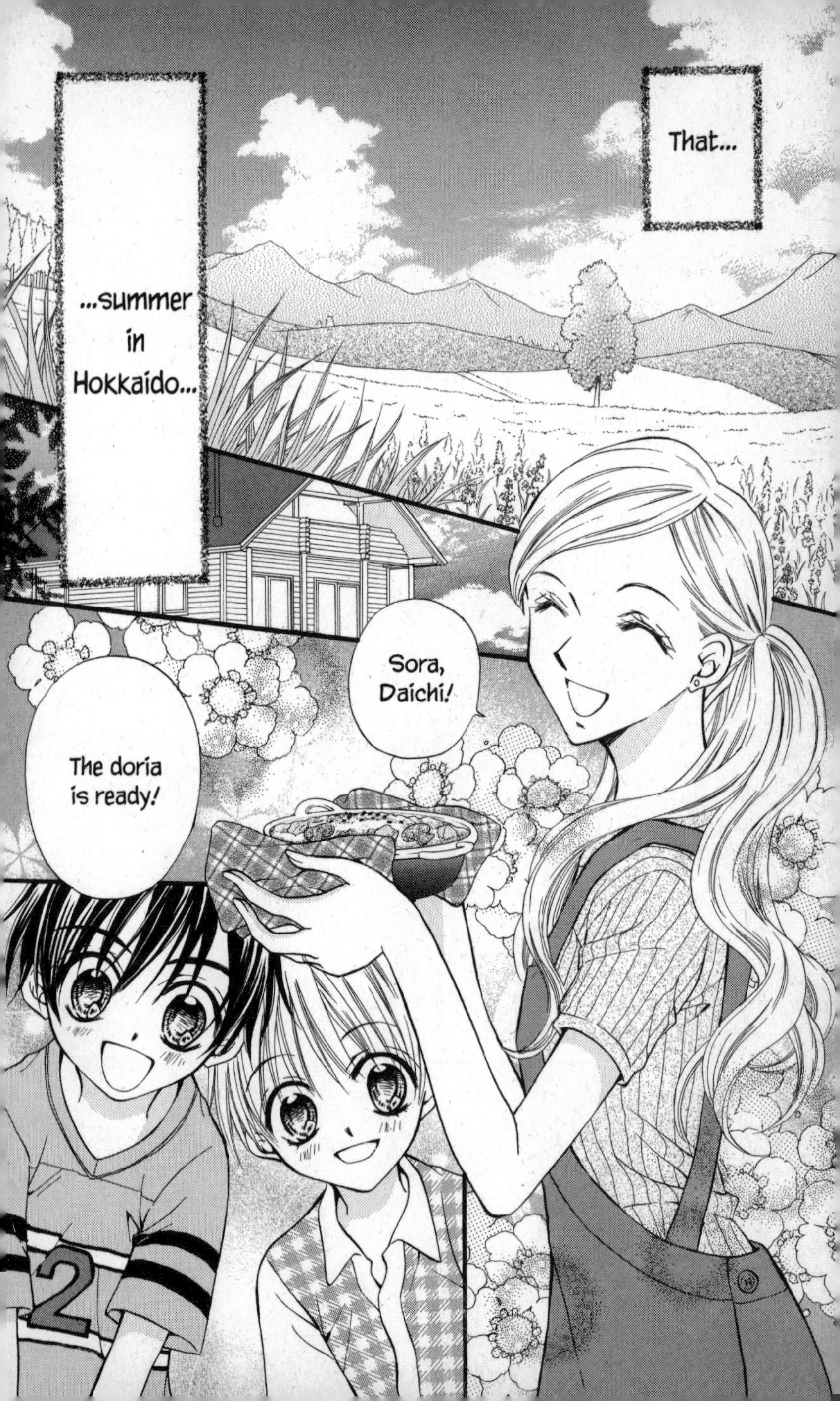
That...
...summer in Hokkaido...
Sora, Daichi!
The doria is ready!

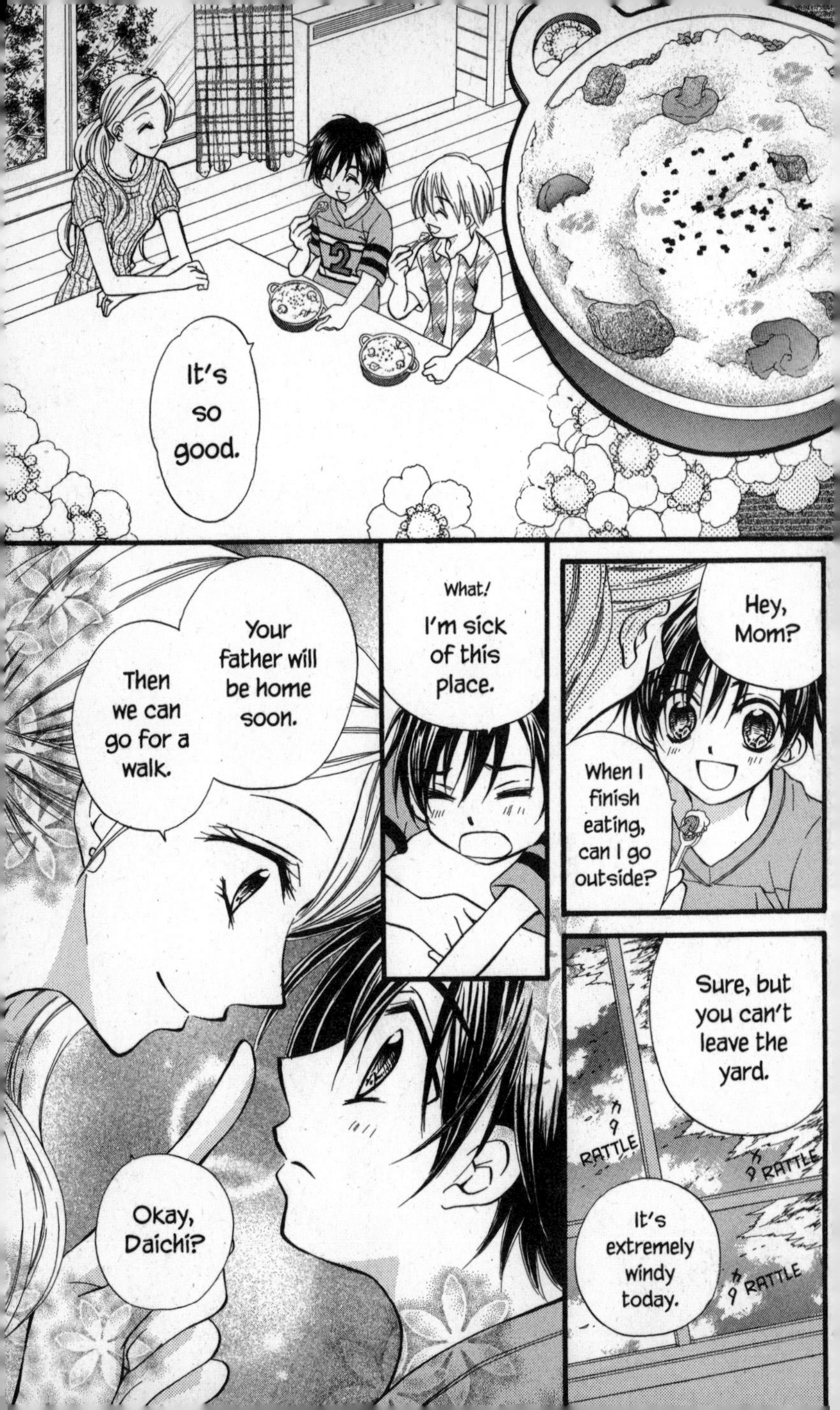

It's so good.
Hey, Mom?
When I finish eating, can I go outside?
Sure, but you can't leave the yard.
RATTLE
RATTLE
It's extremely windy today.
RATTLE
What!
I'm sick of this place.
Your father will be home soon.
Then we can go for a walk.
Okay, Daichi?

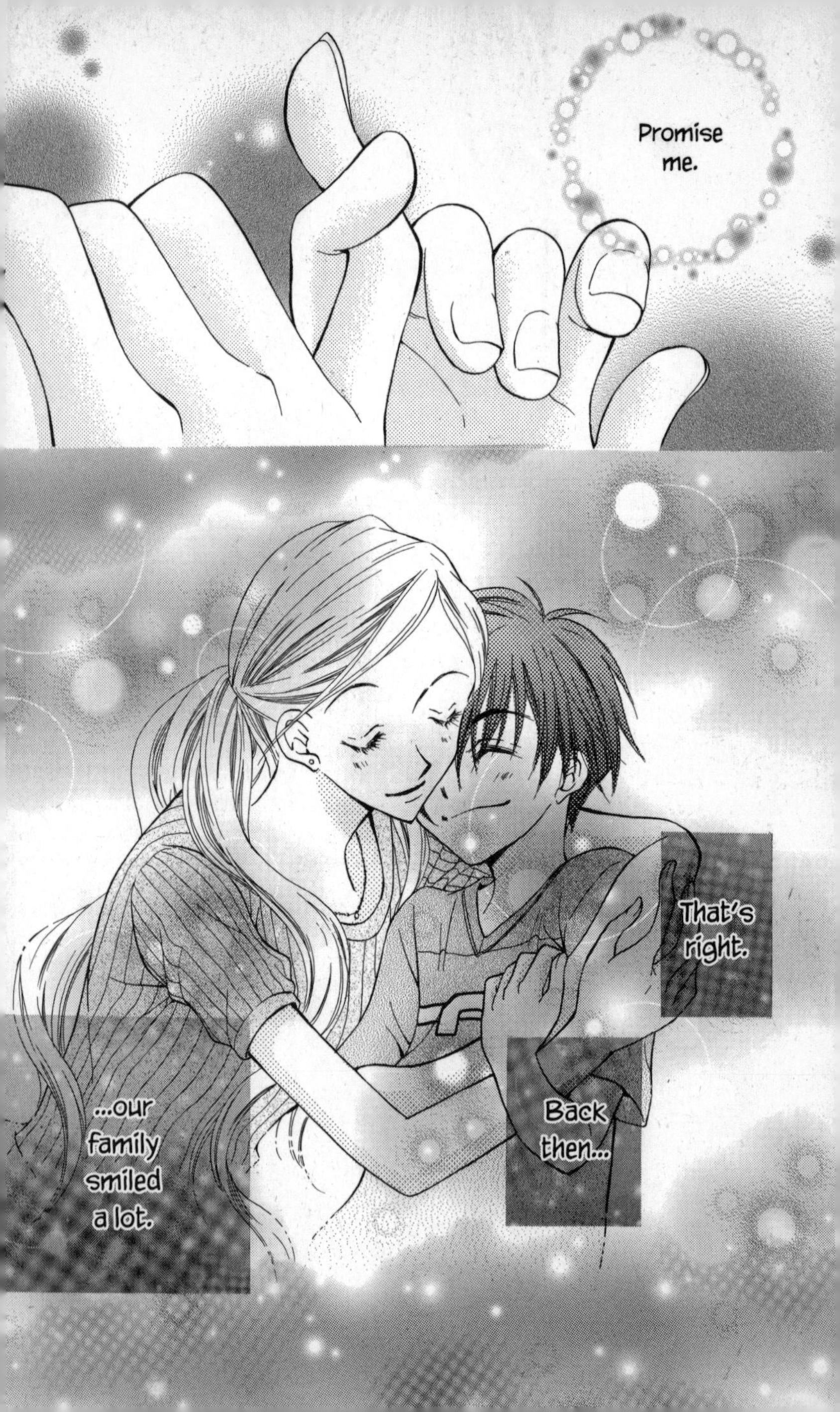
Promise me.
That's right.
Back then...
...our family smiled a lot.

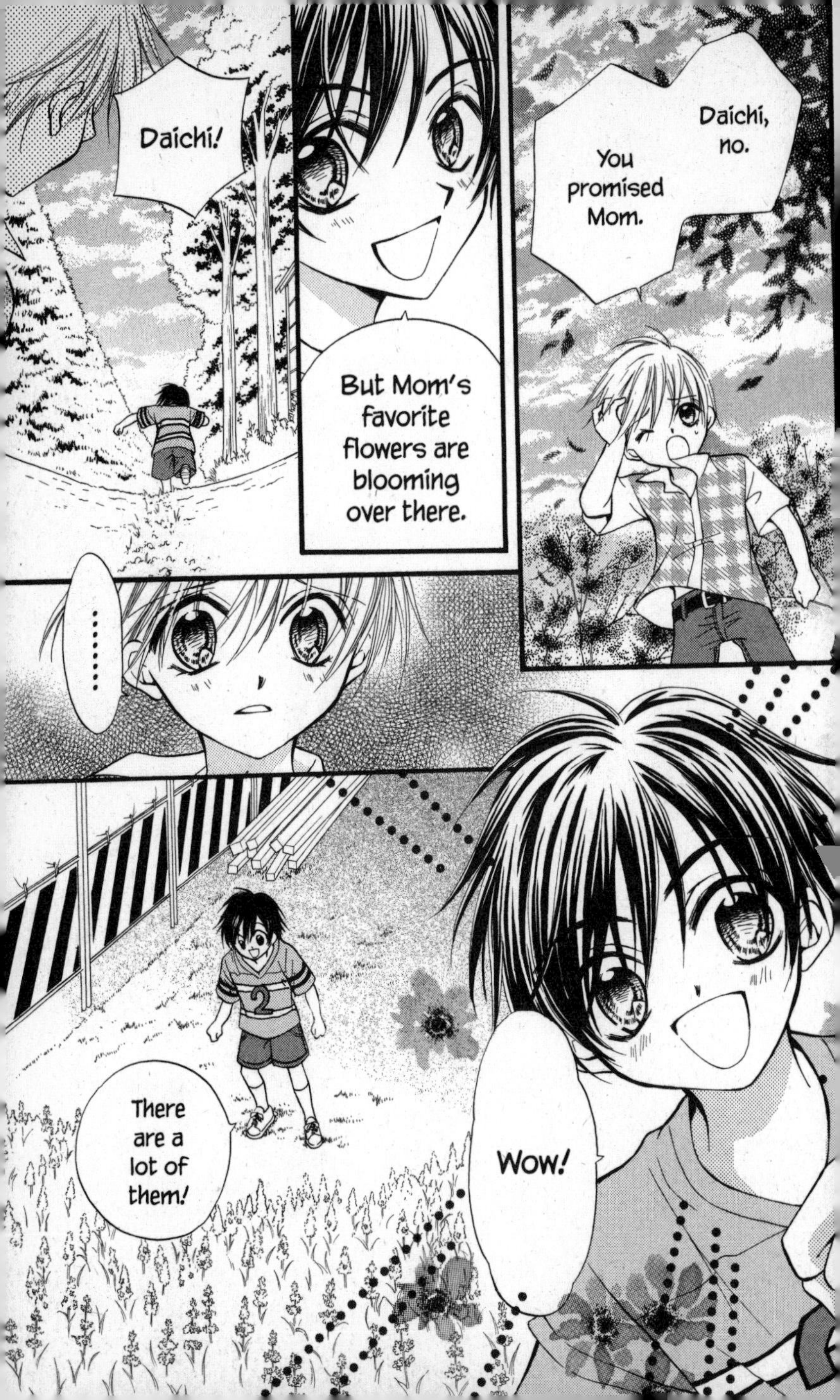

Daichi, no. You promised Mom.
But Mom's favorite flowers are blooming over there.
Daichi!
......
Wow!
There are a lot of them!

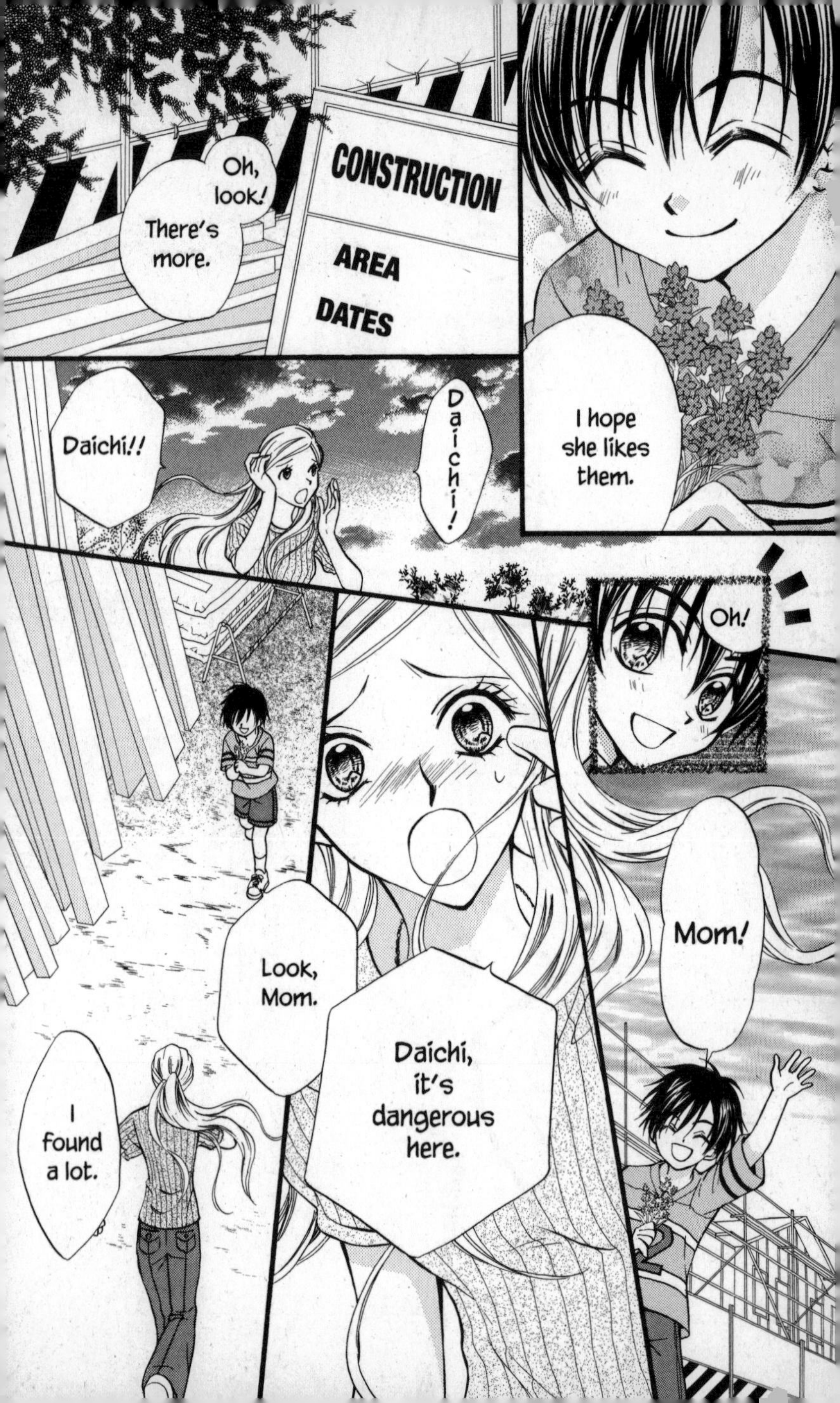
CONSTRUCTION
AREA
DATES
Oh, look! There's more.
I hope she likes them.
Daichi!
Daichi!!
Oh!
Mom!
Daichi, it's dangerous here.
Look, Mom.
I found a lot.

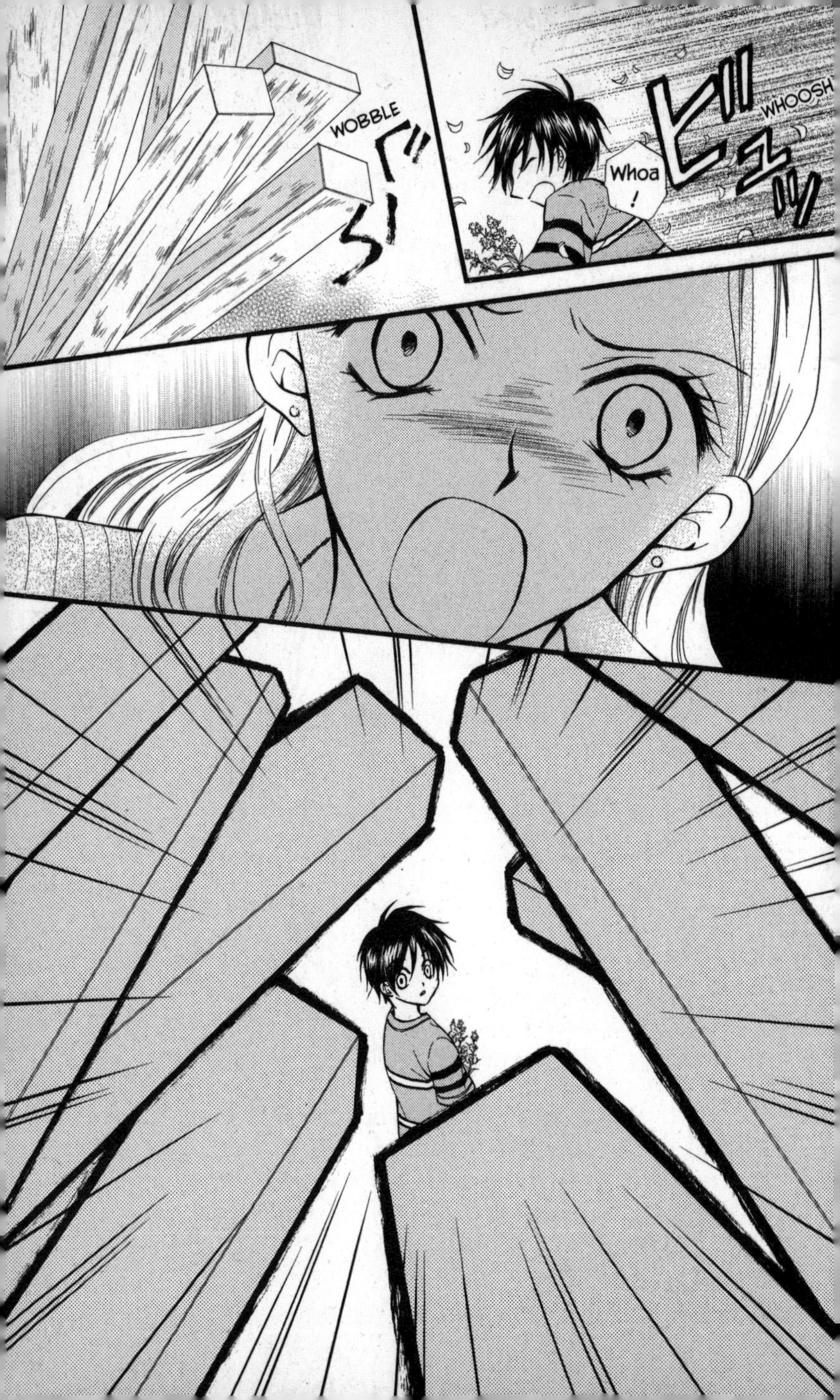
WHOOSH
ビュッ
Whoa!
WOBBLE
ぐら

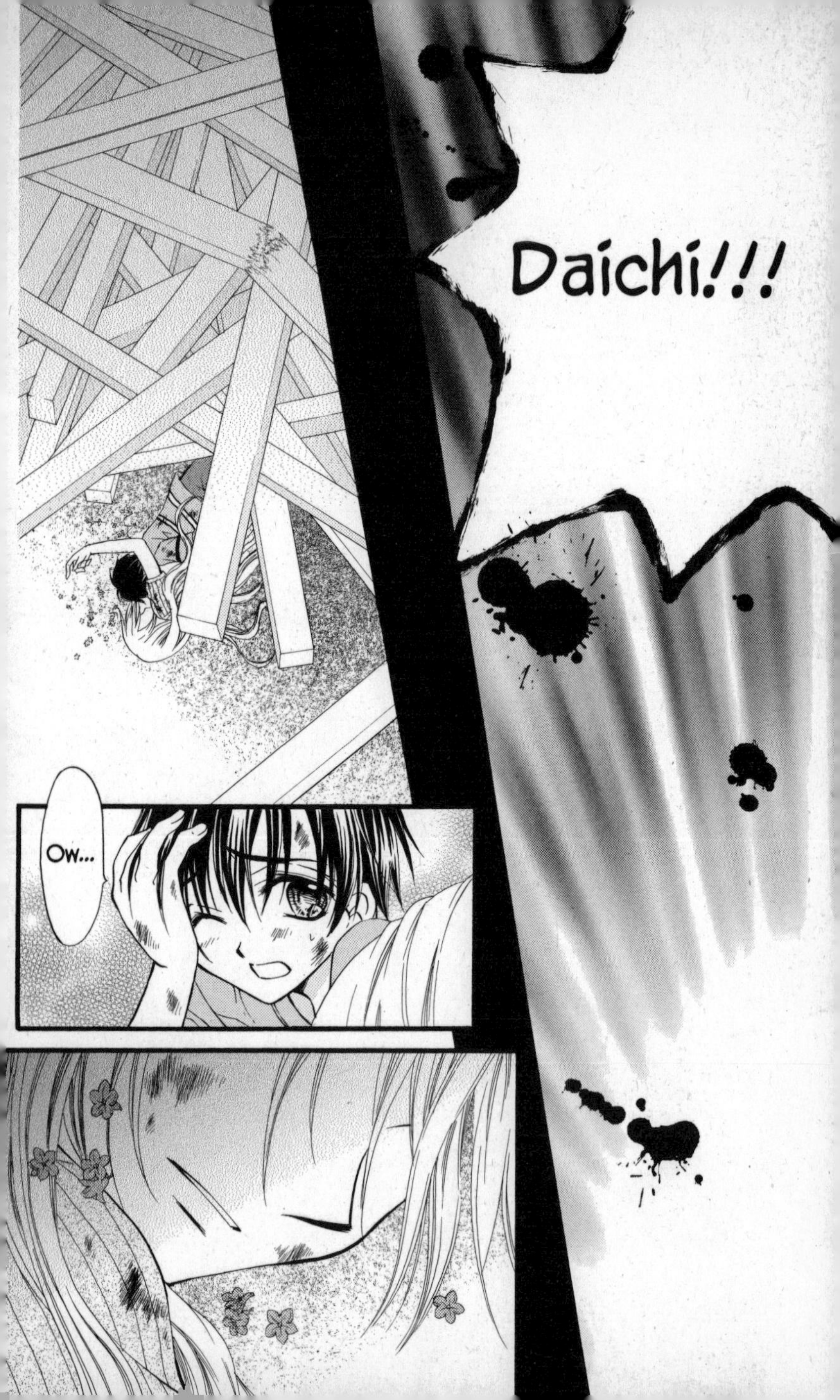
Daichi!!!
Ow...

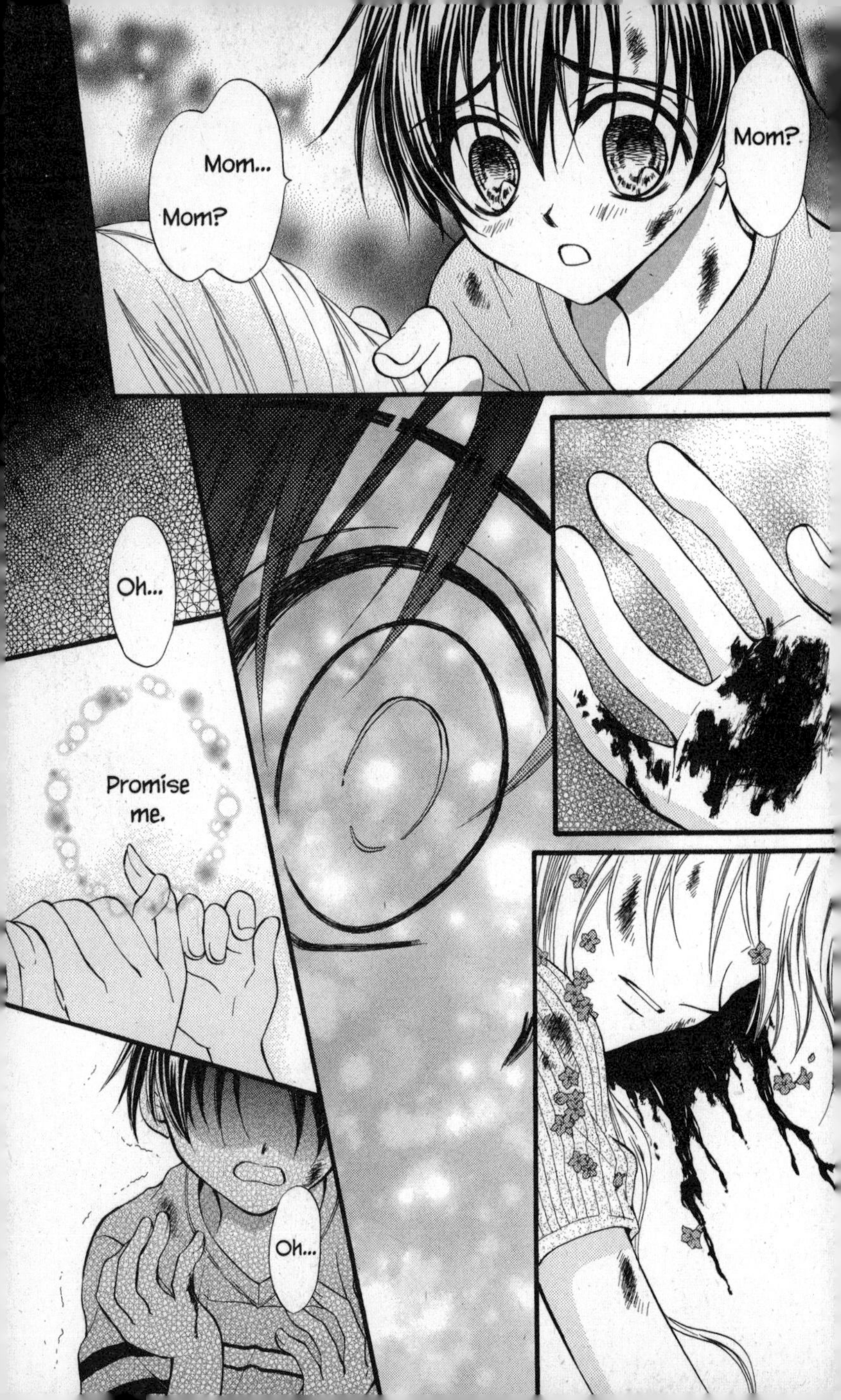

Mom?
Mom... Mom?
Oh...
Promise me.
Oh...

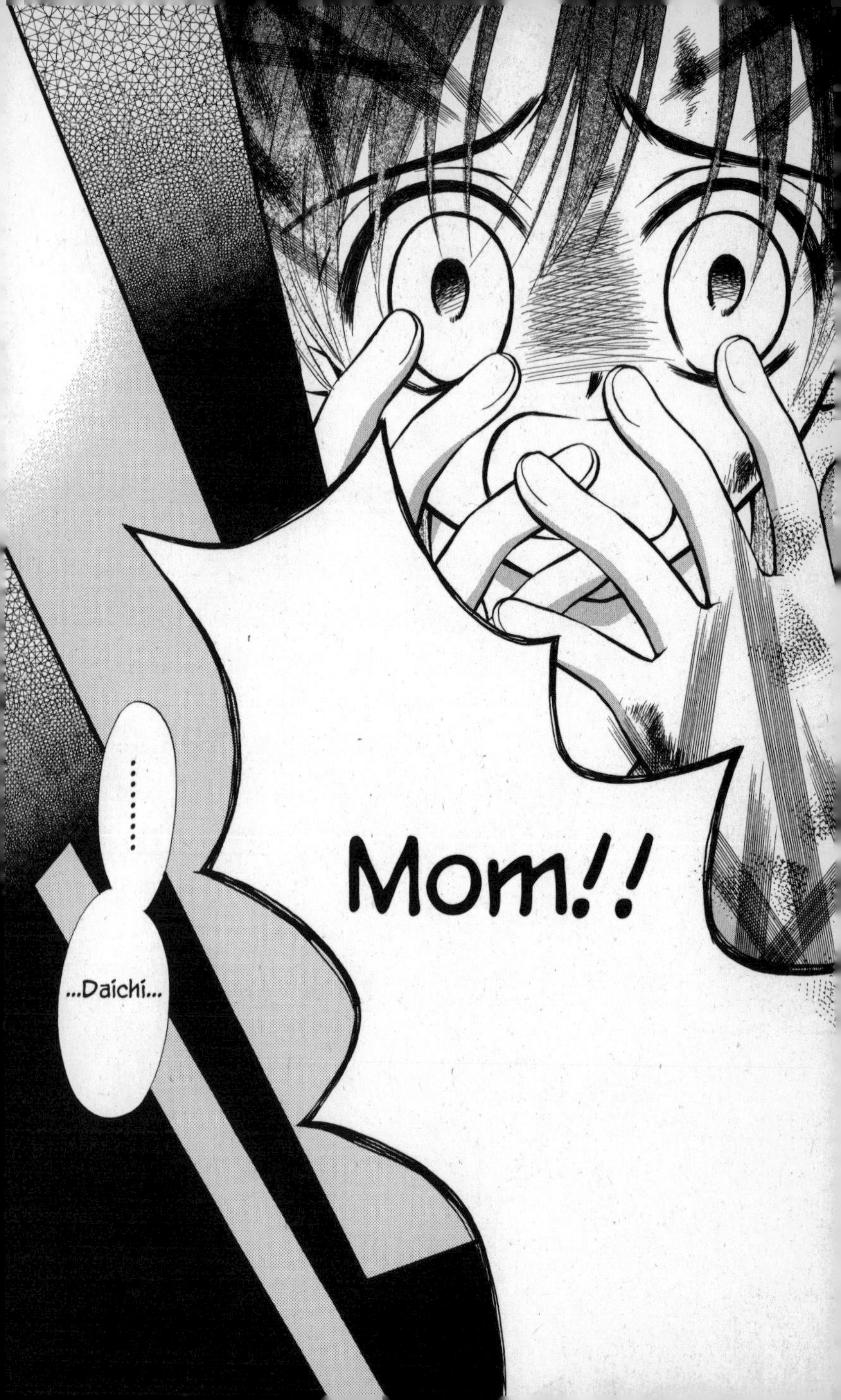
Mom!!
....
...Daichi...

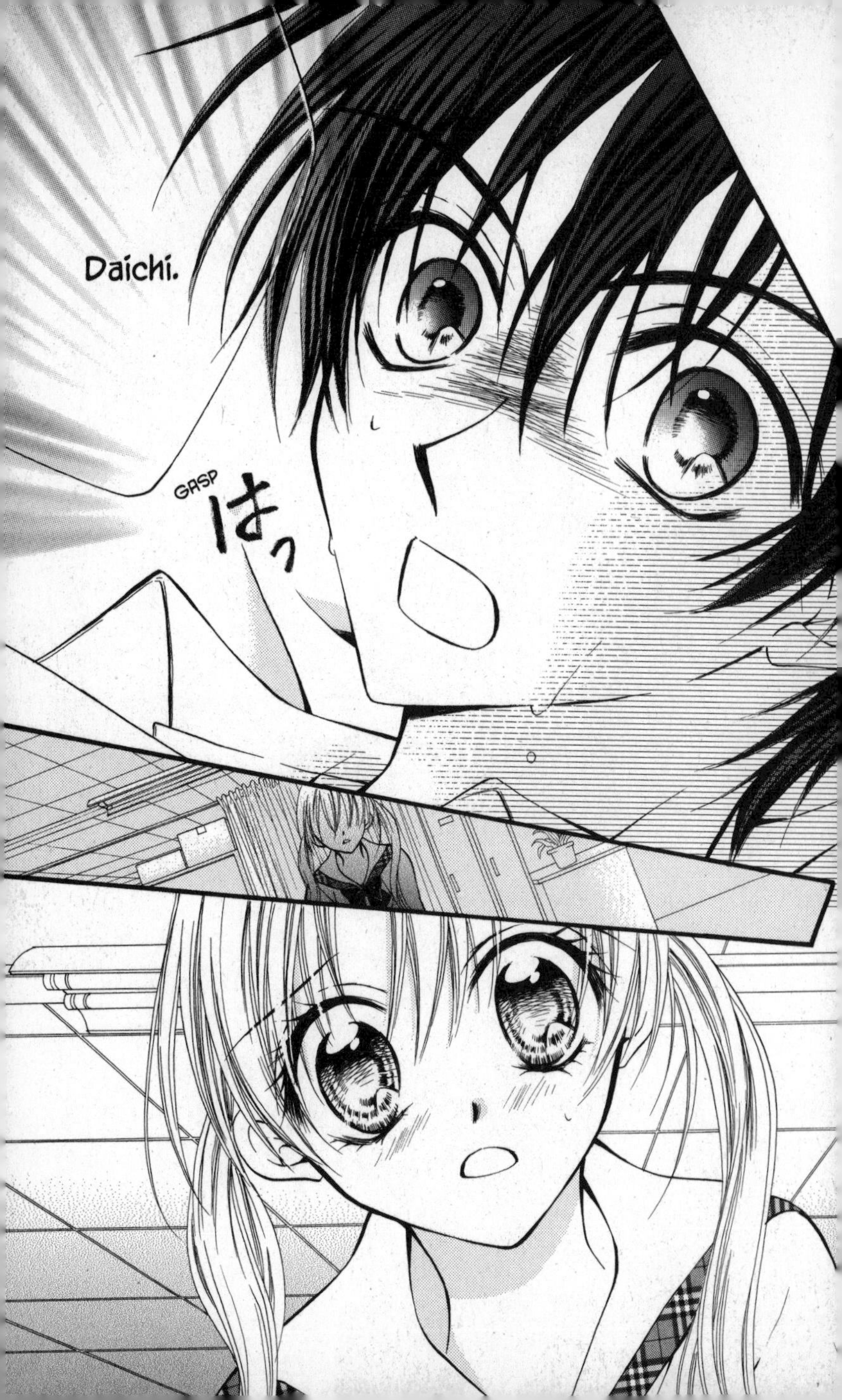
Daichi.
GASP
はっ

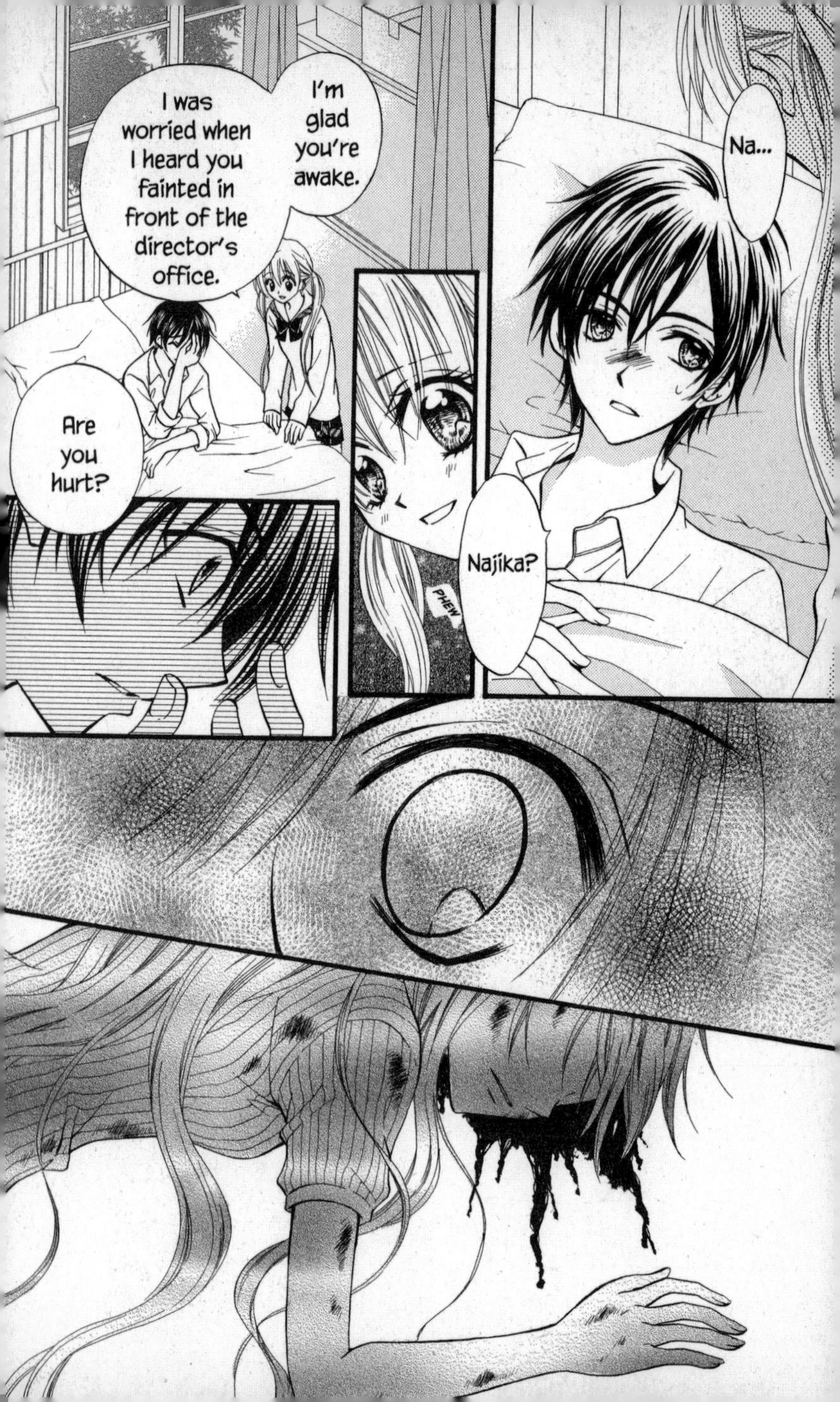
Na...
Najika?
PHEW
I'm glad you're awake.
I was worried when I heard you fainted in front of the director's office.
Are you hurt?

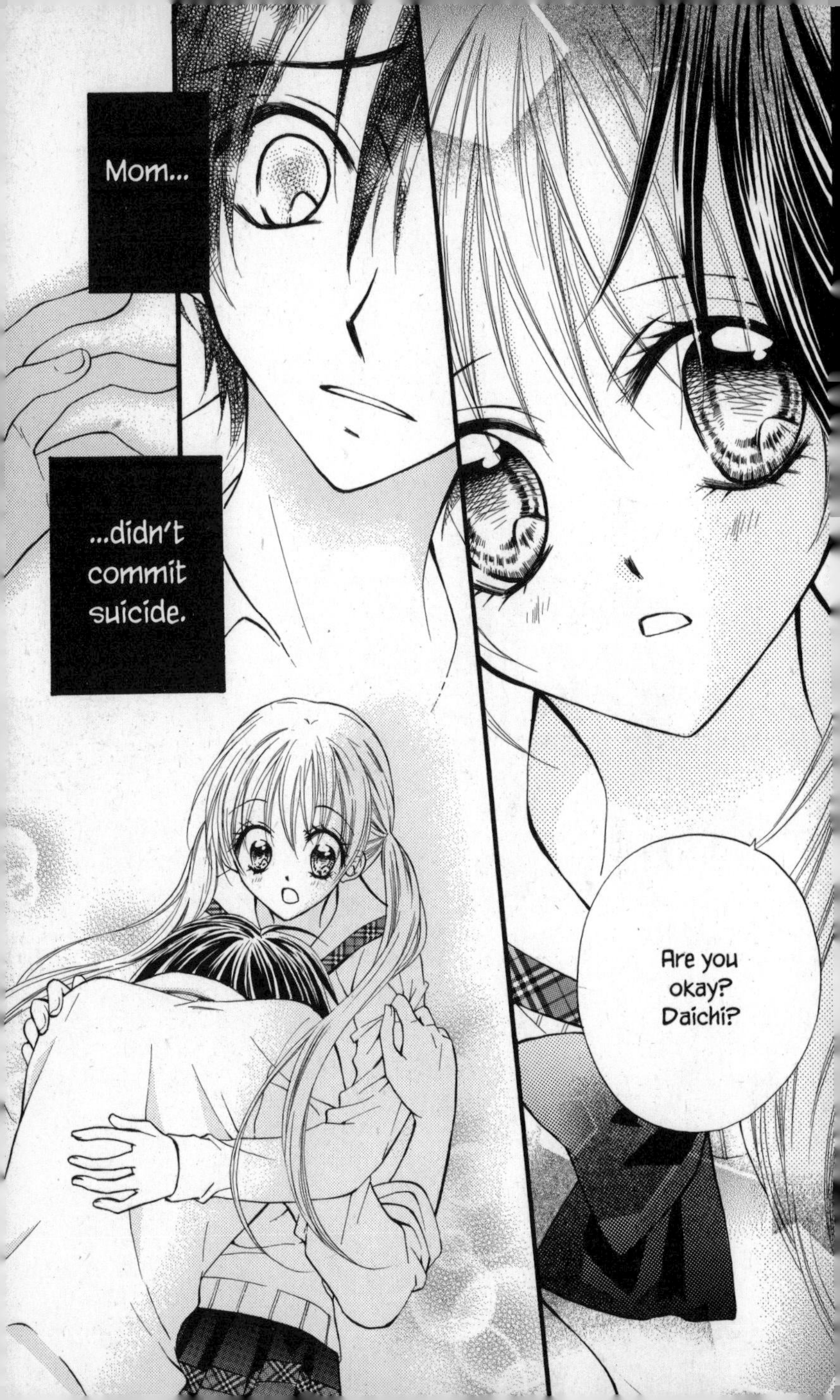
Are you okay? Daichi?
Mom...
...didn't commit suicide.

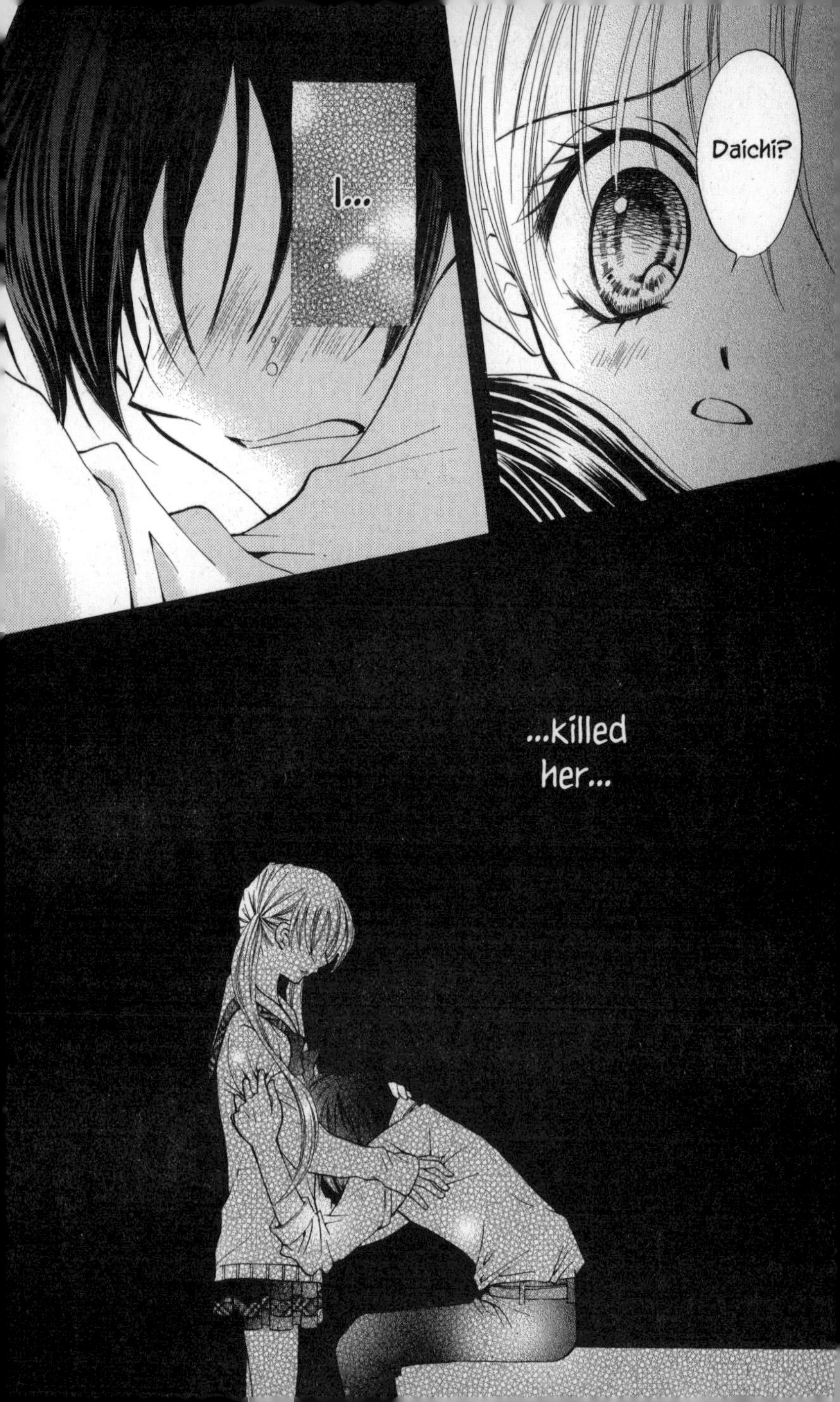
Daichi?
I...
...killed her...

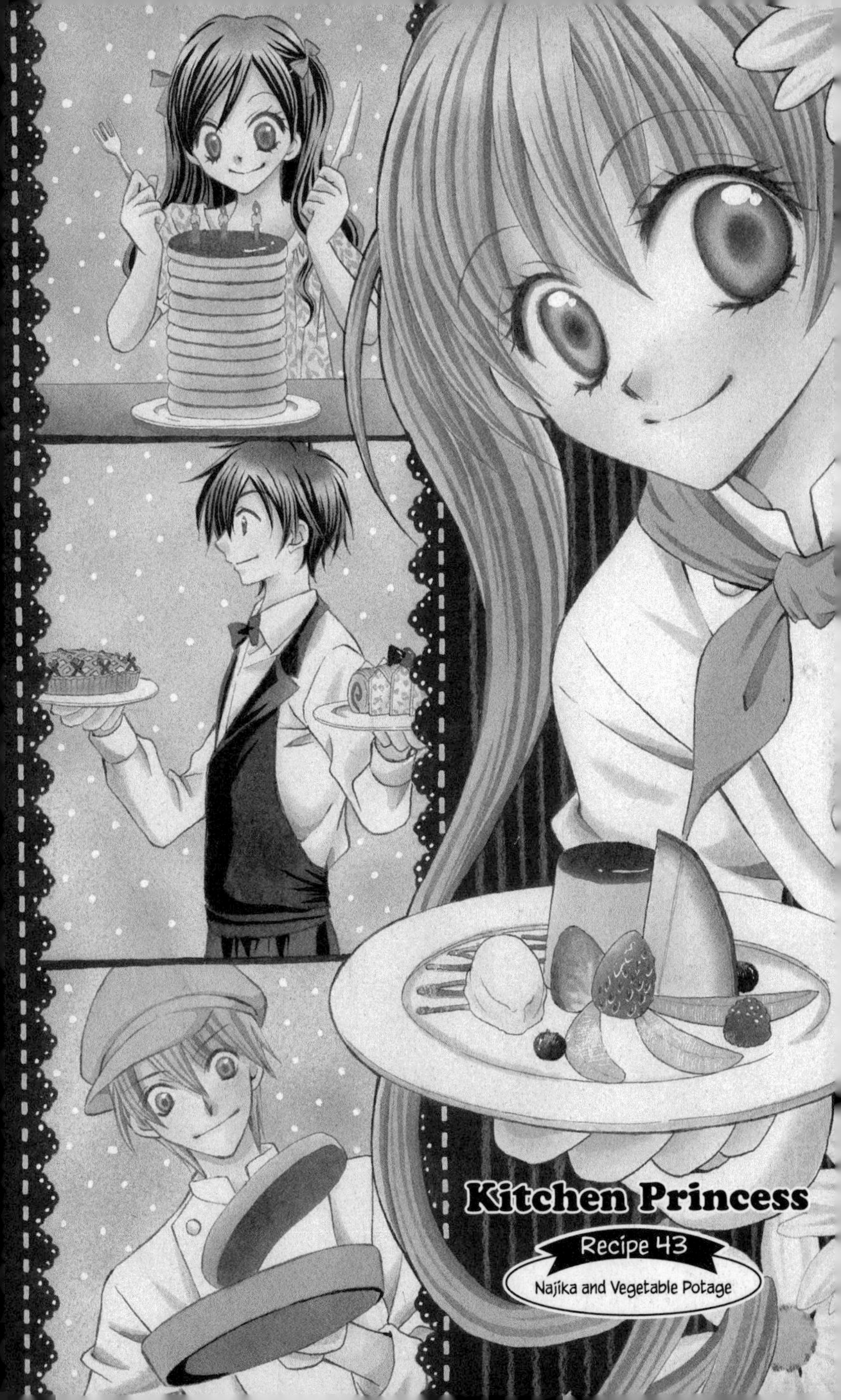
Kitchen Princess
Recipe 43
Najika and Vegetable Potage

Q&A I would like to use this space to answer a few questions I received in the mail.

Q Which recipe do you like the most in *Kitchen Princess*?

A My favorite is hard to pick, but I often make the Black Sesame Castella that was featured in Recipe 21. I really like the texture of the black sesame. And it's healthy, too. ♪

I also make the Yogurt Bread from Recipe 27 often. I don't know how many times I've made it already.
It's great for breakfast, and it goes great with jam, and it's really easy, so I recommend it to everyone. ^.^

Q Who is the most fun to draw, the hardest to draw, and the easiest to draw?

A Fujita-san is the most fun to draw. I can play around with him, and make him do funny things. Hardest...? Hmmm. It might be Daichi. It's hard to style his hair. The easiest is Najika. I like her hairstyle when it is tied in pigtails.

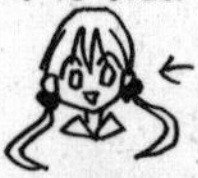
← = LIKE THIS

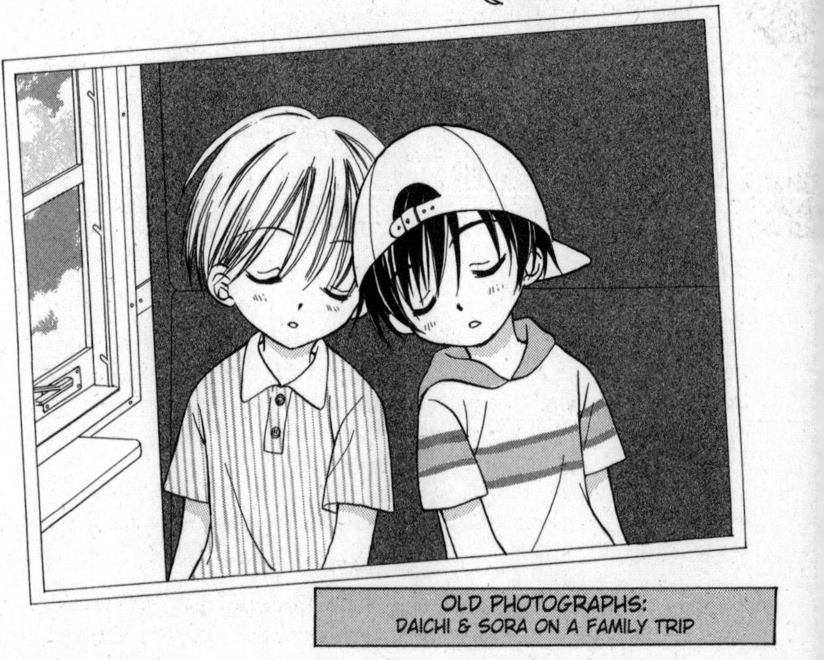

OLD PHOTOGRAPHS:
DAICHI & SORA ON A FAMILY TRIP

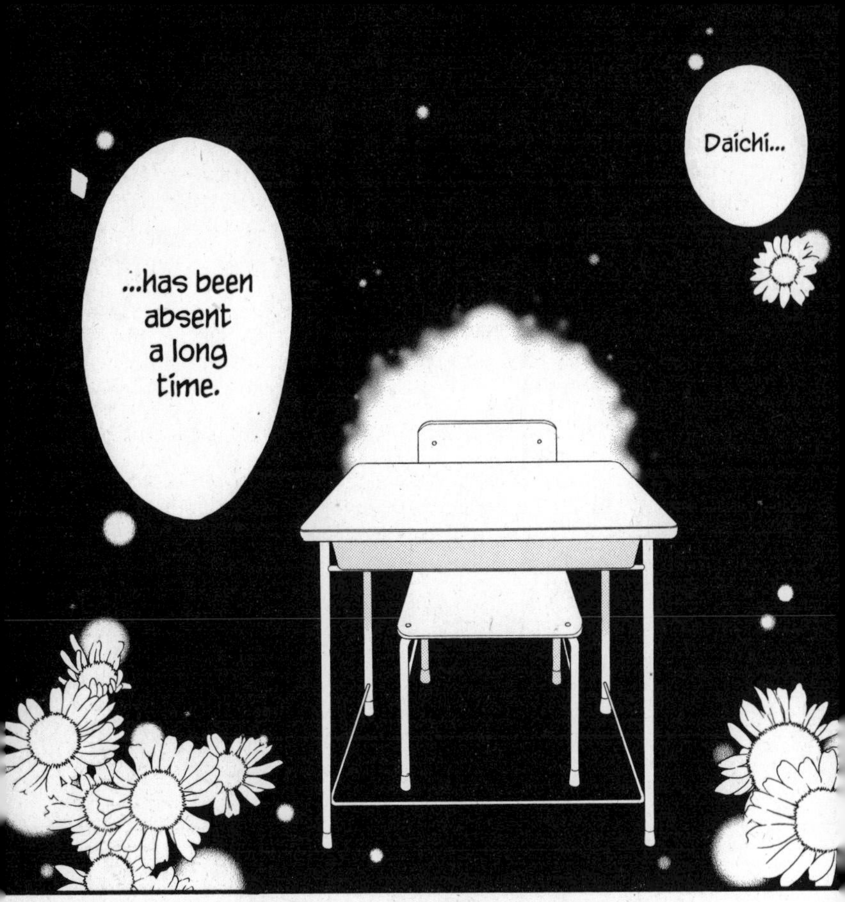
Daichi...
...has been absent a long time.

About the Splash Pages

Recipe 43

This is actually a splash page I had to draw in a hurry because I had a lot of work. I had another composition in mind that had Najika and Daichi, and I couldn't decide which one to choose, since the story was about the two of them. But I wanted the splash page to be cheerful, so I ended up with the one that had Najika smiling.
I used gouache to color it, and when I went to go buy some I was surprised at the number of colors available. I would like to use it again. ♡

The Special

It is a shot of Najika and Fujita-san. It was actually quite refreshing. I wondered if having an old man on a splash page of *Nakayoshi* magazine would be okay, though. But I had a lot of fun drawing this splash page.

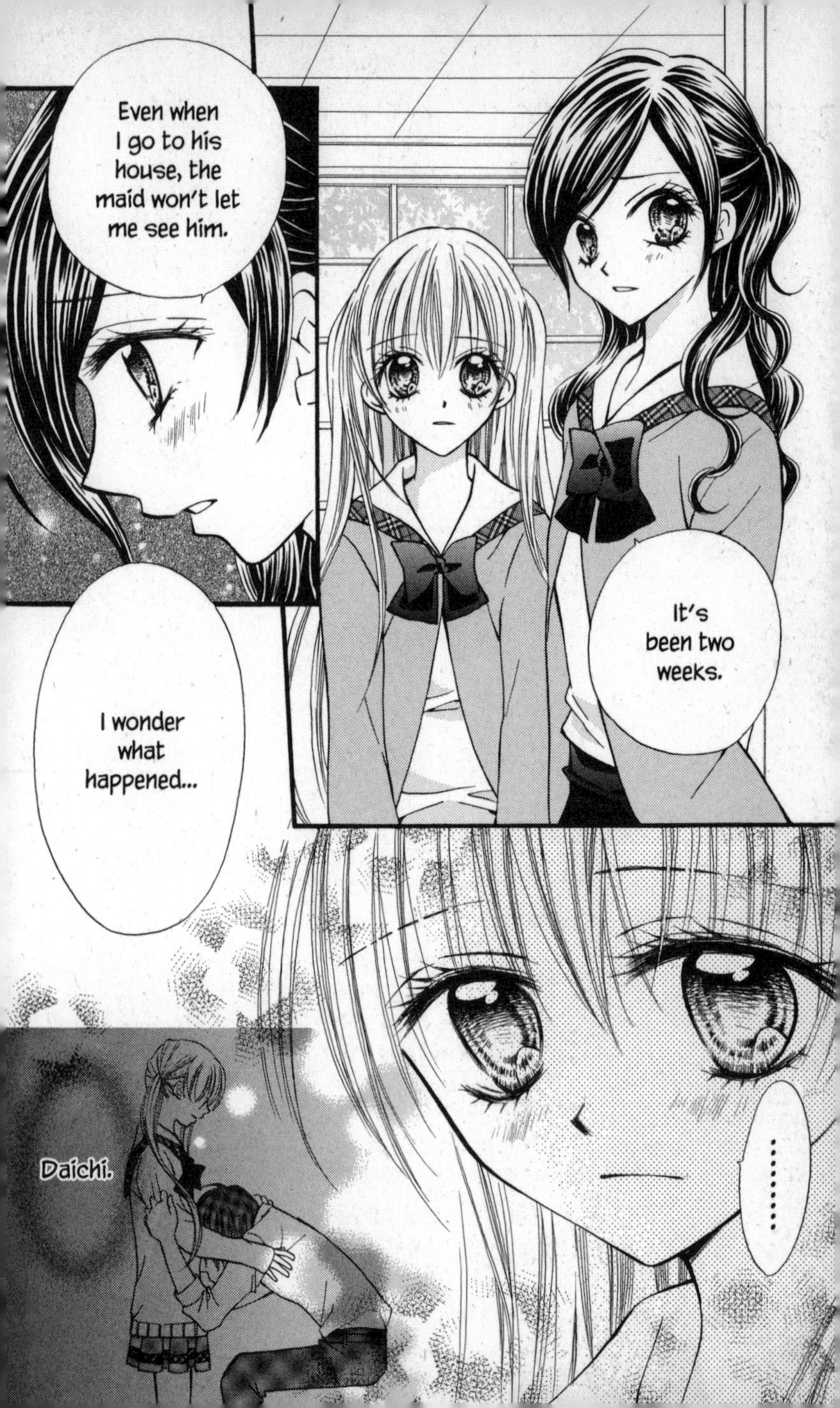
It's been two weeks.
Even when I go to his house, the maid won't let me see him.
I wonder what happened...
......
Daichi.

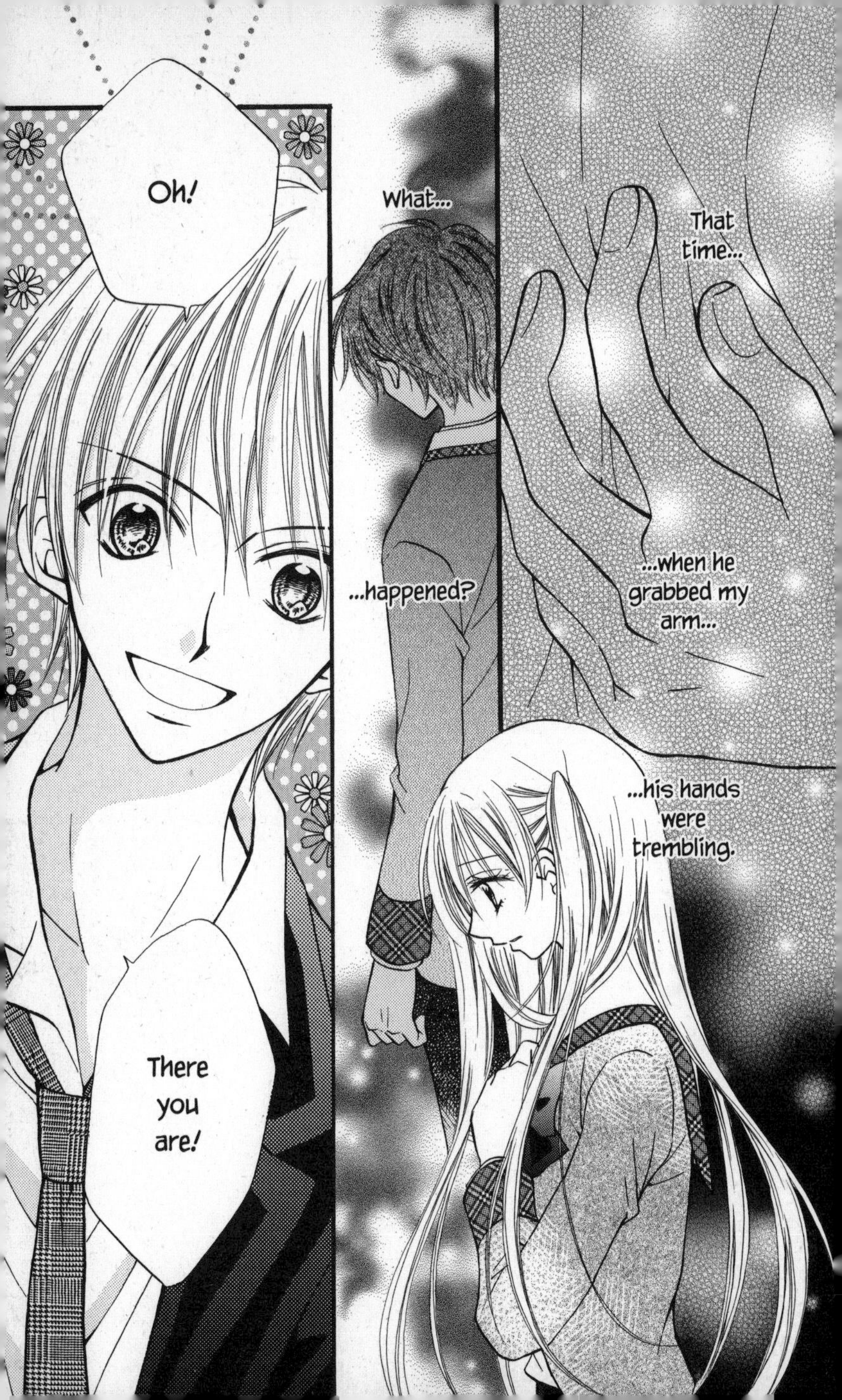
That time...
...when he grabbed my arm...
...his hands were trembling.
What...
...happened?
Oh!
There you are!

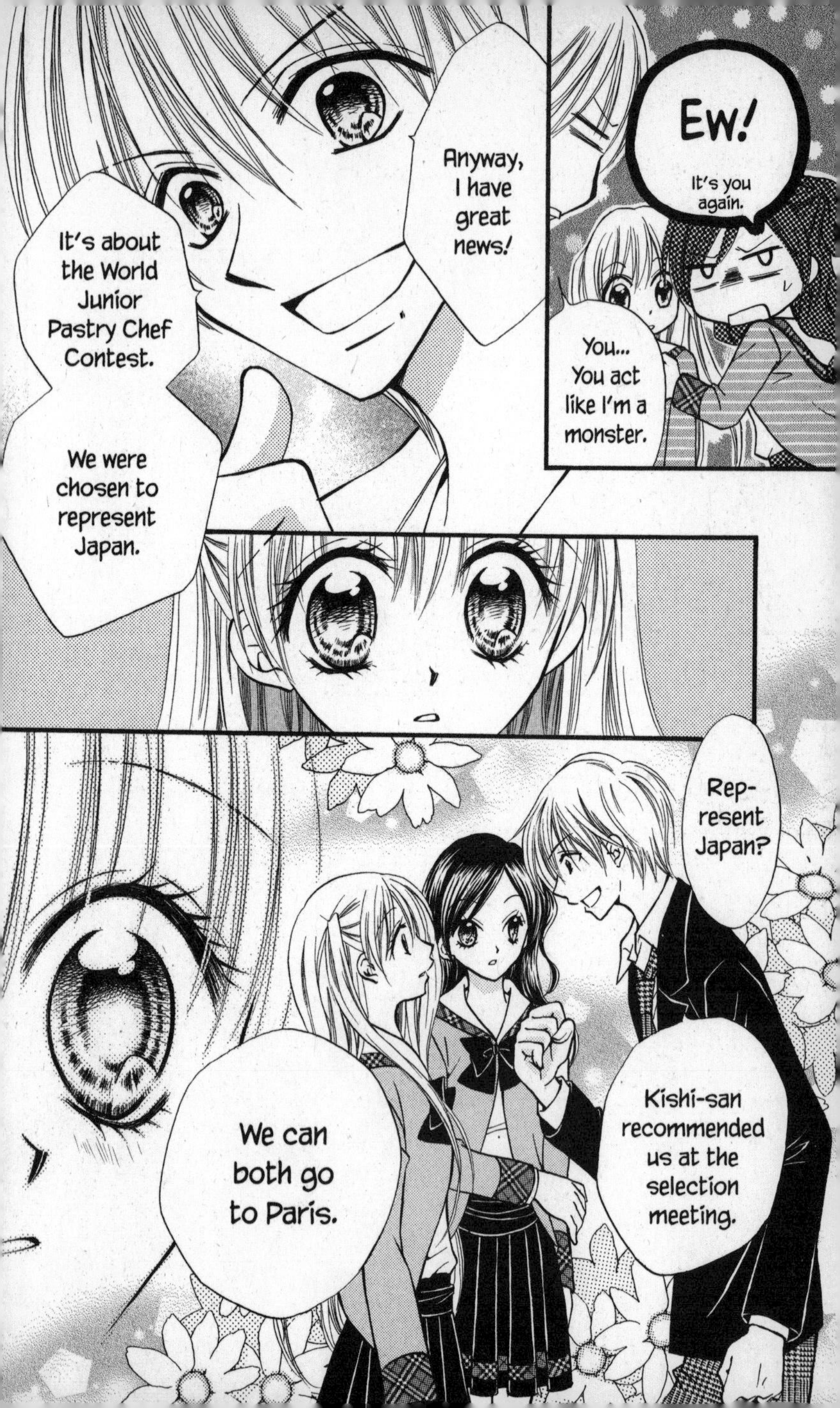
Ew! It's you again.
You... You act like I'm a monster.
Anyway, I have great news!
It's about the World Junior Pastry Chef Contest.
We were chosen to represent Japan.
Rep-resent Japan?
Kishi-san recommended us at the selection meeting.
We can both go to Paris.

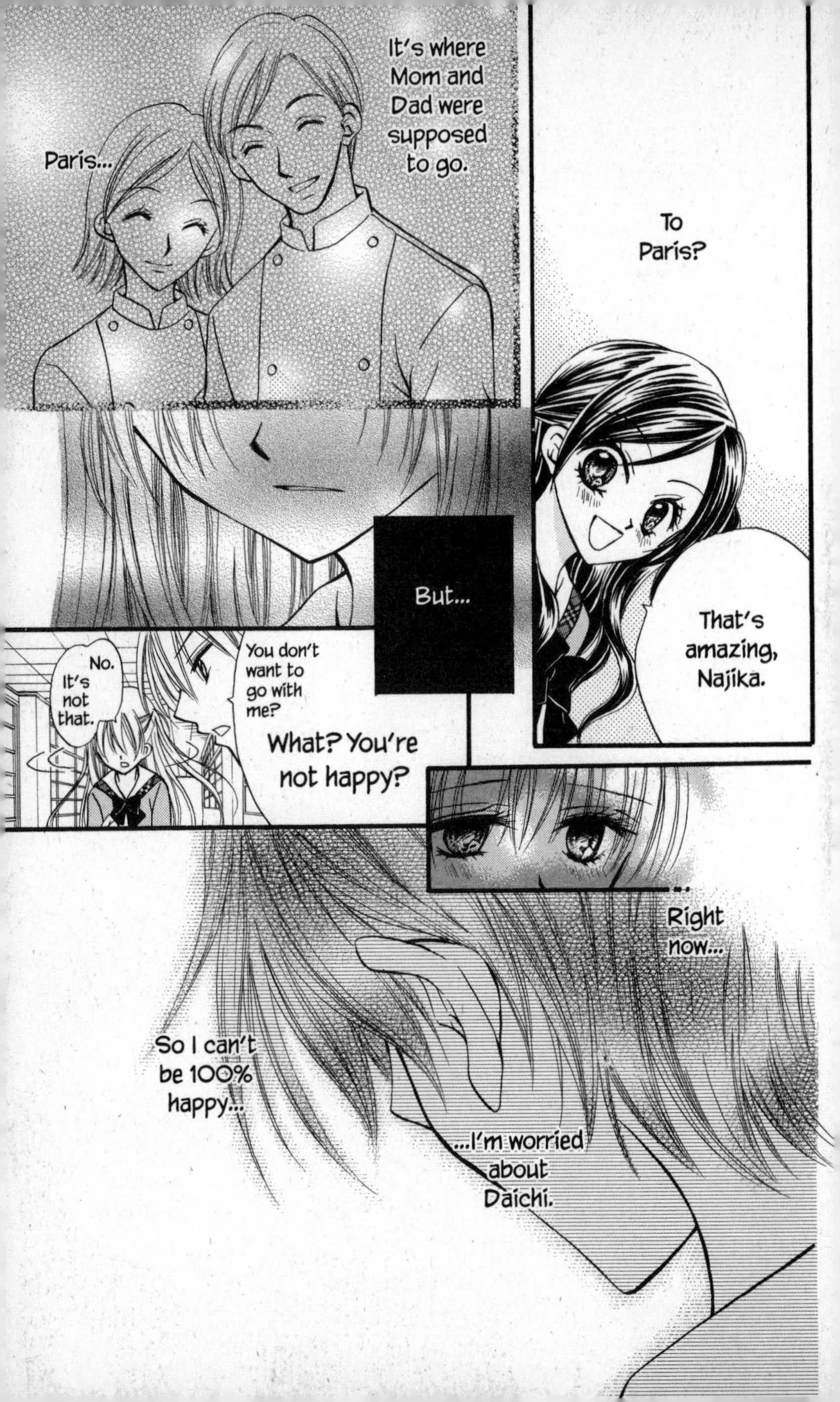

To Paris?
That's amazing, Najika.
It's where Mom and Dad were supposed to go.
Paris...
But...
What? You're not happy?
You don't want to go with me?
No. It's not that.
...
Right now...
...I'm worried about Daichi.
So I can't be 100% happy...

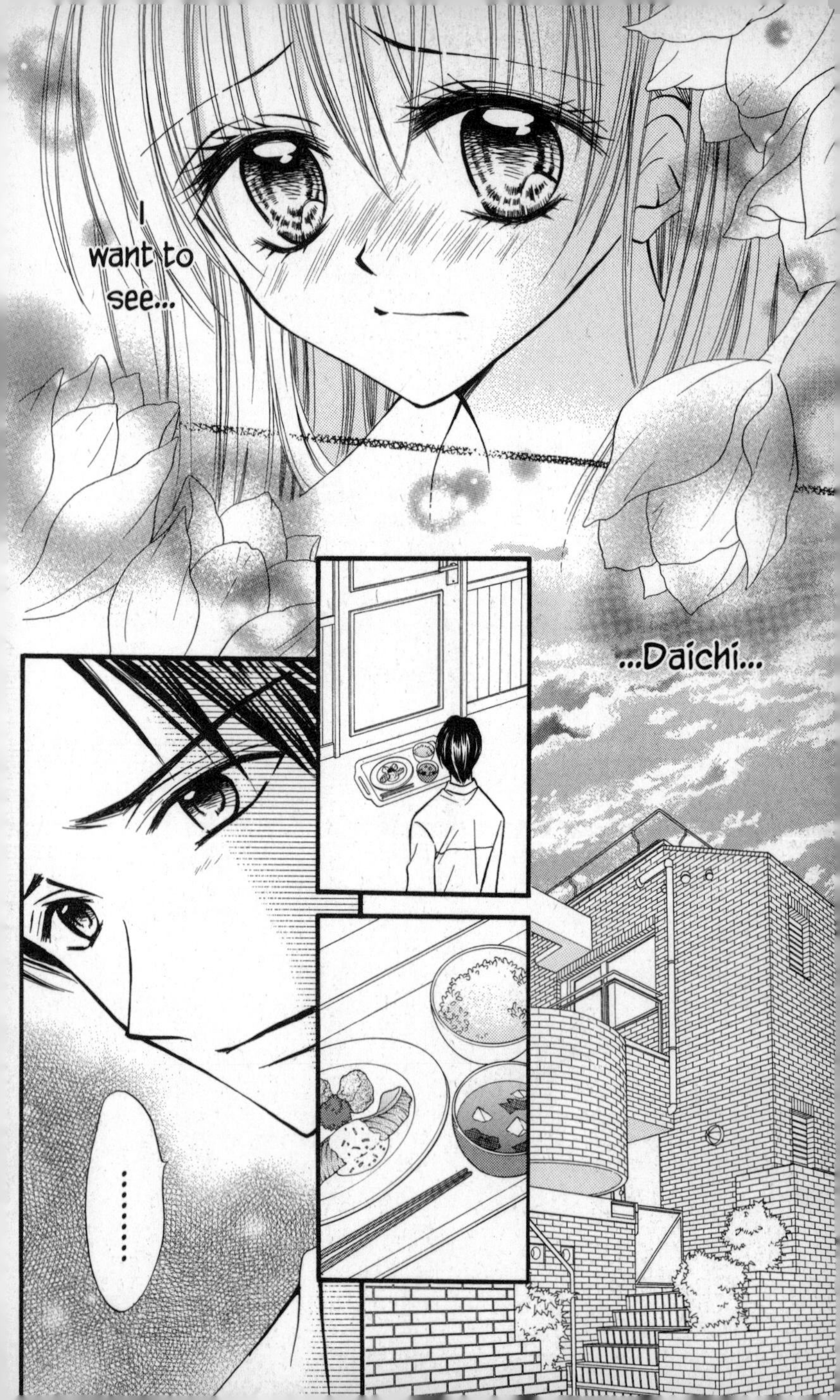
I want to see...
...Daichi...
......

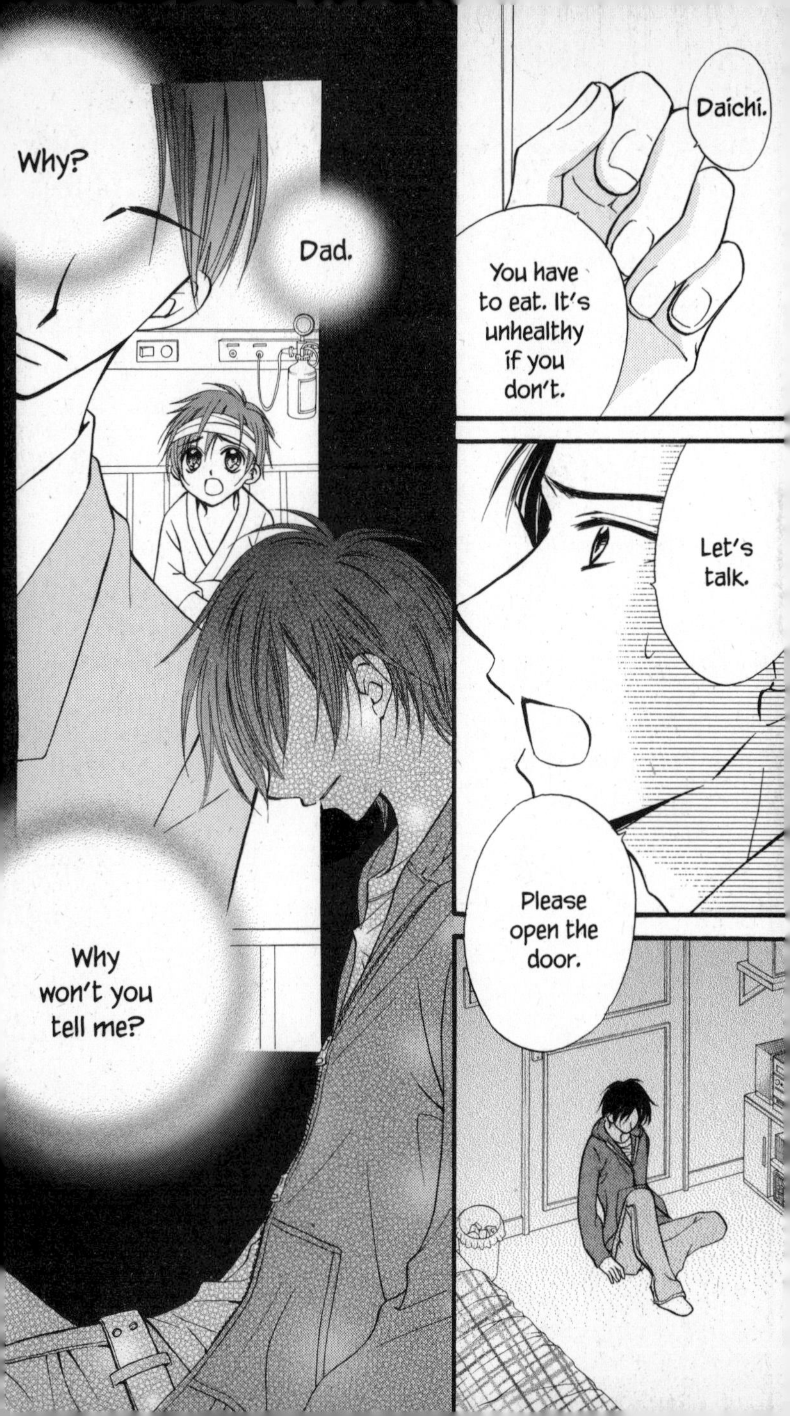
Daichi.
You have to eat. It's unhealthy if you don't.
Let's talk.
Please open the door.
Why?
Dad.
Why won't you tell me?

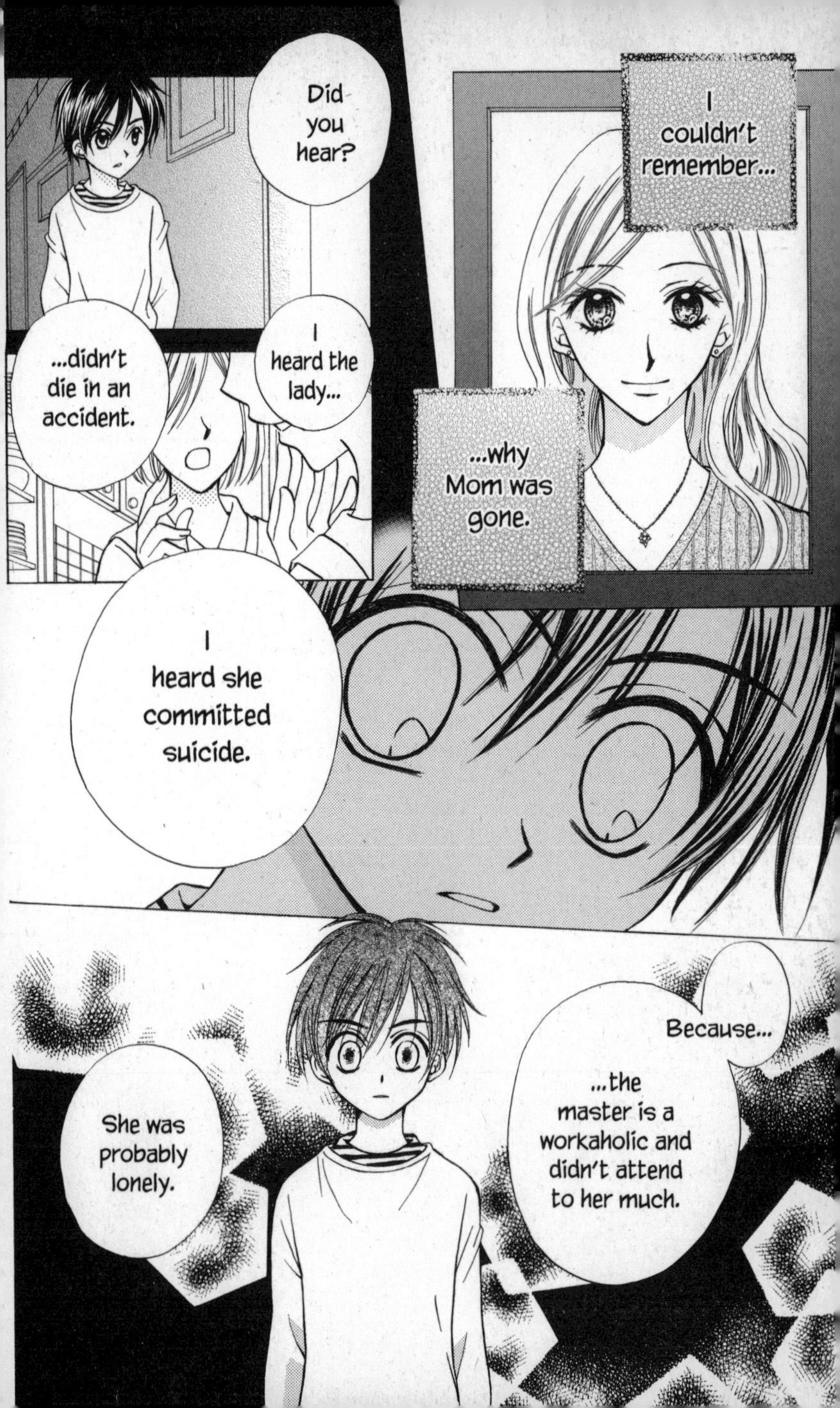

I couldn't remember...
...why Mom was gone.
Did you hear?
I heard the lady...
...didn't die in an accident.
I heard she committed suicide.
Because...
...the master is a workaholic and didn't attend to her much.
She was probably lonely.

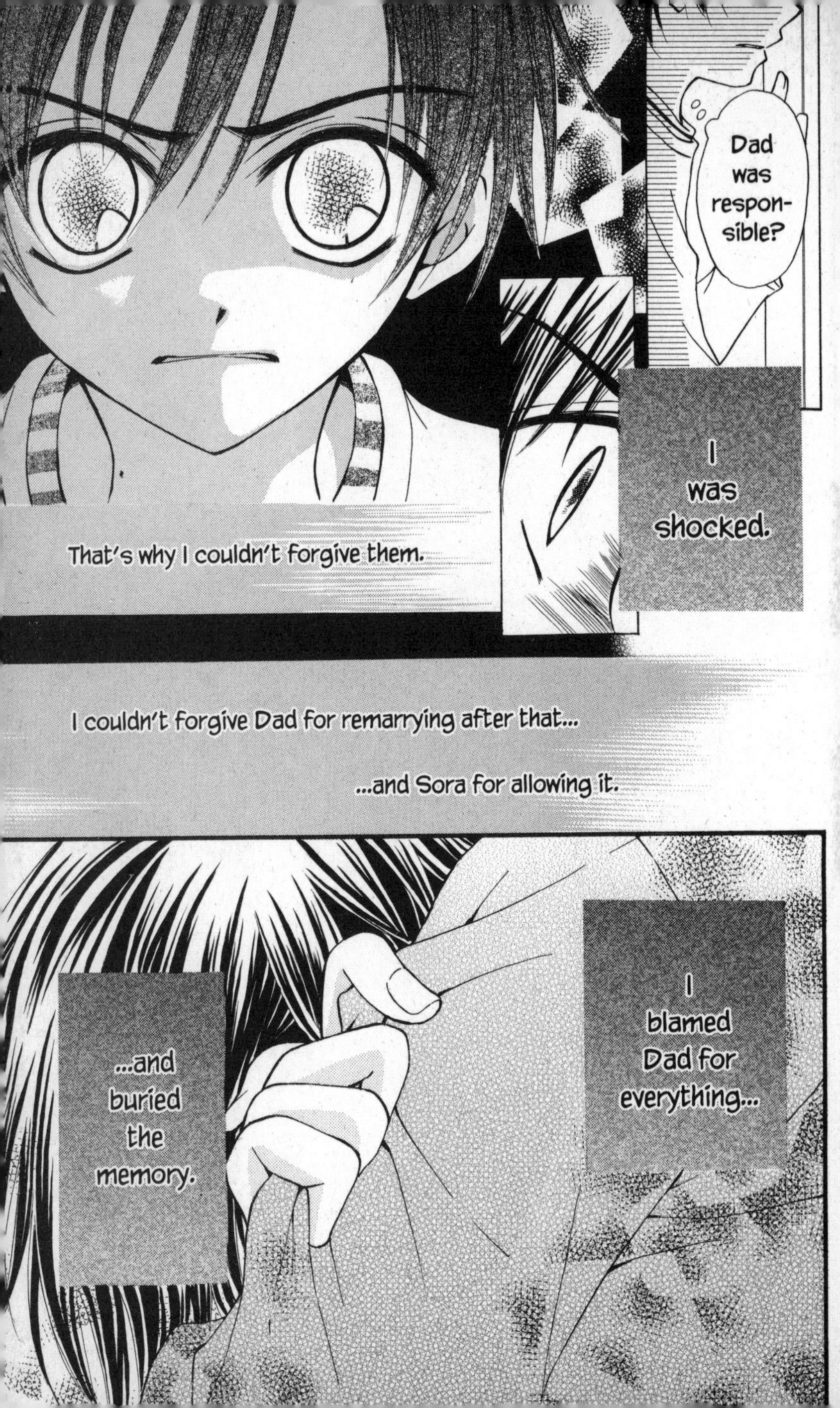
Dad was respon-sible?
I was shocked.
That's why I couldn't forgive them.
I couldn't forgive Dad for remarrying after that...
...and Sora for allowing it.
I blamed Dad for everything...
...and buried the memory.

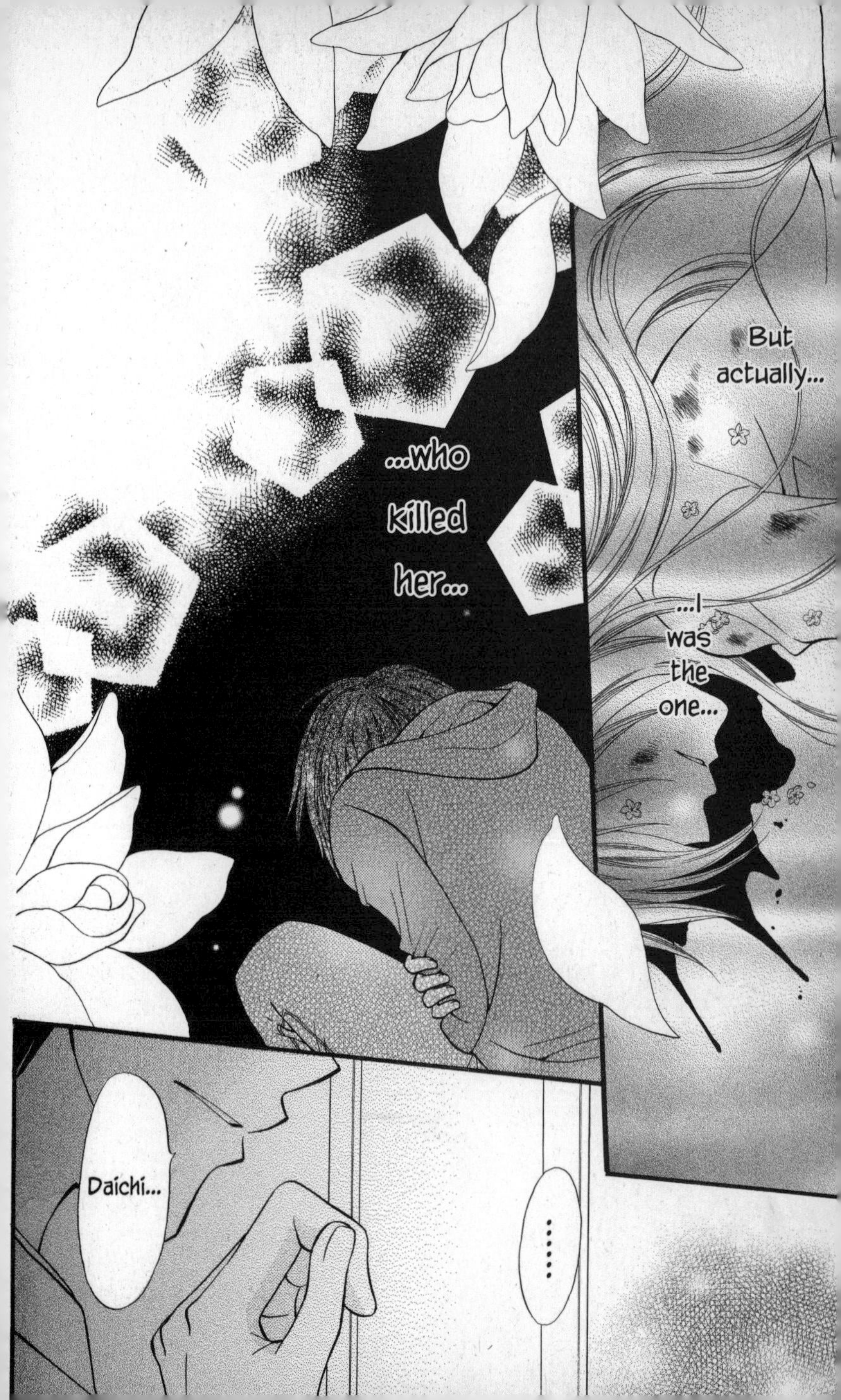
But actually...
...I was the one...
...who killed her...
......
Daichi...

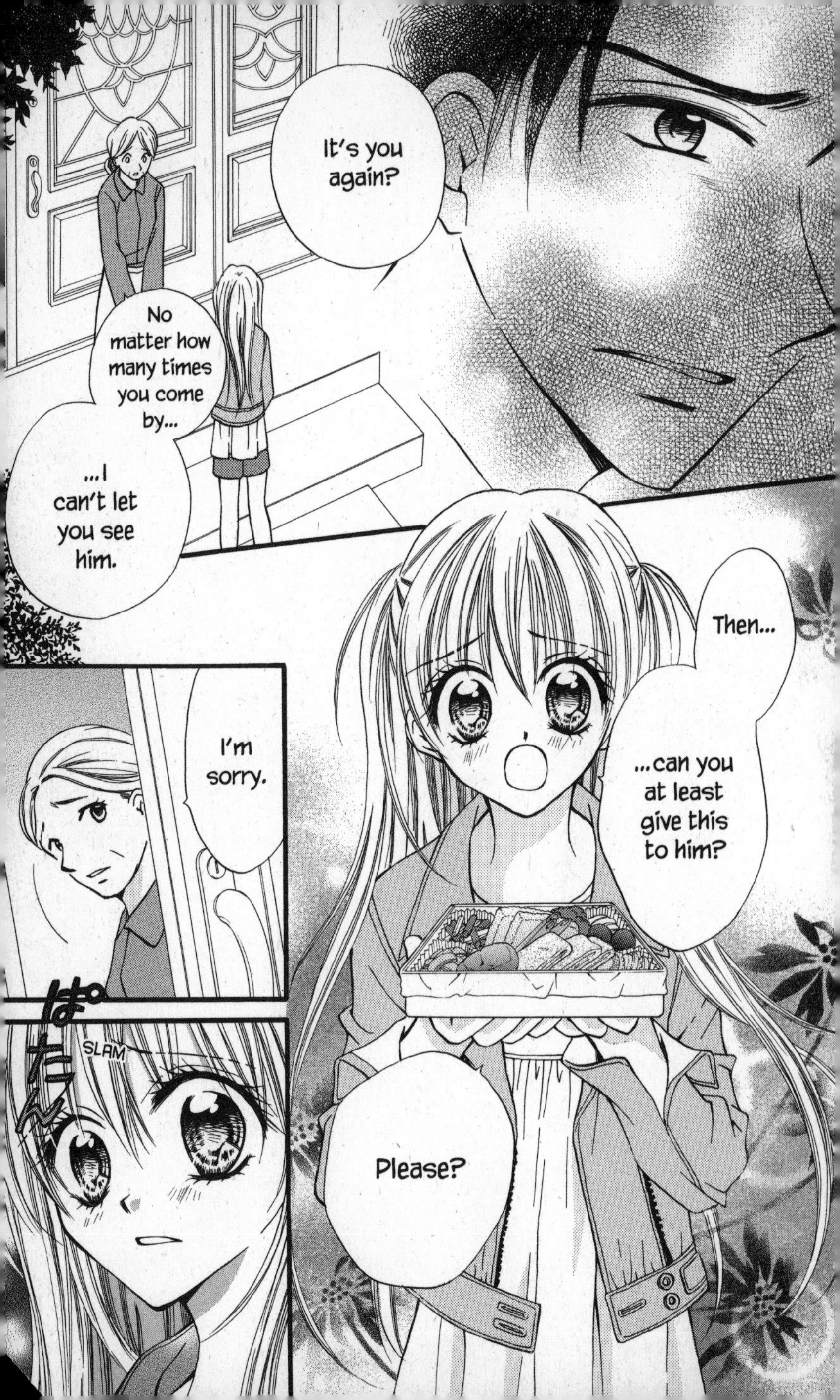
It's you again?
No matter how many times you come by...
...I can't let you see him.
Then...
...can you at least give this to him?
Please?
I'm sorry.
ぱたん
SLAM

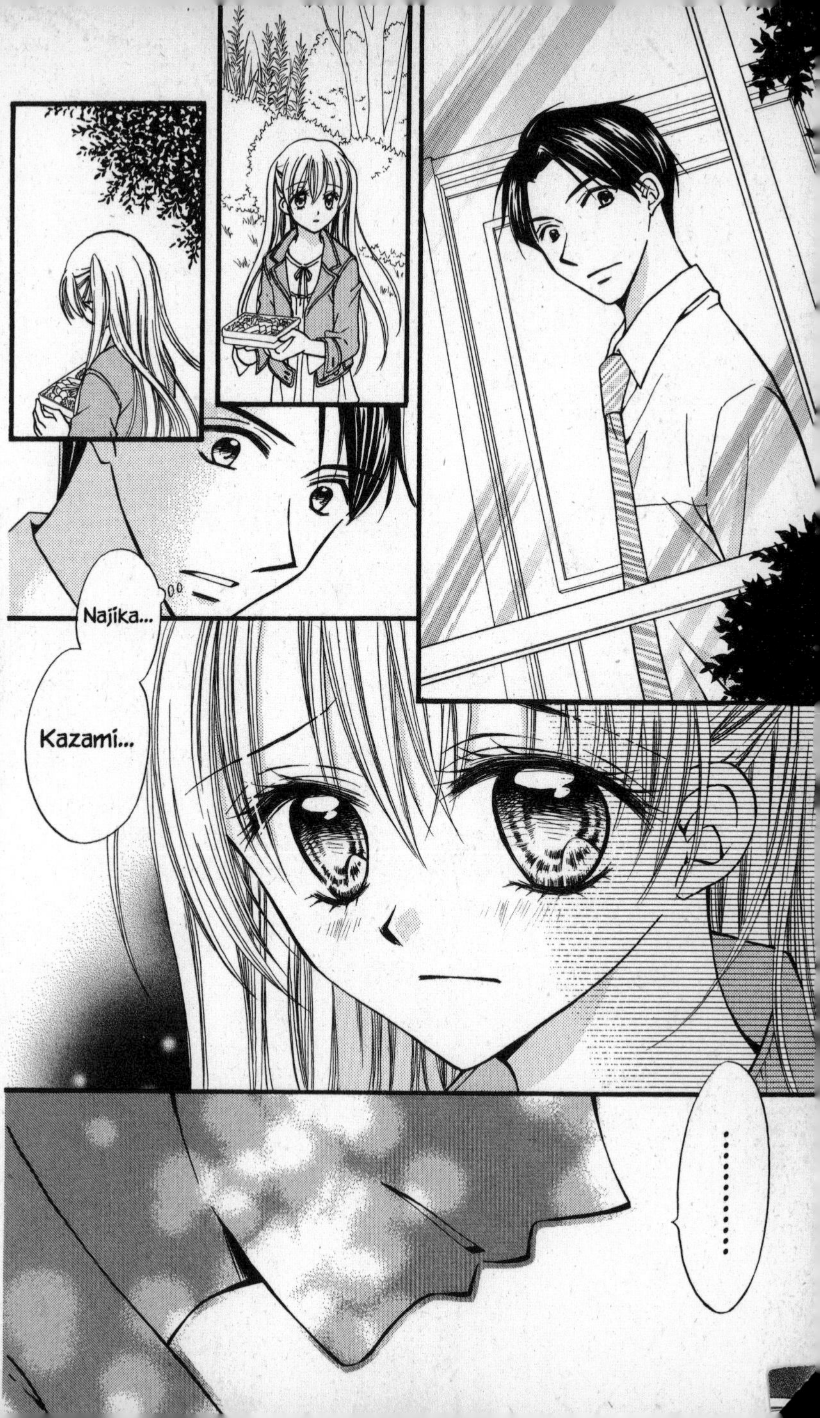

Najika...
Kazami...
....

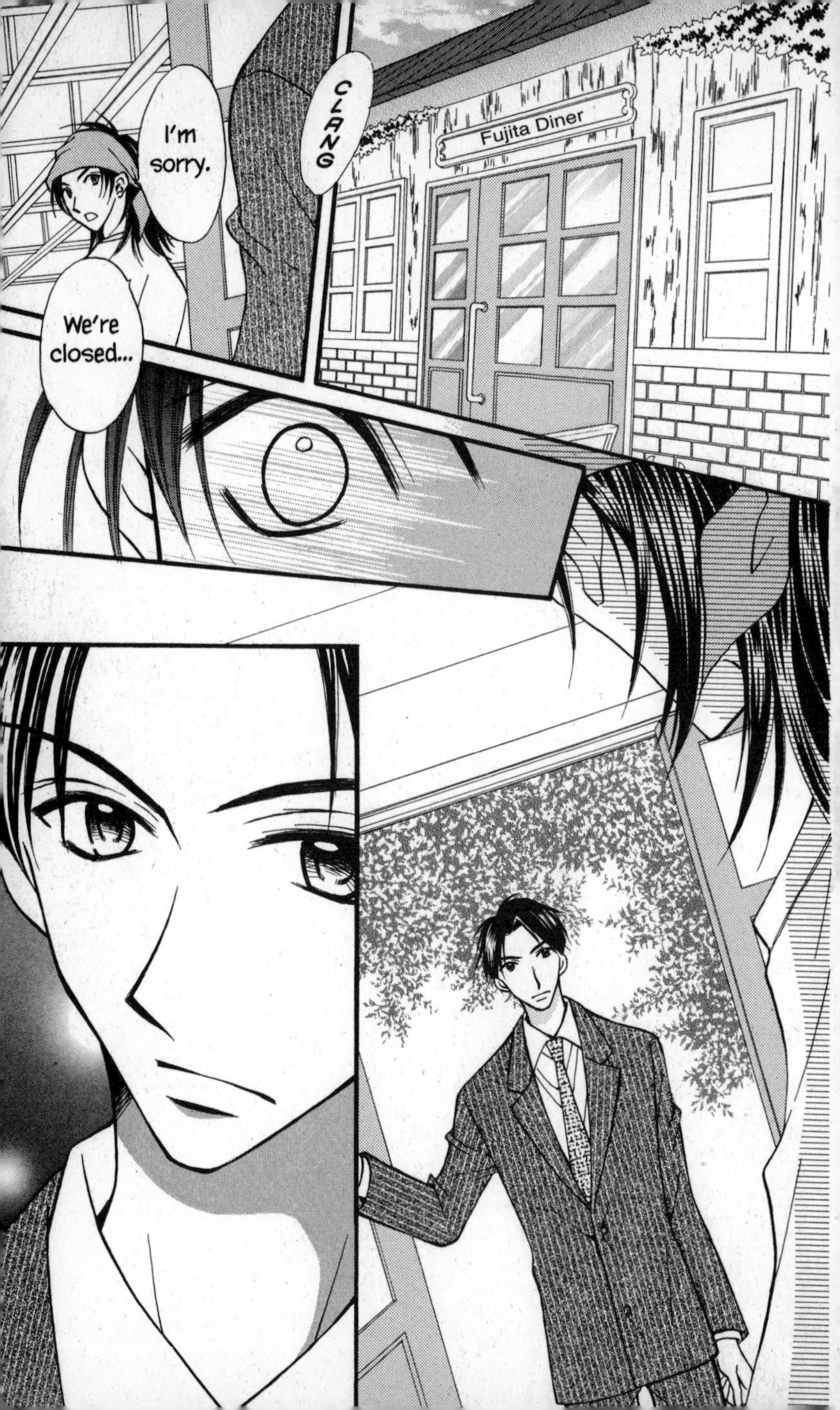
Fujita Diner
CLANG
I'm sorry.
We're closed...

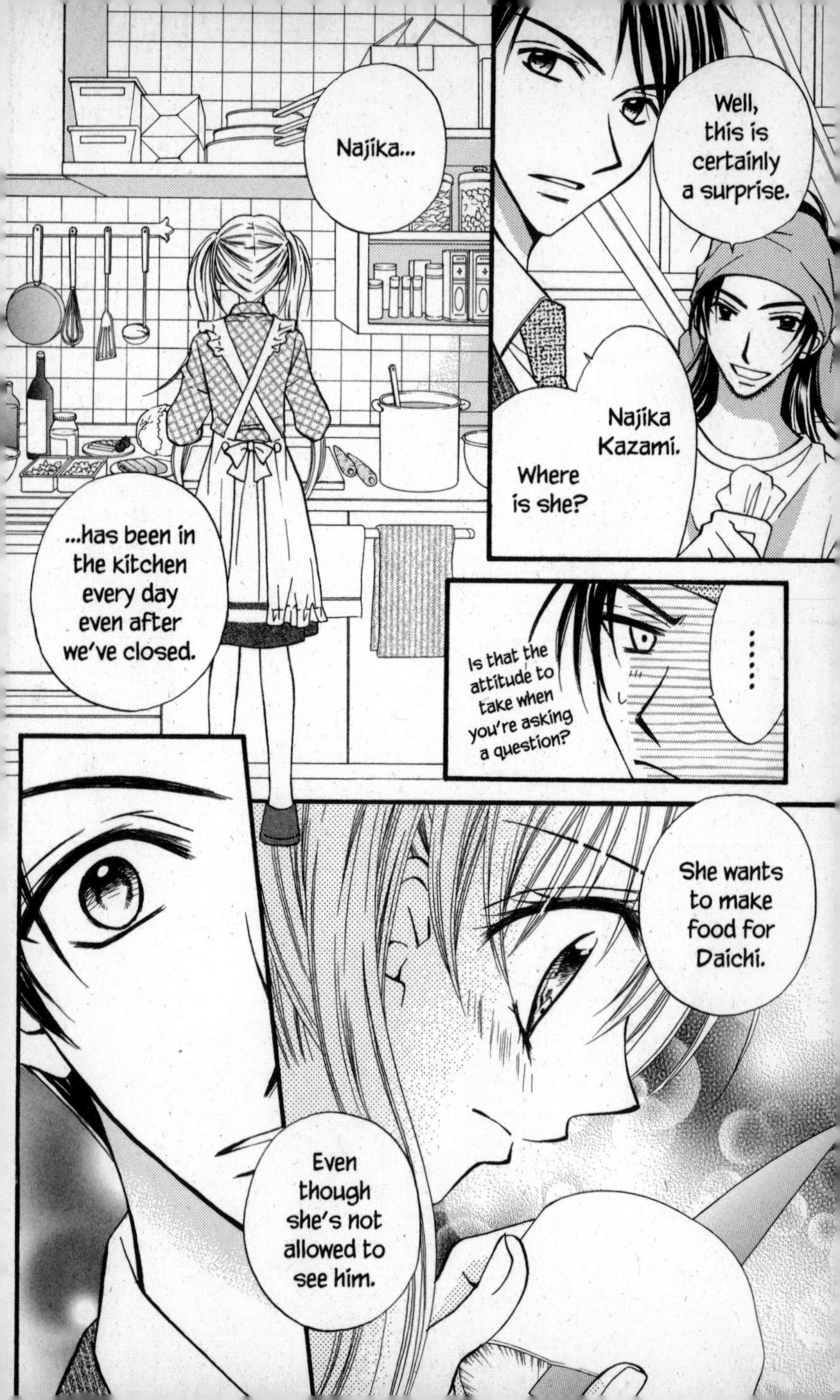
Well, this is certainly a surprise.
Najika Kazami.
Where is she?
......
Is that the attitude to take when you're asking a question?
Najika...
...has been in the kitchen every day even after we've closed.
She wants to make food for Daichi.
Even though she's not allowed to see him.

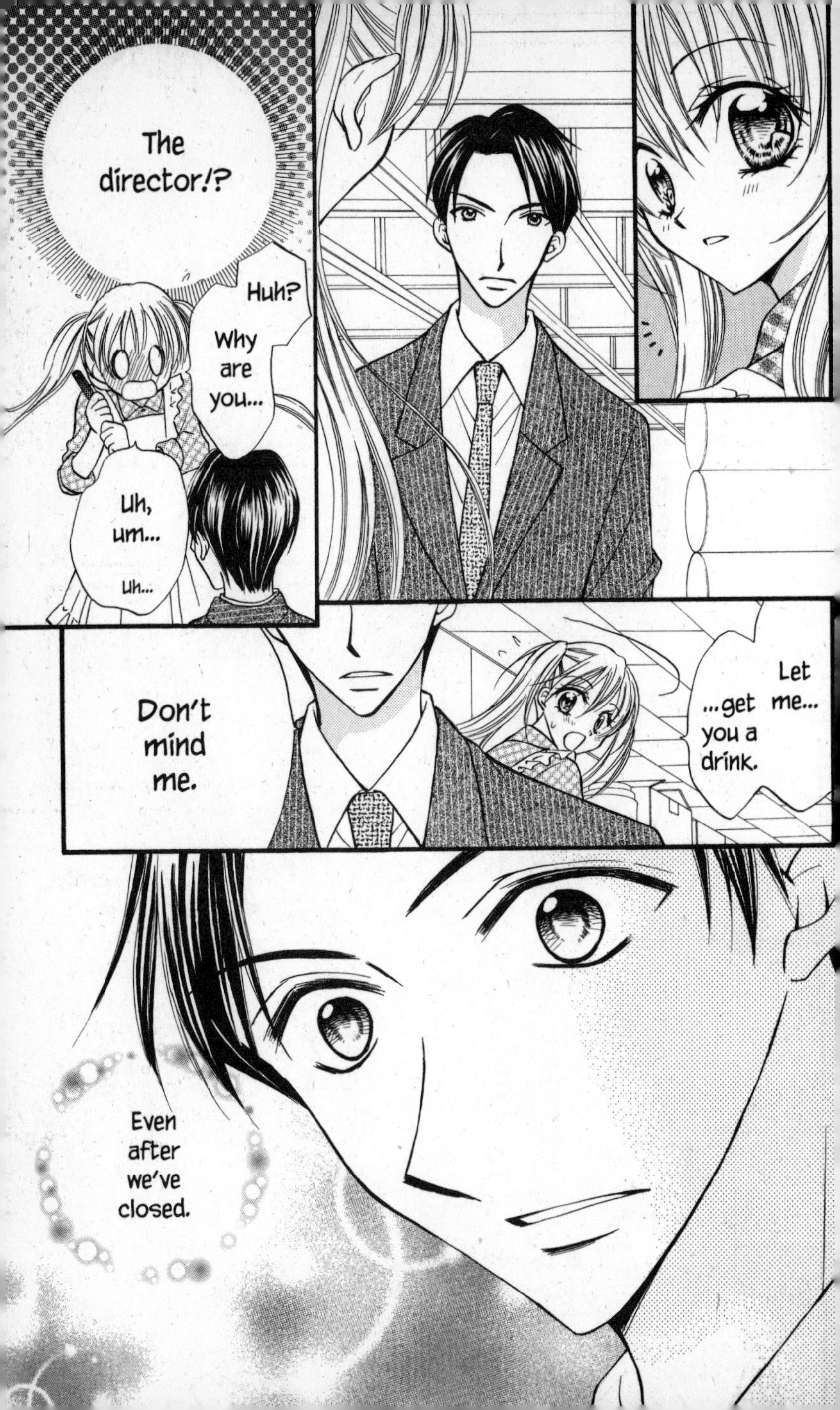
The director!?
Huh? Why are you...
Uh, um... uh...
Let me... ...get you a drink.
Don't mind me.
Even after we've closed.

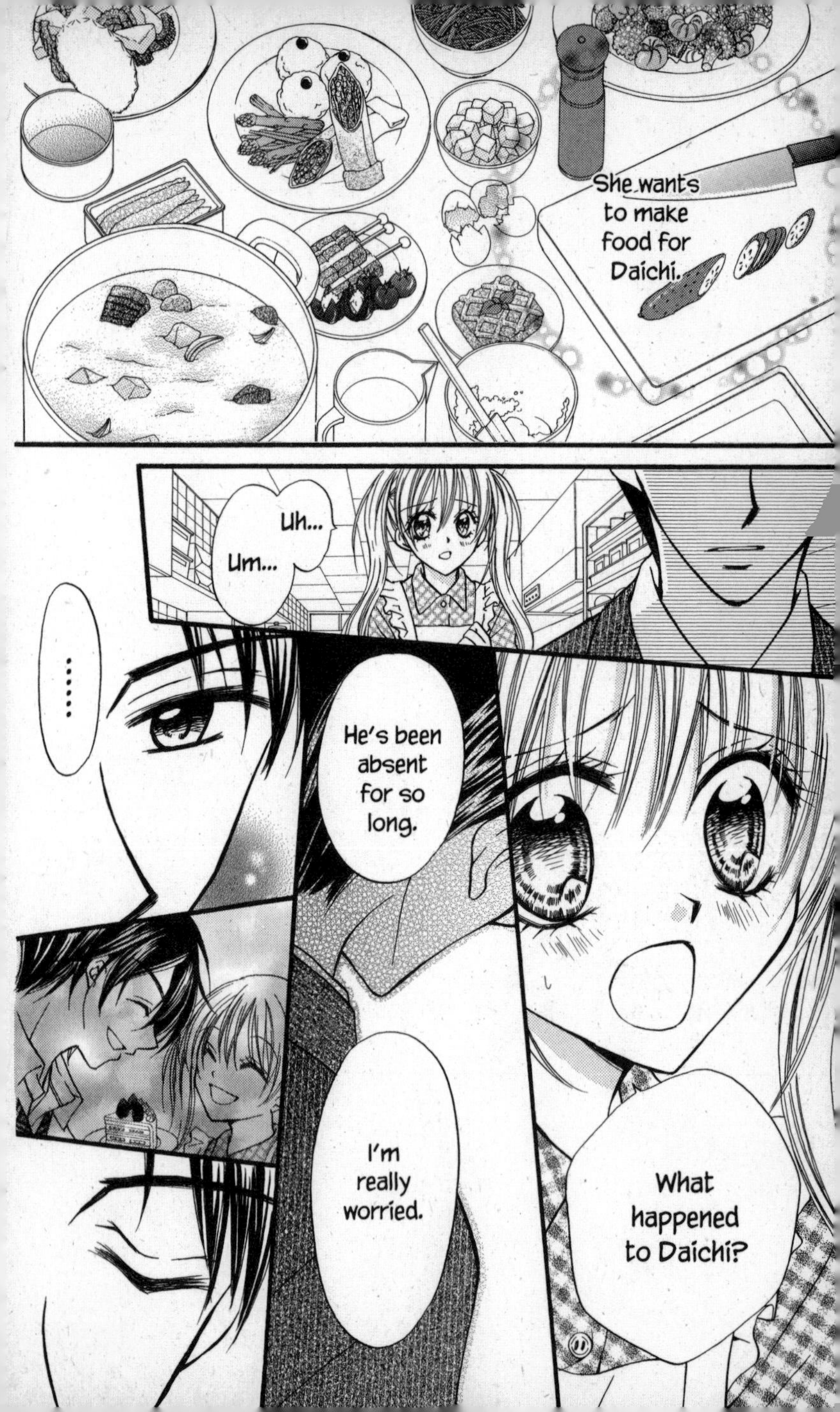
She wants to make food for Daichi.
Uh...
Um...
He's been absent for so long.
I'm really worried.
What happened to Daichi?
......

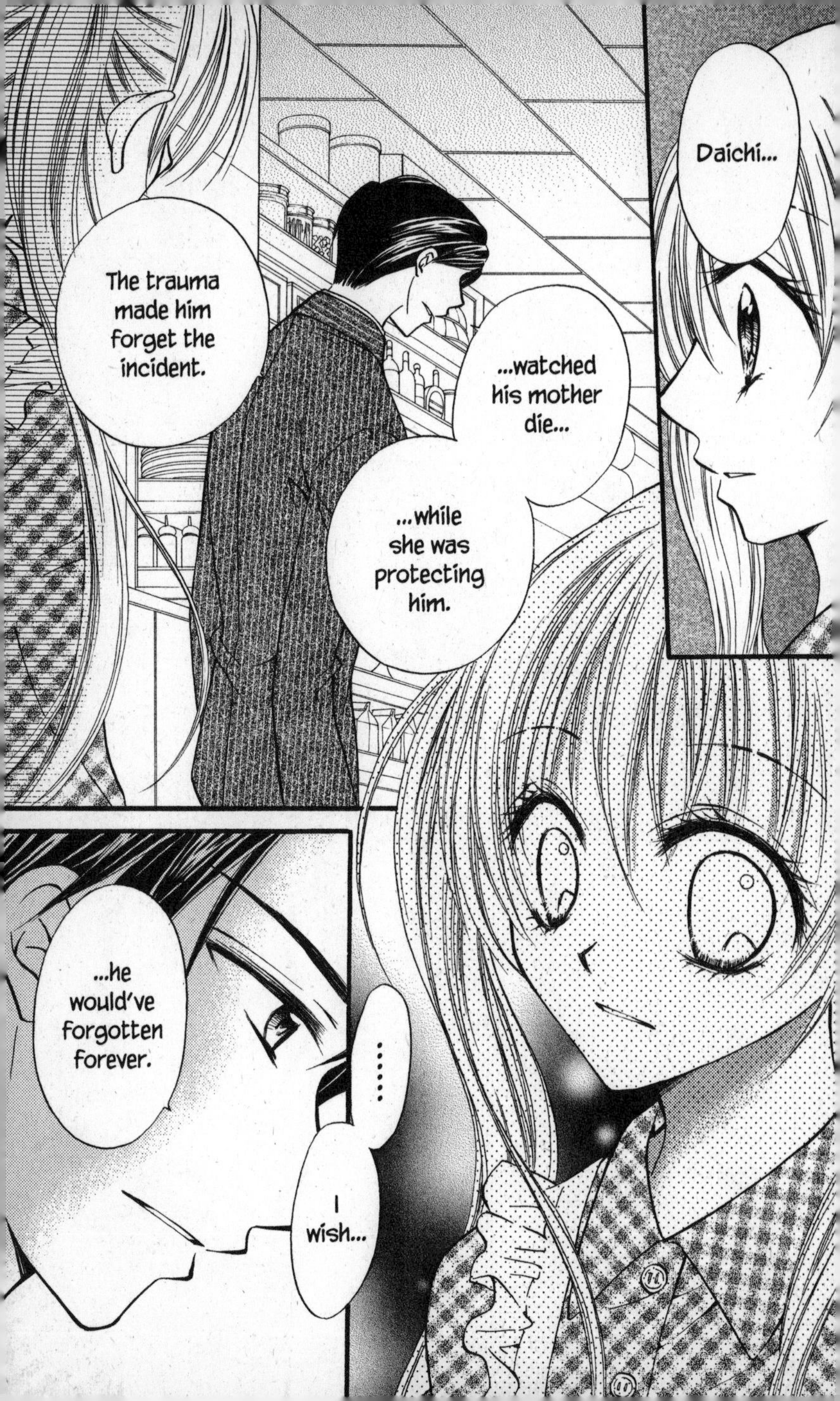
Daichi...
...watched his mother die...
...while she was protecting him.
The trauma made him forget the incident.
......
I wish...
...he would've forgotten forever.

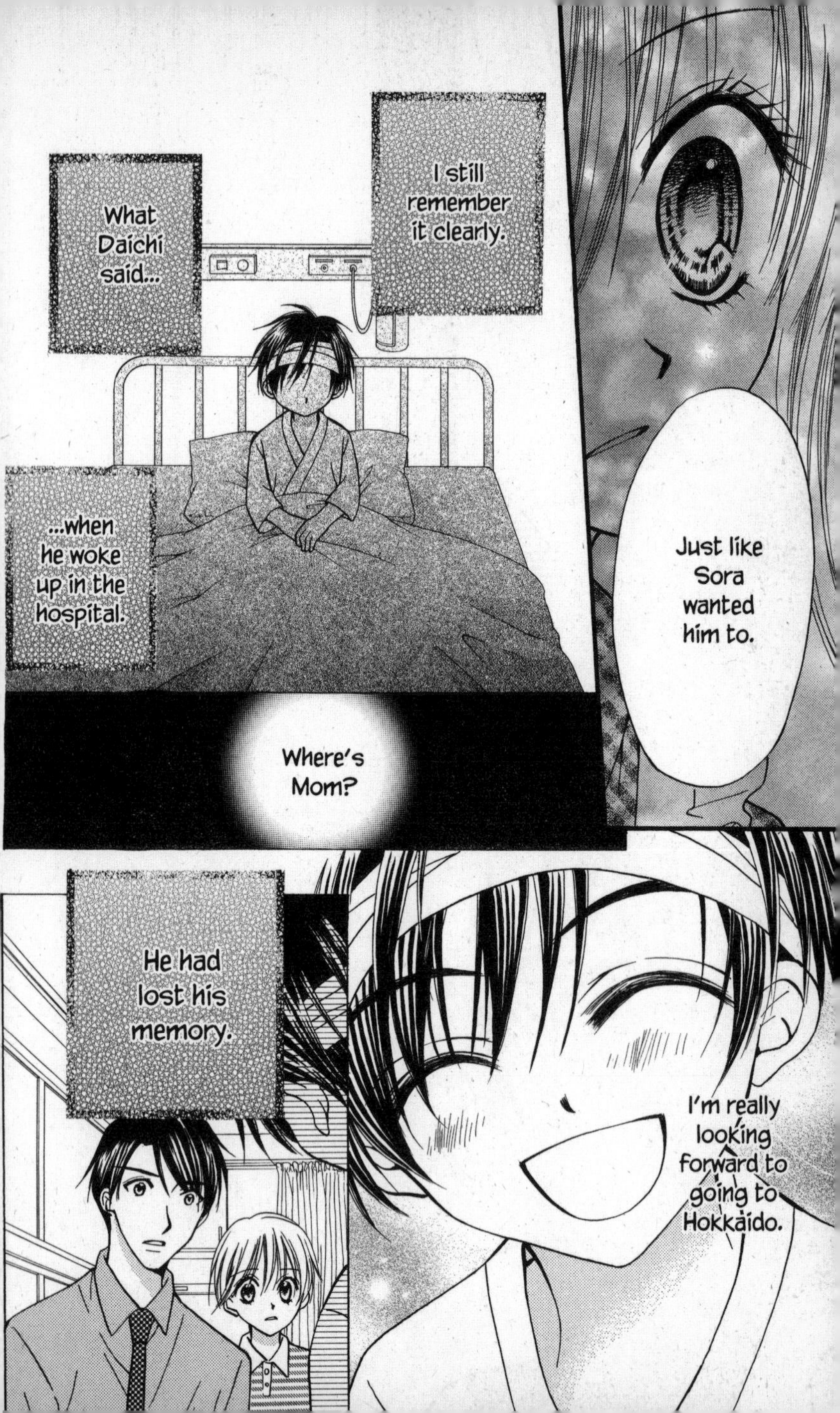
Just like Sora wanted him to.
I still remember it clearly.
What Daichi said...
...when he woke up in the hospital.
Where's Mom?
I'm really looking forward to going to Hokkaido.
He had lost his memory.

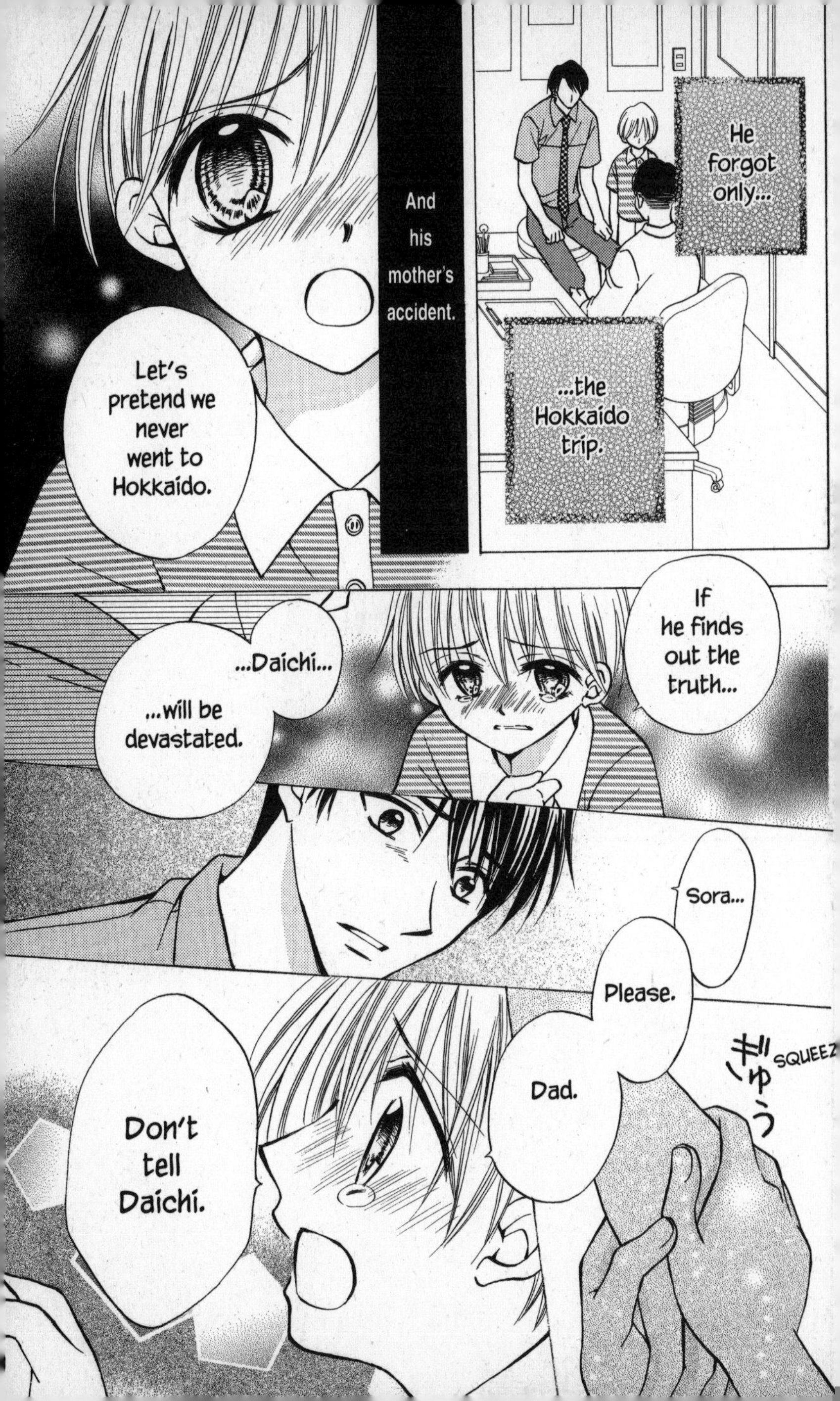
He forgot only...
...the Hokkaido trip.
And his mother's accident.
Let's pretend we never went to Hokkaido.
If he finds out the truth...
...Daichi...
...will be devastated.
Sora...
Please.
Dad.
ぎゅう SQUEEZ
Don't tell Daichi.

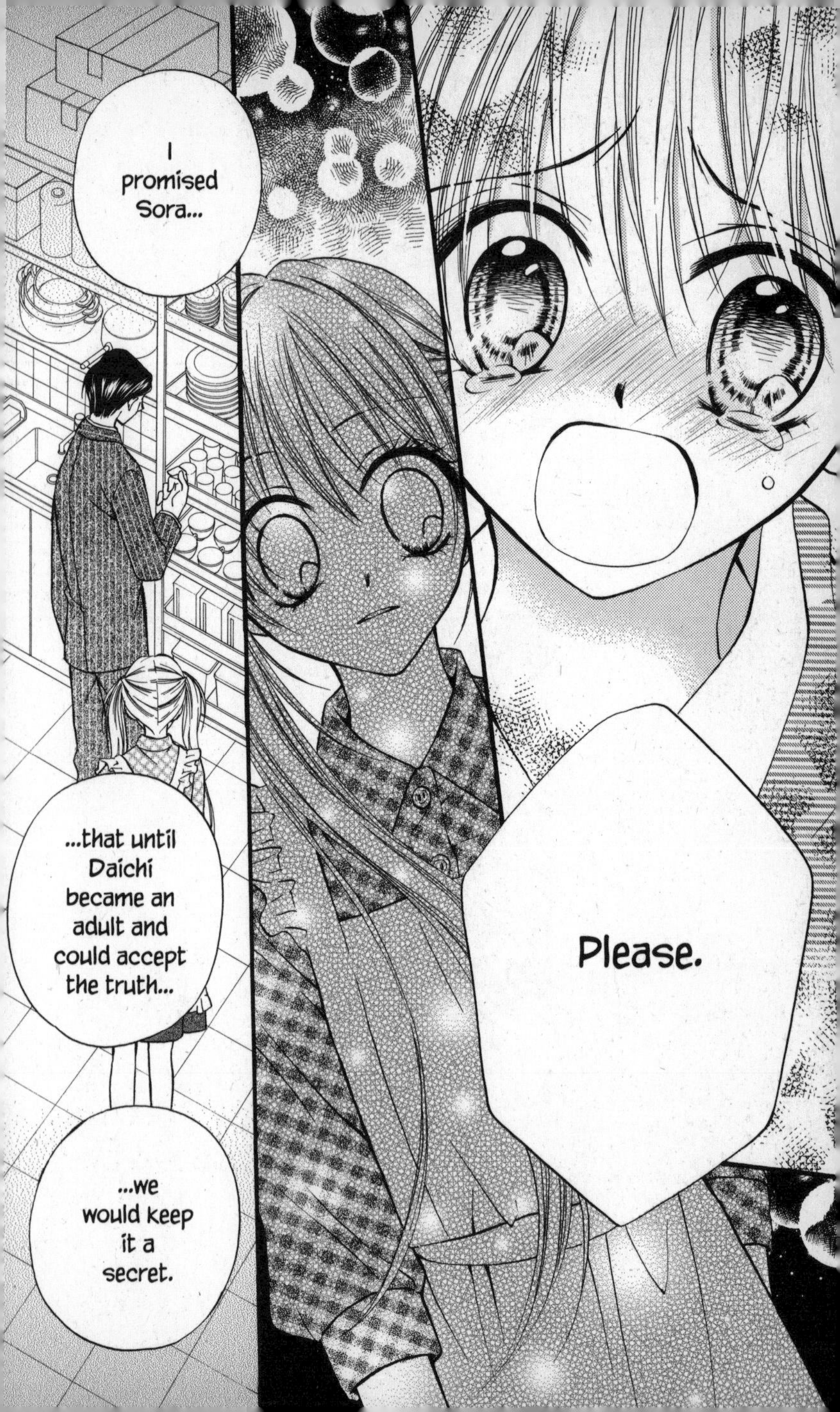
Please.
I promised Sora...
...that until Daichi became an adult and could accept the truth...
...we would keep it a secret.

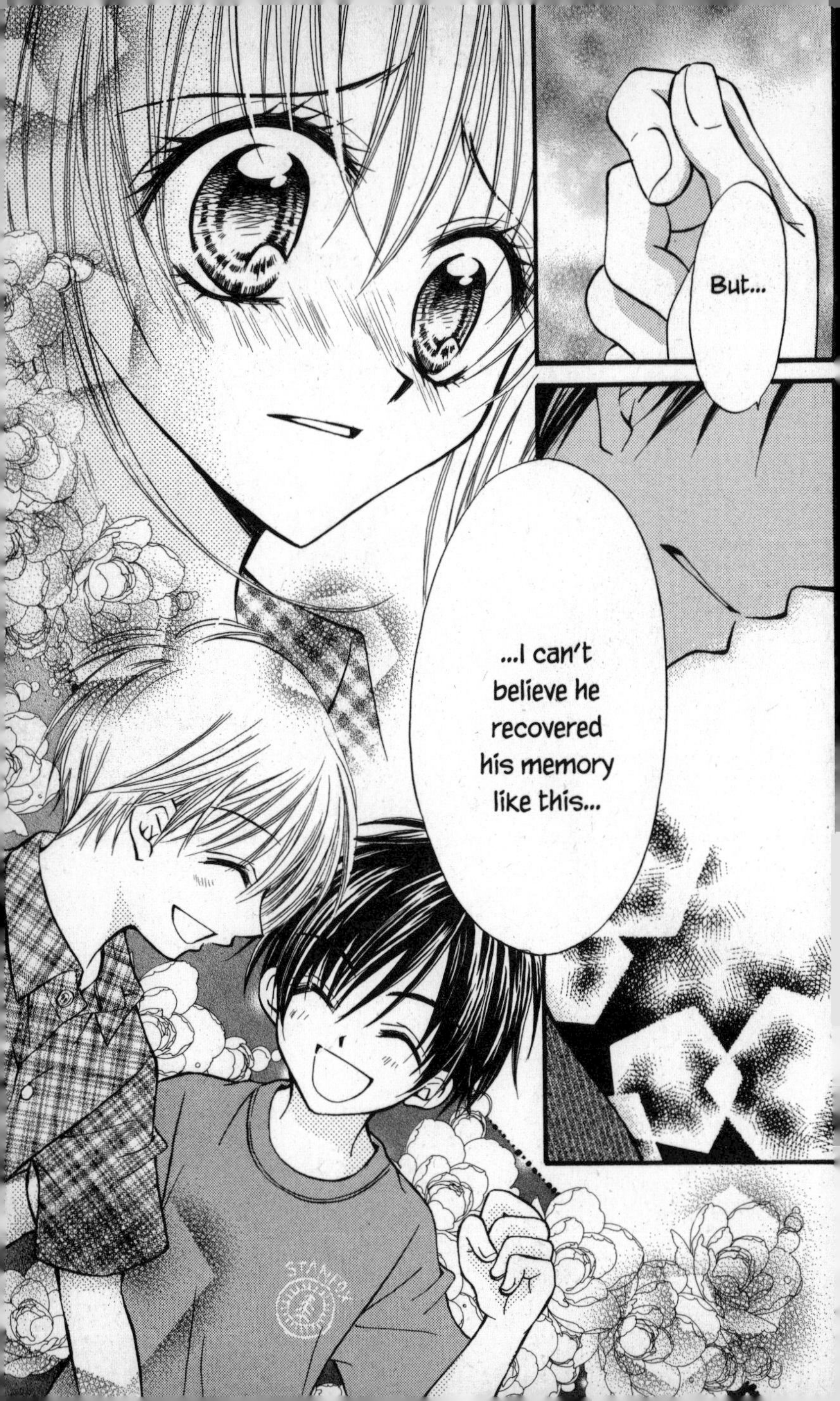
But...
...I can't believe he recovered his memory like this...

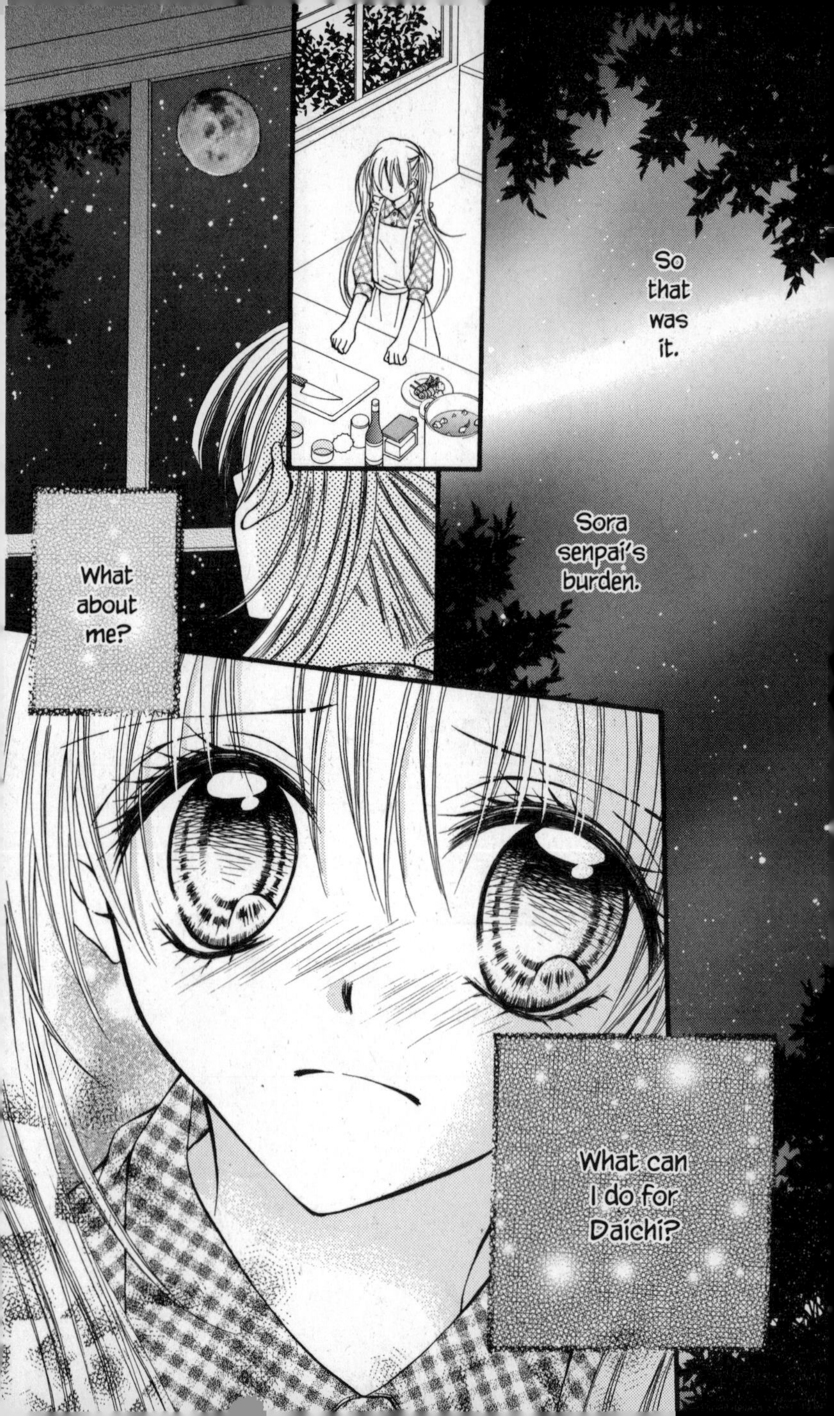
So that was it.
Sora senpai's burden.
What about me?
What can I do for Daichi?

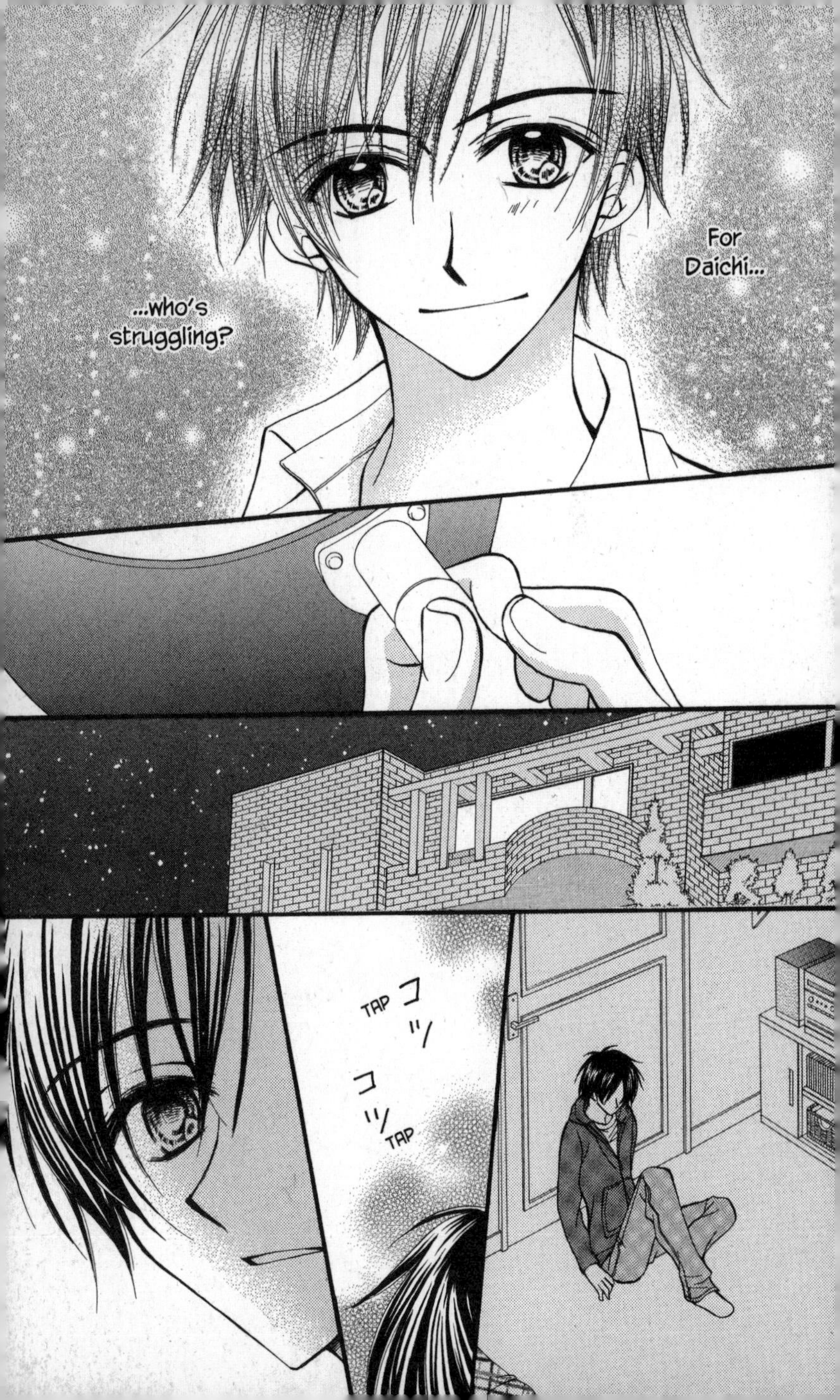
For Daichi...
...who's struggling?
TAP コツ
コツ TAP

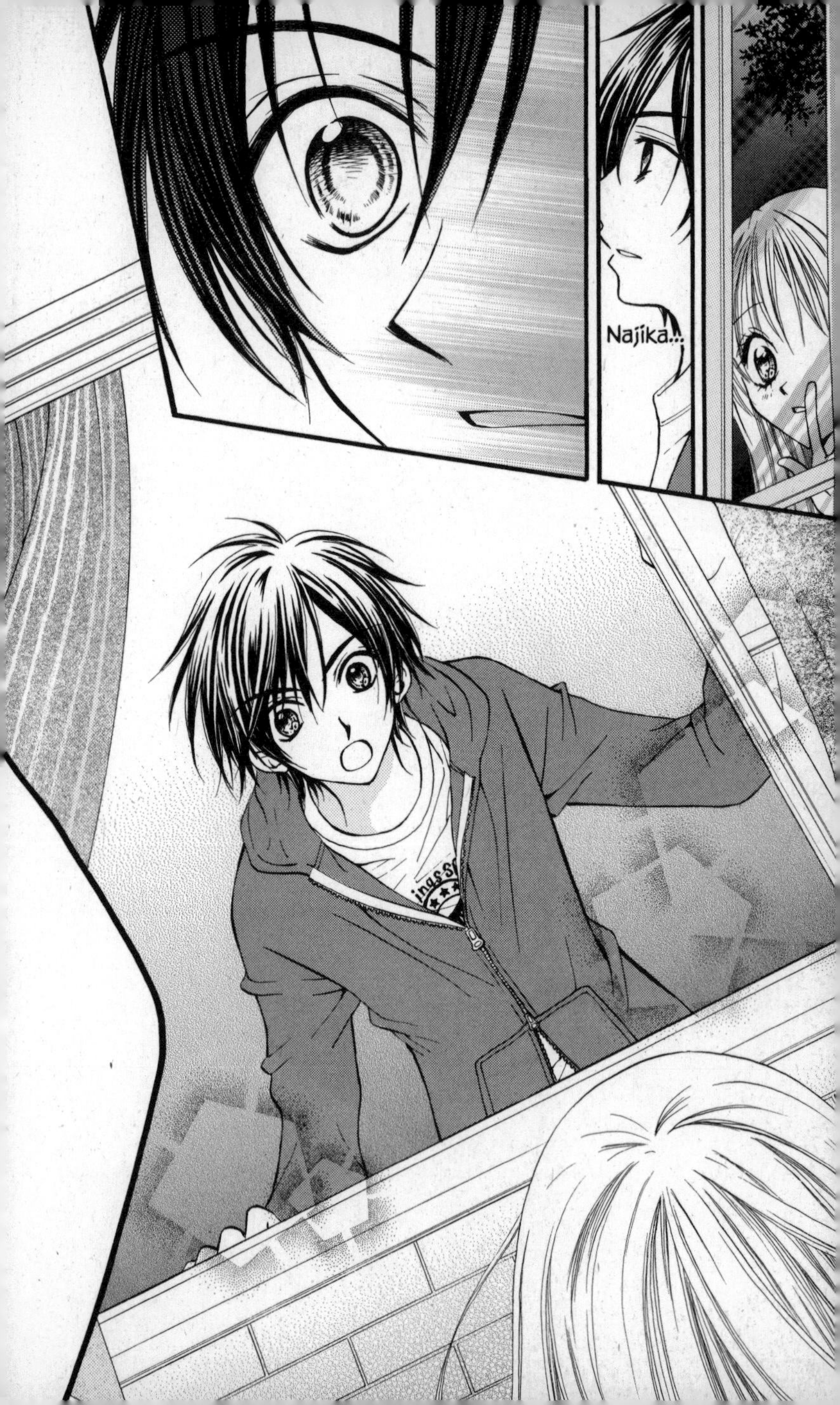
Najika...

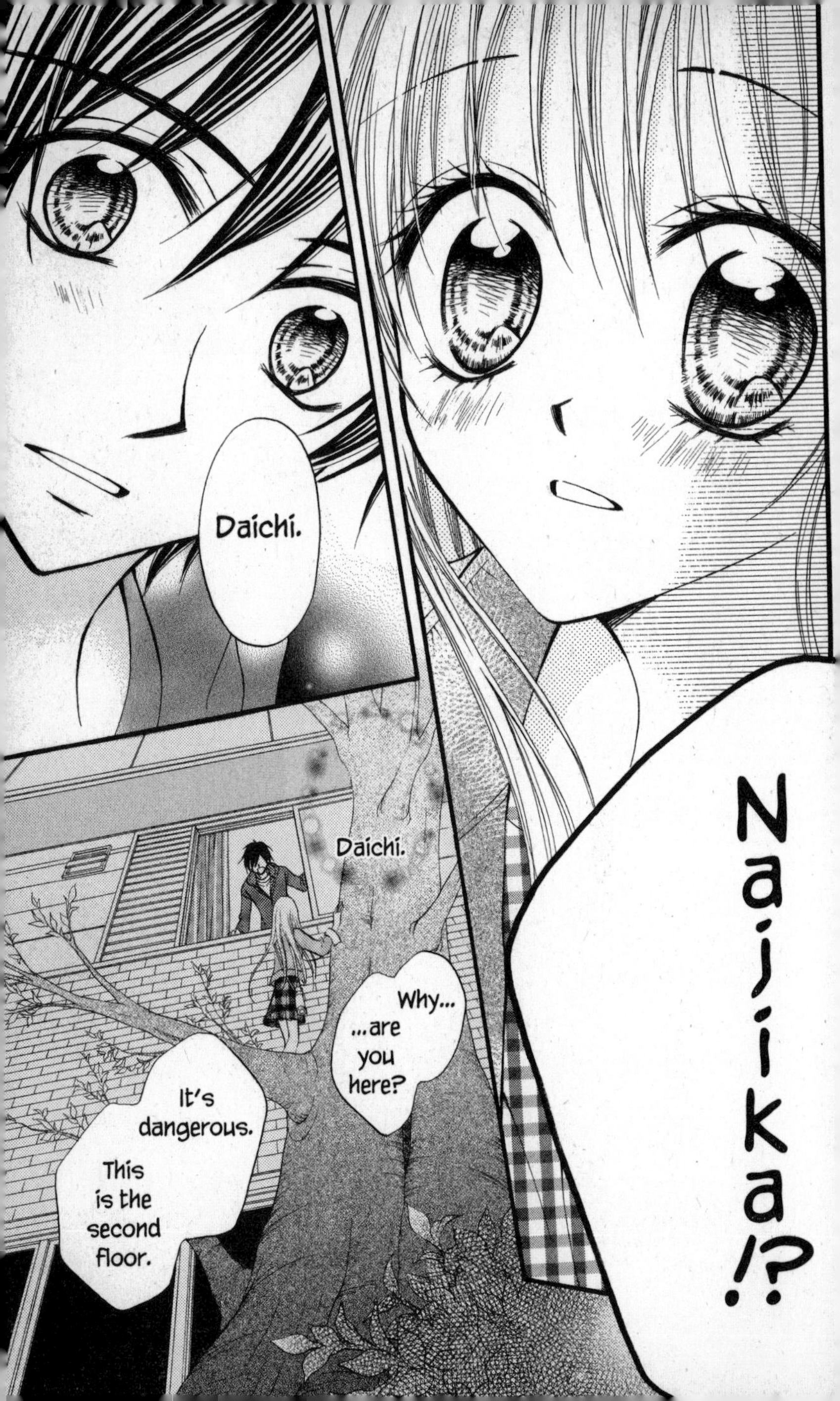

Najika!?
Daichi.
Daichi.
Why...
...are you here?
It's dangerous.
This is the second floor.

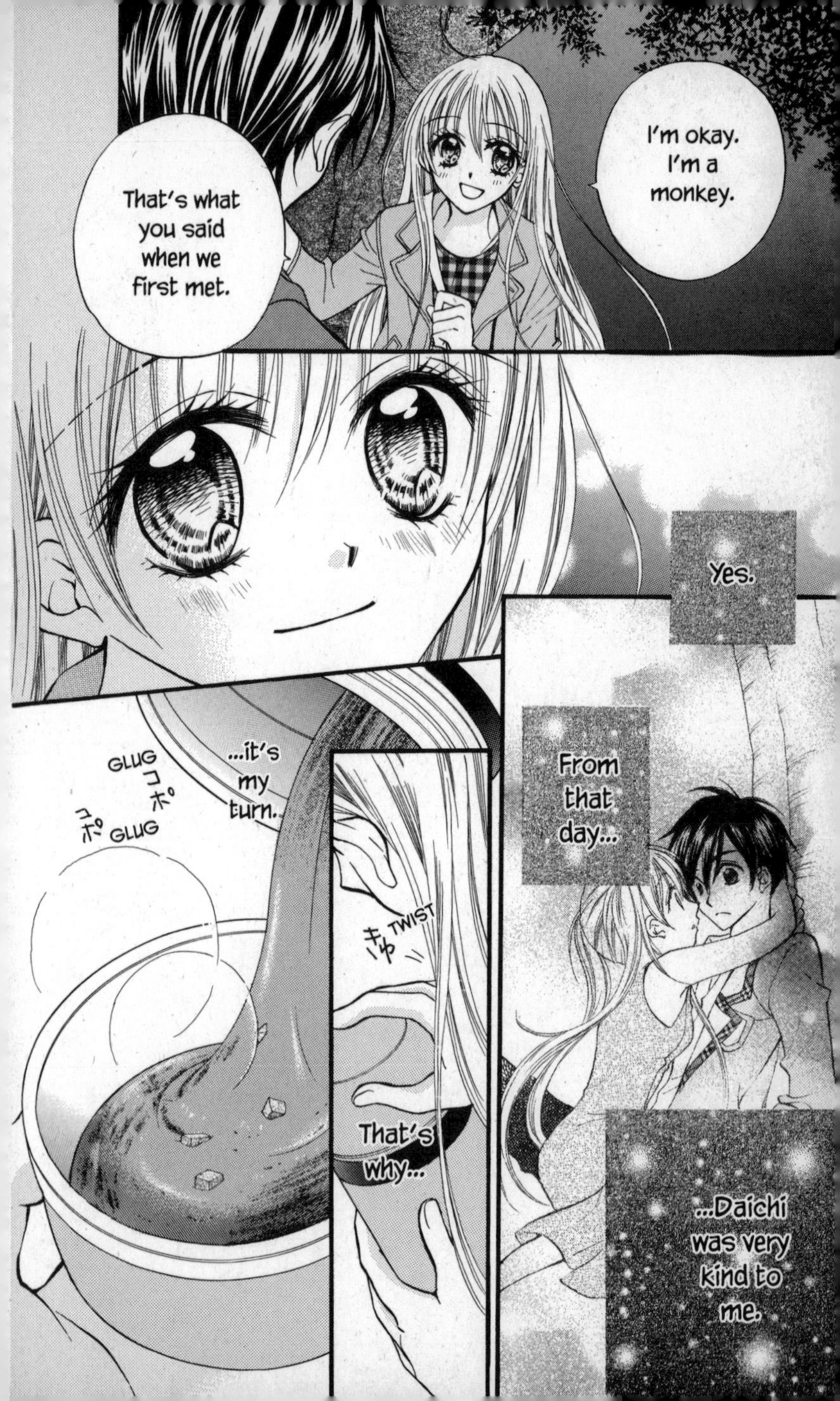

I'm okay. I'm a monkey.
That's what you said when we first met.
Yes.
From that day...
...Daichi was very kind to me.
キュ TWIST
That's why...
GLUG コポ
コポ GLUG
...it's my turn.

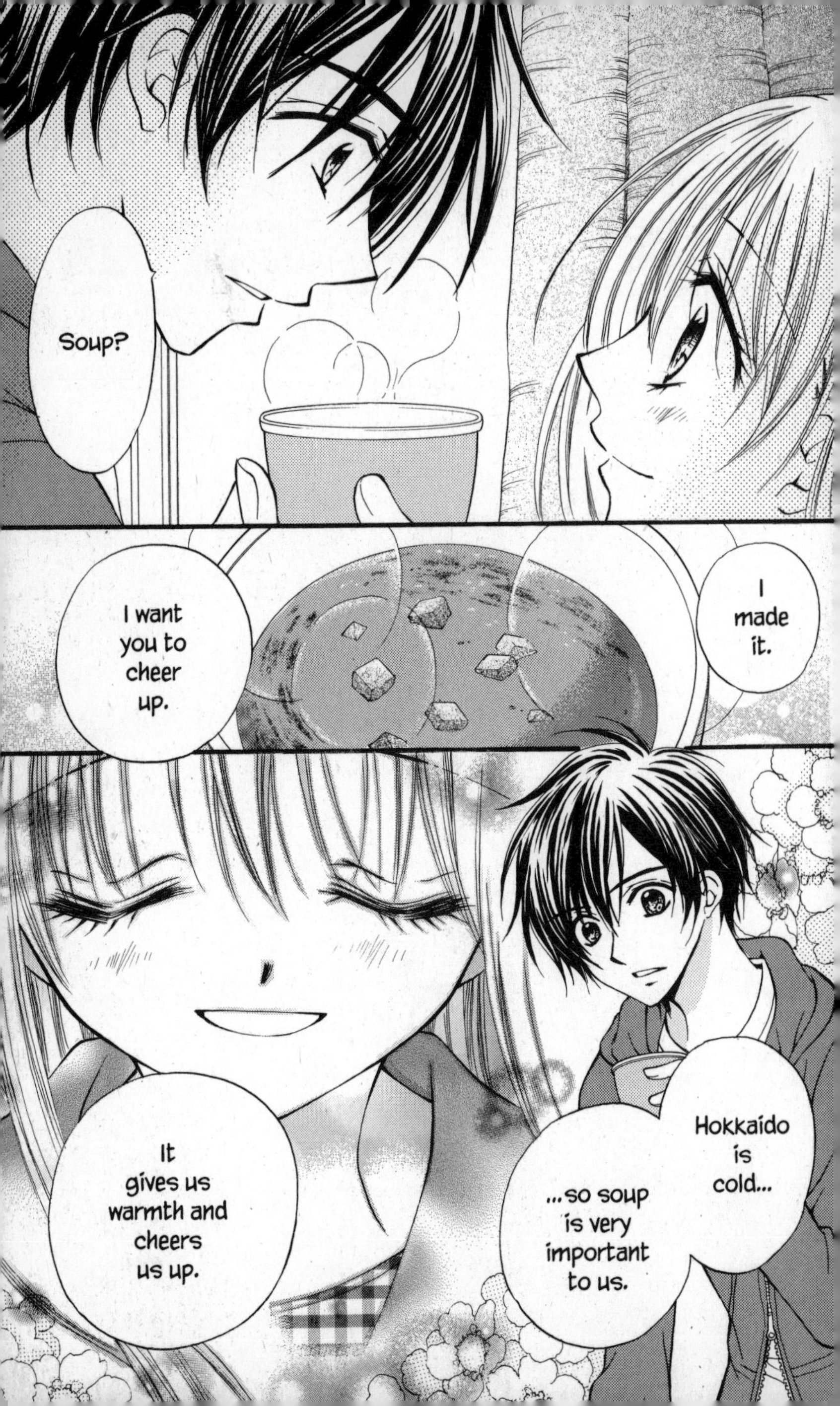
Soup?
I made it.
I want you to cheer up.
Hokkaido is cold...
...so soup is very important to us.
It gives us warmth and cheers us up.

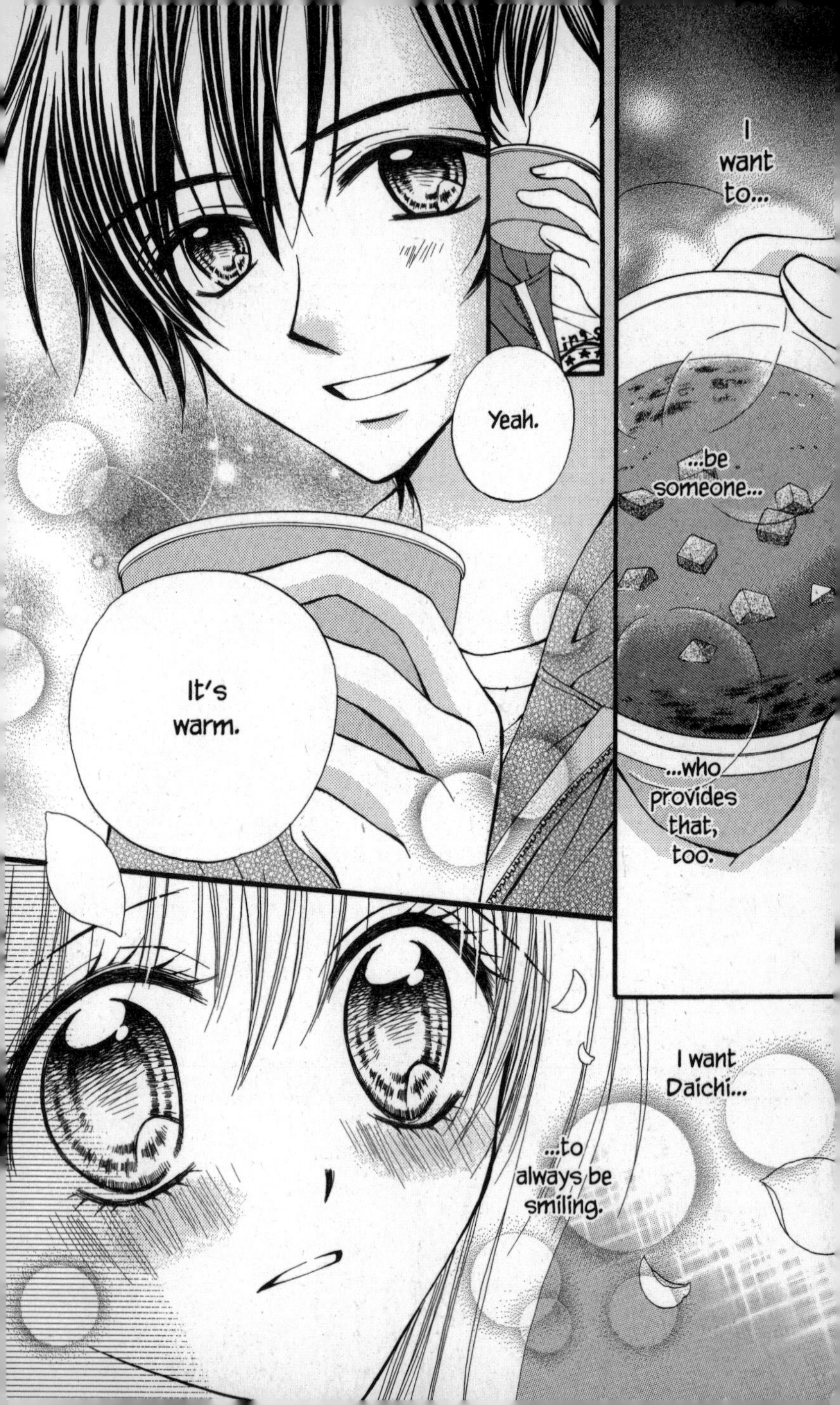
I want to...
...be someone...
...who provides that, too.
Yeah.
It's warm.
I want Daichi...
...to always be smiling.

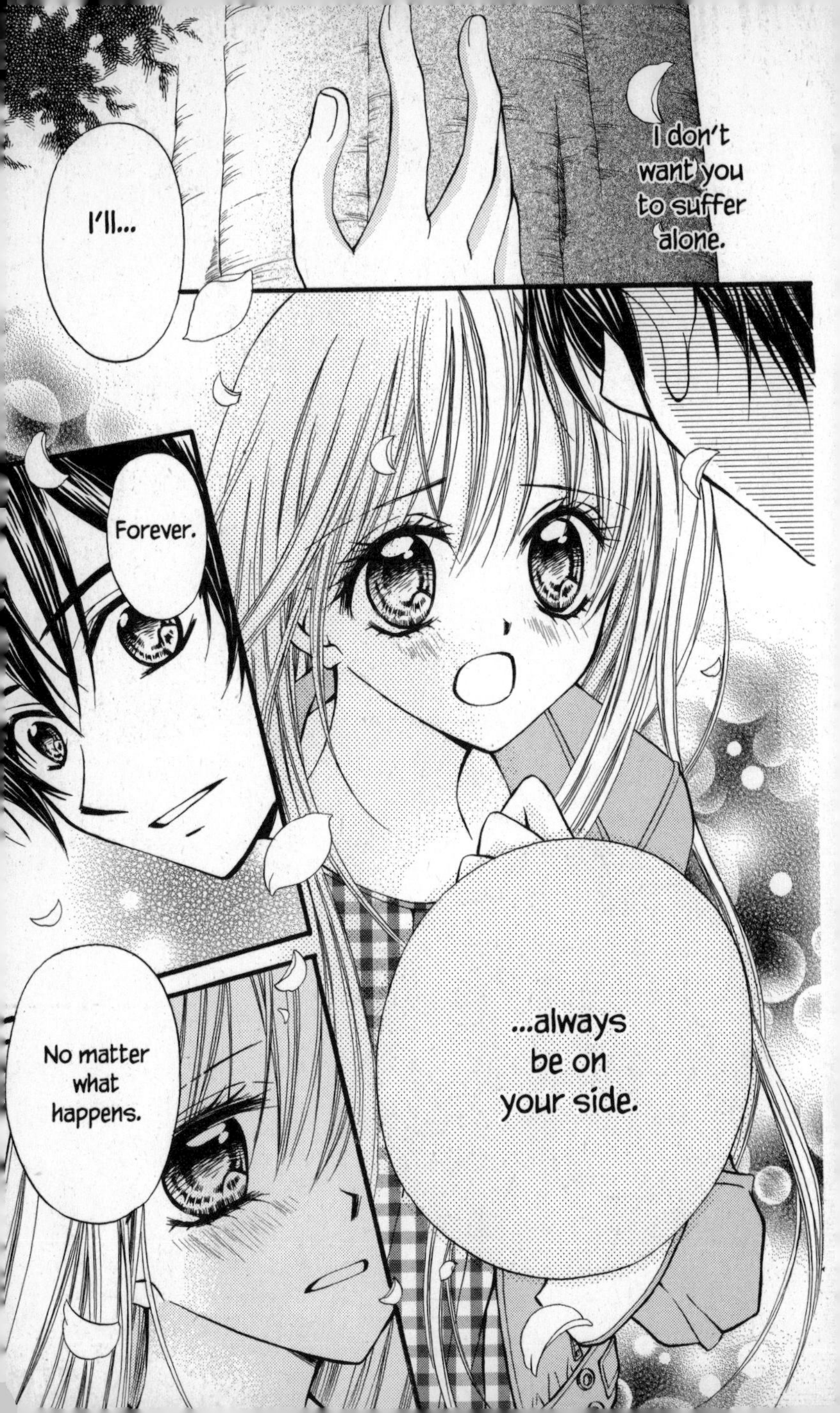
I don't want you to suffer alone.
I'll...
...always be on your side.
Forever.
No matter what happens.

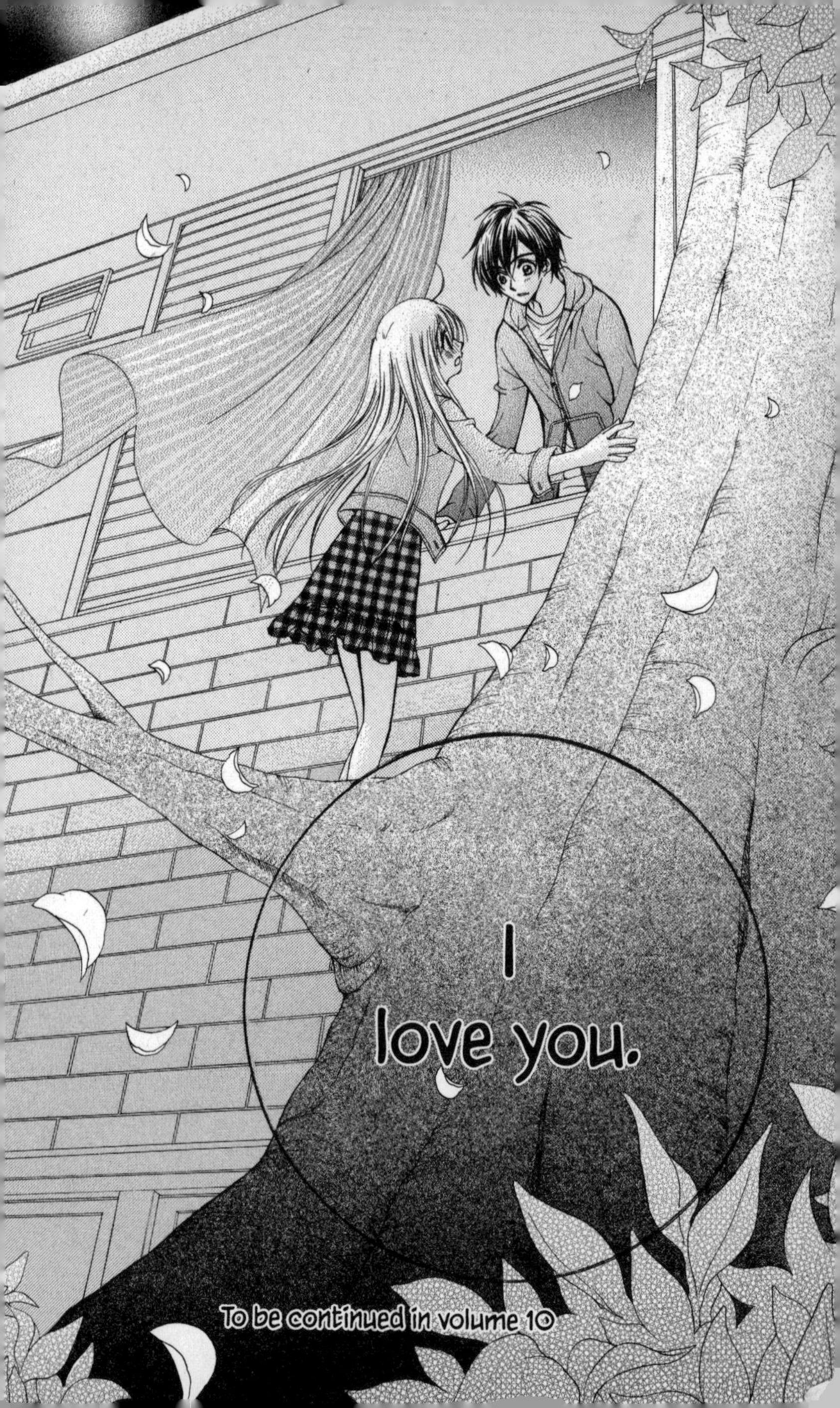

I love you.
To be continued in volume 10

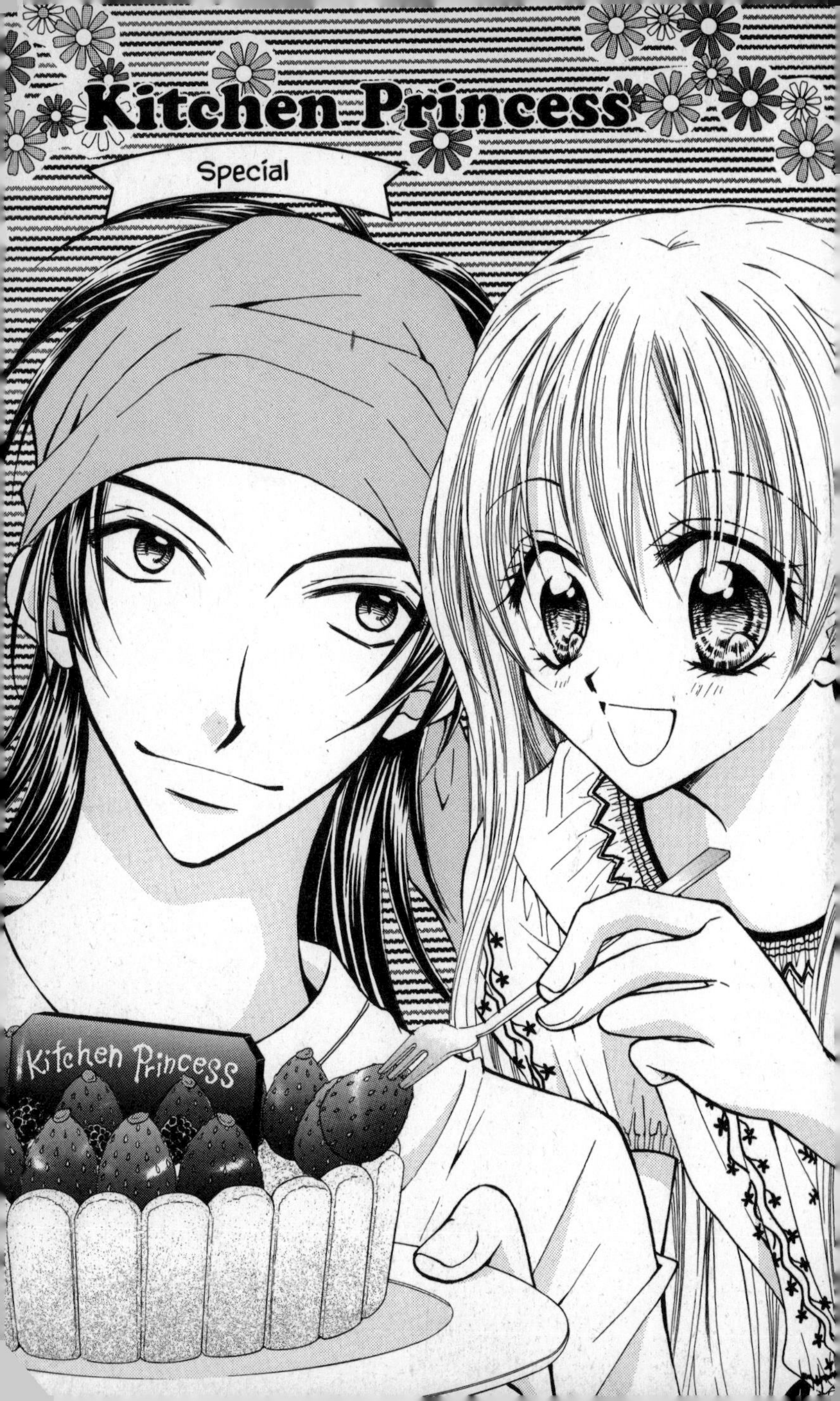
Kitchen Princess
Special
Kitchen Princess

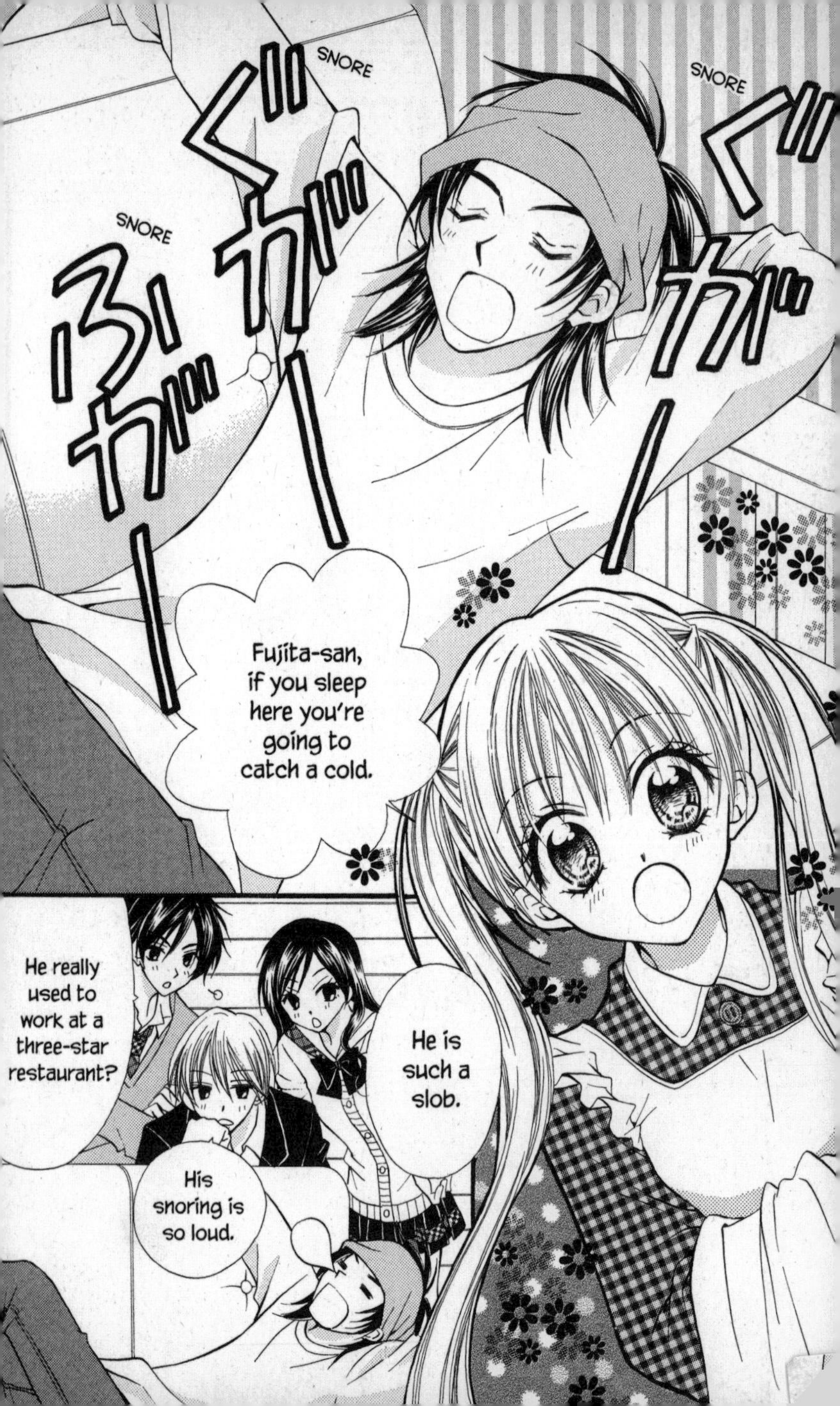
SNORE
ぐがー
SNORE
ぐがー
SNORE
ふがー
Fujita-san, if you sleep here you're going to catch a cold.
He is such a slob.
He really used to work at a three-star restaurant?
His snoring is so loud.

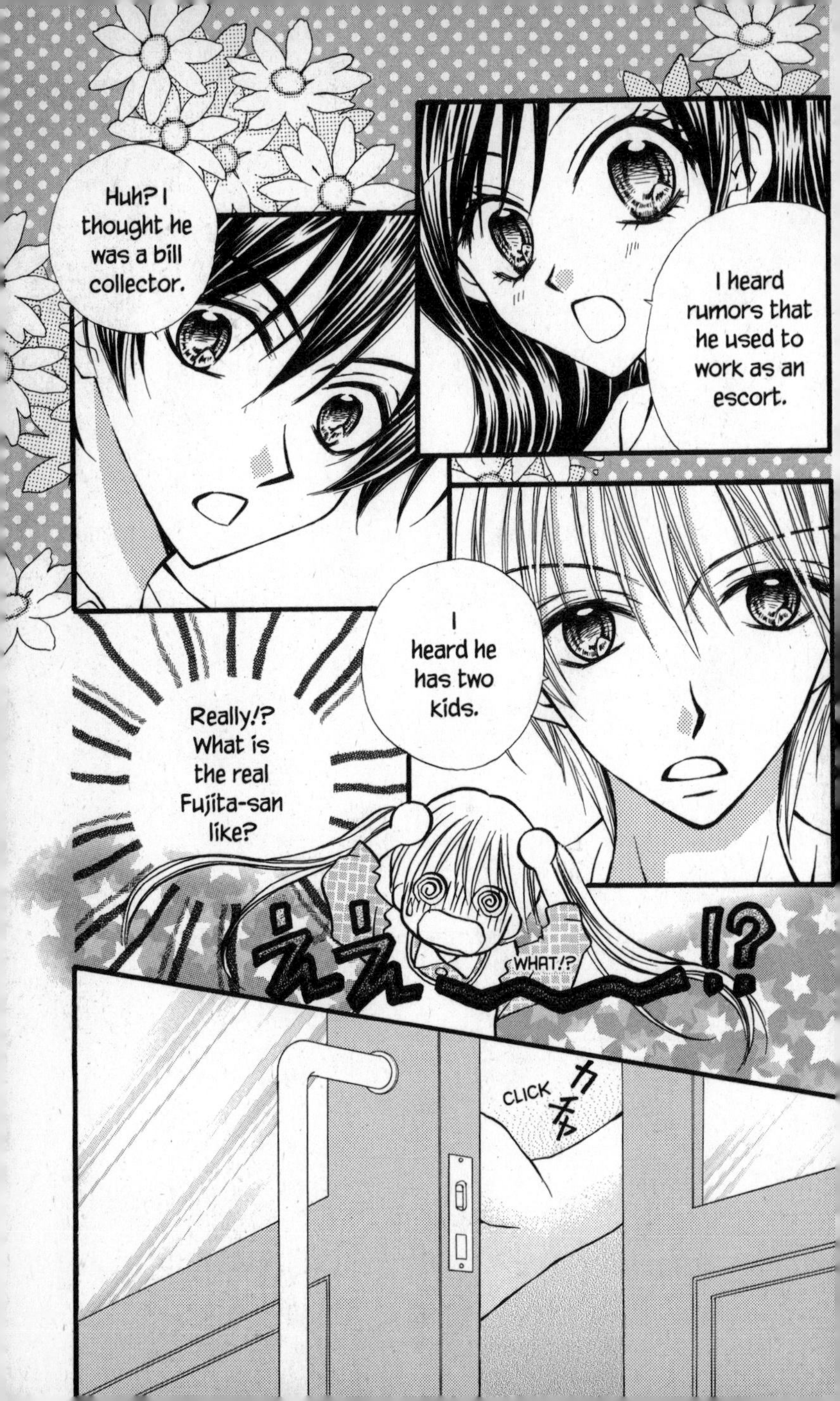
I heard rumors that he used to work as an escort.
Huh? I thought he was a bill collector.
I heard he has two kids.
Really!? What is the real Fujita-san like?
ええーー!?
WHAT!?
カチャ
CLICK

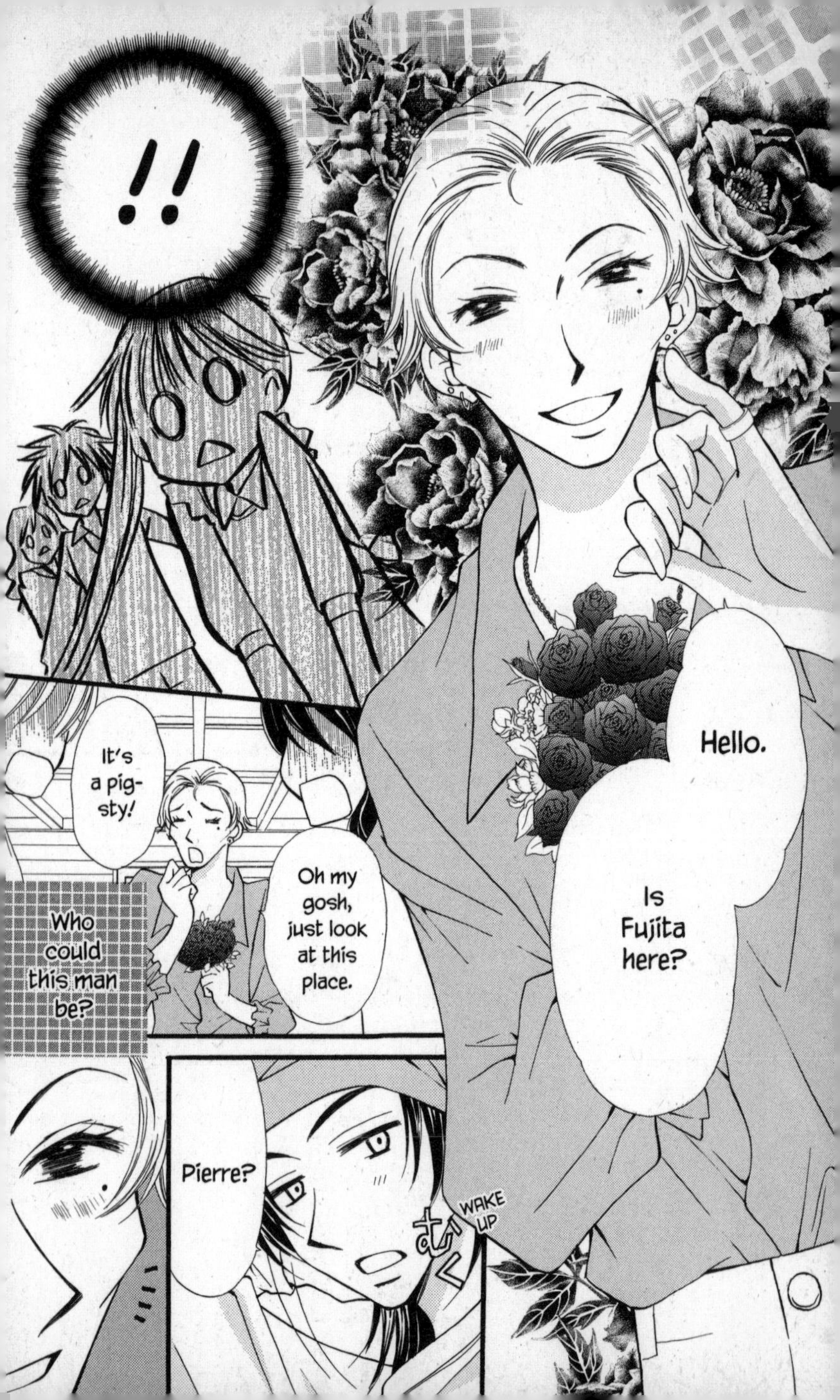
Hello.
Is Fujita here?
!!
Oh my gosh, just look at this place.
It's a pig-sty!
Who could this man be?
Pierre?
WAKE UP

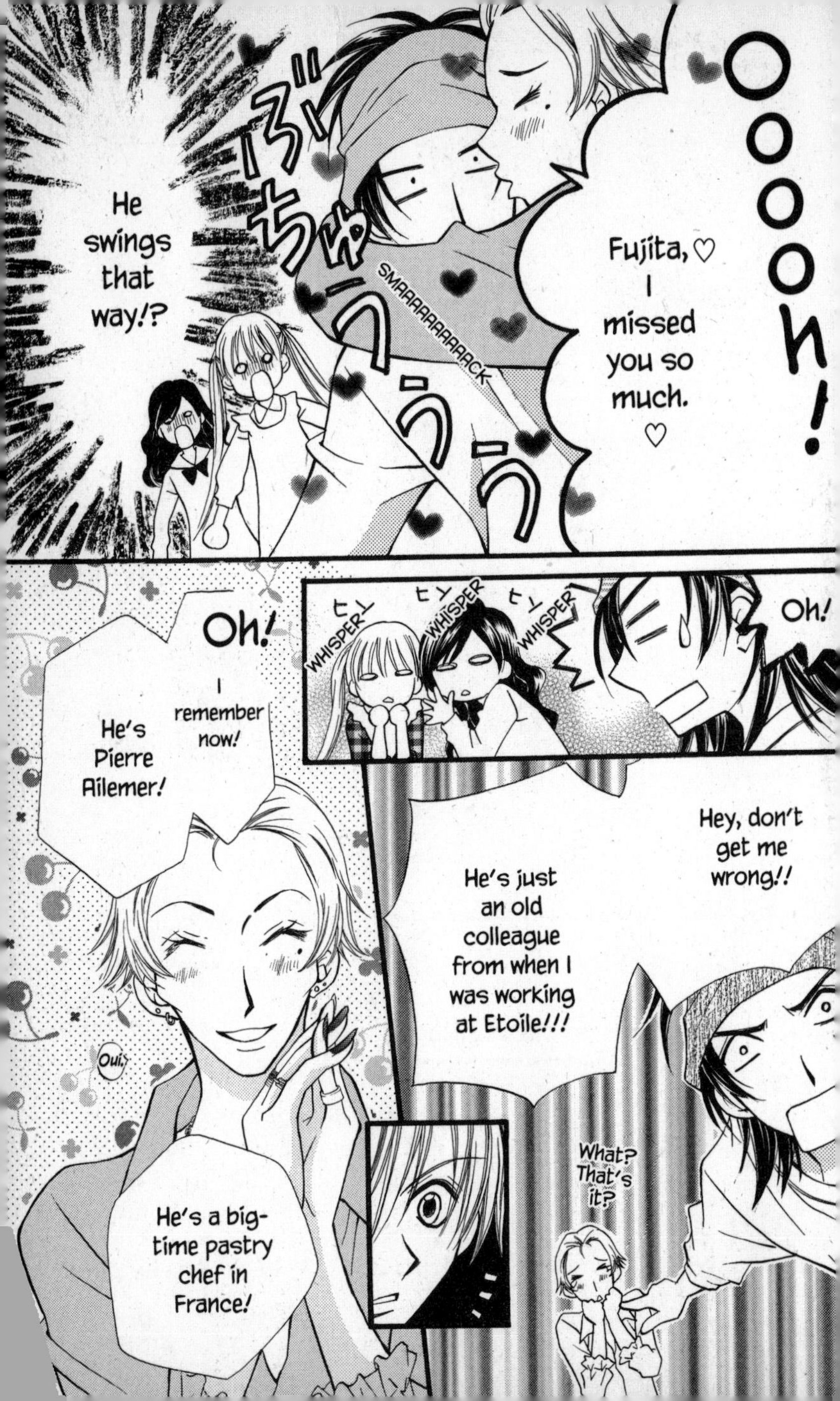

Ooooh!
Fujita, ♡ I missed you so much. ♡
ぶちゅーううう
SMAAAAAAAAAACK
He swings that way!?
Oh!
ヒソ WHISPER
ヒソ WHISPER
ヒソ WHISPER
Hey, don't get me wrong!!
He's just an old colleague from when I was working at Etoile!!!
What? That's it?
...
Oh!
I remember now!
He's Pierre Ailemer!
Oui.
He's a big-time pastry chef in France!

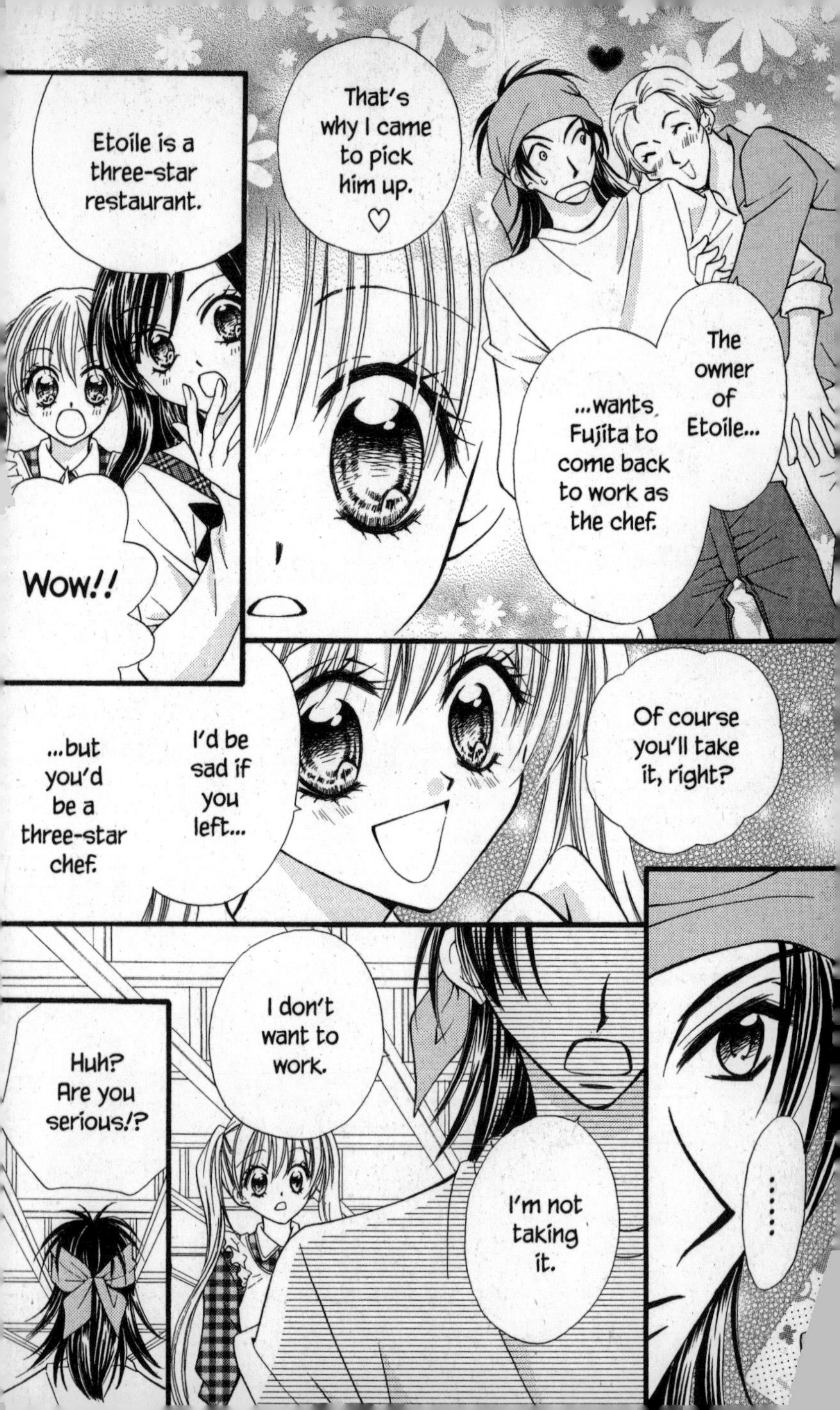
The owner of Etoile...
...wants Fujita to come back to work as the chef.
That's why I came to pick him up. ♡
Etoile is a three-star restaurant.
WOW!!
Of course you'll take it, right?
I'd be sad if you left...
...but you'd be a three-star chef.
......
I'm not taking it.
I don't want to work.
Huh? Are you serious!?

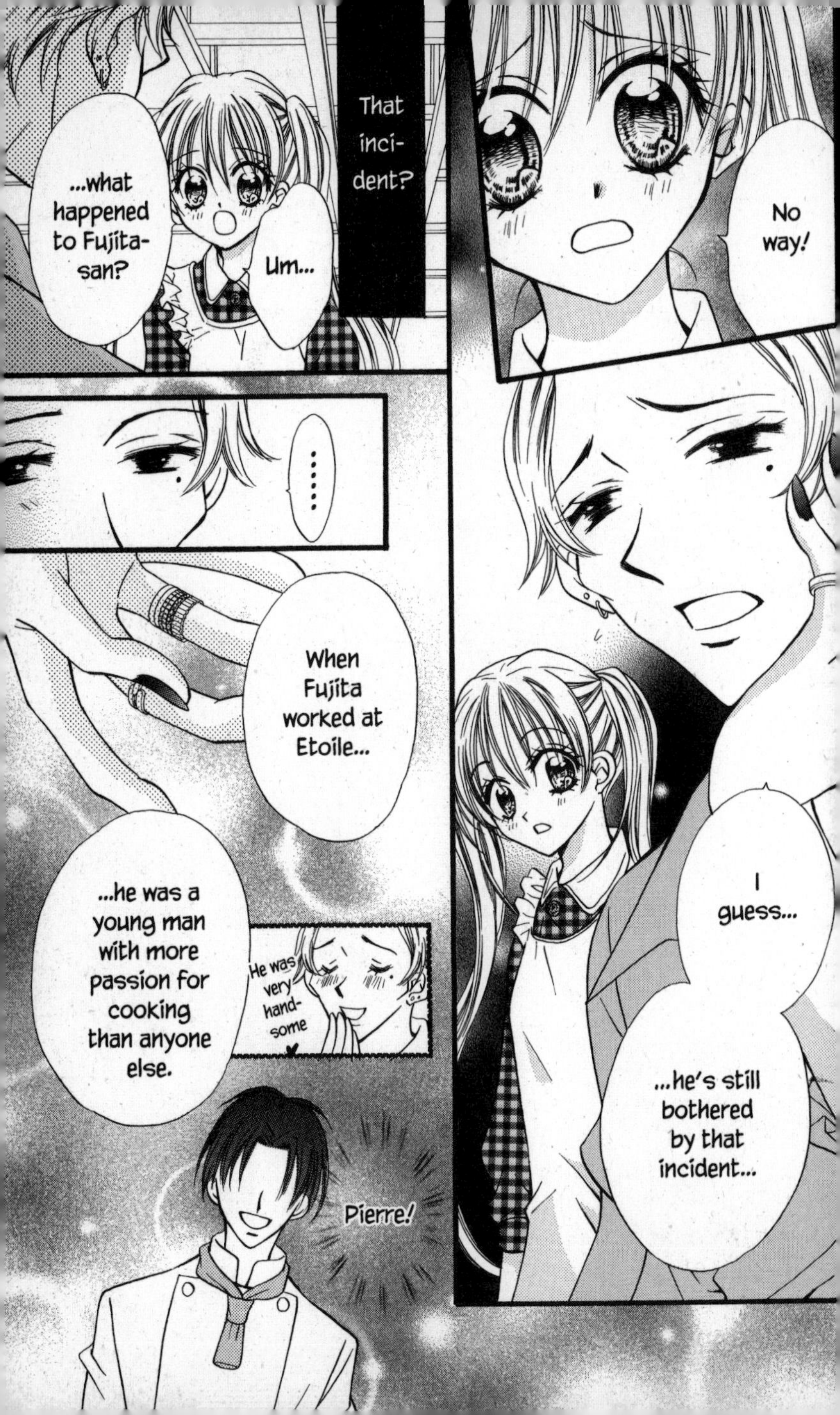
No way!
I guess...
...he's still bothered by that incident...
That incident?
Um...
...what happened to Fujita-san?
......
When Fujita worked at Etoile...
He was very hand-some
...he was a young man with more passion for cooking than anyone else.
Pierre!

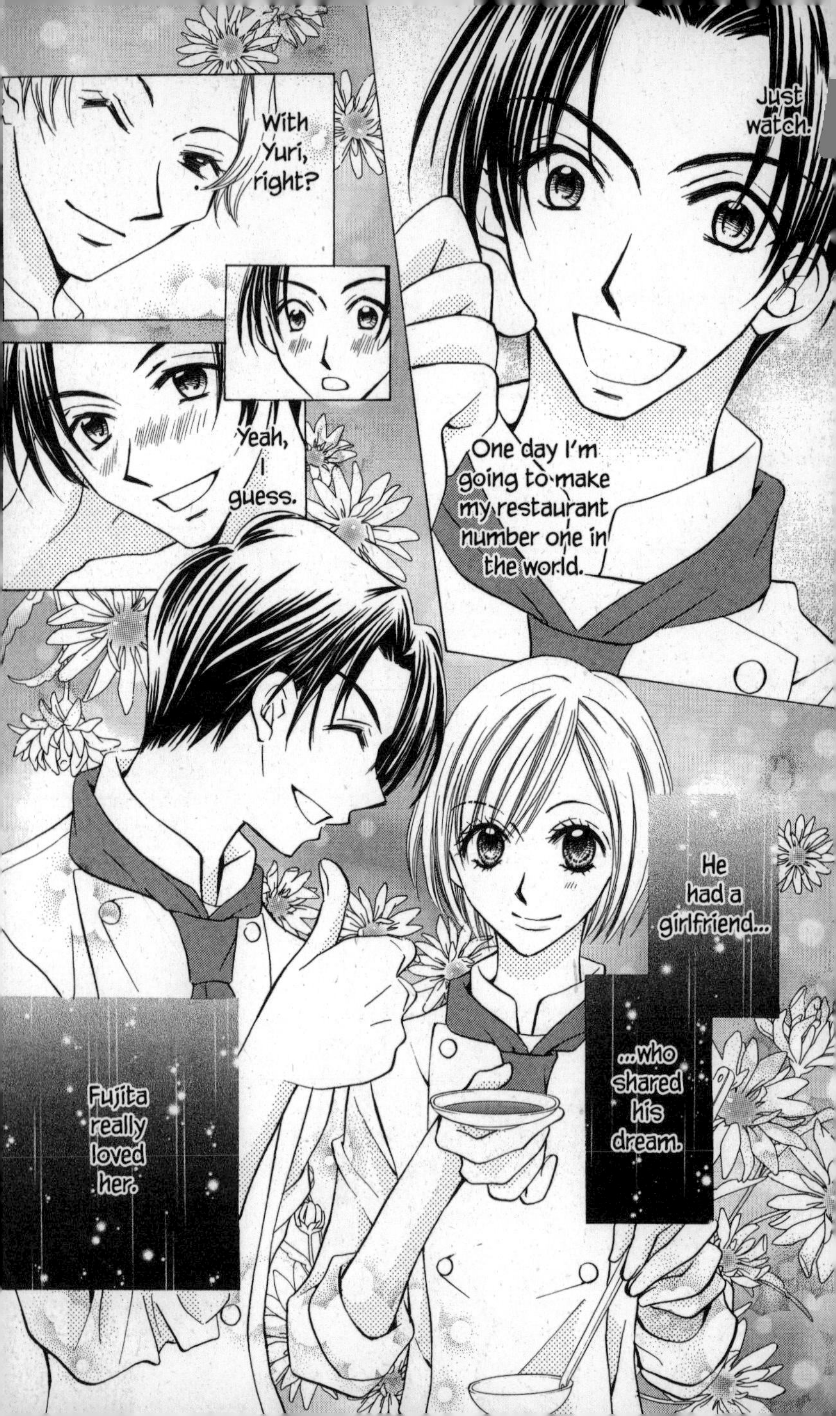
Just watch.
One day I'm going to make my restaurant number one in the world.
With Yuri, right?
Yeah, I guess.
He had a girlfriend...
...who shared his dream.
Fujita really loved her.

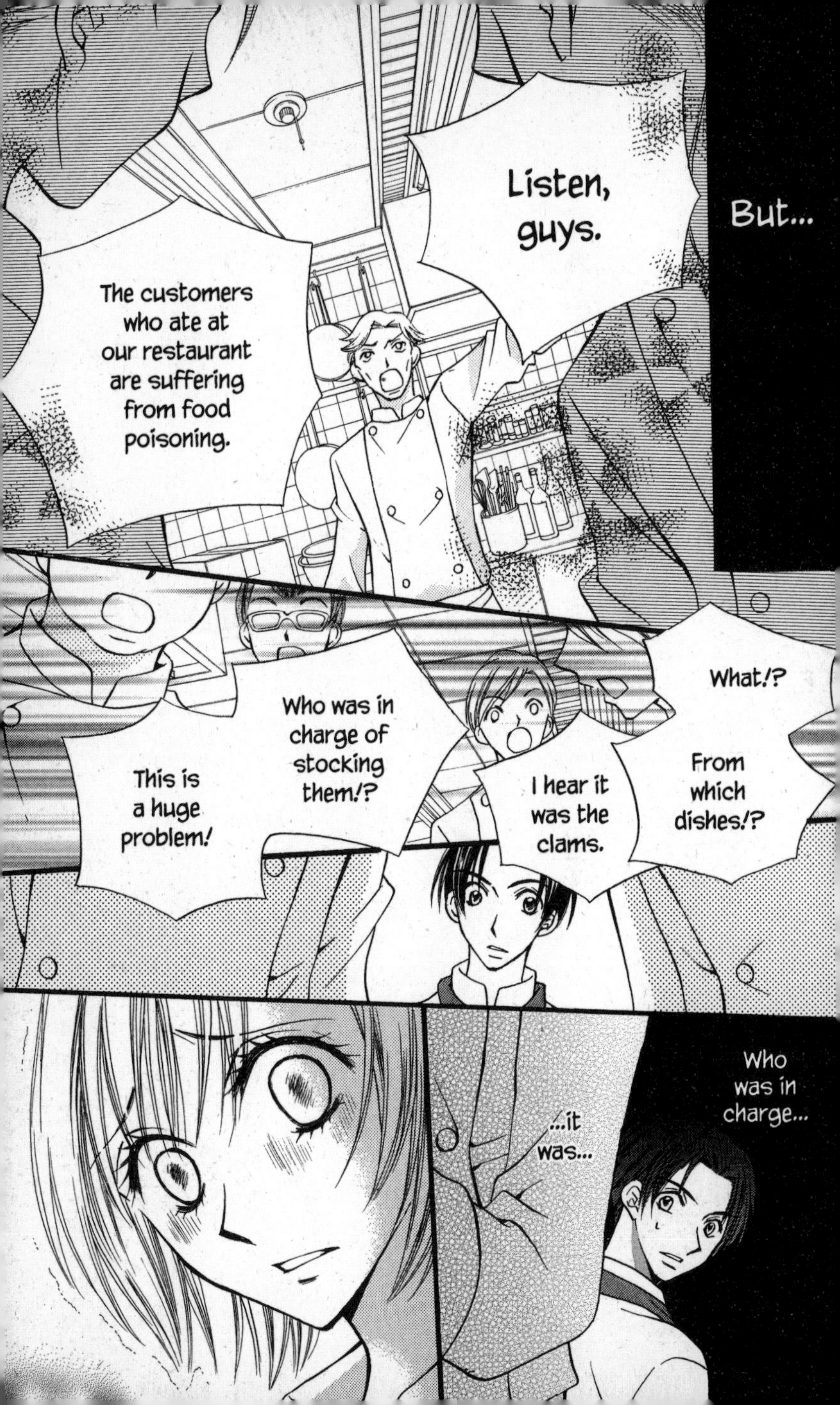
But...
Listen, guys.
The customers who ate at our restaurant are suffering from food poisoning.
What!?
From which dishes!?
I hear it was the clams.
Who was in charge of stocking them!?
This is a huge problem!
Who was in charge...
...it was...

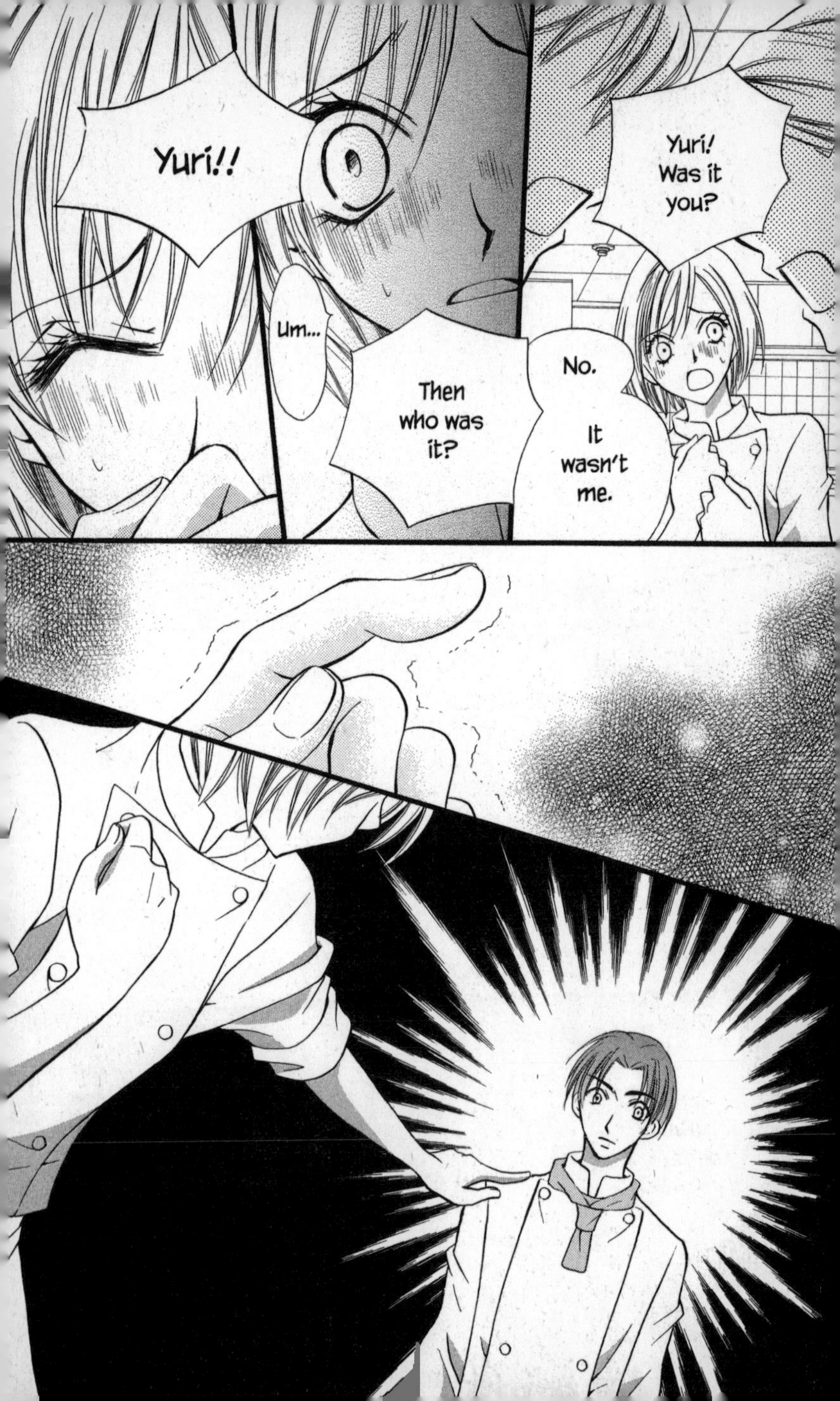
Yuri! Was it you?
No.
It wasn't me.
Then who was it?
Um...
Yuri!!

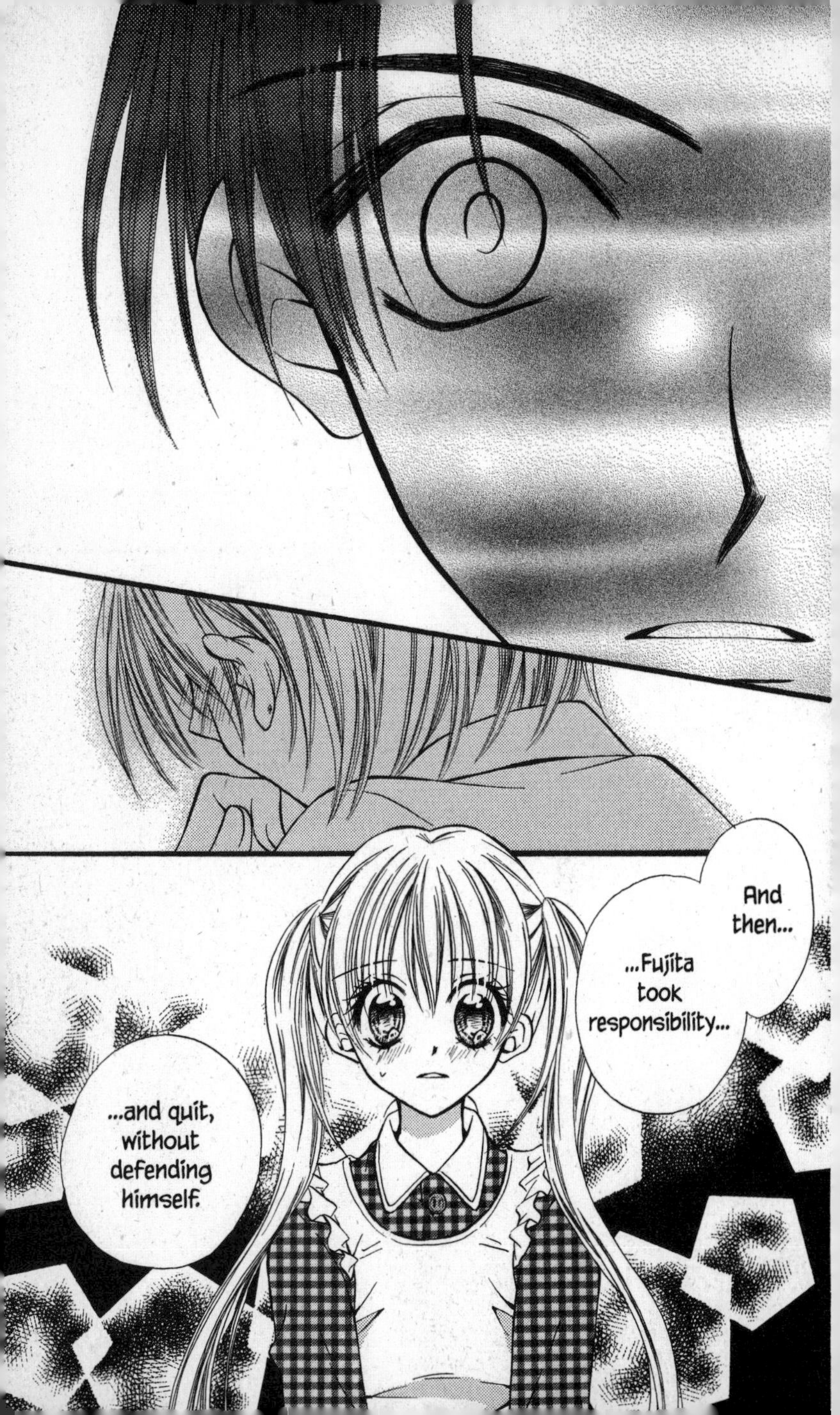
And then...
...Fujita took responsibility...
...and quit, without defending himself.

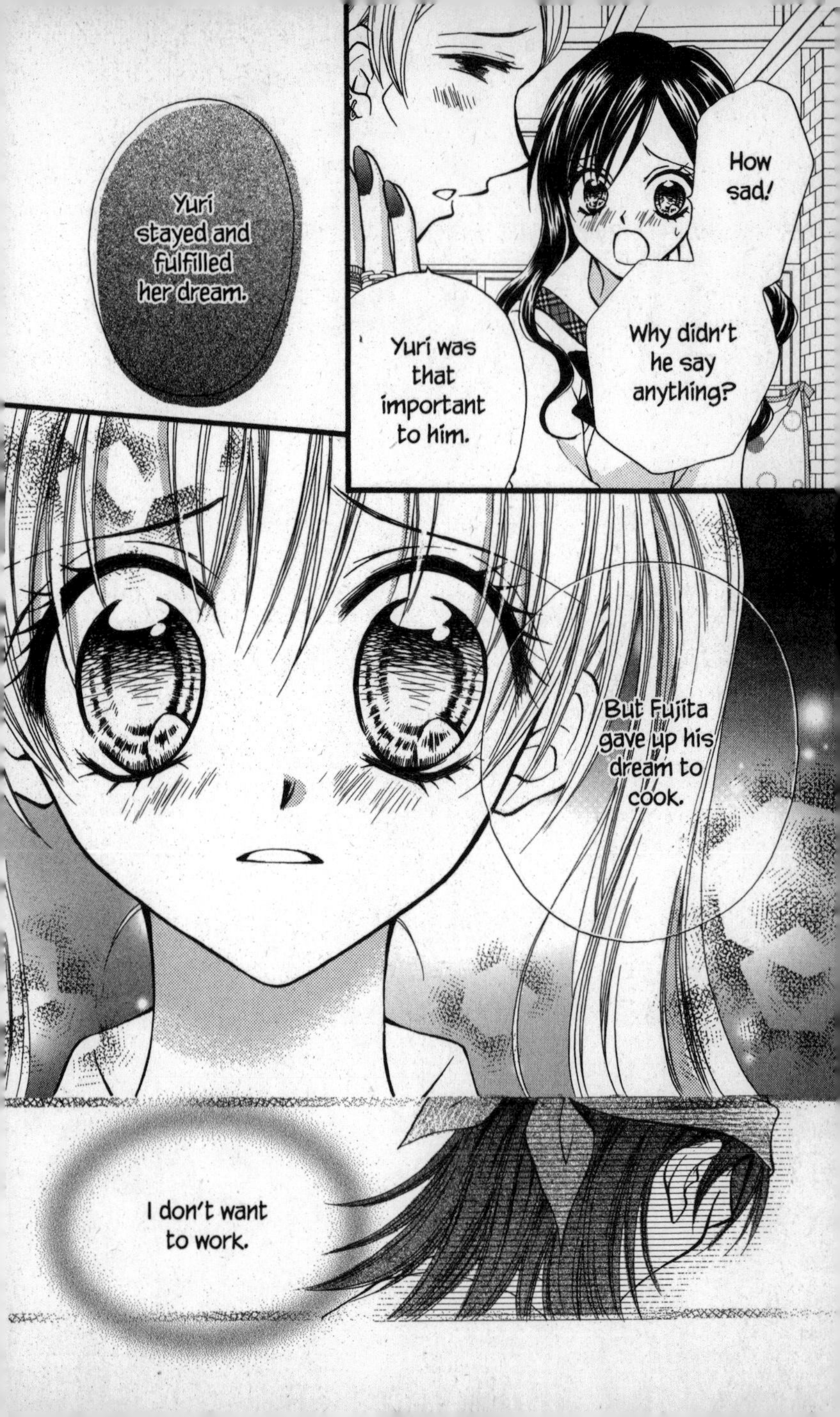
How sad!
Why didn't he say anything?
Yuri was that important to him.
Yuri stayed and fulfilled her dream.
But Fujita gave up his dream to cook.
I don't want to work.

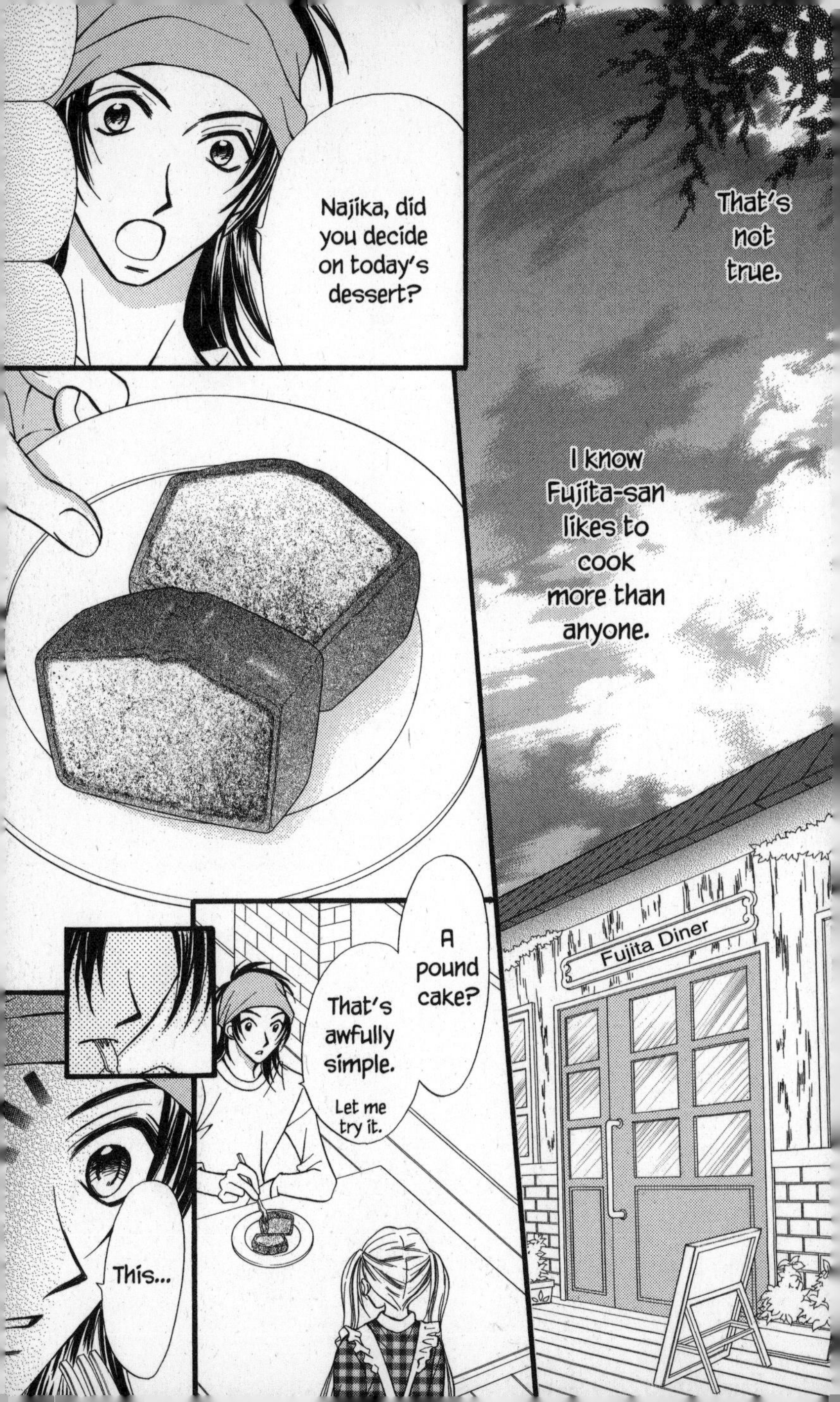
That's not true.
I know Fujita-san likes to cook more than anyone.
Fujita Diner
Najika, did you decide on today's dessert?
A pound cake?
That's awfully simple.
Let me try it.
This...

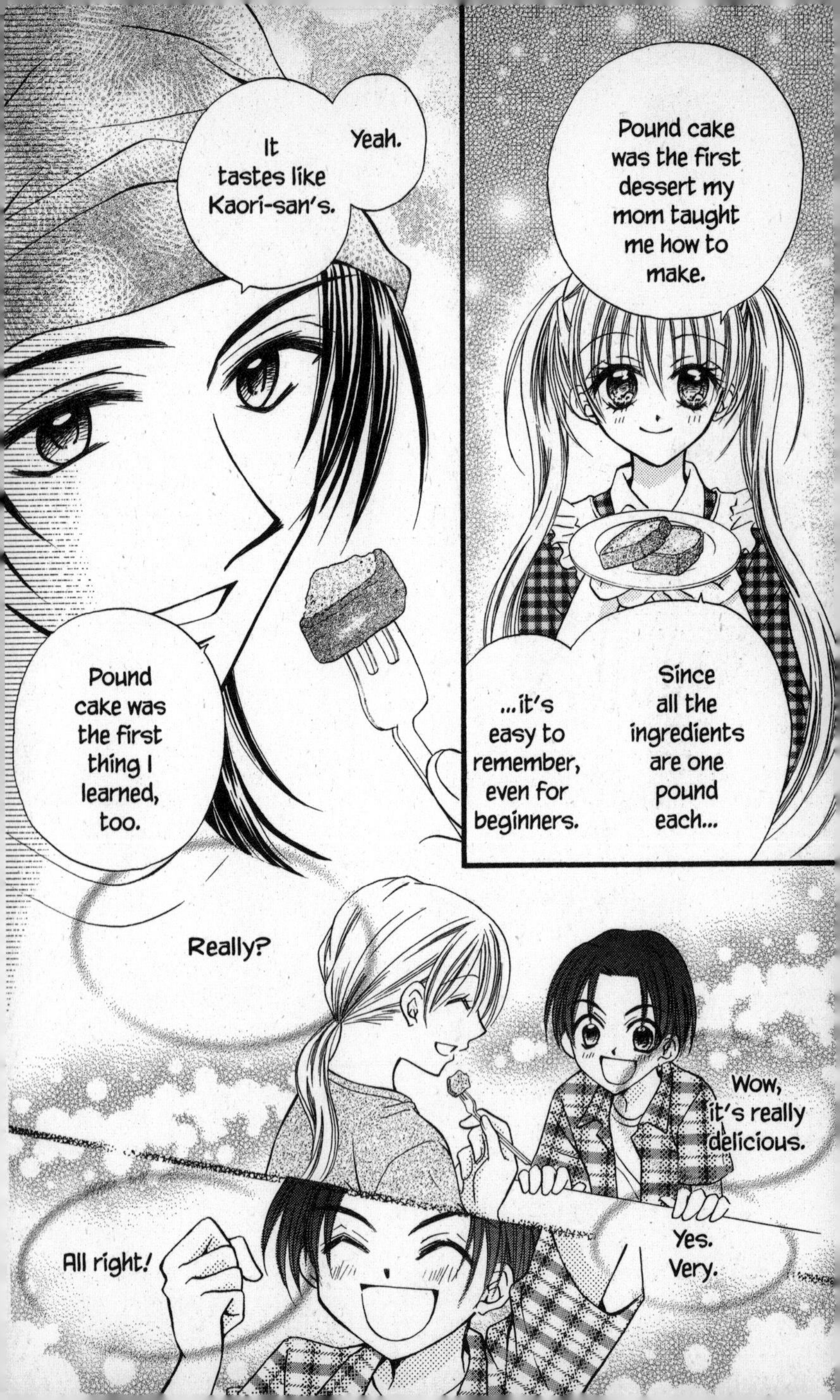
Pound cake was the first dessert my mom taught me how to make.
Since all the ingredients are one pound each...
...it's easy to remember, even for beginners.
Yeah.
It tastes like Kaori-san's.
Pound cake was the first thing I learned, too.
Really?
Wow, it's really delicious.
Yes. Very.
All right!

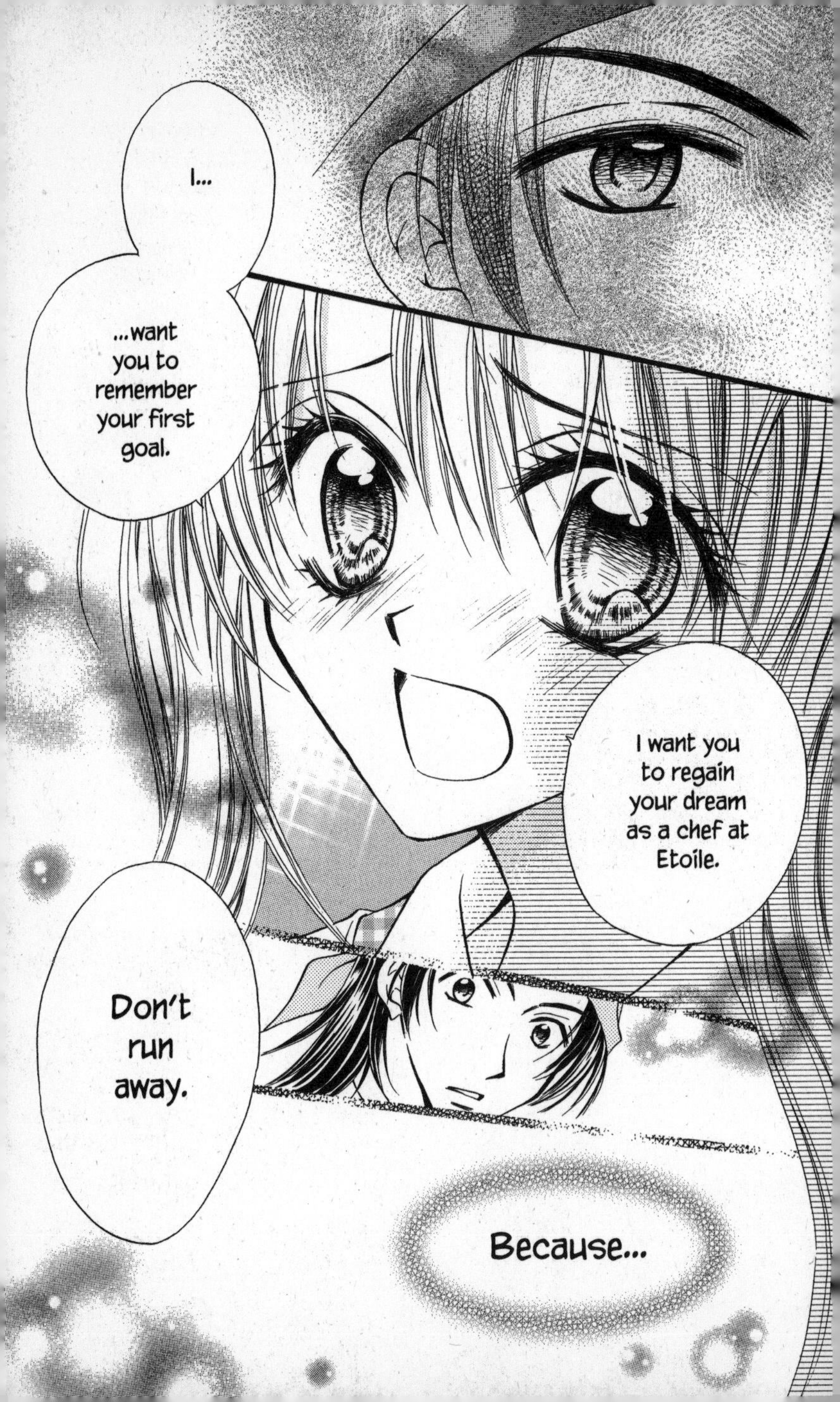
I...
...want you to remember your first goal.
I want you to regain your dream as a chef at Etoile.
Don't run away.
Because...

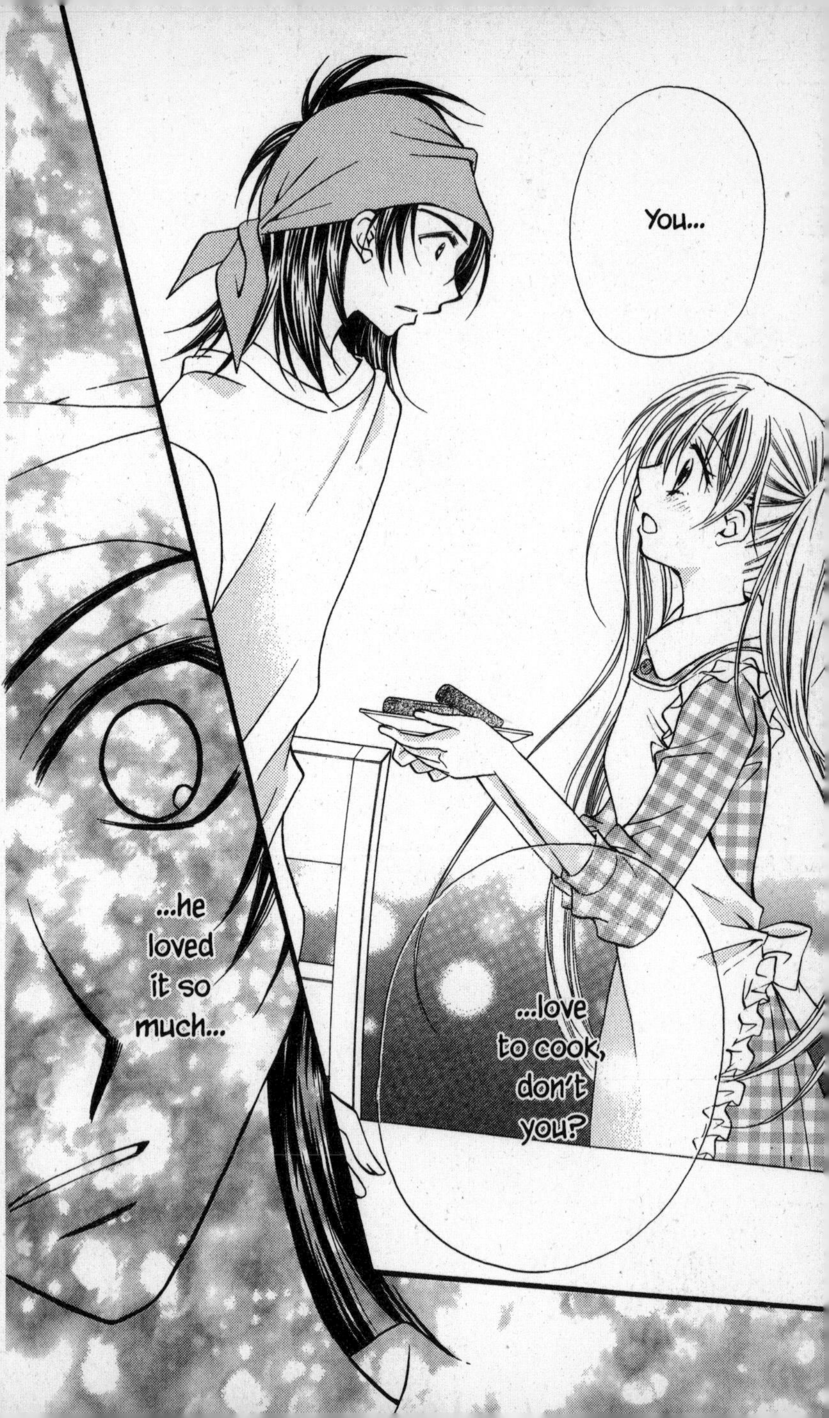
You...
...love to cook, don't you?
...he loved it so much...

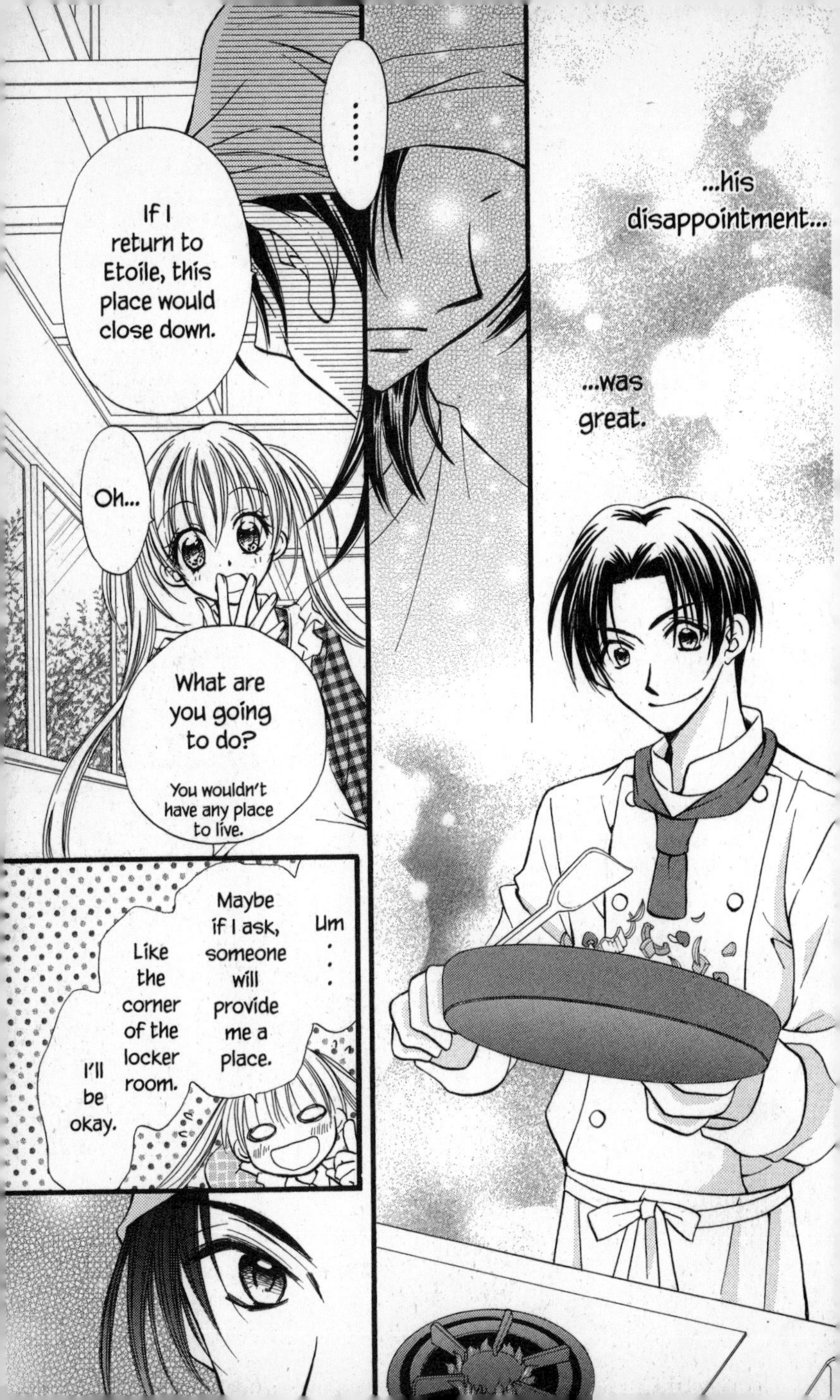
...his disappointment...
...was great.
......
If I return to Etoile, this place would close down.
Oh...
What are you going to do?
You wouldn't have any place to live.
Um...
Maybe if I ask, someone will provide me a place.
Like the corner of the locker room.
I'll be okay.

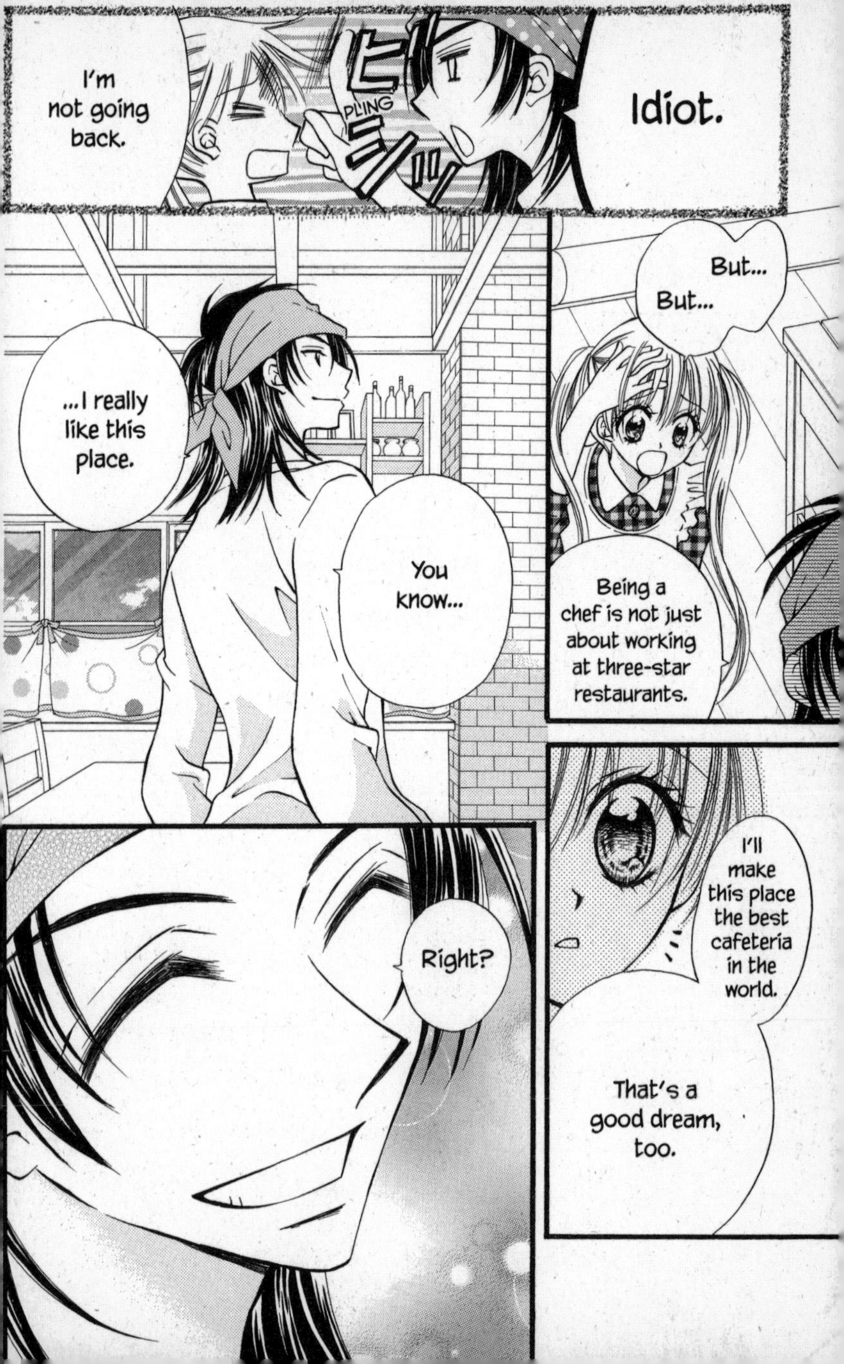
Idiot.
PLING
I'm not going back.
But... But...
Being a chef is not just about working at three-star restaurants.
You know...
...I really like this place.
I'll make this place the best cafeteria in the world.
That's a good dream, too.
Right?

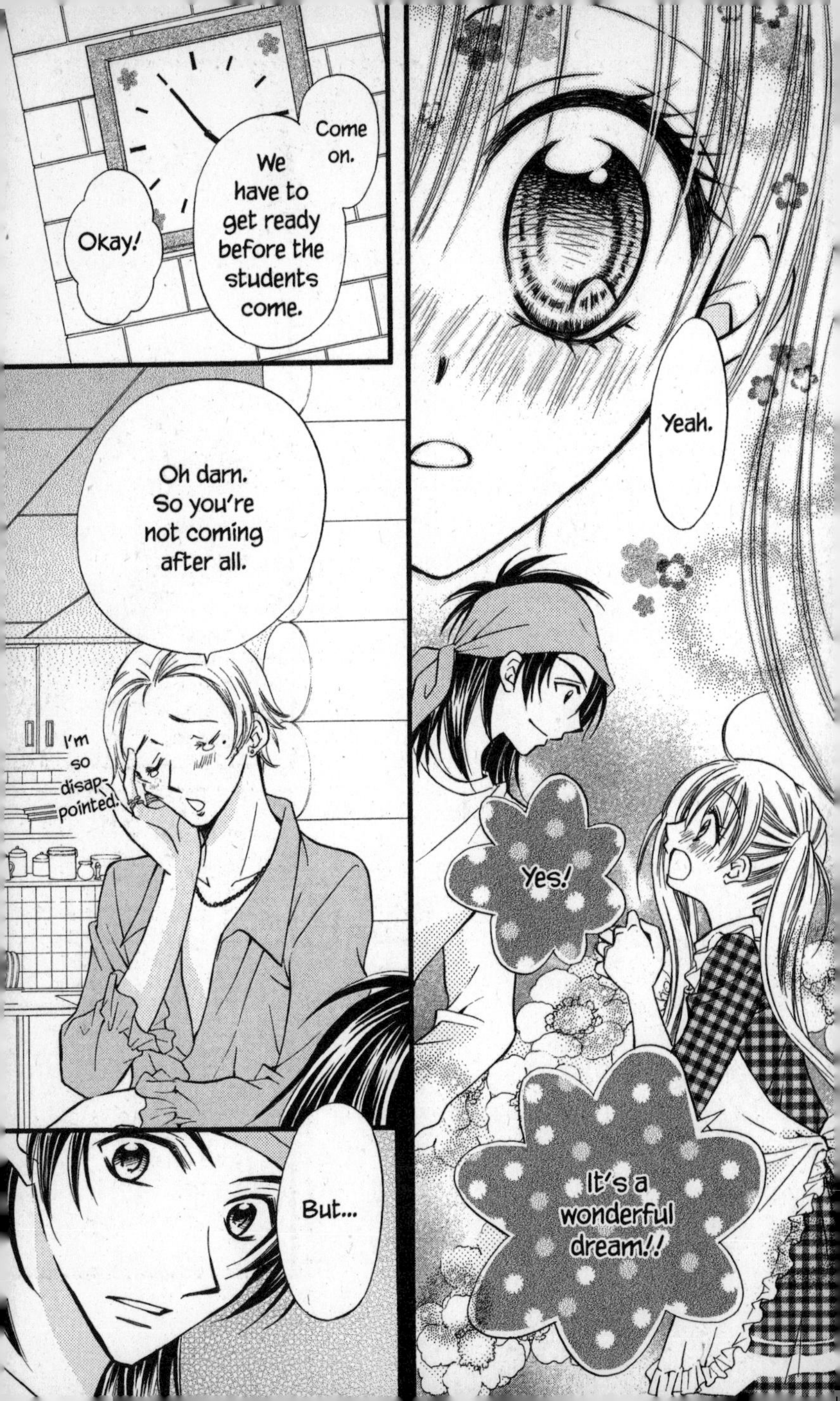
Yeah.
Yes!
It's a wonderful dream!!
Come on.
We have to get ready before the students come.
Okay!
Oh darn. So you're not coming after all.
I'm so disap-pointed!
But...

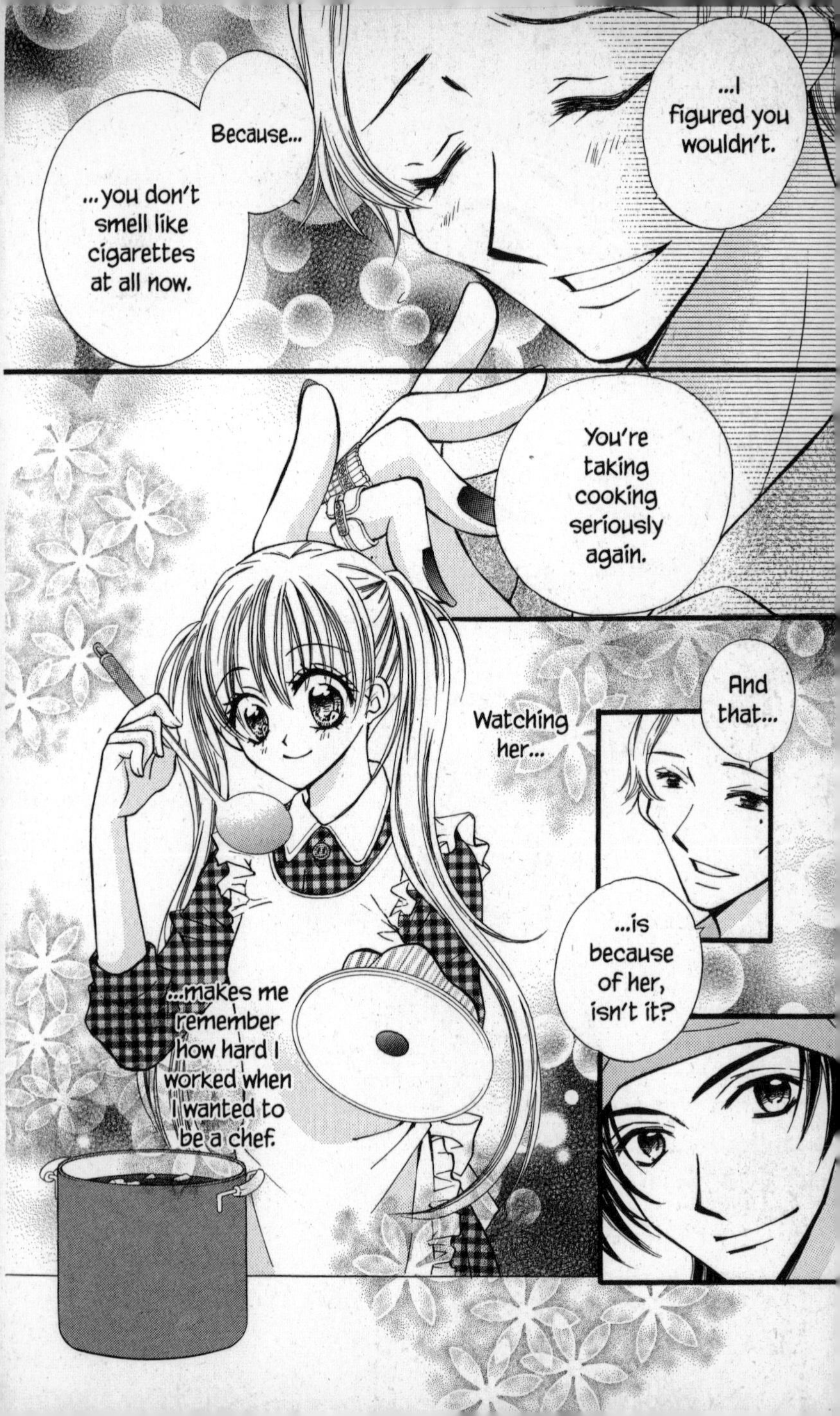
...I figured you wouldn't.
Because...
...you don't smell like cigarettes at all now.
You're taking cooking seriously again.
And that...
...is because of her, isn't it?
Watching her...
...makes me remember how hard I worked when I wanted to be a chef.

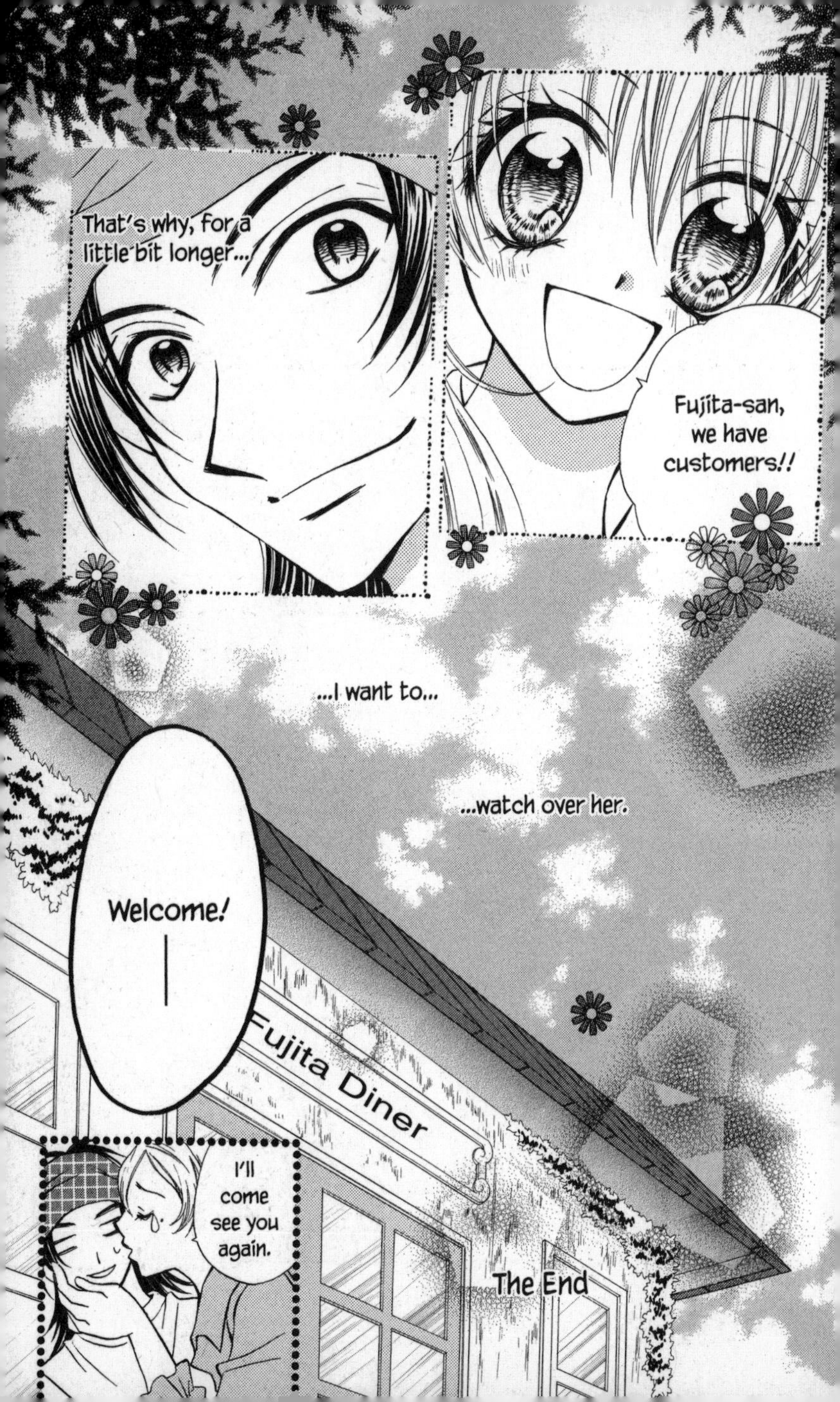
Fujita-san, we have customers!!
That's why, for a little bit longer...
...I want to...
...watch over her.
Welcome!
Fujita Diner
The End
I'll come see you again.

Thank you

Since it's hard to answer the questions I receive in the mail individually, I tried answering them in this volume.

I would like to do it again if space allows it. The next volume is the last volume!! It's Volume 10!!

I was able to come this far because of all the readers who cheered me on...

Please continue to read *Kitchen Princess* until the end.

★ Thank you ★

Yamada-sama
Miyachi-sama
Shirasawa-sama
Sato-sama
&
Miyuki-sensei
Kishimoto-sama

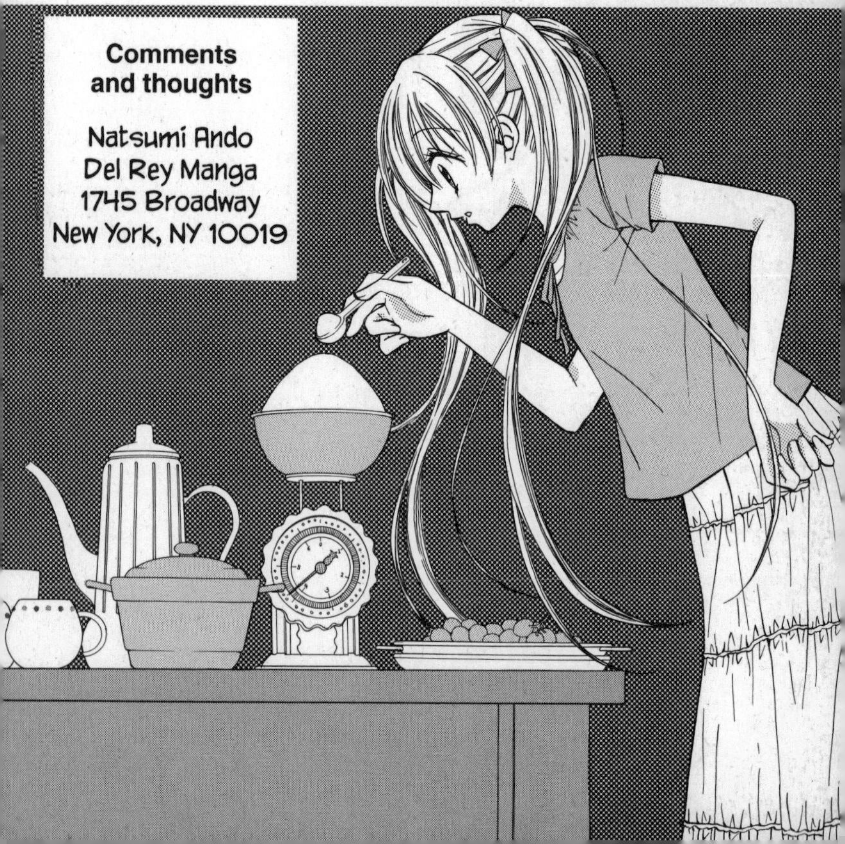

Comments and thoughts
Natsumi Ando
Del Rey Manga
1745 Broadway
New York, NY 10019

Kitchen Palace

Did you enjoy *Kitchen Princess*?
In this section, we'll give you the recipes
for the food that Najika made in the story.
Please try making them. ♥

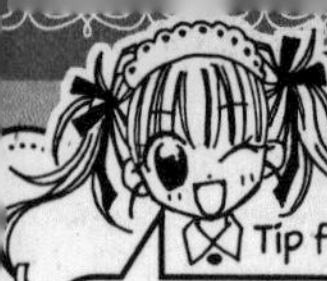

Cinnamon Rolls

Tip from Najika.

Making your own bread is easy once you get the hang of it. You should knead the dough well to ferment it for a fluffy finish.

Cinnamon Rolls

(For 8-9 rolls)

- 1 1/2 cups flour
- 2 tablespoons sugar
- 1 1/2 teaspoons dry yeast
- some salt
- 1/2 cup milk
- 1 egg yolk
- some cinnamon
- some sugar

How to Make

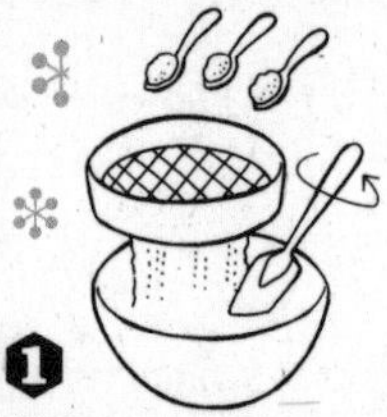

1. Sift flour, sugar, dry yeast, and salt into a bowl and mix using a spatula.

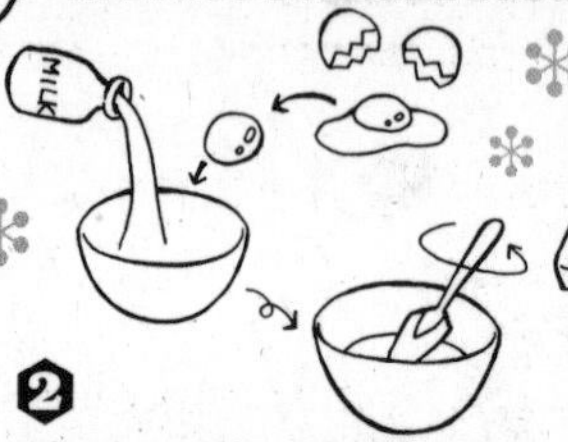
MILK

2. Microwave the milk for about 20 seconds. Add the egg yolk into the milk, and then add the mix to the bowl from step 1. Stir well.

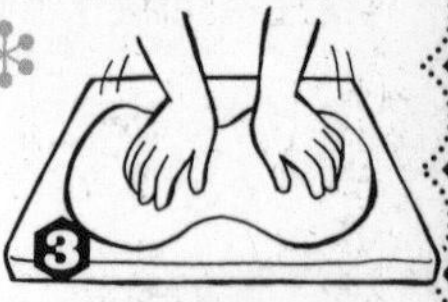

3. Once the dough comes together, put it on a board and knead it for about 10 minutes.

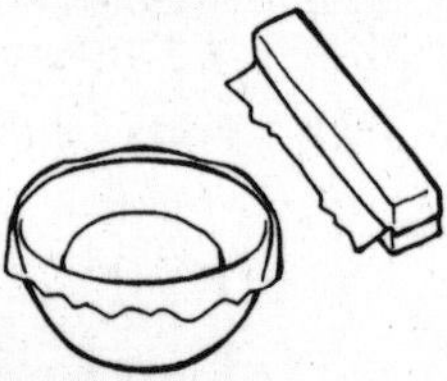

4. Once the surface is smooth, make a ball and put it in a bowl. Cover it with plastic wrap and leave in a warm place (about 30 degrees, approx. 85 F) for 40 to 50 minutes. This will allow the bread to rise.

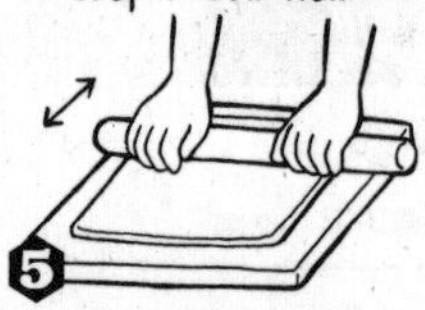

5. Once the dough has doubled in size, roll it out on a board with a rolling pin. The dough should be a rectangular shape of about 8″ x 12″. Sprinkle with sugar and cinnamon.

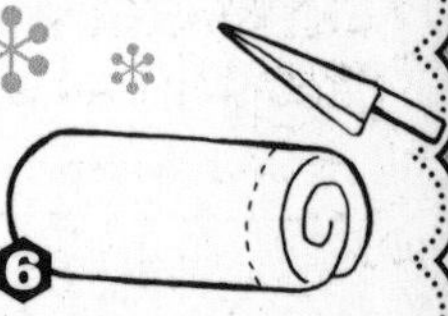

6. Then roll it and press the edges to seal it. Cut it into slices with a knife. The pieces should be about 1 inch wide.

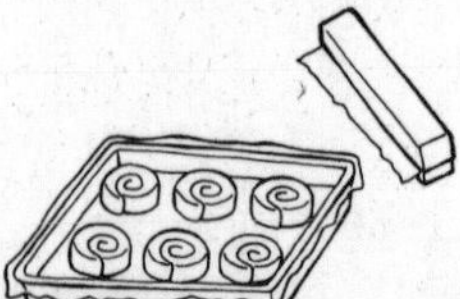

7. Place the slices on a baking sheet and cover with plastic wrap to keep them moist. Leave for 10 to 20 minutes for the rolls to rise some more.

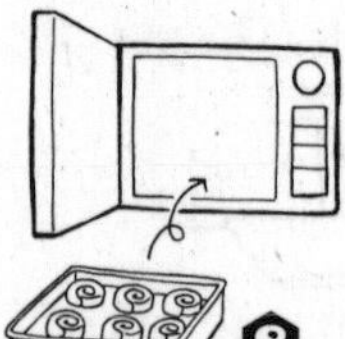

8. Remove the plastic wrap and bake in a preheated oven at 180 degrees (approx. 350 F) for 15 minutes.

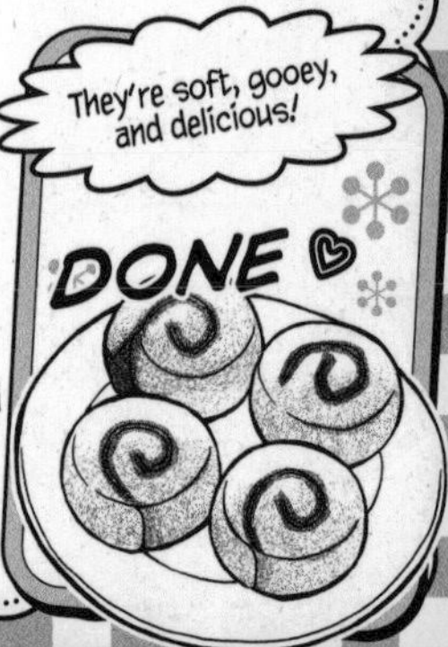
They're soft, gooey, and delicious!
DONE

Hot Chocolate

Tip from Najika.

I'll introduce three hot drinks that are perfect for winter. You can try various kinds of chocolate (such as dark chocolate) according to your taste.

Hot Chocolate (Makes one serving) ● 1 ounce bar chocolate ● 2 cups milk

How to Make

Perfect for Valentine's Day!!

① Cut the chocolate into small pieces using a knife.

② Put the chocolate in a small pot. Add milk and put it over medium heat to melt the chocolate. Stir it with a whisk while you heat. Take it off the heat right before it boils.

③ Pour into a mug and you're done.

Other Hot Drinks

Hot Banana Milk

How to Make (Makes one serving)

● half of a banana ● 1/2 cup milk

① Slice the banana into pieces and put it in a blender with the milk. Mix until smooth. For people who like it sweet, you can add honey or sugar.

② Pour the mixture in a mug and microwave it for about a minute. You can use a spoon to scoop the fluffy parts.

Hot Lemonade

How to Make (Makes one serving)

● half a lemon
● 1 tablespoon honey ● 1/2 cup hot water

① Use a citrus press to squeeze the juice out of a lemon.

② Pour the lemon juice and honey into a mug and stir with a spoon.

③ Pour hot water in it and mix. You can add honey if you prefer it sweeter.

DONE ♡

You can enjoy all different tastes!!

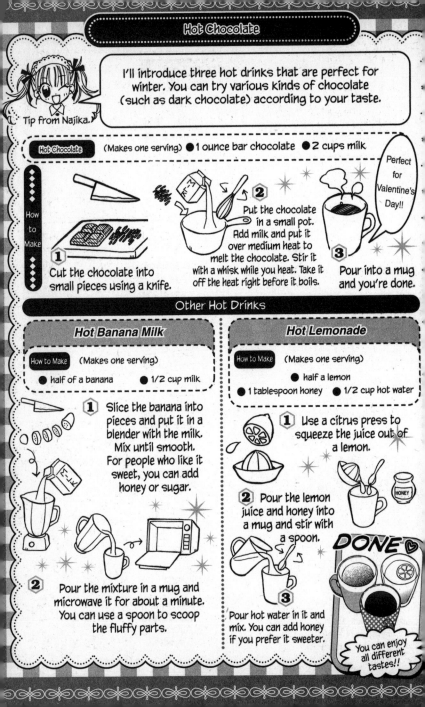

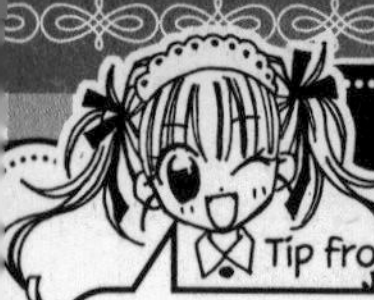

Banana Bread

Tip from Najika.

If you use a really ripe banana, the aroma will be enhanced and the bread will be sweeter. Brown bananas are best for snacks.

Banana Bread (Makes one loaf)

- 1 banana
- 2 1/2 tablespoons salt
- 4 tablespoons sugar
- 1 egg
- 1/2 cup milk
- 1/2 cup flour
- 1 teaspoon baking powder

◆◆◆ How to Make ◆◆◆

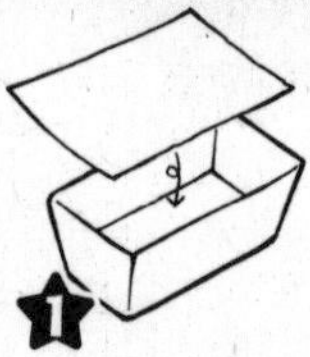

1. Place waxed paper in the bottom of a loaf pan.

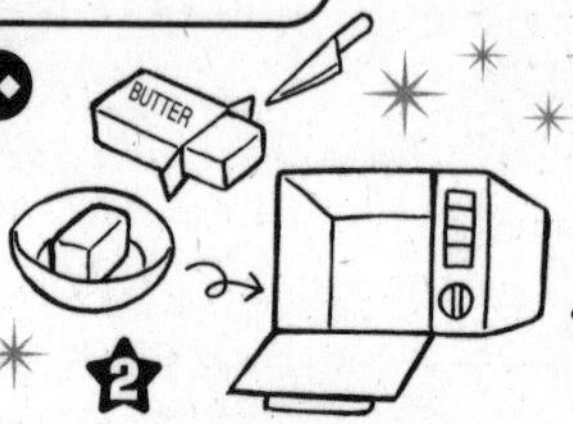
BUTTER

2. Put the butter in a microwave-safe container and heat for 2 minutes.

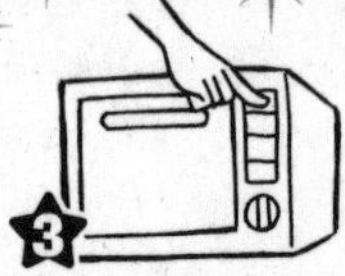

3. Preheat the oven to 180 degrees (approx. 350 F).

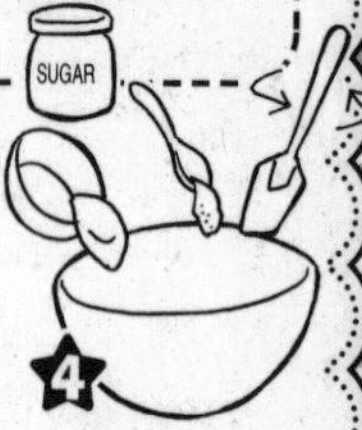
SUGAR

4. Put the butter in a bowl and add sugar. Mix with a spatula.

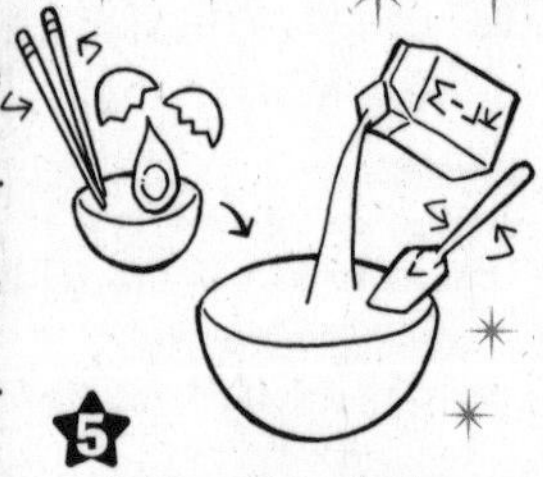

5. Add a whisked egg and milk in the bowl and mix it some more.

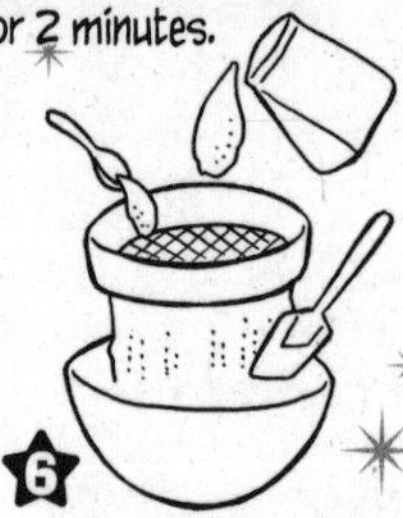

6. Sift flour, baking powder, and salt in the bowl and mix.

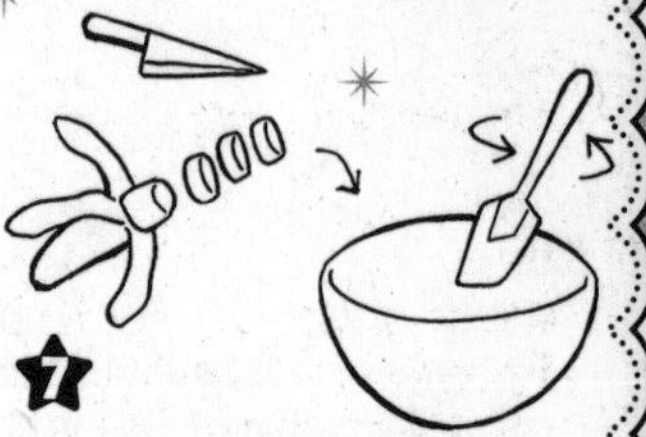

7. Peel the banana and cut into slices. Add them to the bowl and mash them as you mix well.

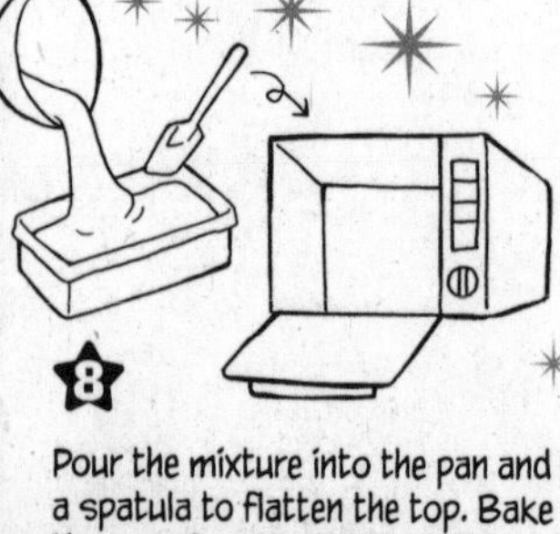

8. Pour the mixture into the pan and use a spatula to flatten the top. Bake in the oven for about 35 minutes.

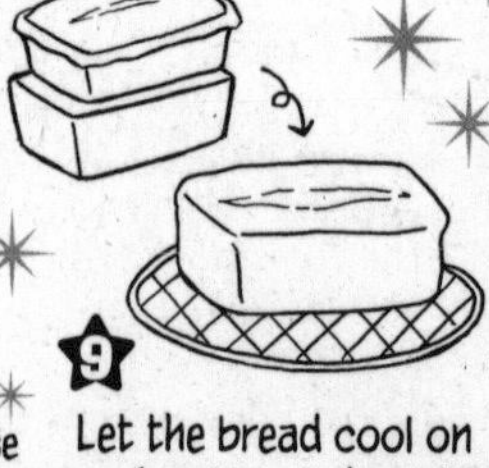

9. Let the bread cool on a wire rack and you're done!

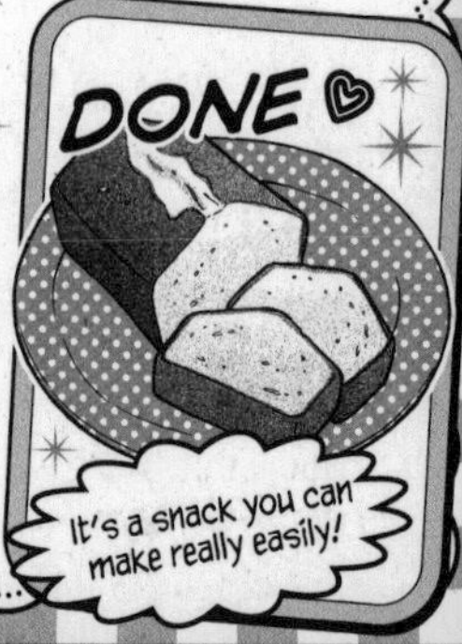
DONE
It's a snack you can make really easily!

Chicken Doria

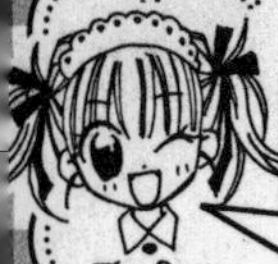

Everyone loves a good Doria. You can add shredded cheese on top to make it even more delicious. Try adding bell peppers, carrots, and mushrooms. Even if you don't like eating vegetables, they taste great in Chicken Doria!

Tip from Najika.

Chicken Doria (Serves four)

<Rice>

- half of an onion
- 1 chicken breast
- 1 tablespoon butter
- 4 tablespoons ketchup
- 4 bowls of cooked rice
- some salt and pepper

<White sauce>

- 1 tablespoon butter
- 1 tablespoon flour
- 1 1/2 cups milk
- some salt and pepper

How to Make

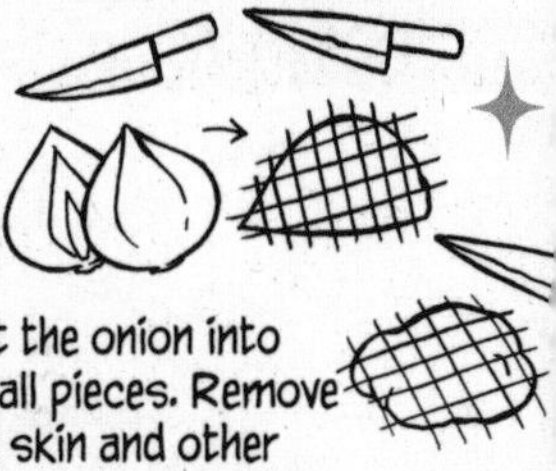

1. Cut the onion into small pieces. Remove the skin and other fatty parts from the chicken and cut into 1/2-inch squares.

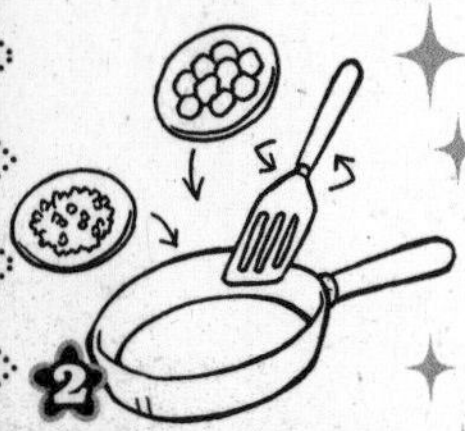

2. Melt the butter in a frying pan and fry the onion over medium heat. Once it turns transparent, add the chicken and fry some more.

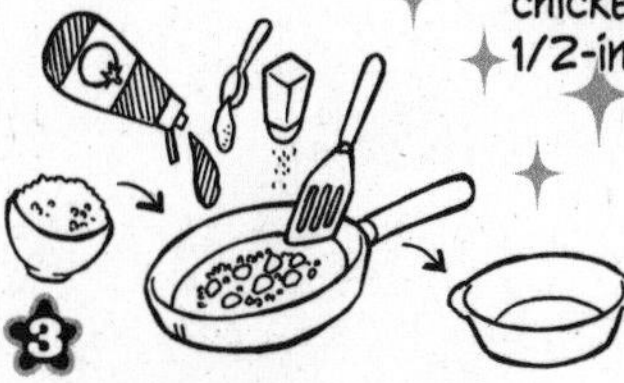

3. Once the color of the chicken changes, add rice, salt, pepper, and ketchup. Stir well. After it's done, put it in an au gratin dish.

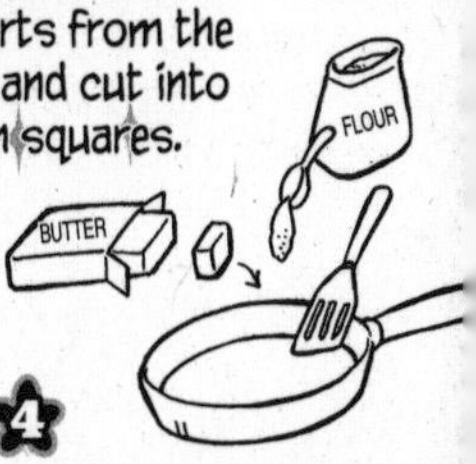
FLOUR
BUTTER

4. Now we'll make the white sauce. In a separate frying pan over low heat, put butter in. Once the butter melts, add flour little by little and mix well.

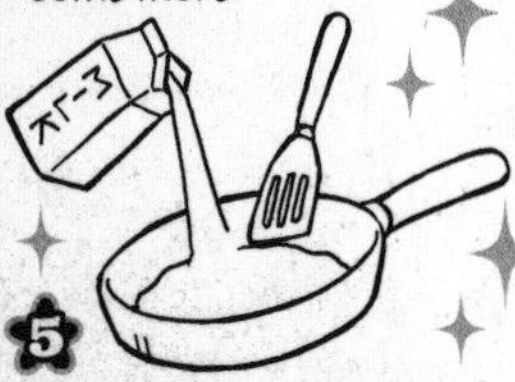

5. Add the milk little by little, trying not to create any lumps. Once the mix is smooth, add salt and pepper.

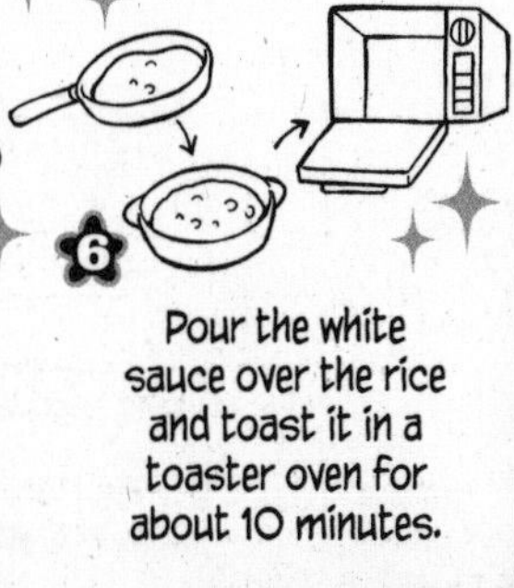

6. Pour the white sauce over the rice and toast it in a toaster oven for about 10 minutes.

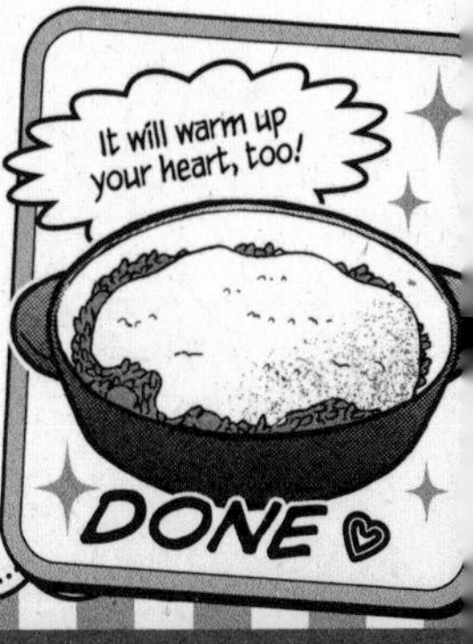
It will warm up your heart, too!
DONE ♡

Vegetable Potage

Tip from Najika.

This is an easy potage to make. The potato makes it thick. You can use other vegetables, too. Try using carrots or broccoli instead of spinach.

Vegetable Potage

(Serves two)

- 1/3 of a pack of fresh spinach
- 1 potato
- an onion
- 2 tablespoons butter
- 1 cup water
- 1 consommé block
- 3/4 cup milk
- salt and pepper

<Croutons>

- 1 slice of white bread

How to Make

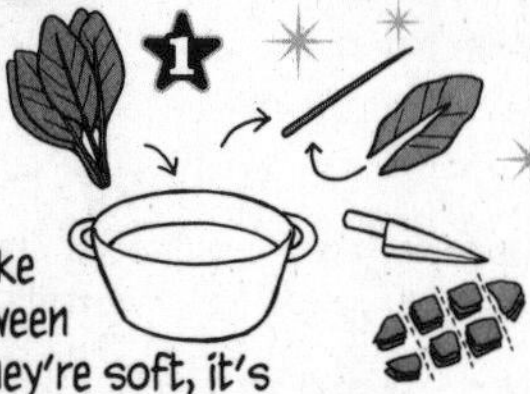

1. Rinse the spinach well. Boil water in a pot and add 1 teaspoon of salt, then put the spinach in. Boil it over high heat. Make sure to flip it over in between and press the roots. If they're soft, it's done. Place in a bowl of water and let cool. Wring the spinach lightly to get the water out, and remove the roots. Cut the spinach into 3/4-inch pieces.

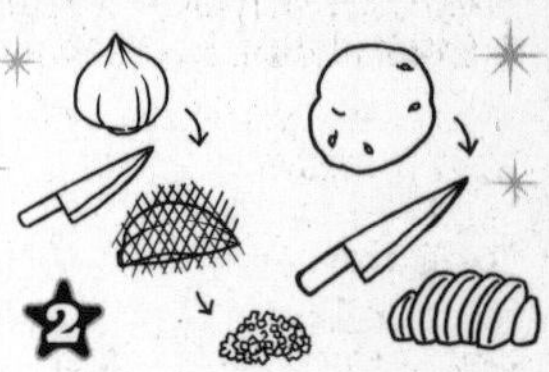

2. Cut the onion into small pieces. Peel the potato and cut it in half, then cut it in thin slices.

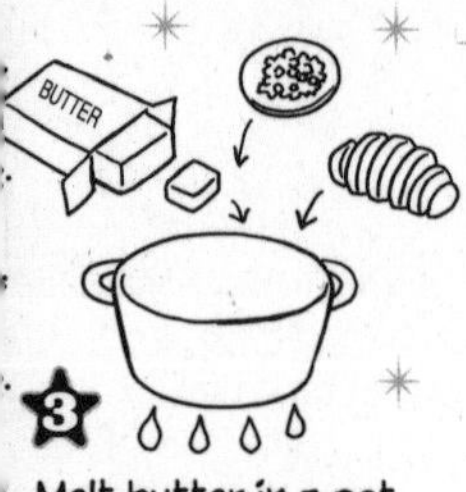
BUTTER

3. Melt butter in a pot and cook the onions and potato over medium heat.

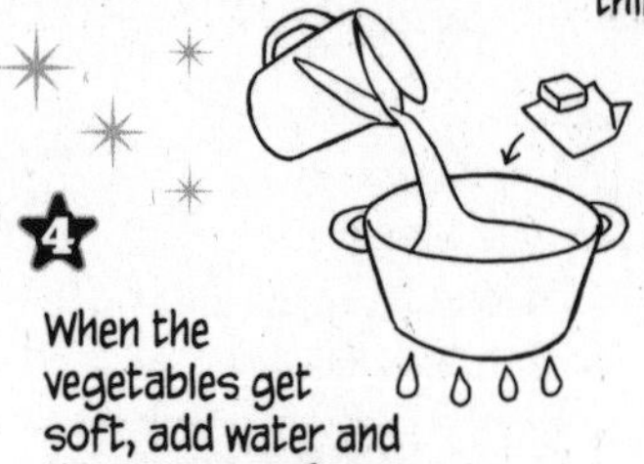

4. When the vegetables get soft, add water and the consommé block. Simmer for 8 to 10 minutes.

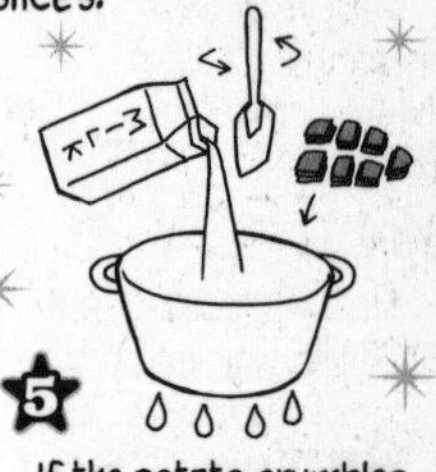

5. If the potato crumbles when you push it, you can turn off the heat. Add spinach and milk, and stir well.

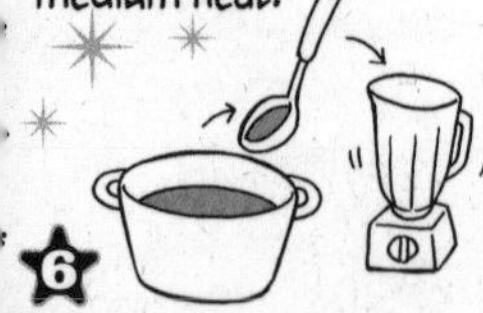

6. Put the mix in a blender and once it's smooth, return it to the pot and warm it up over medium heat.

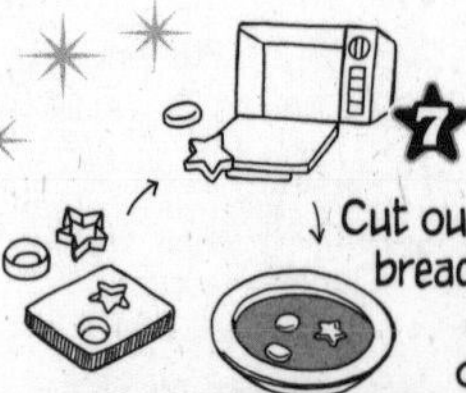

7. Cut out white bread using cookie cutters and toast them in a toaster oven. Float these in the soup and it's done. During the summer, you can have the soup cold.

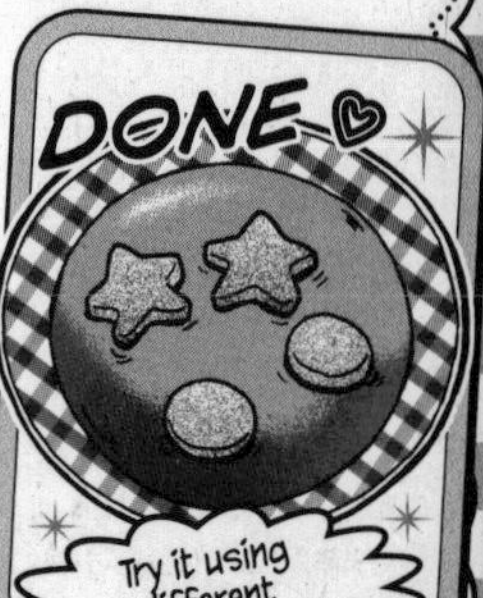
DONE
Try it using different vegetables!

Pound Cake

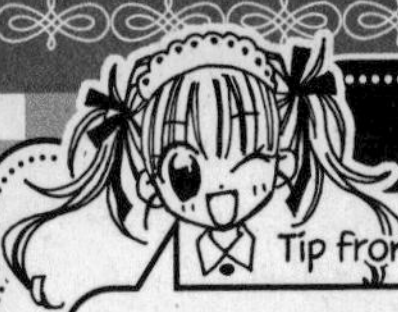

Tip from Najika.

It's called pound cake because you use one pound of flour, eggs, sugar, and butter. So it's a simple recipe where you can just mix the four ingredients. It's delicious if you let it sit for one day, and it lasts a long time (up to a week) if you keep it in the refrigerator.

Pound Cake (Makes one loaf)

- 3/4 cup butter
- 3/4 cup sugar
- 2 eggs
- 3/4 cup flour
- 1 teaspoon baking powder

How to Make

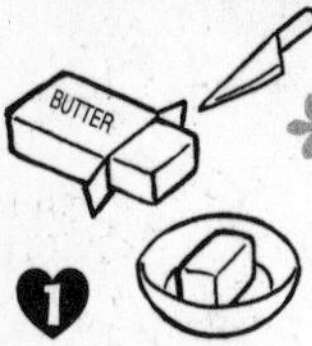
BUTTER

1. Leave the butter out at room temperature to soften it.

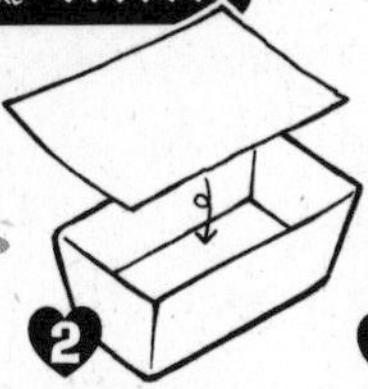

2. Put waxed paper in the loaf pan.

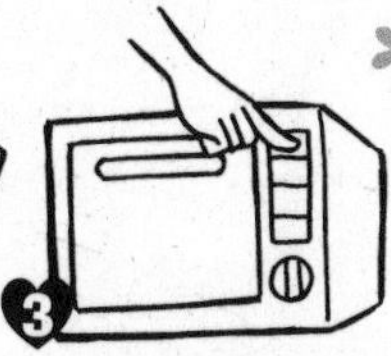

3. Preheat the oven to 170 degrees (approx. 340 F).

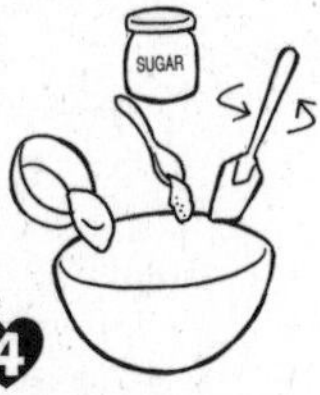
SUGAR

4. Cream the butter with a spatula until it's very creamy. Add sugar and cream some more.

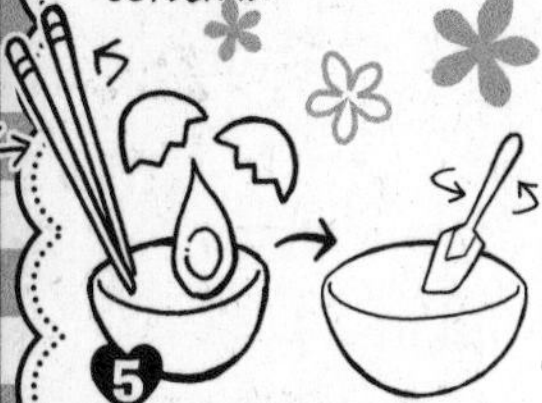

5. Whisk the eggs and add them little by little to the bowl from step 4. Stir more.

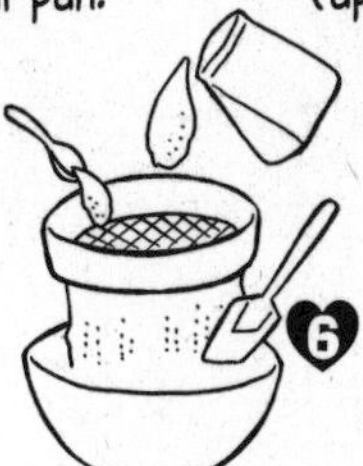

6. Sift flour and baking powder into the bowl and mix.

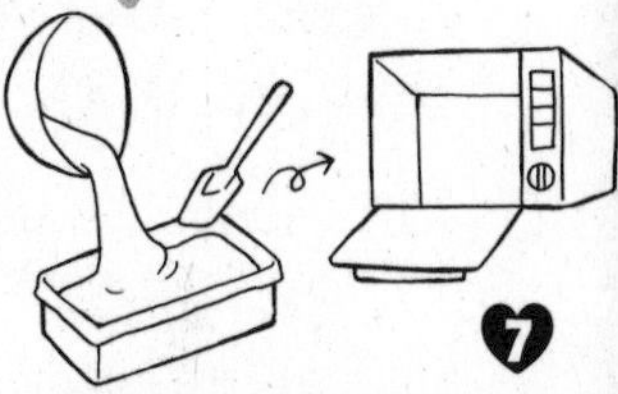

7. Pour the dough into the loaf pan and flatten the top with a spatula. Bake in the oven at 170 degrees (approx. 340 F) for 20 minutes.

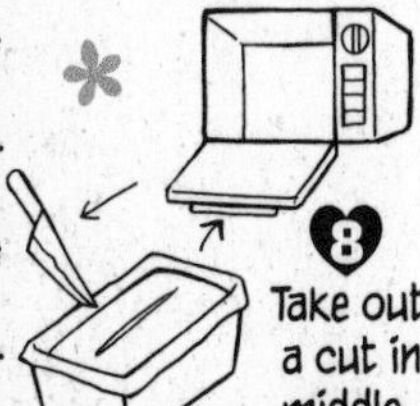

8. Take out, make a cut in the middle. Then bake it for another 20 minutes. It's hot, so make sure you don't burn yourself.

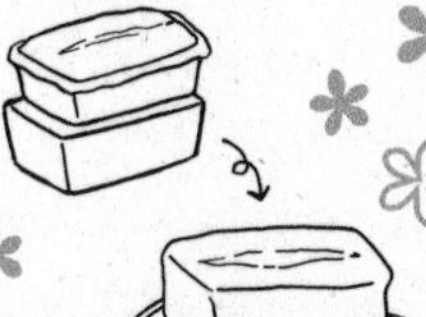

9. Once it's done, cool on a wire rack.

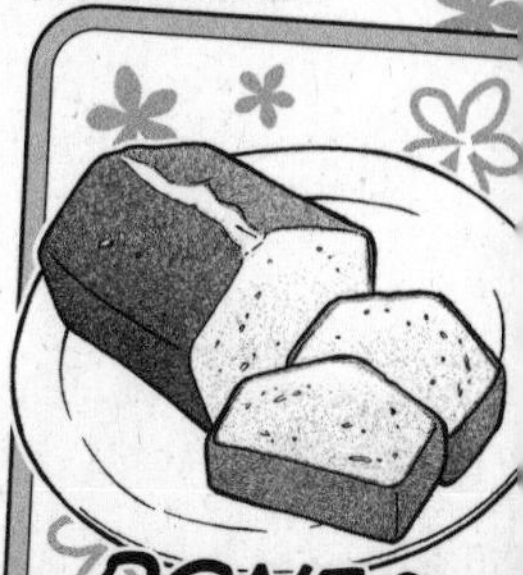
DONE

Kitchen Princess

From the Writer

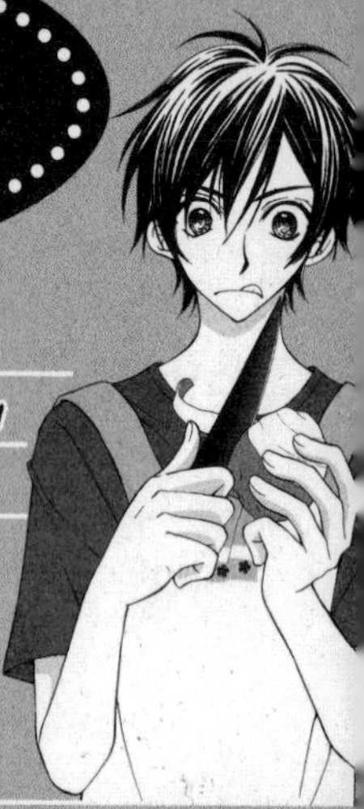

Hello! I am the writer and the person in charge of the recipes, Miyuki Kobayashi. The other day, the *Kitchen Princess* novel came out. It's called *Find the Angel's Cake!* and it's an original story. It features new illustrations by Natsumi Ando-sensei, of course. You can find out Fujita-san's surprising past! If you haven't read it yet, please do!

Oh, so the other day I had a signing for my other book (I write novels for the Tori Bunko label). I love to talk to everyone while signing autographs. One girl came up to me and told me that she reads *Kitchen Princess*, too. She also told me that she wants to be like Najika. I asked her why, and she told me that it's because Najika is positive no matter what sad thing happens. She never gives up.

I was so happy when I heard that! I was happy that my feelings were getting through to the girls who read *Kitchen Princess*. If everyone became like Najika, there would be no teasing or picking on others at school and everyone could be happy.

Anyway, *Kitchen Princess* ends in the next volume. There is still a big twist to come. I hope you're looking forward to it.

Finally, I would like to thank Natsumi Ando-sensei, my editor Kishimoto-san, Saito-san from the editorial staff, and our editor-in-chief Matsumoto-san. I'll see you in volume 10!

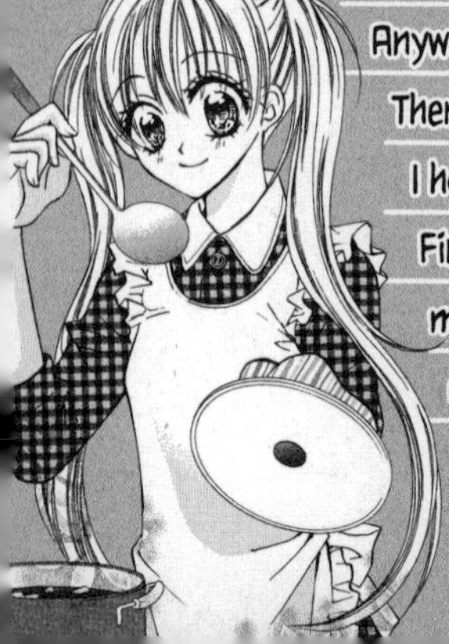

About the Creator

Natsumi Ando

She was born January 27 in Aichi prefecture. She won the 19th
Nakayoshi Rookie Award in 1994 and debuted as a manga artist. The
title she drew was "Headstrong Cinderella." Her other known works are
"Zodiac P.I.," "Wild Heart," and others. Her hobbies include reading,
watching movies, and eating delicious food.

Translation Notes

Japanese is a tricky language for most Westerners, and translation is often more art than science. For your edification and reading pleasure, here are notes on some of the places where we could have gone in a different direction in our translation of the work, or where a Japanese cultural reference is used.

Nabe, page 68

Nabe is a term that refers to various pot dishes in Japan. Common ingredients of *nabe* include vegetables such as nappa cabbage, mushrooms, green onions, tofu, and meat. *Nabe* means "pot."

Doria, pages 114 and 115

Doria is a rice dish, originally created by a restaurant in Paris for a noble Italian family, the Doria family. It used to have tomatoes, cucumbers, and eggs to match the colors of the Italian flag. Today, the term can describe any dish that features white sauce over rice and is toasted in the oven.

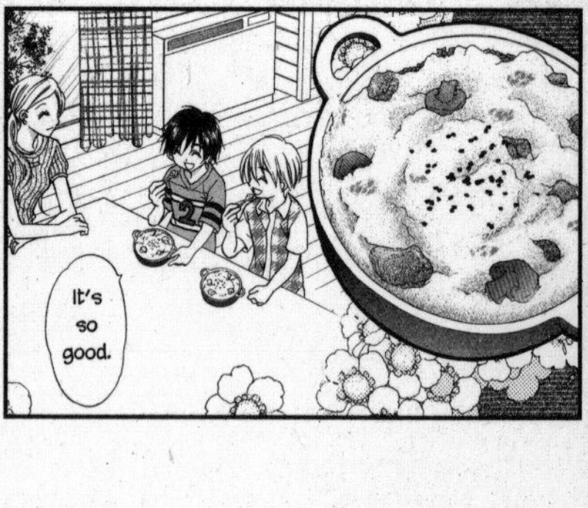
It's so good.

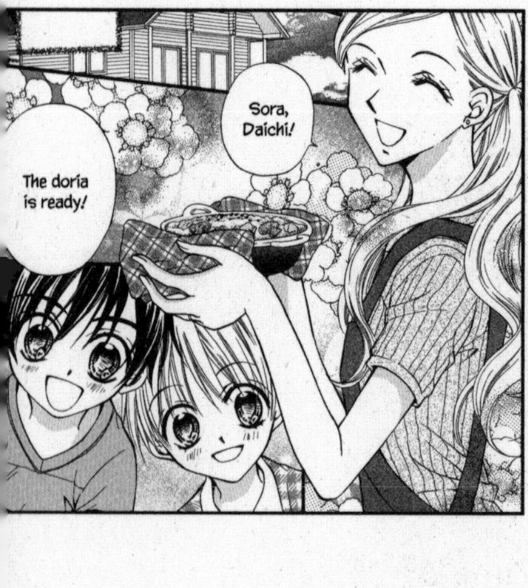
Sora, Daichi!
The doria is ready!

Preview of Volume 10

We are pleased to present you a preview from volume 10 of *Kitchen Princess*. Please check our website (www.delreymanga.com) to see when this volume will be available in English. For now you'll have to make do with Japanese!

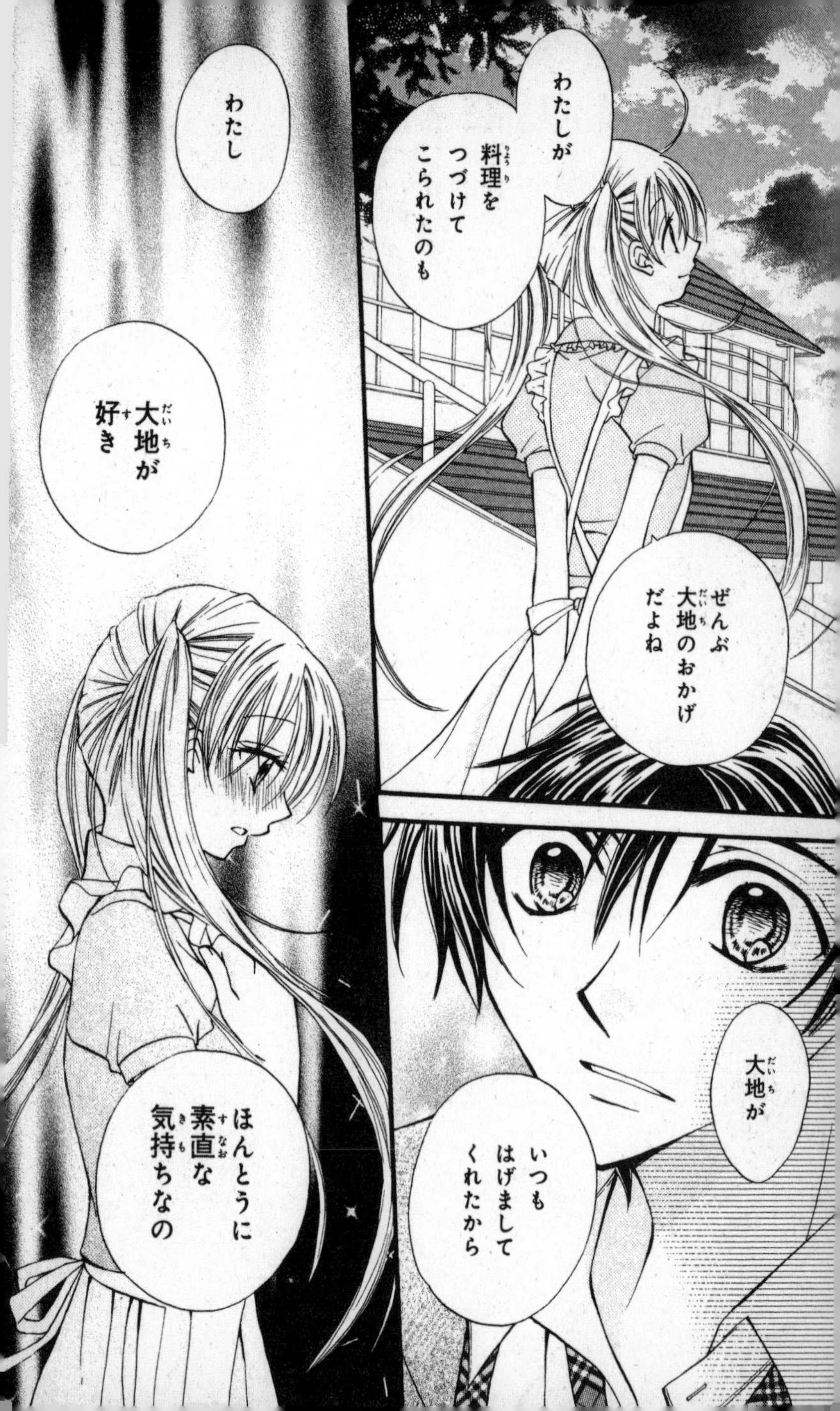
わたしが料理をつづけてこられたのも
ぜんぶ大地のおかげだよね
大地が
いつもはげましてくれたから
わたし
大地が好き
ほんとうに素直な気持ちなの

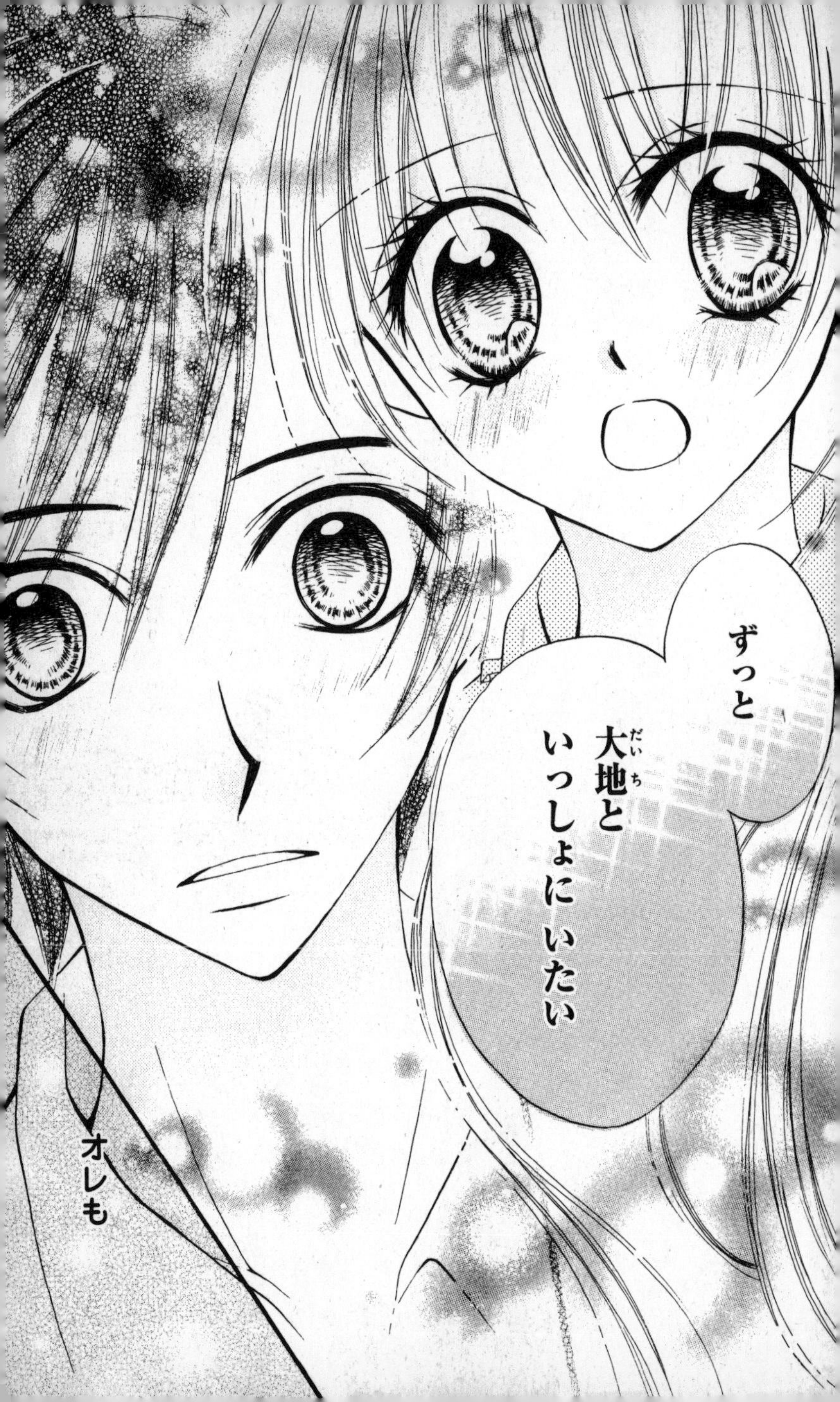
ずっと大地(だいち)といっしょにいたい
オレも

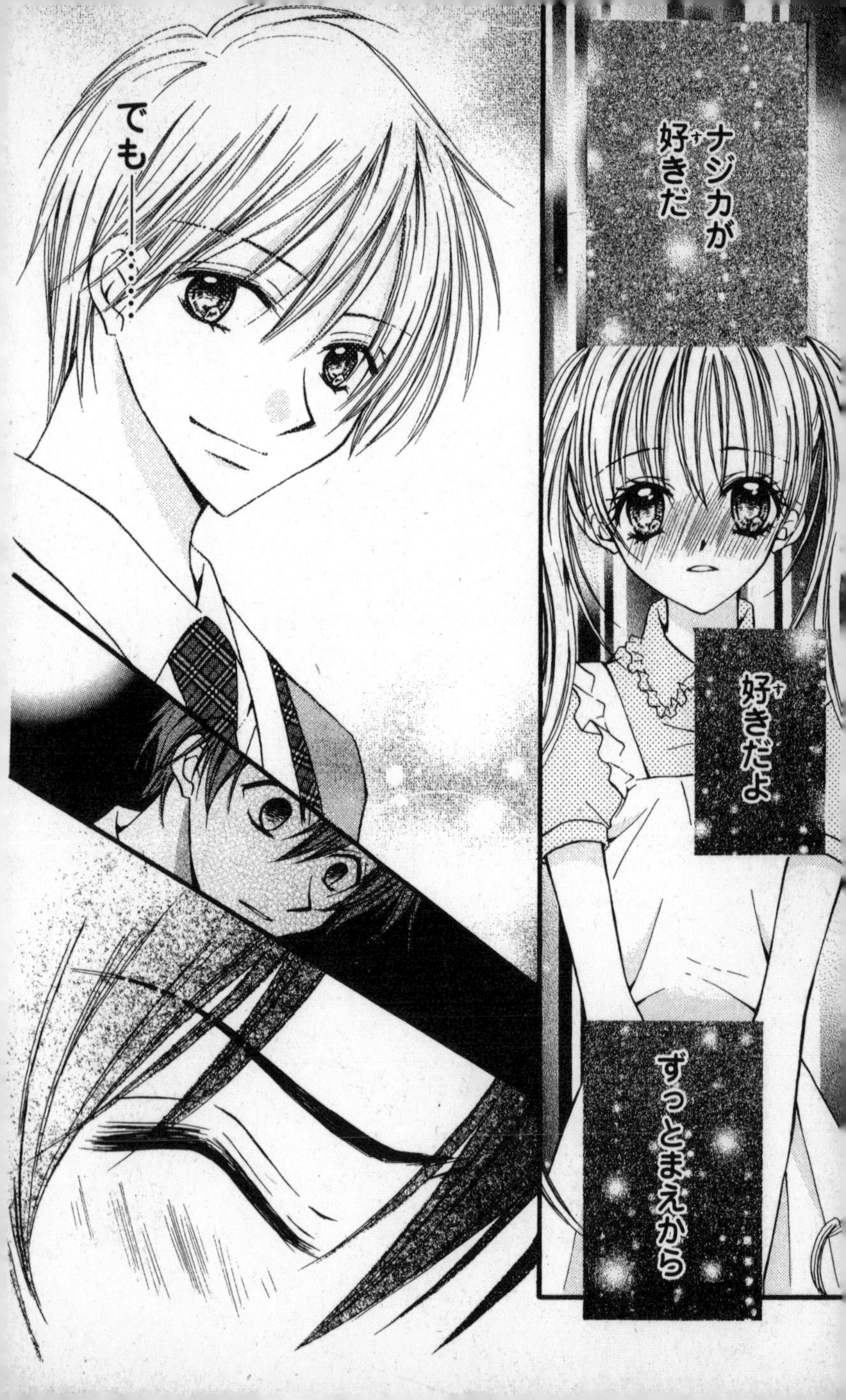
ナジカが好きだ
好きだよ
ずっとまえから
でも――……

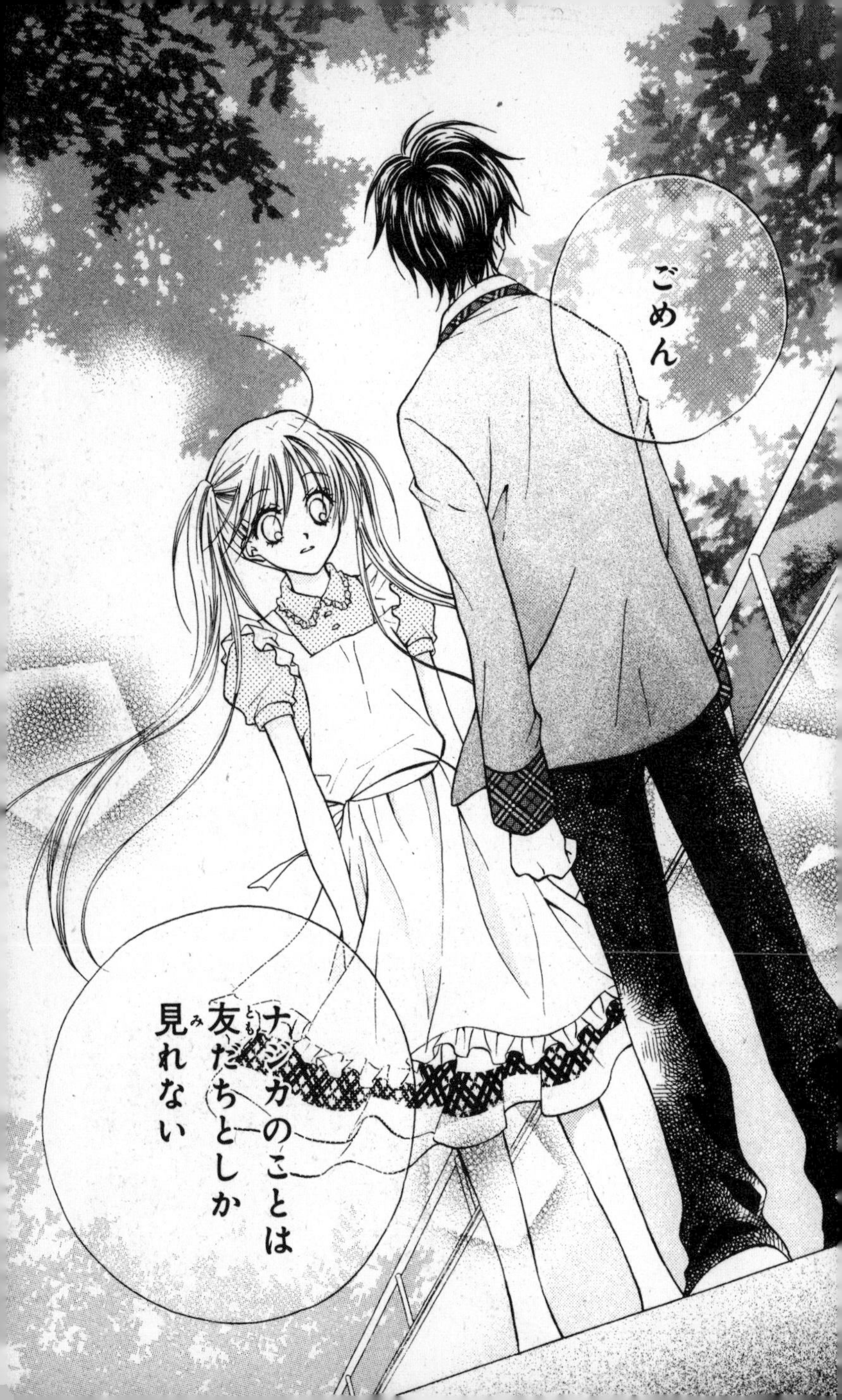
ごめん
ナジカのことは友だちとしか見れない

From Hiro Mashima, creator of *Rave Master*

FAIRY TAIL

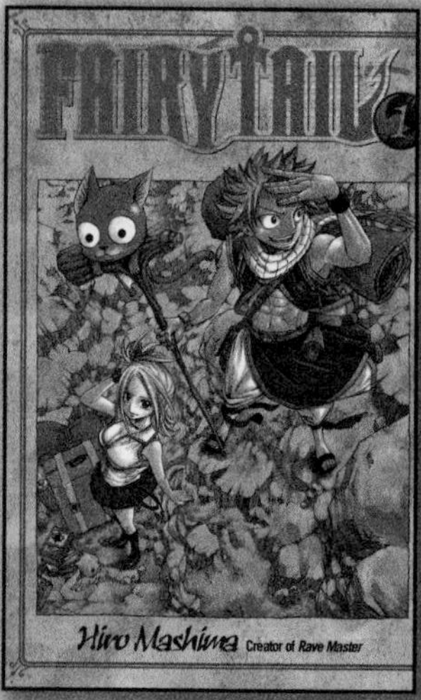
FAIRY TAIL 1
Hiro Mashima Creator of Rave Master

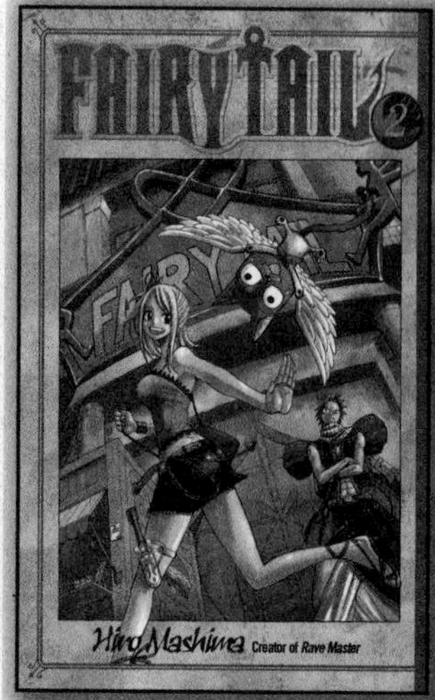
FAIRY TAIL 2
FAIRY
Hiro Mashima Creator of Rave Master

Lucy has always dreamed of joining the Fairy Tail, a club for the most powerful sorcerers in the land. But once she becomes a member, the fun really starts!

Special extras in each volume! Read them all!

VISIT WWW.DELREYMANGA.COM TO:

- Read sample pages
- View release date calendars for upcoming volumes
- Sign up for Del Rey's free manga e-newsletter
- Find out the latest about new Del Rey Manga series

RATING T AGES 13+

DEL REY MANGA デルレイ

The Otaku's Choice™

KASUMI
かすみ

STORY BY SURT LIM
ART BY HIROFUMI SUGIMOTO

A DEL REY MANGA ORIGINAL

Exploring the woods, young Kasumi encounters an ancient tree god, who bestows upon her the power of invisibility. Together with classmates who have had similar experiences, Kasumi forms the Magic Play Club, dedicated to using their powers for good while avoiding sinister forces that would exploit them.

volume
1
KASUMI
かすみ
Story by
Surt Lim
Art by
Hirofumi
Sugimoto

Special extras in each volume! Read them all!

VISIT WWW.DELREYMANGA.COM TO:
- Read sample pages
- View release date calendars for upcoming volumes
- Sign up for Del Rey's free manga e-newsletter
- Find out the latest about new Del Rey Manga series

RATING T AGES 13+

DEL REY MANGA デルレイ
The Otaku's Choice™

BY MACHIKO SAKURAI

A LITTLE LIVING DOLL!

What would you do if your favorite toy came to life and became your best friend? Well, that's just what happens to Ame Oikawa, a shy schoolgirl. Nicori is a super-cute doll with a mind of its own—and a plan to make Ame's dreams come true!

Special extras in each volume! Read them all!

Kamichama Karin Chu

BY KOGE-DONBO

A GODDESS IN LOVE!

Karin is your lovable girl next door—if the girl next door also happens to be a goddess! Karin has a magic ring that gives her the power to do anything she'd like. Though what she'd like most is to live happily ever after with Kazune, the boy of her dreams. Magic brought Kazune to her, but it also has a way of complicating things. It's not easy to be a goddess and a girl in love!

- Sequel series to the fan-favorite *Kamichama Karin*

Special extras in each volume! Read them all!

VISIT WWW.DELREYMANGA.COM TO:
- Read sample pages
- View release date calendars for upcoming volumes
- Sign up for Del Rey's free manga e-newsletter
- Find out the latest about new Del Rey Manga series

RATING T AGES 13+

The Otaku's Choice™

Papillon

BY MIWA UEDA

BUTTERFLY, SPREAD YOUR WINGS!

Ageha is a shy tomboy, but her twin sister Hana is the ultimate ultra-glam teen queen. Hana loves being the center of attention so much that she'll do anything to keep Ageha in her shadow. But Ageha has a plan that will change her life forever and no one, not even Hana, can hold her back. . . .

• From the creator of *Peach Girl*

Special extras in each volume! Read them all!

TOMARE!

止まれ

[STOP!]

You're going the wrong way!

Manga is a completely different
type of reading experience.

To start at the *beginning,*
go to the *end!*

That's right! Authentic manga is read the traditional Japanese way—
from right to left. Exactly the *opposite* of how American books are
read. It's easy to follow: Just go to the other end of the book, and read
each page—and each panel—from right side to left side, starting at
the top right. Now you're experiencing manga as it was meant to be!